THE

D0779689

THE BEST AMERICAN MAGAZINE WRITING

2014

Compiled by Sid Holt for the American Society of Magazine Editors

Columbia University Press   New York

Columbia University Press
Publishers Since 1893
New York   Chichester, West Sussex
cup.columbia.edu
Copyright © 2014 American Society of Magazine Editors
All rights reserved

Library of Congress Cataloging-in-Publication Data
ISSN 1541-0978
ISBN 978-0-231-16957-8 (pbk.)

Contents

Mark Jannot

Introduction

Well, this is an odd little exercise, isn't it?

I mean, you've bought (or are considering buying—in which case, what the hell? Pull the trigger!) a collection of great writing that is defined, in the very title of this book, by its relation to the aggregated, issue-based format for which it was commissioned and in which it was originally published.

It's *magazine* writing!

Which is . . . what, exactly?

Magazine writing is, I guess we can all agree, writing that is published between the covers of a magazine. But. But when you remove it from the magazine, and from the magazine context—to present it between different covers, in the pages of a Best American anthology, for instance—is it still magazine writing? And if so, how so?

It's not an idle question for those of us who are involved in the commissioning and publication of this fine work because more and more—and ever more into the future—magazine writing does appear outside the covers of a "magazine," that wood-pulp-based product that until two decades ago was its sole repository, not to mention the source of its particular identity and appeal. Please excuse this belaboring of the obvious, but today magazine writing can be found also on all manner of screen—computer, tablet, e-reader, smartphone—and in an ever-kudzu-fying range of formats and packages. Does the concept of "magazine writing" lose meaning in such a chaotic universe? Or is there something essential in this sort of work that transcends the physical form itself?

Let's find out, shall we? Here's a fun game, though it probably works best if you haven't already thoroughly consumed the table of contents or so eagerly thumbed through this book that you've committed the lineup to memory and mapped out a plan for how you're going to devour these bonbons. (But of course if you were a devotee of that intensity, you wouldn't be wasting your time reading these words. So I think we're on pretty safe ground.) When you turn to each new story, take care somehow to avoid casting your eyes over the spot where the name of the originating magazine is proudly displayed—put your hand over that side of the page (or screen), or, if the layout allows, just flip swiftly past. And, for Pete's sake, don't read the italicized intro! (You can save that for later.) Then, as you're reading the piece, or once you've finished it, see if you can guess its provenance. (Or at least whittle the candidate magazines down to a "most likely" two or three.)

Ready? Go!

Everybody back? OK, how'd we do? I'm willing to bet that, if you have any sort of magazine awareness to draw upon—and you do—your performance on this mag-identity test was strong, better than you'd have thought. (Or it would have been, if you'd actually gone and tried it.) That was my experience, anyway: It's striking, the extent to which these stories, taken in isolation, as a mere shard of a magazine's DNA, can in fact still be used to reverse-engineer the entire organism.

Tom Junod's celeb profile of Matt Damon, which kicks off this collection, is, for instance, a true exemplar of a particular form, and as the particulars pile up it becomes a form that could plausibly have been published in no more than a handful of magazines. The story gives the reader exactly what the reader always wants out of this sort of story—insider detail, delicious tales told by the celebrity about other celebrities while said celebrity is drinking large beers in the chummy company of your interlocutor and thus you. But the adjacent-barstool nature of this particular narrative and voice certainly narrows the presumptive audience. And the story also *meta*-stasizes its pleasures by making the reader uncomfortably aware of the dark heart of his want and of its insalubrious effect on all who are touched by it. (By the end, you feel you do know Damon better, but you're less sure that you have any right to and almost painfully aware of the gap that exists between you and his celebrity Elysium, though you've enjoyed spending a good chunk of time bathing in its ambrosial waters.) It's smart as hell. Could be *New York*? But no, the discussion of Damon's decamping from New York to L.A. doesn't carry the requisite NY-centric knowingness; gotta be a true national mag. Did I mention that there is much drinking of alcohol? Also smoking of cigars. *Cigar Aficionado*! But no, it has a different kind of ambition—and besides, there aren't *that* many cigars, and the alcohol is beer. Could be *GQ*, but it feels a bit older than that, a bit more self-conscious. The hed, the title, seals it: "The Second Biggest Star in a Remote Little Burg Somewhere in Germany." Gotta be *Esquire*.

BingBingBingBingBing!

Isn't this fun?

We can get a different spin on a similar outcome by considering whether the two "Columns and Commentary" exemplars here—Emily Nussbaum's TV criticism from *The New Yorker* and Witold Rybczynski's architecture reconsiderations from *Architect*—could have swapped publications intact. (Well, from a voice/tone/erudition standpoint, anyway; we can assume that Nussbaum's small-screen meditations would be beyond-scope for *Architect*.) Nussbaum's criticism is bracing, crisp, and straightforward. She beats around no bushes, she comes across as a relatable passionista, yet, however relatable her enthusiasm might be (she made me feel good about liking *Scandal* better than *House of Cards!*), she always delivers a perspective that is clearly her own, entirely fresh, and hard (or at least enjoyably challenging) to refute. Rybczynski is cool and analytical but also personal and passionate and engaged. And quite wry, with that breed of orotund in-the-fullness-of-time wit that I personally prize: "Although the librarians who showed me around boasted of their building's popularity, it's unclear that the experience of using a public library is actually enhanced when it doubles as a tourist attraction." (Oh, *snap*.)

Yeah, from a tone standpoint, it's possible to imagine either of these writers contributing to the other's rag (and, indeed, a search of the Web reveals that Rybczynski did toss a few bones Eustace Tilly's way back around the time the Web itself was being created; *Architect*, however, has apparently yet to find a way to snare Nussbaum's talents). But it's not possible to imagine these particular essays being published in each other's magazines—or any other magazine, for that matter. Rybczynski could write architecture criticism for *The New Yorker*, perhaps—but not *this* architecture criticism, which is too specific, too catering to the concerns and predilections of a relatively narrower audience, to reside comfortably anywhere but where it was created to reside.

This is the core reason that magazine writing retains its particular ATCG encoding even outside of its activating environment. (Which is an even more impressive achievement when you consider also that these pieces were originally published, both in print and online, in beautifully illuminated visual environments, accompanied by powerful photography, extraordinary illustration, etc.—yet here, where you consume them only and entirely in their textual essence, they don't feel diminished at all.) This is one thing that defines magazine writing and that creates and conditions its essence: It's commissioned; it's *assigned*.

The longstanding custom at the National Magazine Awards, whence these selections spring, is that every award, even the ones given to honor an individual article crafted by a lone writer, is accepted by the editor in chief of the magazine that published the work. This may sound like a glory grab perpetrated under the auspices of an organization that is, after all, called the American Society of Magazine Editors, but there is a logic to the practice based on the fact that editors assign (or, much more rarely, acquire) these stories and work with writers to shape them, all with an eye to ensuring that they're *right* for the magazine, will appeal to its particular audience, and will weave nicely into a tapestry of many other stories that, presented together, have an even greater positive effect on its readers.

This is presumably the reason book excerpts, though commonly published in magazines, often after a good deal of additional collaborative massaging between writer and editor, are not eligible for the NMAs: A book excerpt is not, at heart, magazine writing, it's book writing that happened to find itself in a magazine. This is also the reason that I'm personally a bit dubious about the inclusion here of Kathleen Ossip's poetry and Zadie Smith's fiction. I understand the impulse to showcase the full range of writing that gets published (at least occasionally) in magazines, and I celebrate the artistic virtuosity of Ossip and Smith—I sure loved reading and being tortured by every word— but, ultimately, this isn't *magazine writing*, made possible only through the agency of a magazine and bearing its particular genetic imprint.

Here's another game to play while reading these things (for best results, I'd recommend trying it the second time through, so the story can wash over you on first read). This one is called "Where did *that* detail come from?" What sort of reporting delivered that information? Kyle Dickman's "Nineteen," published in *Outside*, is a chilling account of the wildfire that menaced the town of Yarnell, Arizona, and of the nineteen firefighters from the Granite Mountain Hotshots who perished in the blaze. Think of it: These people are *dead*. How do you wrestle a rich, detailed, and psychologically acute narrative from ghosts? How did Sebastian Junger dramatize the plight of the fishermen on the doomed *Andrea Gail* in *The Perfect Storm* (which was once, in its original incarnation in *Outside*, "The Storm") when there were no survivors? Pay attention to how Dickman builds his story from knowable facts woven through highly informed speculation on what was happening, and what was seen by and might possibly have passed through the minds of the men who would ultimately die.

You don't actually have to wonder where the details came from in Luke Mogelson's "The Dream Boat" (*New York Times Magazine*), but it does inspire tremendous wonder at the empathy, commitment, and courage required for Mogelson to accompany a rickety boat's worth of Iranian and Afghan asylum seekers on their desperate attempted passage across 200 miles of tempestuous sea from Indonesia to an Australian territory named (perversely enough) Christmas Island. So many heroic acts of reporting are featured in this volume, in fact, that it provides a handy excuse for me to make the inarguable assertion that there is no great magazine writing without great reporting.

And sometimes the best way to write it is to lay out the reporting as cleanly as possible and simply ensure that its implications speak clearly—as they most assuredly do in "Bitter Pill," Steven Brill's infuriating 24,000-word reportorial masterpiece on the debilitating costs of medical care, which was published as an entire issue of *Time*. It was a bold decision by the magazine's editors, one that, it seems to me, serves as a reminder and celebration of one thing that magazines can do uniquely well, which is to deliver investigations of such depth, nuance, and power that they can transform the debate around an essential issue.

I do have a small quibble, however, about a decision *Time* made when it archived this opus online. It resides behind a paywall, accessible only to those willing to pony up for a subscription to the magazine—with no provision for simply buying the single article. While I support in principle the practice of using such powerful stories as an inducement to subscribe, to experience the report and future reports in situ, I worry that adopting such a blanket proscription is a willful denial of the future. Contrary to popular digital dogma, content doesn't want to be free, but neither does it want to be housed behind a high wall surmounted by coils of razor wire.

Bottom line, while the essence of "magazine" writing arises out of and is still most satisfyingly expressed in its curated, packaged, issue-based, defined, and confined-between-the-covers form, the insistence on constraining its consumption only to that form is distressingly backward-leaning and missing of the point. As the volume you hold in your hands (whether in print or through the magical screen of your smartphone, tablet, or e-reader) and the stories here robustly demonstrate, the best magazine writing retains both its power and its magazine-ness, even when there's no physical magazine in evidence.

Acknowledgments

This collection of stories and poems represents the best magazine journalism published in the United States in 2013. "Represents" because no single volume could contain every example of the often astonishing reporting and writing that appears every quarter, every month, every week, and now every day in American print and digital magazines. These stories appear here not as they were originally published—festooned with illustrations and photographs—but in simple black type. Yet these words have the power to remind us, as Mark Jannot explains in his introduction to this anthology, just how important magazine journalism remains to millions of readers.

"Remains" because many believe magazines are dying, even though the number of Americans who read magazines continues to grow—not necessarily in print, of course. Instead, many of us now read magazines on variously sized screens (no one could have imagined when the National Magazine Awards were founded in the mid-1960s that one day prizes for Multimedia and Video would be presented alongside awards for such magazine staples as reporting and service). Because the truth is, magazines are not dying. Yes, the business of magazines is changing, as it has changed before (before the Internet, there was television), but despite uncertain times, magazine journalism is thriving.

Wherefore this cockeyed optimism? The work collected here answers the question. Americans' growing thirst for magazine storytelling is evidenced by the steady popularity of titles such as *The New Yorker* and *The Atlantic* (in both print and digital incarnations) and the emergence of magazines like *The Atavist*, a digital publication dedicated solely to literary journalism. The stories collected here from these and other titles—*Esquire, Rolling Stone, Time*—attest to the enduring strength of what we now call magazine media (the media being print, Web, tablet, smartphone, and, a world of its own, social). Far from dying, magazines continue to shape our conversations both public and personal—just check your Twitter feed.

The stories in *Best American Magazine Writing* are drawn from publications nominated for National Magazine Awards—yet another reason this anthology can only be said to represent the best of magazine journalism. Hundreds of magazines enter the awards every year; hundreds more do not (the competition is fierce). Only a few dozen are nominated; still fewer win.

This year only seventeen publications received National Magazine Awards. Most of those magazines are represented (there's that word again) in this anthology. Others such as *Glamour, National Geographic,* and *W* won awards for work—websites, tablets, video series, entire print issues—uncontainable between the covers of any book. To find that work, you can visit the websites or download the apps listed with the rest of the winners and finalists at http://www.magazine.org/asme/national-magazine-awards and on the Wikipedia entry for the National Magazine Awards.

Those winners and finalists are chosen by judges—magazine journalists and educators—who gather in New York every spring to read thousands of entries. This year there were 333 judges and 1,586 entries submitted by 251 magazines in 24 categories. In some categories—General Excellence, Design, Photography, Magazine of the Year—the judges read entire print and digital issues of dozens of magazines. In other categories—such as Public Interest, Personal Service, Leisure Interests, Feature Writing—the judges read hundreds of stories, some as long as 30,000 words, all in the matter of a day or two, then pick the finalists and eventually the winners.

Then the judges go home—many live and work in New York, where many magazines are headquartered, but more than a quarter of the judges live and work elsewhere—only to return later in the spring for the presentation of the awards at a sometimes raucous dinner, which this year was hosted by Joe Scarborough and Mika Brzezinski of MSNBC's *Morning Joe.* The winners get copper statuettes modeled on Alexander Calder's stabile *Elephant.* The finalists receive certificates of recognition. Everyone else gets a story to tell until the next deadline comes along.

Hundreds of people work on the National Magazine Awards in one way or another. The judges, of course, deserve our thanks not only for the days they spend sequestered in utterly charmless conference rooms reading and discussing magazines but also for the time they spend preparing for the judging (each judge is assigned several entries to read before they arrive). A list of the judges is posted at http://www.magazine.org/asme. But even before the judging begins, editors up and down mastheads, especially editorial assistants and assistant editors, devote hours to preparing their entries. For this they deserve our thanks as well.

The National Magazine Awards are overseen by the board of the directors of the American Society of Magazine Editors. Board members juggle their ever-growing responsibilities, managing the sprawling operations magazines have become, with planning and supervising the awards. Their dedication and impartiality ensure that a wide range of magazines, from large general interest magazines to less well known special interest titles, receive National Magazine Award honors. Each board member deserves our gratitude, but special recognition is due the irrepressible Lucy Schulte Danziger, who served as president of ASME the last two years.

The National Magazine Awards are sponsored by ASME in association with the Columbia Graduate School of Journalism. ASME is thankful for the support Columbia has given to the awards since their founding a half century ago. On behalf of ASME, I want to thank Steve Coll, the dean of the school and Henry R. Luce Professor, and Abi Wright, who not only worked on the administration of the awards but also served as a judge.

The members of ASME are thankful to our literary agent, David McCormick of McCormick & Williams, for his skillful representation of our interests. I especially want to thank the editors of this book at the Columbia University Press, Philip Leventhal and Michael Haskell, who are not only talented craftsmen and patient friends but together are a constant reminder that even editors need editors.

ASME also thanks our associates at MPA—the Association of Magazine Media, especially the president and CEO, Mary G. Berner. In addition, I want to thank Hendley Badcock, Patty Bogie, John DeFrancesco, Sarah Hansen, and Meredith Wagner, as well as the longtime producers of the National Magazine Awards annual dinner, Leane Romeo and Michael Scarna of the Overland Entertainment Company. And a very loud shout-out goes to Nina Fortuna, who makes sure ASME members and award judges have what they need before they know they need it.

I also want to acknowledge the work of Mark Jannot, vice president, content, of the National Audubon Society and the current president of ASME, who wrote the introduction to this year's anthology. His steady leadership ensures the continuing success of the National Magazine Awards. And finally, on behalf of ASME, I want to thank the writers, editors, and magazines that permitted their stories and poems to be published in *Best American Magazine Writing 2014*. Their work guarantees the future of magazine media.

THE BEST
AMERICAN
MAGAZINE
WRITING

2014

Esquire

FINALIST—MAGAZINE OF
THE YEAR

For many readers, the celebrity profile defines the modern magazine; few consumer titles are published without at least one inside. Yet no matter how well crafted, these stories are often dismissed as the magazine equivalent of a loss leader. But many magazines—and many writers—not only take profiles seriously but also use them to tell us something about the way we live now. Esquire *is one of those magazines, and Tom Junod— whose stories have won two National Magazine Awards and have been nominated for nine more—is one of those writers. This is the third year in a row* Esquire *has been nominated for Magazine of the Year, and this profile of Matt Damon by Tom Junod was one of the cover stories that earned* Esquire *that honor.*

Tom Junod

The Second Biggest Star in a Remote Little Burg Somewhere in Germany

L et's face it, the guy is ridiculous.

He's ridiculously handsome. He's ridiculously accomplished. He's ridiculously smart. He's ridiculously kind to those in need of his kindness. He's ridiculously funny. He's ridiculously magnetic, with a ridiculously white movie-star smile and a ridiculously resonant voice-talent voice. Despite his ridiculous sense of ease and casual aplomb, he cannot go anywhere without making an entrance for the simple reason that people who feel ridiculous staring at him feel even more ridiculous *not* staring at him. All he has to do is smile and open his mouth and he switches on an inner light that turns every head, even Matt Damon's.

Now, just to be clear, Matt Damon is also ridiculous. Indeed, Damon is so ridiculous—so ridiculously handsome, accomplished, smart, funny, etc.—that he has been holding forth on the subject of German Holocaust awareness while drinking beer and eating steak on the patio of a hotel restaurant in Germany without sounding ridiculous himself. Damon does this a lot. He holds forth. He drinks beer. He holds forth while drinking beer, often with members of the crew of the movie he happens to be making, which in this case is *The Monuments Men*, the story of the American soldiers charged with recovering the vast stashes of priceless art stolen by the Nazis. Damon's the most social of movie stars, the most easily conversant, and so he holds forth lightly, his knowledge of history just as much a social lubricant as the beer he keeps ordering for the table. He's sitting with a young actor, a military consultant, a script supervisor, and me, and with a ridiculous lack of anything resembling effort he keeps all eyes trained upon him until—

"Ah, he's back!"

It's Clooney. It's the boss. It's the guy who's directing *The Monuments Men* as well as starring in it, and it's the guy whose unabashed incandescence makes Damon's feel suddenly like the light from a sustainable bulb. Did I say Clooney's ridiculous? Clooney's ridiculous. He's back from a weekend in Berlin, nearly three hours away, and he looks as though he just stepped out of the shower. He's skinny, almost gaunt in a T-shirt and baggy belted jeans, but with the elemental sheen of his swept-back gray hair and his gray mustache, he looks like Clark Gable, circa *The Misfits*, which is to say a movie star in any era, America's gift to the world. There's a small lake next to the hotel patio; earlier, Damon had changed places and put his back to it, because on the other side there gathered a host of photographers and German townspeople—*civilians*. Now Clooney walks over to him and says, "Hey, you folks are the entertainment."

"There are photographers," Damon says, because in the world he shares with Clooney, starstruck civilians are symptoms of a disease; photographers are active agents of infection.

"Yeah, I know," Clooney says. "I saw 'em all. One guy's got a lens like this." He spreads his hands around an imaginary object the size of a beach ball.

"They're all back because you're back," Damon tells him. "Today, I literally walked out the back door and walked up the street. Nobody was there."

"They don't follow you, but they follow him?" I ask.

Clooney leans over slightly and put his hand on Damon's shoulder. His smile is like the cleaver that chefs use in Japanese steakhouses—it looks too big and too sharp to handle, but he's tossing it around for fun. "You have to get your second Sexiest Man Alive," he says to Damon. "You get your second Sexiest, they follow you like crazy."

·　　　·　　　·

In the forthcoming movie *Elysium* (out August 9), the boy who plays Matt Damon's character as a little boy looks a lot like Matt Damon must have looked when he was a child. "When I first saw the photos, I thought someone Photoshopped Matt's face on them," says director Neill Blomkamp. "When Matt saw them, he said, 'Jesus, that looks like me.'"

In the movie, the boy spends most of his time on earth—which is, of course, hellishly "postapocalyptic"—staring into the sky at the enormous wheel of a satellite that provides refuge for the rich, who have abandoned the planet. The satellite is called Elysium, and when the little boy who grows up to become Matt Damon stares at the sky, he vows to get there. He winds up with a shaved head, a shitload of tattoos, a flash drive jacked into his brain stem, and an exoskeleton of body armor screwed into his very bones. He also winds up engaging in the kind of expertly choreographed yet relatively realistic fights Damon mastered in the Bourne series but that the presence of the exoskeleton made challenging—but get there he does, fomenting revolution in the process.

Blomkamp wrote the movie after his *District 9* turned into one of the surprise hits of 2009. Let Damon tell his story because Damon likes to tell stories: "When I first met him, Neill said, 'I grew up in South Africa. I grew up in a nice neighborhood in Johannesburg, but we'd drive a few miles and see poverty as abject as any place on earth. Then, when I was eighteen, we moved to

Canada and the experience of moving to the First World so shocked me that all my life, everything I do, all my work, is a rumination on that incredible difference.'"

Now let Blomkamp: "I wanted to make a film that separated rich and poor in a science-fiction way. And I thought it would be really interesting to take a corn-fed American white boy and put him in a Third World environment—to take someone that America knows well and put him in an America as run-down as possible. And Matt was the right guy for that, not only as an actor but as a *persona*."

He did not film *Elysium* in the run-down parts of America. He filmed it, as he says, in the "most poverty-stricken parts of Mexico City. I very specifically scouted the areas because I wanted them to be as run-down as possible. That was Matt's only trepidation—the security in Mexico City. He's very game, but the whole thing there is kidnapping, and it's different with him than it is with you or me. He's internationally recognized. People know he's in the country. We had to hire a security firm. Our security guys would run different routes to the set in the morning, do reconnaissance, make sure there were in-and-out routes everyplace we went."

Elysium is an interesting movie. But one of the most interesting things about it is that in order for it to exist, it had to be made by people from Elysium. Elysium is not just a metaphor for apartheid or for the growing divide between rich and poor in this country. It is a metaphor for celebrity and the privileges it bestows. Matt Damon plays a man who is willing to sacrifice everything in order to get there, and his portrayal is complicated by the fact that he lives there already.

.　　.　　.

"Would you like a small beer?" a waitress asks.

"No," Matt Damon says. "A *big* beer."

We are sitting at a table in a hotel lobby two and a half hours outside of Berlin. The table is small and round and high, the chairs tall and wobbly. We are meeting in the lobby because we're supposed to go out on a journalistic version of a date, Matt and I. We're supposed to go for a hike and then have a conversation over dinner. But then a waitress comes by and asks the persistent German question: "Would you like a beer?" She is very short, under five feet tall, with jet-black hair and sharp, dark features inked on very white skin. She is wearing the traditional folk costume that every waitress in Germany who works outside a major city has to wear in disconcerting ubiquity. It's just after five o'clock. Dinner is scheduled for eight. There's plenty of time for each of us to drink a beer before the hike, even a big beer.

"The thing that I like about Germany is that Germans are so much *like* us," he says when the beer arrives in tall clear glasses. "It's not like going to some other countries, where the differences are overwhelming and you walk around in a fog. Germans are so similar to Americans. They're, like, only 5 percent different— but then that difference makes *all* the difference. It makes everything that much stranger. You think that everything is going to be *exactly* the same, and when it's not it seems much stranger to you, and you realize that you must seem stranger to them. It's clarifying, man."

Damon is forty-two years old, married, father of four. Along with unfaded jeans, he is wearing black—a black V-neck T-shirt, big black punk-rock boots, a black ball cap imprinted with a pattern of four black stars. He has short brown hair haunted by a blond ghost. He is a shade under six feet tall, in shape but not in action-movie shape, not in ass-kicking *Elysium* shape. He has what Neill Blomkamp saw in him, what everybody sees in him: a broad, friendly American face, not so much youthful as still boyish, interesting primarily for what can be imprinted upon it—the tabula rasa of its blue eyes, turned-up nose, and perfectly even white teeth. In the movies, he has the most useful smile since Tom Cruise's, but whereas Cruise uses his smile to overpower, to silence doubters, and to get out of trouble, Damon uses his to express nuance, as both beacon and shadow. In person, he does the same thing. He smiles a lot, but he has a smile that can operate at cross-purposes with his eyes. Hell, he can smile while turning down the corners of his mouth; more precisely, he can turn down the corners of his mouth and *still* smile, without appearing to smirk or frown. It's either a trick or a talent, but in any case it's nearly impossible to do, and it shows why, when Blomkamp says "He's almost like a regular guy who's a global celebrity," *almost* is the operative word.

He is not a regular guy. He is to regular guys as he says Germans are to Americans—about 5 percent different. For comparison's sake, let's say George Clooney is about 15 percent different. Brad Pitt is about 12.5 percent different, and Leonardo DiCaprio has never *been* a regular guy, so he offers no basis for calculation. But Damon is so close to being a regular guy that he can pass as a regular guy onscreen and off-. He can be the *same* guy onscreen and off-, and so he offers audiences the rarest of combinations— the satisfaction of reliability and surprise. It was a surprise when he was able to both write and star in *Good Will Hunting*. It was a surprise when he was able to pull off the Bourne series. It was a surprise when he was so funny on Jimmy Kimmel and *30 Rock*. It was a surprise when he wore a thong for Michael Douglas in *Behind the Candelabra*. ("Though I've seen Matt's ass quite a lot, it was nice to get an update," says his friend Ben Affleck.) But he can be continually surprising in his performances because he is so reliably unsurprising in his life—because he fulfills expectations instead of confounding them. Matt Damon is a movie star because he always delivers on being Matt Damon. He is a movie star not only because he makes us want to have a beer with him but also because he makes us think that, alone among movie stars, he might actually want to have a beer with us . . .

And then he orders his second big beer ten minutes after his first.

·   ·   ·

We never go on the hike. We never go out to dinner. We never even stand up, except for the necessities. As soon as we start drinking, members of the crew and cast of *The Monuments Men* start stopping by. The hotel is a refuge, with tall, black iron gates and security guards with walkie-talkies. Our table is not. When the actor Bob Balaban walks by, Damon says, "Hey, man!" When the lead gaffer walks by, Damon says, "Hey, man!" When a military advisor named Billy Budd walks by, Damon says, "Hey, man!" And he says the same thing to a young actor named Diarmaid Murtagh. Budd is a Brit, a former marine in the service of the queen, with a silver brush cut, a big hawk nose that casts a shadow on his scorched face, and arms scrawled with fiendish tattoos. Murtagh is an Irishman, with an explosive laugh and an Irish thirst. They're both first-class storytellers, and when they sit with us, they sit with us for the next seven hours. I never get the chance to do a long interview with Matt Damon because Matt Damon is never alone. But that's okay. I've talked to movie stars before. I've never had a chance to hear what movie stars talk *about*, inside the gates of Elysium.

·   ·   ·

Here's a story. Matt Damon told it. But it's not about Matt Damon. It's about Bono. But it's not really about Bono, either; it's about Paul McCartney. But Damon heard it from Bono. One day, Bono flew into Liverpool. Paul was supposed to pick him up at the airport, and Bono was shocked when Paul *picked him up* at the airport alone, behind the wheel of his car. "Would you like to go on a little tour?" Paul said. Sure, Bono said, because Bono, you see, is a fan of Paul's, in the same way that Damon is a fan of Bono's. "Bono's obsessed with the Beatles," Damon said at the table in the lobby of the gated hotel in the little town in Germany. "He's, like, a student of the Beatles. He's read *every* book on the Beatles. He's seen *every* bit of film. There's nothing he doesn't know. So when Paul stops and says 'That's where it happened,' Bono's like, 'That's where *what* happened?' because he thinks he knows everything. And Paul says, 'That's where the Beatles started. That's where John gave me half his chocolate bar.' And now Bono's like, 'What chocolate bar? I've never heard of any chocolate bar.' And Paul says, 'John had a chocolate bar, and he shared it with me. And he didn't give me *some* of his chocolate bar. He didn't give me a *square* of his chocolate bar. He didn't give me a *quarter* of his chocolate bar. He gave me *half* of his chocolate bar. And that's why the Beatles started right there.' Isn't that fantastic? It's the most important story about the Beatles, and it's in *none* of the books! And Paul tells it to Bono. Because he knows how much Bono loves the Beatles."

Now, George Clooney is right—*People* has named Matt Damon Sexiest Man Alive only once. He is not the biggest global celebrity. He's not the biggest movie star, and it's a matter of debate whether he's the most handsome in Jimmy Kimmel's "Handsome Men's Club." But he's pretty damned *close*—close enough to be on the inside, close enough to hear the stories, close enough to tell the stories, close enough to tell stories about those who tell the stories. And the stories—well, they're delicious, sweetened by their exclusivity and by the fact that they're strictly rationed. They're in none of the books, and for good reason: They're occasionally too good to be true.

•   •   •

You want to know what famous people talk about? They talk about you and me, first of all—the people on the other side of the lake, the people peering inside the window, the extent to which they'll go to get a look or a photograph. Then they talk about one another. Those are the best stories because they're also performances. Damon is famous for his Matthew McConaughey imitation, but three or four or five or six big beers into the night, he did quick imitations of nearly everyone he talked about. He did Scorsese and Spielberg and Clint Eastwood. He did Russell Crowe and he did Tom Cruise. He did Russell Crowe talking about his relationship with director Ridley Scott—"Rid's the general, I'm the soldier, and when we make a movie, we go to *war!*"—and he did Tom Cruise talking about the stunt director for one of the *Mission: Impossible* movies who refused to let him climb the side of a building without a stunt double. "I asked Tom, 'Well, what did you do?' And he looked at me"—and here Damon reproduced the Thetanic fixity of Cruise's stare and the martinet hysteria of his voice—"and said, 'I *fired* him, Matt.'"

He told the Tom Cruise story for two reasons. Number one, it is a Tom Cruise story. Number two, Damon doesn't climb buildings. He's afraid of heights, and, he says, "That's what stuntmen are for. That's what green screens are for. But Tom's incredible. I said, 'You have the title. Nobody's ever going to take the title from you. You win.' He laughed. But he also goes, '*It was worth it.*' And it was—for him. It's not for me. I'm way too old to do all my own stunts."

And that's the other thing about the stories famous people tell. They tend to tell stories about people more famous than they are. Matt Damon tells stories about Tom Cruise and George Clooney. He tells a story about Bono telling a story about Paul McCartney. There are rings of fame, like some kind of obverse *Inferno*, and the people inside one ring tell stories about people in another—the ones who are farther inside, closer to some kind of impossible absolute. It's a form of gossip, sure, and also of adulation, but it's also an education, often the best education they've received. Damon left Harvard without graduating, but he's something of a polymath who, no matter the subject, can tell you what he's learned about it not just from the book he's read but also from the person who wrote the book he's read. He drops names like crazy, but he's not so much a name-dropper as he is a student citing his sources. He talks about talking to Tom Cruise, Jodie Foster, Michael Strahan, Tom Brady, Martin Scorsese, Brad Pitt, Joaquin Phoenix, Emily Blunt, and his friends Ben and Casey Affleck, but he also talks about talking to Bill Clinton, Jeffrey Sachs, Paul Farmer, Ray Kurzweil, Dave Eggers, and other assorted writers, economists, scientists, and advocates. He has access to them all in the same way that he has access to tables at the most exclusive restaurants, and it no longer matters that he dropped out of Harvard—fame has become his Harvard. In the globalized world, the false currency of celebrity has turned out to be the only one that resists devaluation because it has become the price of access and access has become the price of knowledge. We like to think that fame insulates its denizens from the real world. It is painful to contemplate what everyone drinking beer in that hotel lobby seemed to know—that fame brings the famous closer to the heart of things, or at least closer than the people clustered outside the gate can ever get.

·   ·   ·

My mother thought it was child abuse," he says. "She literally did. She was a professor who specialized in early childhood development, and she thought putting a child onstage or in a commercial or in a movie was child abuse. So when I did *Elysium* with Jodie Foster, I asked *her*. I mean, she's basically been acting since she was born. I figured if anyone's going to know, it should be her, right? So I asked her. And she sort of smiled and said, 'It depends on the child.'"

Matt Damon was not a child actor. He was a child and then an adolescent enriched by progressive education in Cambridge, Massachusetts—by Howard Zinn as his neighbor, by Cambridge

Rindge and Latin as his high school, by immersive-language study with Mom in Mexico and Guatemala as his summer vacation. But his friend Ben Affleck was a child actor, and acting became the ambitious way Matt separated himself from his mother's ambitions. He not only acted in school plays; he also worked as an extra in Boston and can do an imitation of the guy who was, like, "the king of the extras, because he'd worked on Scorsese movies. And he was like, 'Me and Marty, we're like *this*. I give Marty exactly what he wants.' And I'm sitting at this guy's feet, thinking, *Hey, one day, maybe that could be me.*"

At the time, Affleck was the star, both in school plays and at auditions. But Damon permitted himself to learn from him, and they became not just friends but also a team. "The summer after freshman year in college, we got a job together. I was eighteen. There was a theater in Harvard Square called the Janus. They had only one screen, and Ben and I got a job there. We were ticket takers and served popcorn—we basically did everything. But the kicker was that the movie we showed that summer was a movie Ben and I got relatively close on—*Dead Poets Society*. We got down the line; we got called back. Ben got even closer than I did. And that was the one movie they showed that summer. It was a constant reminder. We'd sit there, these young ambitious guys in our maroon vests, our black pants, our white shirts, and our fucking name tags, watching people coming out of the theater *bawling* their fucking eyes out.

"It was like, 'Whatever doesn't kill you makes you stronger.' But it underscored the difficulty of breaking in, enough that we were convinced we had to start writing."

Good Will Hunting began as a lark, the fanciful idea of two kids who loved to learn but didn't want to go to school. "We were like, 'Wouldn't that be cool if you could read every book in the world and remember everything you read?'" But it became, Damon says, "an act of desperation." Multiple drafts, written in multiple rented apartments over multiple years, developed by multiple studios: "We had an unlimited amount of time. It wasn't like anybody cared. It wasn't like anybody was waiting to see what we were doing . . ."

But then, of course, it changed everything. The Best Screenplay Oscar changed everything. "Being known as a writer did change the relationships I had with directors. The rap on actors is that they always want to inflate their parts. But when directors know you write screenplays and have a different view of things, you really get invited into the huddle in a much fuller way. And those collaborations end in friendships. That's how it works. It really is all about relationships. If you enjoy working with someone, you'll find a way to work with him or her again. It's human nature."

When Damon was in high school and in college, he had a Mickey Rourke poster on the wall of his bedroom. (Affleck: "I don't remember that. I remember the Michael Jackson.") Mickey Rourke was his favorite actor; he wanted to be Mickey Rourke. And so when he was still very young—before *Good Will Hunting* made him a star—and he got the lead role in *The Rainmaker* alongside Mickey Rourke, "I was really excited just to meet him. And then the first day of filming, he pulls me aside and just reads me the riot act. We were shooting in a really bad neighborhood in Memphis—we had security and everything—and I'm standing on a street corner and my boyhood idol is *yelling* at me. He's saying, 'Francis Ford Coppola wanted you for this movie—that's a big deal. That sends a message to everyone in Hollywood that you have a future. So don't do what I did. *Don't fuck it up!*'"

And Damon hasn't. He might give the appearance of being a regular guy, but he hasn't done what regular guys always do—he hasn't fucked it up. He understands better than anyone else that celebrity is a social contract, and he has fulfilled it to the last jot and tittle. He's passed every possible test of citizenship that fame could offer, and what you understand when you spend time with him is simply this:

He's a member of the club.

•   •   •

There's a young actor with a big role in *The Monuments Men*. His name is Dimitri Leonidas, and he was, until Clooney cast him, a so-called unknown. He's not one of the cast members who walk through the hotel lobby on either night that Damon is drinking beer. But Damon talks about him and says how bright his future is. He doesn't say that his future is bright as an actor, though. He says, "He could be a movie star."

What does that mean, exactly? It's uttered by a movie star, so it must mean something—it must mean that there are some qualifications for the job, and you don't know what they are until you get it. It must mean that Matt Damon recognizes some kindred quality in Dimitri Leonidas, some degree of difference that only those with their own inexplicable difference can see. It also means that Damon thinks about these things *a lot*. He thinks about stardom and he thinks about fame, not to glory in them but to assess his own degree of difference and dislocation. He talks about *what happened* to him when he became a movie star as though it's irrevocable:

"When it happens to you, it's not that you change. Everybody says you change, and you do eventually. But what happens, almost overnight, is that nothing and everything changes at the same time. You're aware that everything that mattered yesterday still matters today. Everything is the same, and intellectually you understand that. But the world is completely different—for *you*. Everybody has changed their relationship to you, but you still live in the same world. So when people talk about the surreality of fame, that's what they're talking about. That's what it was for me. It's walking into a restaurant and everybody turns their head and starts whispering—and you're like, 'But I ate at this restaurant last *week*.' And so the world is still the same—it's just never going to be the same for me. And that's a real mind-fuck. The world is one degree stranger. It's not like the houses have suddenly turned to gingerbread and you go, 'Oh, it wasn't like that before.' You live in the same house, you go to the same market, you get coffee in the same place. It's just that somebody has hired an unlimited amount of extras and given them very specific directions—for you. It's as if a director has gotten there before you and grabbed a bullhorn and said, 'Okay, when he comes in, if your name begins with A through M, count to ten and then notice him. N through Z, notice him right away.' It's very strange."

·   ·   ·

Here's another story. Matt Damon tells it, but it's not about Matt Damon. It's about Brad Pitt. But it is also about Matt Damon because it's about fame and Matt Damon is famous. But is he as famous as Brad Pitt? Is he as big a movie star? In some ways, he's bigger—with the Bourne movies, he created the action franchise that Pitt hopes to create with *World War Z*. But there are measures of stardom other than weekend grosses, indices of which ring you occupy other than money. One is your degree of convergence with Bono. Another is pain.

"If you can control the celebrity side of celebrity," Damon says, "then it's worth it. I look at Brad—and I have for years—and when I'm with him I see the intensity of that other side of it. And the paparazzi and the insane level of aggression they have and their willingness to break the law and invade his space— well, I wonder about that trade. I remember telling him that I walk my kids to school, and his face just fell. He was very kind, but he was like, 'You bastard.' Because he should be able to do that, too. And he can't."

Damon can. He lives in New York, and he walks his kids to school. Photographers occasionally dog his steps, but generally from a distance, and if he asks them to back off, they will after they get their shots. He can do this because of what he didn't do—or whom he didn't marry. "I got lucky," he says. "I fell in love with a civilian. Not an actress and not a famous actress at that. Because then the attention doesn't double—it grows exponentially. Because then suddenly everybody wants to be in your bedroom. But I don't really give them anything. If I'm not jumping up and down on a bar, or lighting something on fire, or cheating on my wife, there's not really any story to tell. They can try to stake me out, but they're always going to get the same story—middle-aged married guy with four kids. So as long as that narrative doesn't change too much, there's no appetite for it."

The narrative, however, is about to change. Damon and his wife, Lucy, and their four children are about to move to LA, despite knowing they will lose some of their privacy to an entrenched apparatus of snoops. There are a few reasons for this. First of all, Ben Affleck and Jennifer Garner live there, and even though "there are five or six photographers outside their house all the time," Damon and his family have bought a house on the same street. Second, Damon and Affleck have started a production company, Pearl Street Films, "and we finally just rented offices and it's like, Let's get serious." And third, "Most of our old friends with kids live in LA, and their kids don't know me. I don't like that." (Affleck: "It's like being in the neighborhood again.")

But the fourth and final reason is the most interesting. Damon is buying a house in Los Angeles because he couldn't buy one in New York. "We tried to find a place for four years and couldn't find one. We made five offers, and we had two places where we had a verbal agreement, the last of which I absolutely loved. And in both cases, they used my name to sell to someone else. In a lot of transactional situations, fame is a good thing—people are much nicer to you. But in this case, it worked against me. Or maybe people think I'm an actor, so I must be stupid."

•　　　•　　　•

I drank beer for seven hours with Matt Damon on one night and four hours on another. I learned a lot of things. Because Damon knows the director Doug Liman, I learned that Tiger Woods kept missing the ball in that famous Nike commercial until the camera was turned on, whereupon he bounced it on the face of an iron and then whacked it two hundred yards. Because he knows Casey Affleck, I know that Joaquin Phoenix's "breakdown" really *was* a piece of performance art intended for the Affleck-directed documentary *I'm Still Here*, and that David Letterman really was pissed off when Affleck and Phoenix revealed the hoax to the *New York Times* instead of on his show. And because he knows Christopher Hitchens's agent, I know the last thing Hitchens said before he died.

I found out like this. Damon was talking about going to watch a TED Talk in the company of Paul Farmer, the great physician to the poor and one of Damon's heroes. They went to see Gordon Brown, the former British prime minister and, as Farmer told Damon, one of the handful of people "who know how the world works." Damon went and was amazed that every single one of Brown's sentences was complete and every single one of his thoughts conformed to the shape of a paragraph—and that he didn't use a teleprompter.

"Christopher Hitchens was like that," I said. "I saw him speak once, drunk, and if someone had written the whole thing down, he could have handed it in as an essay."

"I know his agent," Damon said, for he is both possessor and habitual proprietor of upstream knowledge. "And he told me Hitchens's last words."

We all waited. It was our chocolate bar.

"They were *capitalism fail*."

When I came home, I discovered that Andrew Sullivan knows the same agent and wrote on the *Daily Beast* that Hitchens's last words were "capitalism downfall." I have no idea which version is correct. But that's not the end of the story. The end of the story comes the next day, when Damon returns to his hotel room after a morning of filming and is inspired by the words "capitalism fail" to go online and watch a lecture by one of his former professors at Harvard, Michael Sandel. "I took his class twenty-three years ago, and now I'm taking it again," he says a few hours later on the patio. The same tiny waitress in the same traditional frock asks him if he'd like a beer, and this time he says, "Yes, a large beer" and begins speaking about what he learned from Sandel.

"He was asking about the things that money can't buy," Damon said. "He was saying that we've gone from a market economy to a market society, where we're essentially trying to monetize everything. He gave all these examples, like this jail in Santa Barbara where you can pay for a nicer cell and better treatment. The world changes in a fundamental way when you can buy your way out of any situation."

I mentioned an experience I'd had over the summer, when I took my daughter to a water park we'd been to many times and found it transformed by the availability of a "Fast Pass," which allows visitors to pay an extra forty-five dollars to go to the head of the lines. "It changed everything," I said, "because people were now paying to cut the line, and everybody knew that it was unfair. I knew it, my daughter knew it, and so did the people doing the cutting."

Damon nodded. "If you really want to know what it's like to be famous, all you have to do is go to that water park and pay your forty-five bucks. Go to the water park and that's what it's like.

"You jump the line."

. . .

Here's one last story. Matt Damon tells it, but it's not about Matt Damon. It's about George Clooney. But it's not really about George Clooney, either, because Damon wouldn't be telling it if it weren't also about Russell Crowe. Damon loves telling Russell

Crowe stories, in Russell Crowe's voice. But the story's all about the questions of selling out and hypocrisy, so maybe it's about Damon after all. He's been wrestling with these things because he recently began lending his ridiculously believable speaking voice to commercials. It frankly seems an unnecessary inner struggle, given that everybody in his business, from Jeff Bridges to Jon Hamm to Denis Leary, is allowing himself to be used as voice talent.

"I know," he says. "but it's still a *commercial*. What's the line that Paul Newman used to say—'shameless exploitation in pursuit of common good'? I tell myself that. I mean, I give all the money to [Damon's foundation] Water.org. I couldn't imagine keeping it. But let's face it—the money I contribute from the commercial is money I don't have to contribute from my pocket. One way or another, I'm getting paid. So maybe I'm a big hypocrite."

Of course, Clooney does a lot of voice work, too, especially in Europe. And one day, Damon says, "Russell called him out for doing a commercial in Italy. He called him a sellout—George, who never got full boat. George, who's always cutting his deal to work with the directors he wants to work with. So George said, 'Wait a minute. The only way I could live is if I do this fucking espresso commercial. What the fuck? Why are you attacking me? You're calling me a sellout? Look at your fucking movies, man!'

"And George is the best prankster. But he doesn't do anything. He's furious—but he sits on it. And then Russell wins a [British Academy of Film and Television Arts] award, and he goes up in front of the BAFTAs and reads a poem he wrote. He goes on for so long that when they show it that night, they edit it. They're at a party and they're all in tuxedos and they're playing the thing back, and Russell sees that his speech is truncated. And he famously grabs the producer of the show and throws him against the wall, and it has to be broken up.

"So the next year, George gets nominated. He's got *Good Night, and Good Luck* and he's got *Michael Clayton*, and he's up for, like, fifty fucking BAFTAs. And he wins one of them. So he gets onstage. But a few weeks before, he was in a bookstore and saw a book by Russell Crowe. It's called *My Heart, My Song*, and it's a book of Russell's poetry.

"So George gets up in front of the BAFTA audience, and they're cheering him on, and he goes, 'I hear you like poetry.' And instantly the place goes dead quiet. Then he just reaches into his tux and pulls out the book, and he goes, '*My Heart, My Song*, by Russell Crowe.' And the place instantly goes wild. He picks a poem to read, and every line people are falling out of their chairs and he's gotta hold twenty seconds for their laughter.

"And he reads the whole thing and he says, 'Thank you. Good night, good luck.'

"And he walks off."

It's a delicious story, too good to be true. Russell Crowe did, in fact, read a poem at the BAFTA awards in 2002, but not one of his own. He made a CD called *My Hand, My Heart*, but he has never published a book of poems. George Clooney never won a BAFTA until this year, when he won as a producer of Affleck's *Argo*. Does any of this make the story any less delicious? It does not, because the story's flavor does not derive from its veracity. It derives from proximity—from the fact that you are listening to Matt Damon tell it on the patio instead of watching him tell it from the other side of the lake.

•   •   •

The sun's going down when his BlackBerry pings. He pulls it out of his pocket, and when he looks at it he almost seems to flinch, but it's the quick jolt of his smile snapping his head back an inch. He's at a table full of people, but he does not take his eyes off the screen. His face fills with light, and what can be heard, in the sudden silence, is the voice of a little girl reporting the news from home: the fact that one of Damon's other daughters has lost a tooth. Then we hear what he hears—"I love you, Daddy!"—and his smile deepens as his shoulders sag, and we see that look of pride and pain common to every father in the world who has to experience the love of a child from a helpless distance. He can't answer because what he's just seen is a video that his children made and his wife attached to an e-mail. So he doesn't say anything, just slides the BlackBerry back in his pocket, and for the first time since I've met him, Matt Damon is, for the moment, alone.

There are a few more stories and a few more beers, but the dusk deepens to darkness, and he stands up to go back to his room. George Clooney is long gone, but along and across the lake they are still clustered, and now they wave to him. They have been waiting for him to go before they disperse, and he waves back. They are all Germans, 5 percent different from him, but he is 5 percent different not just from them but also from everyone else. When he turns his back on them one last time, they call "Goodnight" to him, in English.

Fast Company

When the National Magazine
Awards judges chose the
Magazine of the Year for 2014,
one of the reasons Fast Company
won was the editors' coverage
of industrial design—on their
network of websites, especially
Co.Design, and in print iterations
such as the tenth annual
Innovation by Design Issue.
The cover story of that issue was
this oral history of Apple design.
There may, of course, be some
readers who think an oral history
is not, well, writing, but nowhere
is the skill of the interviewer and
editor more evident than in a piece
like "Apple Breaks the Mold"—a
story about what is for many
Americans not a business but a
way of life, told only in the words
of the people who created it.

Max Chafkin

Apple Breaks the Mold

An Oral History

"This is our signature," Apple's gauzy television ads proclaim, referring to the familiar words that the company stamps on the undersides of its products: DESIGNED BY APPLE IN CALIFORNIA. The ads fall in the grand Apple tradition—beginning with the "1984" Super Bowl spot—of seeming to say a great deal while revealing little. The singular Cupertino computer company is one of the most intensely competitive, pathologically secretive organizations in the world.

If there is one thing that CEO Tim Cook doesn't want people to know, it's what dwells behind his company's "signature." As a result, most efforts to explain design at Apple end up reducing a complex thirty-seven-year history to bromides about simplicity, quality, and perfection—as if those were ambitions unique to Apple alone.

So *Fast Company* set out to remedy that deficiency. It wasn't easy. Precious few designers have left Sir Jonathan Ive's industrial design group since he took over in 1996: Two quit; three died. (We talked to the two who quit, among dozens of other longtime Apple veterans.) What we found is that the greatest business story of the past two decades—how Apple used design to rise from near bankruptcy to become the most valuable company in the world—is completely misunderstood.

Outsiders have tended to assume that because longtime CEO Steve Jobs was a champion of products in which hardware and software work together seamlessly, Apple itself was a paragon of collaboration. In fact, the opposite was often true.

What's more, the myth of Jobs's exile in 1985 and restoration in 1997 has obscured the fact that much of the critical design work that led to Apple's resurgence started while Jobs was running Pixar and NeXT. Ive—of whom Jobs once said, "He has more operational power than anyone else at Apple except me"—joined the company in 1992. And since Ive added software to his domain, in 2012, the industrial designer has even more power now.

Neither Ive, nor anyone else at Apple, was willing to speak on the record for this article. As a result, this story is different from any other you've read about Apple. It is an oral history of Apple's design, a decoding of the signature as told by the people who helped create it. Its roots go back to the 1980s, when Jobs's metaphor that the computer is a "bicycle for the mind" became a touchstone for design at Apple, an expression of the ambition to turn high tech into simple and accessible devices. In the immediate aftermath of Jobs's 1985 ouster, Apple had some commercial success, thanks in part to the work of Hartmut Esslinger's Frog Design (now Frog). But Esslinger followed Jobs to NeXT in the late 1980s, and as the 1990s wore on, Apple struggled as a me-too PC maker, and its market share plummeted. Our creative conversation starts in those dark days, when a hardy few trying to hold onto Jobs's ideals are heartened by the arrival of a soft-spoken, young industrial designer from the United Kingdom.

1992: "Here Lies the Guy Who Hired Jonathan Ive"

ROBERT BRUNNER, founder, Apple's industrial design group (now founder of Ammunition and the designer of Beats headphones): I sometimes joke that when I die, my tombstone will say, "Here lies the guy who hired Jonathan

Ive." Jonathan had shown up at my old firm, Lunar, on a
bursary scholarship. He was this quiet, polite English kid
with these models. They weren't just well-designed
objects; he'd actually engineered them. I thought, Wow,
this is someone I'd like to have on my team.

When I first got to Apple in 1989, I called Jony [Ive] to
see if he was interested in coming to work at Apple. He
said no. He'd just started his own firm, Tangerine, and he
wanted to see it through. In 1992, I hired Tangerine for
this mobility project called Juggernaut. I have to admit
part of the reason was because I wanted to see if I could
get him interested in Apple. They built some wonderful
models. When Jony came over to show them, it was a
beautiful, sunny weekend in California. And when
I asked again if he was interested, he said yes.

THOMAS MEYERHOFFER, senior industrial designer, Ive's first
hire (now runs his own design firm): We wanted to put
design forward as a competitive tool for Apple, but
nobody really understood what design could do. There
was a great urge from us in the design group to say:
Apple is different, Apple has always been different.

BRUNNER: There was a guy on our team, Thomas Meyerhoffer, who was working on the eMate. We took the guts and
the operating system of the [proto tablet] Newton and put
it in a clamshell. The idea was a very simplified computer
for kids. That's where the whole translucent, bulbous form
of the iMac got started.

MEYERHOFFER: Every laptop you'd seen before was square
and a big chunk of beige plastic. I wanted to make this
product look light and fun. And because nobody knows
what's inside those beige boxes, I wanted to give the
feeling that there was something intelligent in there.
I used a translucent plastic because that's the only way
you can do that. It gave the product more life.

DOUG SATZGER, industrial design creative lead (now VP, industrial design, Intel): We worked on a lot of cool concepts. But still, under [then-CEO] Gil Amelio, design didn't mean anything. You'd design a product and marketing would say, "Well, we only gave you fifteen dollars to do this and it's gonna cost us twenty dollars, so we're gonna badge a Dell computer or Canon printer." We were a marketing-driven company that wasn't focused on design, or even delivering a product. I saw that if this was the way it was going to continue, then I should probably leave. Jony knew that, and we had discussions about how the whole team would move if that were to happen.

Meanwhile, things were even worse in the software division, where Apple's operating system had been surpassed by the far-superior Windows 95.

CORDELL RATZLAFF, manager, Mac OS human interface group (now a user experience director at Google): There was a project code-named Copland, which was supposed to be Apple's next-generation operating system. It was probably one of the worst-managed projects ever at Apple. After a couple of years, it was clear that it was never going to ship.

DON LINDSAY, design director, Mac OS user experience group (now VP, user experience, BlackBerry): Shortly after that, Apple acquired NeXT—and, of course, along with that package comes Steve Jobs.

1998: "Good Enough to Lick"

The deal to acquire NeXT for $429 million closed in December 1996. Jobs would be named interim CEO of Apple the following summer. One of his first moves: teaming up with Ive, who replaced Brunner as head of the industrial design group in 1996, to redesign the company's desktop computers. Ive was just thirty years old at the time.

SATZGER: For Steve's first interview with us, we cleaned up in the studio. We knew Steve was a loud talker but that he wanted his voice to be focused on whom he was talking to. When he walked in the door, we turned up the music, so his conversations stayed between the person he was with.

JEFF ZWERNER, creative director, packaging (now a VP at Evernote): Jony manufactured every facet of that space as if to make Steve feel comfortable—from what they wore to the ambient techno music that was playing. There was an unwritten rule that if Steve came in, everyone had to slowly and deliberately move to the other side of the space.

JON RUBINSTEIN, senior VP, hardware engineering, Ive's boss until 2004 (now an Amazon board member): Steve spent a lot of time in the studio because it was his happy place. Running the business wasn't as much fun as hanging around with the design team.

SATZGER: Steve told us he wanted an Internet computer. His daughter was going to college, and he wanted to develop a computer that he felt was good enough for her to take to school. He had this idea for a product that didn't need a hard drive.

RUBINSTEIN: The network computer just didn't work. There wasn't enough bandwidth. The original design looked like a shrunk-down version of what became the iMac. It had a tunnel underneath where you could put the keyboard, because there was almost nothing inside it.

KEN SEGALL, creative director, Chiat/Day (now a writer and consultant): When we first saw the iMac prototype, it was shocking. Somebody lifted a cloth and you could see the guts of the computer. It looked like a cartoon version of the future.

Tɪᴍ Kᴏʙᴇ, cofounder, Eight Inc., an architecture firm that initially worked on display designs at Macworld conferences (now works on the design of the Apple Stores): Steve said, "All it takes is for the word *color* to get out, and we're screwed." He was really sensitive to the fact that that core idea—that it had color and a personality—was a shift in thinking.

Sᴀᴛᴢɢᴇʀ: We delivered the Bondi Blue iMac, and as soon as Steve got offstage after the announcement, he said, "I love the iMac, but we just delivered it in the wrong color."

Tʀɪᴘ Hᴀᴡᴋɪɴs, former marketing and product manager, Apple Lisa group (later founder of Electronic Arts): I was like, "Man, he managed to make a monitor look sexy." No one had done that, ever.

The iMac, which was offered in five candy colors, was a hit, the first computer that felt like a consumer product and not a business appliance. The next step in Jobs's companywide redesign was software.

Lɪɴᴅsᴀʏ: Shortly before the unveiling of the iMac, Steve turned his attention to the user experience on the Mac OS X. He hauled the entire software design team into a room, and in typical Steve style, he just declared everybody in the room to be an idiot.

Rᴀᴛᴢʟᴀғғ: It went downhill from there. We spent the next few weeks working night and day building a prototype of what we wanted Mac OS X to be. We started by thinking about every other operating system out there. They were all big, dark, gloomy, and chunky. Our approach was, Let's do the exact opposite. In that prototype, there were the initial ideas for the dock, the Mac as your digital hub, a completely new color scheme, and the animations.

LINDSAY: Steve was taking his knowledge from the hardware, which at the time was about translucency and glossiness and color, and he was bringing that to bear on the interface.

RATZLAFF: We'd meet with Steve on Tuesday afternoons. He would come up with the craziest ideas. At one point, Steve wanted to do all of our error messages as haikus. He would leave, and we would all think, What is he smoking?

In one of our meetings, Steve said, "I want this to look good enough to lick." After that, one of the designers stuck a half-sucked Life Saver to his monitor.

The new user-interface system was known as Aqua. Using a fixed dock on the bottom of the screen and relying heavily on visual metaphors and animation, it would evolve into the modern versions of both OS X and iOS while exerting an obvious influence on operating systems offered by Microsoft, Google, and pretty much every other major software company.

2000: "He Wanted to Control Everything That Touched His Product"

DAN WALKER, chief talent officer (now an HR consultant): I was in my kitchen in Orange County, and my wife answers the phone and says, "Sure, he's right here." She hands me the phone and says, "It's Steve Jobs." He said, "Mickey Drexler is on our board of directors, and he told me that I should give you a call because I'm thinking about opening retail stores for the Apple brand. Would you come up and talk to me?" [Walker had worked with Drexler at Gap.]

I went to the fourth floor of the Loop. The side opposite the elevators, that's where Steve dwelled. Valhalla. He told me that he was creating a premium product that really needed to have a story told. He wanted to control everything that touched his product—the creation, the manufacturing, how it went to market, and how the customer interacted with it.

With advice from Walker as well as Drexler, Jobs began assembling a team for retail stores, led by a former Target executive named Ron Johnson. The goal was to capitalize on the excitement over Ive's wildly successful iMacs and to begin selling people on the idea that would become central to Apple's design over the next decade: the digital hub.

KOBE: My partner, Wilhelm Oehl, and I were the first ones hired on the Apple Stores program. We started in 1999, on a whiteboard with Steve. He was asking us a lot of questions like, "How big is the Nike store?" He wanted to do a store with a large presence, but at the time Apple had two laptops, two desktops, and not a lot of software. So we had to come up with a lot of other things: the photo zone, the kids area, the Genius Bar, the theater. Those were all outcomes of trying to create an experience that was distinctly Apple and different from the kind of experience most people would have had with technology.

WALKER: Ron Johnson wanted to brainstorm what it was going to be. We had the global head of customer service for the Ritz-Carlton and two kids who sold Macs at CompUSA. We had the architects who were going to design the store. We had this incredibly brilliant graphic artist. We sat in that room for a couple of days. That's where the Genius Bar was invented. I still remember Ron sketching it out.

Michael Kramer, CFO, Apple Retail (later COO, JCPenney): When Ron told me about the Genius Bar, I asked, "So how big is it?" He said, "Five people in every store." "So you're going to take away 20% of the sales floor?" "Yeah." "What are we going to charge?" "Nothing." Most CFOs would say, "Are you fucking crazy?" But even as a financial guy at Apple, you have to have a reverence for the creative side of the business. You have to figure out ways to say yes.

Kobe: I got the sense that Ron was quite frustrated by Steve. Ron would always give a textbook answer to any retail question, and Steve would always go a few degrees off of that. I always thought Steve was just being mean, but later I realized that he was using Ron as a barometer of conventional wisdom of what his best competitors would do. I think it drove him crazy.

George Blankenship, VP, real estate (now a VP at Tesla Motors): Retail was Ron's show, but Steve was the guide. We had a meeting every Tuesday morning with Steve for three hours where we went over store design. We built three full stores in a warehouse in Cupertino before we opened the first one—and trashed three-and-a-half designs. One was very trade-show feeling, like at a Macworld. One was very much museumlike. We ended up with the design of those early stores with those kidney-shape tables.

Kobe: We started with the white Corian tables because the first products were brightly colored and we needed a neutral palette for them to look good on. And then as the products started getting whiter, we switched to the maple tables.

Satzger: The alignment of those big five-by-ten-foot tables that are 36 inches high? That came from the industrial design studio. If you think about how stark the Apple Stores are, that's the ID studio.

BLANKENSHIP: We had to go to the heart of the malls and
have people stumble on us when they weren't thinking
about buying a computer.

KOBE: We were trying to get emotion as an outcome, as
opposed to utility. That's a core attribute of the design
at Apple.

The first Apple Store opened in Tysons Corner, Virginia, on May
19, 2001. The following day, *BusinessWeek* ran a column entitled,
"Sorry, Steve: Here's Why Apple Stores Won't Work." The piece—
remarkable for its improvidence—derided Jobs's "perfectionist
attention to aesthetics," his decision to lease extremely expensive
real estate, and his "focus on selling just a few consumer Macs."
Today, there are 412 Apple Stores, averaging roughly $6,000 in
sales per square foot per year—or more than twice that of any
major retailer.

KOBE: For the first two or three years, people didn't talk about
the stores; they talked about the experience in the stores.
Because the people who worked there were so different,
and the way you engaged with technology was so different.

MIKE FISHER, director, visual merchandising (later chief
creative officer, JCPenney): There was nothing except the
computer. We had to sell the sexiness of just a computer.

2001: "Then Apple's Design Became Experiential"

TONY FADELL, senior VP, iPod division (now CEO, Nest
Labs): Design at Apple was product, product, product
until about 2001. Then Apple's design became experien-
tial. There was a product—the iPod—and then software
that hinged to the product, iTunes. And then a retail
experience. That's what created the Apple design
philosophy as we know it today.

WALKER: All of the wonks were saying the personal computer was dead. And then one day—you never quite knew where Steve would get his ideas because he would sometimes lay claim to others' ideas as his own—Steve woke up and decided not only was the computer not dead, but it was more important than ever. The computer was the center of this ecosystem and there were spokes: pictures, work, music.

Jobs unveiled the "Digital Hub" strategy at Macworld in January 2001, announcing a simple MP3 application, iTunes, that would allow Mac users to burn custom playlists and listen to Internet radio stations.

RUBINSTEIN: We were looking at all the devices you could use with a Mac. We looked at cameras, and we just didn't see where we could add enough value. With cell phones and PDAs [personal digital assistants], we concluded that the PDA was just going to get consumed by the phone. Music players really stood out as the one thing where there were no entrenched competitors. The products on the market were crap.

WALKER: I'd like to tell you the iPod was because of some deep skunk works R&D operation, but it didn't happen that way. It started because Jon Rubinstein was at the Toshiba factory in Japan. They had these tiny hard drives, and Ruby saw the potential.

RUBENSTEIN: I would do regular visits with all of our suppliers to review all the products they were doing and see how they fit into our product road map. We went into Toshiba, and at the end of the meeting, they showed us the 1.8-inch hard drive. They didn't know what to do with it. I said, "We'll take all you can make." I went to Steve: "Hey, I'm gonna need about 10 million bucks." That's

when I went looking for someone to manage the team—
and that's when I found Tony.

FADELL: That hard drive—there was nothing else like it on
the planet. It was the enabler that made the iPod work.
At Fuse Systems [Fadell's previous company], we were
creating this MP3 player for home stereos. It was
rack-mounted because there was no storage that was
small enough.

RUBENSTEIN: Tony has tried to rewrite history where he says
that he came up with the idea, that he was working on it
independently. That's total nonsense.

SATZGER: If you look up iPod creator, they called Jony "Jony
iPod." The "Godfather of the iPod" is Tony. And there's
"Mr. iPod" Rubinstein. It's like none of those three guys
can accept that it was a team of people who changed the
world when they created this product.

FADELL: I started in January 2001 as a contractor. The idea
was "1,000 songs in your pocket"—a long-battery-life
device that syncs with the Mac. In the fourth week of
March, I showed the first design to Steve. It had a
navigation control, and [marketing chief] Phil Schiller
said, "You should do a jog shuttle wheel." And that was it.
It all happened in a one-hour meeting. I made the device
in foam models. We gave it to Jony to skin it.

SATZGER: Tony brought in a stack of foam models about
the size of a cigarette package. We looked at soft shapes,
metals, and the double-shot plastic that we ended up
using. It couldn't get too wild. The package size was really
defined by its components.

FADELL: It was basically a two-piece shell—a plastic top with
a metal back—because we could get that done really fast.
Once the iPod came out, all of the other products started
looking like it: It was all the same language.

The minimalist design for the iPod did not come out of nowhere. Ive's team had been toying with similar designs for years, beginning with the G4 Cube desktop computer as well as the Titanium PowerBook G4, which was released shortly before the iPod.

RUBENSTEIN: The Cube was our only real crap-out, which was too bad, because it was actually a great product, just too expensive. We learned a lot about materials, curved plastics, touch switches—and it was a tremendous piece of industrial design. It set the foundation for almost all of our future products.

SATZGER: The market had outgrown the transparent stuff. Shortly after the iMac, we did the Titanium PowerBook, and then we redesigned the iBook in white. The white definitely came from Jony. I had to go to a couple of suppliers and say, "We want to do the whitest white." We pushed them to the limit of adding titanium to the base resin, and then we had to make sure we adjusted the blue levels, because too much blue makes it look like a washing machine.

LINDSAY: Steve always wanted to stay one step ahead. When the industry started to become very colorful and lickable, then he realized—and Jony and I realized—that we needed to take a different path. Let's go minimalistic, less color, focus more on patterns and textures, and different inspirations for design.

ZWERNER: We were kind of like, Who needs another Walkman? While the design [of the iPod] was great, it was just an MP3 player. The iPod languished for a while. It wasn't until the iTunes Store that everyone was like, Holy shit, this is gonna be phenomenal.

2004: "The Holy of Holies"

The third-generation iPod, released in April 2003, was thinner and featured a new navigation wheel. At the same time, Jobs unveiled the iTunes Store. Apple would sell 2 million iPods in 2003, more than twice as many as it had from its debut in September 2001 through 2002. With 2004's release of the iPod Mini, the figure would increase fivefold. The division was split from the rest of Apple, with Rubinstein at the helm. Ive, who had reported to Rubinstein, would now report directly to Jobs, concentrating power in the hands of his elite group of industrial designers.

> SATZGER: Those of us in the industrial design studio were locked down. Steve made it really clear that if you don't have any reason to be there, you don't belong there, and that it was important that we didn't talk about the designs with anybody else outside the team.
>
> ERIK LAMMERDING, senior manager, developer relations (now cofounder, N3twork): I was never allowed in the secret room. Do you remember the show *Get Smart*? *Duh-dun, duh-dun, duh-dun—chish chish chish.* Multiple keycards, frosted glass. The Holy of Holies.
>
> BOB STEVENSON, chief creative officer, Ngmoco (now cofounder, N3twork): We went in there once. Do you know the end scene of *2010* [the 1984 sequel to Kubrick's *2001: A Space Odyssey*]? It was like an entire set of humans from the future.
>
> JEREMY KUEMPEL, intern, iPad product design: I made it to the door. Have you seen the scene in Star Wars where he goes to Jabba the Hut's palace, and the eyeball sticks out and looks at him? It was like that.
>
> SATZGER: The studio is about 10,000 to 15,000 square feet. It's an amazing space. When you walk in, you go through

this little stainless-steel corridor that's probably about ten feet long and that opens up into this expanse of concrete floor and glass. The ceiling is covered with metal. There are these huge concrete pillars and right in the middle is a glass section—like a giant fishbowl—and Jony has a three-wall room. I remember that Jony had a desk that was custom-designed by Marc Newson, a chair, and two standing drawer shelves. He had a whole series of colored pencils laying on his table, a Tolomeo lamp, a computer, and that's it. There wasn't a picture of his family, his kids, nothing—in fact, there wasn't an image of anything on any wall in the whole studio.

RUBENSTEIN: My job was to manage all the different requirements from all the different teams, and make it work. And that means you're the bad guy. Steve didn't like being the bad guy, so that was my role.

SATZGER: Jony and Steve spent a lot of time together outside the office, and they'd talk about business plans and products and things like that. Jony complained that a lot of the things that Steve took credit for were his ideas. Jony has a very political agenda when it comes to his positioning within the company. He would tell me, "Anytime you meet with Steve, I gotta know." He projects this soft-spoken English gentleman persona.

RUBENSTEIN: It's a good image: "Shaken, not stirred."

SATZGER: But if you challenge the VP of design—and you're not a designer—there are going to be consequences. There are many people who are not at Apple because Jony has decided that person was in his way.

RUBENSTEIN: There was an antenna on one of the PowerBooks, and Jony and I were arguing how big the enclosure should be. And we compromised, which, frankly, compromised performance. You can't violate the laws of physics.

According to Walter Isaacson's book, *Steve Jobs*, Ive threatened to leave Apple if Rubinstein did not. In 2006, Rubinstein announced his retirement (unretiring a year later to be CEO of Palm), leaving Fadell in charge of the company's iPod division as it was preparing to spin off a new, top-secret product.

MATT ROGERS, firmware engineer, iPod division (now Fadell's cofounder at Nest): When we started working on this skunk works project in 2005, our team was super small. One hardware engineer, one antenna guy, one project manager. There were a lot of people at Apple who thought we'd maybe sell a million units a year. That was the high bar.

FADELL: We started with an iPod Mini and tried to make it a phone. We actually built a phone with a click wheel—it worked like a rotary dial.

ROGERS: There's a reason nobody wants rotary phones anymore.

ANDY GRIGNON, senior manager, iPhone division (now founder, Quake Labs): Apple had just acquired a company called FingerWorks, which made multitouch keyboards. So the idea was born to do a full touch-screen-based platform for the phone.

SATZGER: The initial concept of multitouch was from a tablet-computer brainstorm. We were always trying to shove a PC into a tablet. Duncan Kerr [a designer in Ive's group] sat people down for a couple of hours and just talked about multitouch. Wouldn't it be great if you could just turn a page like you were turning a page? Wouldn't it be great if you could just zoom in and out by doing some kind of gesture? We had all those ideas on paper in the ID team. And I'm sure Duncan was talking to the sensor people and the hardware people about multitouch. A couple of weeks later, we were all just blown away by the prototype Duncan and his team built. We were zooming in and out on Google Maps and rotating it.

RUBENSTEIN: It was pretty cool. But it wasn't good enough. And so the technology wound up in the iPhone before the iPad.

GRIGNON: This was around when Scott Forstall [then in charge of Mac software] got wind of the project. He really wanted to do Mac OS on a phone.

ROGERS: The iPhone was done in these vacuums. The software and hardware teams didn't even talk. One of my early tasks was to build a parallel software system for the iPhone so we could actually use it to make calls.

GRIGNON: We called it "skankphone." Of Tony's whole hardware team, which was maybe sixty people at full strength, only me and three guys were allowed to see the real user interface. Before you got UI access, you had to sign a separate legal document, Steve had to approve it, and then you'd go to Forstall, who was the ultimate owner of the secret list. He would tell you, "Don't talk to anybody. Don't tell your wife."

ABIGAIL SARAH BRODY, user interface designer: I'd been working on a new design language for what we called Pro Apps—Final Cut Pro, Logic Pro, Aperture. One day around 2005, I got a call to move up to the fourth floor, the executive floor. I wasn't told I'd be working on a phone. They just said, "Create a user interface for multitouch."

SATZGER: When we developed the first iPhone, we developed around a screen size and a home button.

BRODY: I had a crude prototype and a sense of the dimensions. I rendered some finger-size images and looked at how far my thumb would reach across the screen. I had to create some sort of menu, so I just created a screen with rounded rectangular buttons.

SATZGER: We had a screenshot that we put on every model, and that's all we knew about the UI. Jony knew what was going on, but most of the ID group didn't know how the gestures worked, how you did basic functions, visual voice mail—all the amazing things that came out of that first product.

NITIN GANATRA, director of engineering, iOS applications (now executive director, Jawbone): Everyone on the team knew that Apple had attempted to ship a device with a touch input with the Newton—and was laughed at by the industry. Scott was very focused on the fine points around the look and feel. When we launched an app, it had to come up instantly. When you moved your thumb up or down, the scrolling had to track your movement with no delays.

LOREN BRICHTER, graphics engineer (later inventor of the Twitter app Tweetie, which introduced the pull-to-refresh gesture to iOS): The UI was mind-blowing: 3-D graphics, sixty frames per second. Nothing like it existed.

ROGERS: Before we launched at Macworld in January 2007, I was sitting in the bathroom using one of the devices, and I was like, This is revolution. I'm checking e-mail in the bathroom. That was the moment when I realized this is a totally different kind of device.

BRODY: Steve showed it with clown-fish wallpaper and some green sea anemones in the background. It was the same sample image I used: the black UI, the glossiness, the big numbers. Later, I saw Steve in the hall, and I said, "Is it a coincidence that it looks like my design?" And he said no. One of my fondest memories from my time at Apple was that launch day. Even if it was finished by a completely different team, and even though my contribution is maybe 0.1 percent, there is still something in there that I helped make a difference with.

HORACE DEDIU, analyst, Nokia (now an independent analyst and founder of Asymco): The day after the first iPhone launch, I went to the Nokia cafeteria and asked people about it. They were like, "Meh, there's nothing here." The compromises Apple took on design were legendary: You didn't have copy-paste, you didn't have multitasking, you didn't have apps. Apple said, We just want to have a cool phone. Everybody else was focusing on being smart. Apple focused on being loved.

The iPhone would become the most successful Apple product of all time, accounting for more than half its revenue. Over the next few years, Ive's team would crank out a succession of refinements—and the company would return to the original idea it had for a multitouch device: a tablet computer.

GANATRA: I first heard about this tablet in late 2008. Steve was saying, "Just think of it as a big iPod Touch." It was one of the few times that Steve was arguing that we didn't have to do that much work.

MATT MACINNIS, marketing manager: There's no magic to the product planning cycle at Apple beyond a ruthless focus on a limited set of use cases. What each product does in the first iteration is going to be narrow, but those things are going to be airtight. For the iPad, there were ideas about having docks on two sides. Depending on where you put it in your house, it would behave differently. If you put it on its side by your bed, it would be an alarm clock. But if you put it upright in the kitchen, it'd be a recipe book. Those got cut back.

SEGALL: Back in the Apple II days, they had a tagline, the "most personal computer." But this, the iPad, is really the most personal computer ever made. I mean, you touch it. It responds to your voice.

2010: "It Started as This Green Felt Thing"

In the years following the launch of the iPad, there were no major new product releases, and competitors such as Samsung and Google started catching up to Apple with their own touchscreen phones and tablets. A sense of drift was perhaps best epitomized by Game Center, a social networking app for iPhone games released in September 2010. Game Center took Jobs's preference for visual metaphors and realistic 3-D icons—known as skeuomorphism—to garish new extremes.

> GANATRA: Game Center was a rough one. All the faults with skeuomorphism were front and center. It started as this green felt thing, and they struggled to come up with something that was a true metaphor.
>
> JASON WILSON, senior UI designer (now lead product designer, Pinterest): Forstall took Steve's design taste without understanding the sensibilities behind it. I left Apple because I couldn't stand the design under Forstall.
>
> GANATRA: A lot of the press latched on to the fact that Forstall was the guy who was really pushing skeuomorphism. The truth is, it was Steve. He would look at wood and leathers, and there would be these extensive reviews of materials just to see what would look best on the calendar app or the bookshelf app.
>
> ZWERNER: The hardest thing at Apple is recruiting. You are going to the best designers in the world and saying, "Can you imagine coming to Apple and putting pictures of things on white, with one line of typography—for years?" I really admire the people who stayed there, and their ability to see the big picture. Steve saw this as kind of a life's work. And the question is, in the absence of that careful management, that thread that ties everything together, how will it stay intact?

With Jobs's death in 2011, Apple's software problems only seemed to get worse. The release of a new version of Apple Maps, which had nice visuals but had highly publicized problems directing users to the right location, prompted a public apology from CEO Tim Cook. The debacle reportedly led to Forstall's resignation in October 2012. Ive, who had rarely had any input in Apple's software decisions, took over for Forstall and began working on an ambitious redesign of iOS.

> MacInnis: One of the key ingredients in Amazon, Facebook, and Google is data. Those businesses were built on deep technical understanding of how to manage swaths of data. Apple doesn't know how to do that.
> Wilson: The software has been falling off. The web services have all been failures. And Google is kicking ass.

This past June at its Worldwide Developers Conference, Apple unveiled Ive's new modernist reworking of iOS 7, which includes a new gesture-based interaction model; a futuristic Mac Pro desktop; and, perhaps most important, a sense of swagger. "We completely ran out of green felt," quipped Craig Federighi, senior VP of software engineering. "Can't innovate anymore, my ass," groused Phil Schiller, Apple's marketing chief.

> Segall: Surprise was always an important factor to Steve. That's the feeling I get from the new Mac Pro. I look at that and think of the G4 Cube. Apple will probably get slammed for it, but the way it opens up, the turbine fan, and the thermal core—it's very Apple. Who on earth but Apple would redesign a desktop computer? That makes me feel good about Apple as an innovator.
> Brichter: I have nitpicks with iOS 7, but I'm really happy they did something big. It's more than just the veneer. The way they're reimplementing the UI framework with

physics—it just feels natural. They're mimicking the real world. So in a way, the skeuomorphism, which was previously going into visual design, is now going into interaction design.

2013: "Apple Branches, Grafted Onto New Trees"

BRODY, now working on a stealth startup: I watched WWDC online, and they were all trying so hard. But for me, Apple is a different place without Steve. It's a good place, but it's different. What really makes me happy is to see people like Tony Fadell doing new things. They're like Apple branches, grafted onto new trees.

FADELL, now CEO, Nest: At Apple, we were always asking, What else can we revolutionize? We looked at video cameras and remote controls. The craziest thing we talked about was something like Google Glass. We said, "What if we make visors, so it's like you're sitting in a theater?" I built a bunch of those prototypes. But we had such success with the things we were already doing that we didn't have time.

MACINNIS, now founder, Inkling, an e-book publisher: Visual design and interaction design are things I learned at Apple. Marketing, branding—I learned a lot of that at Apple. What I have learned since I've left is that confidentiality doesn't work. If you try to replicate it, you just look like an asshole.

KUEMPEL, former intern (now founder, Blossom Coffee, manufacturer of an $11,000 coffeemaker): I worked on the iPad SIM-card ejector. It's got a really nice click. You're welcome, world. There were opportunities to stay at Apple, but I didn't want to because I realized that I wouldn't be designing a product—I'd be designing a SIM ejector. I wanted to create whole products and define an industry in the way that the iPad created the tablet market.

DAVE MORIN, former Apple marketing manager (now cofounder, Path, a mobile social-networking app): The pursuit of quality above all else is something we aspire to learn from Apple and that drives us at Path.

PHIL LIBIN, CEO, Evernote, a note-taking app: There had always been products that had been beautifully designed. But they were high end, and very few people actually owned them. Apple was the first company that took high design and made it mainstream. It taught the world taste.

HAWKINS: In 500 years, Steve Jobs will be the only guy from our generation that anybody knows about.

GADI AMIT, founder, NewDealDesign (designer of the Fitbit activity tracker and the Lytro camera): Around 1990, I was in Israel, working at a company called Scitex, but I was spending a lot of time at the Frog Design office in San Francisco. The guy next to me was working on NeXT for Steve Jobs. I saw three identical mice on his desk, and I couldn't tell the difference between them, so I asked. He said, "Can't you see?" And he pointed to the bottom plate of the mouse. One was 1 millimeter thick, one was 1.5 millimeters, the other 2 millimeters. And then I saw the difference—and it transformed my worldview about details in design. That's the reason I moved to California.

That is Apple's contribution: this dogmatic, beautiful, striving for perfection, that chasing for the last millimeter. It drove the world of design to a completely new level.

Additional reporting by Skylar Bergl, Austin Carr, and Mark Wilson.

New York Times Magazine

WINNER—REPORTING

Luke Mogelson's work earned two National Magazine Award nominations for Reporting this year. His story "The River Martyrs," about the Syrian civil war, was one of six New Yorker entries to be nominated in 2014 (five New Yorker pieces are included in this anthology), but it was this story for the New York Times Magazine, then edited by Hugo Lindgren, that won the award. Posing as a Georgian asylum seeker, Mogelson joined dozens of refugees on a 200-mile open-boat voyage from Indonesia to Australia. The publication of "The Dream Boat" was further distinguished by the work of the photojournalist Joel van Houdt, who accompanied Mogelson throughout the reporting of this story. Mogelson was not yet thirty years old when "The Dream Boat" was written.

Luke Mogelson

The Dream Boat

It's about a two-and-a-half-hour drive, normally, from Indonesia's capital city, Jakarta, to the southern coast of Java. In one of the many trucks that make the trip each month, loaded with asylum seekers from the Middle East and Central Asia, it takes a little longer. From the bed of the truck, the view is limited to a night sky punctuated by fleeting glimpses of high-rise buildings, overpasses, traffic signs, and tollbooths. It is difficult to make out, among the human cargo, much more than the vague shapes of bodies, the floating tips of cigarettes. When you pass beneath a street lamp, though, or an illuminated billboard, the faces thrown into relief are all alive with expectation. Eventually, the urban pulse subsides; the commotion of the freeway fades. The drooping wires give way to darkly looming palms. You begin to notice birds, and you can smell the sea.

In September, in one of these trucks, I sat across from a recently married couple in their twenties, from Tehran. The wife, who was seven months pregnant, wore a red blouse stretched over her stomach; the husband a tank top, thick-rimmed glasses and a faux hawk that revealed a jagged scar (courtesy, he said, of the Iranian police). Two months had passed since they flew to Jakarta; this was their fourth attempt to leave. Twice, en route to the boat that would bring them to Australia, they were intercepted and detained and paid bribes for their release. Another time, the boat foundered shortly after starting out. All the same, they were confident this trip would be different. Like everyone else's in the truck, theirs was a desperate kind of faith. "Tonight we will succeed," the husband assured me. They were determined that the child be born "there."

Our drive coincided with a violent tropical downpour that seemed to surge, under pressure, more than fall. Each asylum seeker had brought a small bag with spare clothes and provisions. Those who packed slickers dug them out. The storm was amusing at first, then just cold and miserable. The children, who earlier delighted in our clandestine exit from the city, now clung to their parents. An old man, sitting cross-legged beside me with a plastic garbage bag on his head, shivered uncontrollably, muttering prayers.

Around three in the morning, the truck braked and reversed down a rutted dirt road. The rain had stopped as abruptly as it started. No one spoke. We knew we had arrived. The rear hatch swung open, and we piled out. A second truck was parked behind us; people were emerging from it as well. We were in a dense jungle whose tangled canopy obstructed the moon. Several Indonesians corralled the crowd and whispered fiercely to keep moving. "Go! Go!" they urged in English. The road led down a steep hill and ended at a narrow footpath. As people stumbled in the dark, the Indonesians prodded them along. At the bottom of the footpath was a beach. It appeared as a pale hue through the trees, its white sand giving off a glow. The asylum seekers, fifty-seven of them, huddled at the jungle's edge.

We were in the shelter of a wide bay, its arcing headlands, dotted with lights, repulsing the windward waves. Two open-hull skiffs with outboard motors idled offshore, bobbing gently in the swells. Behind us, the clamor of the truck grew distant and was gone. Suddenly, the Indonesians began pushing people toward the sea.

"You, you. Go!"

Two at a time, the asylum seekers raised their bags above their heads and waded out. The cool water rose to waists and armpits.

It was a struggle to climb aboard. Whenever someone had to be hauled up, the skiff pitched steeply, threatening to tip.

We were ferried to a wooden fishing boat: a more substantial vessel than the skiffs, though not much. About thirty feet long, with open decks, a covered bow, a one-man cockpit, and a bamboo tiller, it was clearly not designed for passengers. Noting the absence of cabin, bridge, bulkheads, and benches, I wondered whether anyone else shared my deluded hope: that there was another, larger ship anchored somewhere farther out and that this sad boat was merely to convey us there.

With frantic miming, the two-man Indonesian crew directed us to crowd together on the deck and crouch beneath the bulwarks. They stretched a tarp above our heads and nailed its edges to the gunwales. Packed close in the ripe air beneath the tarp, hugging knees to chests, we heard the engine start and felt the boat begin to dip and rise.

·　　·　　·

Our destination was an Australian territory, more than 200 miles across the Indian Ocean, called Christmas Island. If the weather is amenable, if the boat holds up, the trip typically lasts three days. Often, however, the weather is tempestuous, and the boat sinks. Over the past decade, it is believed that more than a thousand asylum seekers have drowned. The unseaworthy vessels are swamped through leaky hulls, capsize in heavy swells, splinter on the rocks. Survivors sometimes drift for days. Children have watched their parents drown, and parents their children. Entire families have been lost. Since June, several boats went down, claiming the lives of more than a hundred people.

I first heard about the passage from Indonesia to Australia in Afghanistan, where I live and where one litmus test for the success of the U.S.-led war now drawing to a close is the current exodus of civilians from the country. (The first "boat people" to seek asylum in Australia were Vietnamese, in the mid-1970s, driven to the ocean by the fallout from that American withdrawal.) Last year, nearly 37,000 Afghans applied for asylum abroad, the most since 2001. Afghans who can afford to will pay as much as $24,000 for European travel documents and up to $40,000 for Canadian. (Visas to the United States, generally, cannot be bought.) Others employ smugglers for arduous overland treks from Iran to Turkey to Greece, or from Russia to Belarus to Poland.

The Indonesia-Australia route first became popular in Afghanistan before September 11, mostly among Hazaras, a predominantly Shiite ethnic minority that was systematically brutalized by the Taliban. After the Taliban were overthrown, many refugees, anticipating an enduring peace, returned to Afghanistan, and for a while the number of Afghans willing to risk their lives at sea declined. But by late 2009—with Afghans, disabused of their optimism, fleeing once more—migration to Australia escalated. At the same time, Hazaras living across the border in Pakistan, many of whom moved there from Afghanistan, have also found relocation necessary. In a sectarian crusade of murder and terror being waged against them by Sunni extremists, Hazara civilians in the Pakistani city of Quetta are shot in the streets, executed en masse, and indiscriminately massacred by rockets and bombs.

In 2010, a suicide attacker killed more than seventy people at a Shiite rally in Quetta. Looming directly above the carnage was a large billboard paid for by the Australian government. In Dari, next to an image of a distressed Indonesian fishing boat carrying Hazara asylum seekers, read the words: "All illegal routes to Australia are closed to Afghans." The billboard was part of a wide-ranging effort by Australia to discourage refugees from trying to get to Christmas Island. In Afghanistan, a recent Australian-funded TV ad featured a Hazara actor rubbing his eyes before a black background. "Please don't go," the man gloomily implores over melancholic music. "Many years of my life were wasted there [in detention] until my application for asylum was rejected."

In addition to the messaging campaign (and the hard-line policies it alludes to), Australia has worked to disrupt smuggling networks by collaborating with Pakistan's notorious intelligence services, embedding undercover agents in Indonesia, and offering up to $180,000 for information resulting in a smuggler's arrest. The most drastic deterrence measure was introduced this July, when the Australian prime minister at the time, Kevin Rudd, announced that henceforth no refugee who reaches Australia by boat would be settled there. Instead, refugees would be detained and eventually resettled in impoverished Papua New Guinea. Several weeks later, the resettlement policy was extended to a tiny island state in Micronesia called the Republic of Nauru.

Since then, there have been more boats, more drownings. In late September, a vessel came apart shortly after leaving Indonesia, and dozens of asylum seekers—from Lebanon, Iran and Iraq—drowned. That people are willing to hazard death at sea despite Australia's vow to send them to places like Papua New Guinea and the Republic of Nauru would seem illogical—or just plain crazy. The Australian government ascribes their persistence partly to misinformation propagated by the smugglers. But every asylum seeker who believes those lies believes them because he chooses to. Their doing so, and continuing to brave the Indian Ocean, and continuing to die, only illustrates their desperation in a new, disturbing kind of light. This is the subtext to the plight of every refugee: Whatever hardship he endures, he endures because it beats the hardship he escaped. Every story of exile implies the sadder story of a homeland.

·   ·   ·

It's surprisingly simple, from Kabul, to enlist the services of the smugglers Australian authorities are so keen to apprehend. The problem was that every Afghan I spoke to who had been to Indonesia insisted that no Western journalist would ever be allowed onto a boat: paranoia over agents was too high. Consequently, the photographer Joel van Houdt and I decided to pose as refugees. Because we are both white, we thought it prudent to devise a cover. We would say we were Georgian (other options in the region were rejected for fear of running into Russian speakers), had sensitive information about our government's activities during the 2008 war (hence, in the event of a search, our cameras and recorders), traveled to Kabul in search of a smuggler, and learned some Dari during our stay. An Afghan colleague of mine, Hakim (whose name has been changed to protect his identity), would pretend to be a local schemer angling for a foothold in the trade. It was all overly elaborate and highly implausible.

When we were ready, Hakim phoned an elderly Afghan man, living in Jakarta, who goes by the honorific Hajji Sahib. Hajji Sahib is a well-known smuggler in Indonesia; his cell phone number, among Afghans, is relatively easy to obtain. Hakim explained that he had two Georgians—"Levan" and "Mikheil"—whom he wished to send Hajji Sahib's way. Hajji Sahib, never questioning our story, agreed to get Joel and me from Jakarta to Christmas Island for $4,000 each. This represents a slightly discounted rate, for which Hakim, aspiring middleman, promised more business down the road.

A few days later, we visited Sarai Shahzada, Kabul's bustling currency market. Tucked behind an outdoor bazaar on the banks of a polluted river that bends through the Old City, the entrance to Sarai Shahzada is a narrow corridor mobbed with traders presiding over stacks of Pakistani rupees, Iranian rials, American dollars, and Afghan afghanis. The enclosed courtyard to which the corridor leads, the exterior stairwells ascending the surrounding buildings, the balconies that run the length of every floor—no piece of real estate is spared a hard-nosed dealer hawking bundled bricks of cash. The more illustrious operators occupy cramped offices and offer a variety of services in addition to exchange. Most of them are brokers of the money-transfer system, known as *hawala*, used throughout the Muslim world. Under the *hawala* system, if someone in Kabul wishes to send money to a relative in Pakistan, say, he will pay the amount, plus a small commission, to a broker in Sarai Shahzada, and in return receive a code. The recipient uses this code to collect the funds from a broker in Peshawar, who is then owed the transferred sum by the broker in Sarai Shahzada (a debt that can be settled with future transactions flowing in reverse).

In Afghanistan, where many people have family living abroad and lack bank accounts, the *hawala* system mostly facilitates legitimate remittances. It also, however, offers an appealing space for illicit dealings. In 2011, the U.S. Treasury Department blacklisted one of Sarai Shahzada's main businesses for laundering millions on behalf of Afghan narcotics traffickers. The Taliban, as well, are thought to get the bulk of their donations, from Persian Gulf and Pakistani patrons, via *hawala* transfers.

The refugee-smuggling business is conducted almost entirely through *hawala*. Hajji Sahib's man, Mohammad, keeps a third-story office overlooking the courtyard in Sarai Shahzada. When we got there, we found Mohammad sitting behind a desk papered with receipts pinned down against a squeaky fan by half-drunk glasses of tea. With long unkempt hair, bad posture, and acne, Mohammad looked as if he could still be in his teens. Other young men lined the walls, hunched in plastic chairs, working cell phones and calculators. When Hakim introduced himself as an intermediary for Hajji Sahib, they all glanced up from their computations, stiffening a little.

Mohammad immediately gave a spirited endorsement of Hajji Sahib's integrity, as well as of his own. He was eager to assure us that we were in capable hands. "We represent lots of smugglers," Mohammad boasted. "For Australia and also for Europe. Every month, dozens of people give us their money." He picked up a black ledger and waved it in the air. "Look at this notebook! I write every customer's details in here."

We gave him our fake names and origins. ("Gorjestan?" we were asked for the first but by no means the last time.) Then, a bit reluctantly, I counted out $8,000 in cash. In return, Mohammad handed me a scrap of paper with our *hawala* codes scribbled in pen. Levan: 105. Mikheil: 106. Mohammad would withhold the money from his counterpart in Jakarta until we reached Christmas Island. This, theoretically, would preclude Hajji Sahib from retrieving it prematurely. It would also ensure he would not get paid if our boat sank or if we drowned.

•   •   •

Most asylum seekers bound for Australia arrive in Jakarta by air. The day after we landed in the sprawling capital, I called Hajji Sahib and arranged to be picked up the next morning at a 7-Eleven on a busy intersection. Joel and I were sitting outside the 7-Eleven when an Indonesian man in a Hawaiian shirt appeared at the appointed time. He eyed us doubtfully, then handed me a cell phone.

"You will go in a taxi with this guy," Hajji Sahib told me. "He will bring you to a safe place."

We drove in silence, for about an hour, to the northern edge of the city, where gated communities vied for waterfront with ramshackle slums on the garbage-heaped banks of Jakarta Bay. We pulled into the parking lot of a massive tower-block apartment complex and took an elevator to the twenty-third floor. Midway down a poorly lit hallway, our escort knocked on a metal security door. A young girl in a dress decorated with images of Barbie let us in. An Iranian man sat at a glass table, tapping ash from a cigarette into a water-bottle cap. A small boy lay on a bare mattress, watching cartoons. "OK?" asked the Indonesian, and, before anyone could answer, he was gone.

The man, Youssef, had been living in the apartment for a couple of weeks with his eight-year-old son, Anoush, and six-year-old daughter, Shahla. (All the names of the asylum seekers in this story have been changed for their protection.) Youssef had been a laborer in Tehran, refurbishing building exteriors. In order to pay Hajji Sahib, he had sold all his possessions and gave up the house he was renting. He left his wife with her parents, planning to bring her to Australia legally once he and the children were settled there. "In Iran, there is no work, no life, no future for these children," Youssef told me, nodding at Anoush and Shahla. "I want them to go to school so that they can get a position."

We were sitting at the table, in one of the apartment's three rooms. A TV and refrigerator stood against the far wall, opposite a sink and counter, with a two-burner camping stove. Whereas Youssef, plainly, was less than thrilled to have new roommates (there were only two beds, one of them a narrow twin), Anoush and Shahla were competing to one-up each other with hospitality. After Shahla complimented Joel and me on our "beautiful beards," Anoush set about preparing us a lunch of chicken-flavored instant noodles.

Shahla said, "People become thieves there, in Iran."

"In Australia, I want to be a policeman," Anoush announced. "I want to arrest thieves, and say, 'Hands up!' "

Youssef seemed to disapprove. "They will study," he said.

On different floors throughout the tower block, other apartments housed about thirty more asylum seekers. Some were Hajji Sahib's; some belonged to rival smugglers. A majority, I was surprised to discover, were not Afghan but Iranian. Most were from cities and the lower middle class. They were builders, drivers, shopkeepers, barbers. One man claimed to be a mullah; another, an accomplished engineer. Their reasons for leaving varied. They all complained about the government and its chokehold on their freedoms. A few said they had been targeted for political persecution. They bemoaned the economy. International sanctions—imposed on Iran for refusing to abandon its nuclear program in 2006 and later tightened—had crippled their ability to support their families. They were fathers who despaired of their children's futures, or they wanted children but refused to have them in Iran. The most common word they used to describe their lives back home was "*na-aomid*"—hopeless.

Shortly after we settled into the apartment, an Iranian named Rashid stopped by for a visit. Rashid had the sickly, anemic look that I would soon come to associate with asylum seekers who languished in that place for two months or more—a combination of malnourishment and psychological fatigue. As he collapsed into a chair, elbows propped on knees, chin propped on palm, he seemed to lack even the most basic gravity-resisting vigor. After a month in Jakarta, Rashid told me, he got aboard a boat bound for Christmas Island. The engine promptly failed, leaving them adrift for days. In lieu of a bilge pump, Rashid and the other men had to use buckets to bail out the water splashing into the hull and seeping through its wooden planks. They ran out of food and water. People might have begun succumbing to dehydration if the tide hadn't carried them to a remote island. There they were arrested and obliged to pay the Indonesian police before they could be freed.

"We came back to this place," Rashid said. "The smuggler said, 'Don't worry, we will take you again soon.'"

I glanced at Joel. Over the phone, while we were in Kabul, Hajji Sahib urged us to get to Jakarta as soon as possible, saying the next boat was ready to depart.

"Our smuggler told us we were leaving tomorrow," I said.

Rashid laughed. "Yes, they say that."

．　　　．　　　．

The waiting was brutal: doing nothing became the most onerous of chores. The fact that your smuggler could call at any time, day or night, meant that you were forever suspended in a state of high alert. It also meant you couldn't venture far. Most of the asylum seekers, additionally fearful of police, never left the building. Generally, they spent their days sleeping as much as possible,

smoking cigarettes, and rotating through one another's rooms—
for a change of scenery, presumably, though they were all identical. Everyone was broke, and meals, in our apartment anyway,
consisted of instant noodles, once or twice a day, on occasion
served with bread. To sleep, Youssef, Anoush, and Shahla shared
one of the two beds, while Joel and I alternated between the other
and a thin mattress on the floor. Mattress nights were coveted
because it lay at the foot of the refrigerator, which you could open
for a brief but glorious breath of cool air when you woke drenched
in sweat and because, compared with the bed, it was relatively
free of fleas.

Although many of the asylum seekers in the building had
children, only Youssef had brought his with him. (The others
expected to be reunited with their families in Australia.) It's difficult to imagine how Anoush and Shahla processed the whole
experience. My sense was that the thrill of the adventure eclipsed
its hardships and hassles. With nothing and no one, except each
other, to play with, they kept themselves remarkably well enter-
tained. A feather duster found beneath the sink made for a superb
tickling instrument; plastic grocery bags were turned into balloons; the hot-sauce packets, included in every ration of instant
noodles, could be squirted on the tabletop to create interesting
designs. There was also much to explore. The tower block was a
kind of self-sufficient microcity, its four lofty wings flanking a
private courtyard with shops and fish fries servicing outdoor
tables clustered around a concrete bandstand. Every night, wiz-
ened Indonesian men belted out karaoke covers of John Denver
and Johnny Cash. There was a Muslim mosque, a Christian
church, a Buddhist temple. There were giant roaches and tailless
cats to chase. And most delightfully, there was a pool.

As neither of the kids had swimming trunks or a spare pair of
clothes, underwear had to suffice. Applying their talents for im-
provisation, Shahla found a used dish rag they could both share
for a towel while Anoush, with a kitchen knife, removed a length

of flexible tubing from the back of our air-conditioner (which was broken anyway), repurposing it as a snorkel. Their resourcefulness continued at the pool itself: each day, they seemed to come into possession of some new equipment—a pair of goggles, a bar of soap, an inflatable flotation ring.

While Youssef made the rounds of the rooms, Joel and I would end up watching them at the pool. We were both distressed to see that neither Anoush nor Shahla could really swim.

When I asked Anoush, who had never been on a boat before, whether he was nervous about the journey, he clucked his tongue. "I have no fear," he said. "I'll be smiling."

Their father was less carefree. Not long after we joined them, it became clear that Youssef had no money, and if Joel and I didn't buy food and water, they would simply go without. Whenever the fleas or heat would wake me in the night, I would find Youssef sitting by the window, staring out at the fires—bright islands of flame and eerily colored smoke—where the slum dwellers were burning trash. Everyone was stressed; the strain of two kids and no cash, however, rendered Youssef especially edgy. He was given to fits of anger and with the slightest provocation could fly into rages at Anoush, as well as at the other asylum seekers, many of whom avoided him.

Then one day Youssef's family wired money. I was sitting with him in the apartment, smoking, when he got the call. The news transformed him. Beaming with joy, Youssef leapt into the air and began to sing and dance.

That night Joel and I found him in the courtyard drinking with Rashid. Anoush and Shahla ran from shop to shop, swinging bags of candy. When he saw us, Youssef insisted we sit down, then shouted loudly, at no one in particular, for more beer. A group of elderly Indonesian men, playing dominoes nearby, regarded him impatiently. Youssef didn't notice. He was slumped over the table, doodling on its surface with a permanent marker.

Rashid seemed embarrassed for his friend. "His head is messed up," he explained. "Waiting here, with his kids, not knowing when we'll go. It's hard."

Youssef nodded glumly.

"My head is messed up, too," Rashid said. "I'm going crazy. I have two sons in Iran. I haven't seen them or my wife in a year."

Rashid said that before Australia, he tried to get to Europe via Greece. He made it from Turkey to Athens, where he was fleeced by a smuggler. Rather than return to Iran, he came to Indonesia. "Every day, they tell us, 'Tomorrow, tomorrow,'" Rashid said. "But tomorrow never arrives."

Anoush and Shahla appeared and asked Youssef for money. They wanted chips. Youssef pulled out a wad of bills and threw some in their direction. Several fluttered to the ground.

"Beer!" Youssef yelled at a woman passing by. Then he looked guiltily at Rashid, and added: "Please! Thank you!"

.   .   .

Australia's decision to send all boat people to Papua New Guinea or the Republic of Nauru only compounded everyone's anxiety. Although no one allowed himself to take it seriously (if he did, he would have no option but to do the unthinkable—give up, go home), the news was never decisively explained away. "It's a lie to scare people so that they don't come," Youssef told me when I brought it up. Another man became agitated when I asked him what he thought. "How can they turn you away?" he demanded. "You put yourself in danger, you take your life in your hand? They can't." A third asylum seeker dismissed the policy with a shrug. "It's a political game," he told me.

In many ways, he was right. It's hard to overstate how contentious an issue boat people are in Australian politics. From an American perspective, zealousness on the subject of immigration is nothing unfamiliar. But what makes Australia unique is the disconnect between how prominently boat people feature in the national dialogue, on the one hand, and the actual scale of the problem, on the other. Over the past four years, most European countries have absorbed more asylum seekers, per capita, than Australia—some of them, like Sweden and Liechtenstein, seven times as many. All the same, for more than a decade now, successive Australian governments have fixated on boat people, making them a centerpiece of their agendas.

In the summer of 2001, a Norwegian freighter, the MV *Tampa*, rescued 433 asylum seekers, almost all of them Afghan, from a stranded fishing boat. Rather than return them to Indonesia, the captain of the *Tampa*, Arne Rinnan, consented to their demands to be taken to Christmas Island. Australia forbade the ship to enter its territory, and the standoff that ensued led to Australia's threatening to prosecute Rinnan and Norway's complaining to the United Nations. John Howard, a conservative prime minister, who, in the midst of a reelection campaign, was trailing his opponent in most of the polls, declared, "It remains our very strong determination not to allow this vessel or its occupants to land in Australia." When Rinnan, concerned over the welfare of the asylum seekers on his ship, proceeded toward the island anyway, Howard dispatched Australian commandos to board the *Tampa* and stop it from continuing. The impasse was resolved only when New Zealand and Nauru agreed to accept the asylum seekers instead. Howard's action was widely popular with voters, and two months later he was reelected.

Diverting boat people to third countries for processing—albeit with the possibility of someday being resettled in Australia—was subsequently adopted as an official strategy. Under an arrangement popularly known as the Pacific Solution, asylum seekers trying to get to Christmas Island were interdicted by the navy and taken to detention centers on Nauru and Papua New Guinea (both of which rely heavily on Australian aid). The Pacific Solution was denounced by refugee and human rights advocates, who criticized the harsh conditions of the centers and the prolonged periods of time—many years, in some cases—that asylum seekers had to spend in them while their applications were considered. Depression and other mental disorders proliferated; incidents of self-harm were common. In 2003, detainees on Nauru protested with a weeks-long hunger strike, during which some of them sewed their lips together. Last September, Arne Rinnan, the captain of the *Tampa*, told an interviewer that he had recently received a letter from Nauru, written by one of the Afghans he had rescued. According to Rinnan, the man said that "I should have let him die in the Indian Ocean, instead of picking him up."

After the Labor Party regained control of parliament in 2007, and the new prime minister, Kevin Rudd, abolished the Pacific Solution—his immigration minister condemning it as "neither humane nor fair"—the UN and just about every other organization involved with refugees lauded the move. Rudd lost his leadership of the Labor Party in 2010, and his successor, Julia Gillard, resurrected the offshore-processing strategy. When Rudd returned to power in 2013, apparently having learned his lesson, he kept Gillard's policies in place. It was in the context of another reelection bid in July that Rudd eliminated the possibility of any boat person ever settling in Australia. "I understand that this is a very hard-line decision," he acknowledged in a national address. He seemed anxious to make sure that voters understood it too.

Rudd's conservative opponent, Tony Abbott, would not be outdone. One of the two rallying cries that had come to define Abbott's campaign was "Stop the boats!" (The other, referring to carbon-emissions penalties, was "Axe the tax!") Proclaiming the influx of boat people a "national emergency," Abbott proposed an even tougher scheme than Rudd's, dubbed "Operation Sovereign Borders." Among other proactive measures, this militaristic plan called for deploying warships to turn asylum seekers back at sea before they reached Australian shores.

The elections were scheduled to be held less than a week after the night I found Youssef and Rashid drinking in the courtyard. Whichever candidate prevailed, one thing was certain: neither Youssef nor Rashid nor Anoush nor Shahla were going to get to the place they believed they were going. Rashid would never be reunited with his wife and sons in some quaint Australian suburb; Youssef would never see his children "get a position" there; Anoush would never become an Australian policeman; Shahla would never benefit from a secular, Western education. What they had to look forward to instead—after the perilous voyage, and after months, maybe years, locked up in an isolated detention center—was resettlement on the barren carcass of a defunct strip mine, more than 70 percent of which is uninhabitable (Nauru) or resettlement on a destitute and crime-ridden island nation known for its high rates of murder and sexual violence (Papua New Guinea).

How do you tell that to someone who has severed himself utterly from his country, in order to reach another? It was impossible. They wouldn't believe it.

·   ·   ·

Joel and I were walking along the bay, where dozens of residents from the slums had gathered to watch backhoes on floating barges scoop refuse out of the shallows and deposit it onto the banks, when Youssef called my cell phone and shouted at us to get back to the tower—we were leaving. In the apartment, we found two young Iranian women, Farah and Rima, sitting at the table with large backpacks, while Youssef hurriedly shoved dates and lemons—thought to alleviate seasickness—into a canvas messenger bag. I noticed, too, that he was bringing the inflatable flotation ring Anoush and Shahla had found at the pool.

An Iranian man named Ayoub appeared and told us our car was waiting. By the deferential way Youssef and the women treated him—and by his assertive self-possession, in contrast to our rather panicky excitement—I gathered that Ayoub was a smuggler. He wore a military haircut and a handlebar mustache, and his sleeveless shirt displayed the words "Life is hard" tattooed in English across an impressively sculptured left deltoid.

The asylum seekers braced against strong wind and waves.

We all crammed into a new car with tinted windows, driven by a squat Indonesian man with long rapier-like pinkie nails that tapered into points, who belched every couple of minutes and chain-smoked flavored cigarettes. Anoush and Shahla were elated. As we pulled onto the highway, they could not stop talking about the boat and the sea. The women adored them instantly. Farah hauled Anoush onto her lap, while Rima set to braiding Shahla's wild hair. The kids received this affection like sustenance, with a kind of delirious gratitude and appetite. It made me remember that since arriving in Jakarta, they had not only been without their mother but without any mother.

We stopped at three gas stations along the way and linked up with other drivers. By the time we made it out of the city, several hours later, we led a convoy of six identical cars, all packed with asylum seekers. It seemed a bit conspicuous, and sure enough, as we climbed a narrow, winding road up a densely forested mountain, people came out to watch whenever we passed a shop or village. It was maybe eight or nine at night when our driver got a call that caused him to accelerate abruptly and career down a side road that led into the woods. The other cars followed. Pulling to a stop, shutting off the lights and engine, our driver spun around and hissed: "Shh! Police."

He got out to confer with his colleagues, and when he returned, it was in a hurry. Recklessly whipping around blind turns, we retreated down the mountain in the direction from which we came. Emerging from one sharp bend, we encountered a dark SUV blocking the way. A siren whined; blue lights flashed. We slammed to a halt. A police officer in civilian clothes and a black baseball cap approached the driver's side. He peered in through the open window, registering the women and children. Then, after a moment's hesitation, he reeled back and smacked our driver hard and square in the face.

With the SUV behind us, we returned to the turnoff for the side road. The other five cars were there, surrounded by several police vehicles and a four-wheel-drive truck. A crowd had gathered. It was hard to tell what was happening. Some of the officers were taking pictures of the license plates and asylum seekers; others appeared to be joking affably with the drivers. Everyone was making calls on cell phones. At one point, our driver stuck his head in the window and rubbed his thumb and fingers together. "Money, money," he said. But the next instant he disappeared again.

Eventually, with a police car ahead of us and the truck bringing up the rear, we continued along the road. It was useless to try to get an explanation from our driver, who, in a torpor of self-pity, only muttered to himself and stroked a red mark on his cheek. When Rima got hold of Ayoub, he said not to worry, Hajji Sahib was taking care of it.

We were taken to a police station, in the city of Sukabumi. There, an older, bespectacled man in army fatigues and a beret seemed to be in charge. Once more, all the drivers were pulled out of their cars, pictures were taken, phone calls were made. After about an hour, with the same escort in front and behind, our convoy was on the move again. It's hard to say for how long we drove or where we finally stopped: all I could make out were a couple of shuttered storefronts on an otherwise empty road. Curiously, when I looked out the rear window, every police vehicle save one was turning around and heading back toward Sukabumi.

The sole remaining officer, a young man in a tan uniform, leaned against a chain-link fence, smoking a cigarette, apparently uninterested in us. Soon the asylum seekers began getting out of their cars. After the officer watched with indifference as a group of Afghan teenagers briskly walked away, everyone started flagging down trucks and hopping into communal passenger vans. When a large commuter bus happened by, the officer signaled for it to stop. Those of us who hadn't yet absconded piled on.

I found myself sitting toward the front of the bus with an Iraqi family from Baghdad—a young woman in a hijab, her husband, father-in-law, and three children.

"Where are we going?" the Iraqi woman said in English.

"I don't know," I said.

Someone asked the driver.

"Bogor," he said.

"Where's Bogor?" the Iraqi woman said.

"I don't know," I said.

It turned out to be the end of the line. When the bus stopped, about thirty asylum seekers from Iran, Iraq, and Afghanistan got out. No one quite knew what to do. It was nearly dawn, and everything in Bogor was closed. We all walked to the highway— a motley, exhausted crew, carrying backpacks and plastic bags with food and clothes—and started hailing taxis. Youssef, the children, Rima, Farah, Joel, and I managed to persuade a commuter with a minivan to take us back to the tower block for twenty dollars. The sun was coming up by the time we got there. The apartment was still filthy. It still stunk. It was still hot. Youssef lit a pot of water for the noodles.

.   .   .

A few days later, Joel and I were on our way to one of the shops downstairs when a young Middle Eastern man we had never seen before approached us. "Come with me," he said.

We followed him to the courtyard, where we found Ayoub sitting at one of the tables, absorbed in a hearty lunch.

"Get your bags and the apartment key," Ayoub told me, dropping a chicken bone onto his plate and loudly sucking the grease off his fingers, one at a time, from thumb to pinkie.

When we got up to the apartment and I told Youssef the news, he only nodded. The reaction was not what I expected. "Ayoub is here," I repeated. "We're leaving."

"Did he say us too?" Youssef asked. "Or just you?"

I didn't understand. "We're all going together, of course."

Youssef seemed unconvinced and made no move to pack. A few minutes later, Hajji Sahib called me. I stepped into the hall.

"Are you with the Iranian family?" he said.

"Yes. We're almost ready."

"Ayoub is already gone," Hajji Sahib said. "You have to take a taxi to another place. And you have to leave the Iranians there. They can't come. There is a problem with their money."

Back in the apartment, I found Youssef at the stove. He had put Shahla in the shower. Anoush was watching cartoons.

"What's going on?" I said.

Youssef shook his head. When I told him Joel and I had to go alone, without them, there was no objection or rebuke; however miserable, Youssef was reconciled to what was happening, and I realized he must have seen it coming. He lit a cigarette and lay down on the mattress. Shahla was still in the shower. Anoush, I could tell, hadn't missed a thing. His eyes, though, stayed fastened on the TV.

·   ·   ·

We took a taxi to a much nicer building on the opposite side of Jakarta. A tall, skinny Iranian in his early twenties met us in the lobby and took us to the top floor. In the apartment, we found Farah and Rima sitting with three Iranian men around a coffee table with a row of cell phones on it. The women greeted us warmly and introduced one of the men, Siya, as the "boss." Muscular and shirtless, with intricate tattoos of feathered wings spread across his chest, Siya was busy fashioning a sheath for a long wood-handled knife out of folded magazine pages and rubber bands.

Noticing me notice the knife, Farah said, "For security."

Siya told us to put our cell phones on the table and informed us that we would no longer be allowed to use them.

"Who told you to come here?" he asked.

"Hajji Sahib," I said.

"Who introduced you to Hajji Sahib?"

"Hakim. From Kabul."

"Hakim from Kabul?" Siya nodded knowingly. "OK, good."

After a while, a middle-aged man and his son joined us. Siya embraced each of them for a minute or more. The father, Amir, was a shop owner from the Iranian side of the border with Iraq. He and Sami, a pudgy nine-year-old with glasses, were two of the friendliest people I met in Jakarta. Although he was older than Siya, Amir's meek nature relegated him definitely subordinate: a somewhat awkward dynamic that Amir, loath to make anyone uncomfortable, deflated by clicking his heels and saluting the boss (who, in turn, ordered him to execute a series of squats and lunges, counting out the sets in a mock drill-sergeant voice). Later, when Siya asked to inspect his weapon, Amir reached into his pocket and produced a flimsy steak knife.

It was around midnight when Siya got the call. He gave us back our phones, and we took the elevator to an underground parking garage, where another caravan of new cars with tinted windows was waiting. Every vehicle was already packed beyond capacity. We were all greatly relieved when, a few miles down the highway, our driver pulled into an alley, stopped behind the truck and told us to get out.

• • •

After the hard rain on the way to the beach, and wading out chest-deep to the skiffs, everyone was drenched. It was still dark out when the two Indonesian crew members pulled back the tarp they had nailed over our heads. The coast was a vague shadow growing vaguer. The Indonesians distributed life vests: ridiculous things, made from thin fabric and a bit of foam. The youngest children, including a girl in a pink poncho who appeared no older than four or five, were directed with their parents to a small square of open deck in the stern. The reason for this was that the farther aft you went, the less violent was the bucking as we plowed into the swells.

As the sun broke, we got our first good look at one another. Rashid had made it, as well as several other men from the tower block. There were nine children and more than a dozen women. Aside from one Afghan man, from Kunduz Province, everyone was Iranian. Most of the elderly crowded into the covered bow or leaned against the bulwarks. The rest fit where they could on the open deck. The sea was choppy enough so that each time the boat crashed from a peak into a trough or hit a wave head-on, large amounts of water splashed against us.

The first person to become sick was Siya. It was still early morning when he started throwing up. He was a natural leader, that man, and almost everyone soon followed suit. By late afternoon, we'd lost sight of land completely, and the swells grew to a size that blocked out the horizon when they loomed above us. Some people bent over the gunwales, some vomited into plastic bags. It quickly became apparent that there were not enough bags to go around: rather than toss them overboard, full ones had to be emptied, rinsed, and reused.

Siya would not be cowed. Peeling off his soaking tank top, revealing his tattooed wings—seeming to unfold them, actually, as he threw back his shoulders—he began to sing. Others joined in, breaking now and then to retch.

It was slow going. The Indonesians took turns manning the tiller and hand-pumping water from the bilge. One was older and taciturn and wore a permanent scowl; the other looked to be in his teens, smiled enough for the both of them, and called everybody "brother." The tremendous racket of the engine belied its less-than-tremendous horsepower. Like the rest of the vessel, it was built for neither such a heavy load nor such high seas. Our typical speed was four to five knots, less than six miles per hour, and at times we seemed to make no headway whatsoever against the strong southeasterly trade winds, which whipped up white caps on the waves and kept us all alert with stinging gusts of spray. Depending on the direction of the swells, the Indonesians would signal the men to consolidate themselves on the starboard or port side of the deck and thereby mitigate our listing—which, now and then, felt alarming.

The sea was still big when the sun went down, taking with it the warmth. Those of us who had spent the day on our feet now began staking claims on places to try to sleep. The deck became a claustrophobic scrum of tangled limbs. Few could recline or stretch their legs. Each time someone tried to reposition a foot or knee, say, to restore some circulation, the movement would ripple out in a cascade of shifting and grumbling as the surrounding bodies adjusted to the new configuration.

The tarp was unfurled. There was not enough of it to cover everyone. If you found yourself on an edge or corner, someone from the opposite side would invariably pull it away the moment you relaxed your grip. In any case, it was too worn and porous to do much. The water ran down its folds and creases, streaming through the many tears along the way.

·   ·   ·

In the morning, everyone looked different. Sallow. Haggard. Reduced. Amir and Sami slouched limply against each other, passing between them a bulging plastic bag. The man with the faux-hawk was curled up in a fetal ball: he stayed that way the rest of the trip. His pregnant wife sat cross-legged near the bow, pale and wet and trembling. Rima was clutching Siya's arm, as if it were a lifeline. Their eyes were squeezed tightly shut, but they were too ill to sleep.

Another problem arose. There was no toilet, and absent any railing to hold on to, going over the side was too risky. The men urinated on the hull, the women in their pants.

The Indonesians had brought a box of sealed plastic cups of water, but hardly anyone could hold them down. Siya continued to sing and puke. Although a couple of the children had begun to cry, none complained. In the afternoon, two dolphins appeared and spent the better part of an hour playfully showing off. As they darted under the boat, and launched into the air, the spectacle cheered up everyone, adults and kids alike. Even Amir and Sami rallied from their stupor to watch. A few grown men became positively gleeful, vying to be the first to spot the gray shadows flitting from the deep.

That night, several of us tried to sleep atop the engine room, trading the shelter of the hull for a little extra space. It was a poor call. Every ten minutes or so, a bucket's worth of cold water took your breath away or you were pitched against a hot pair of vertical pipes spewing noxious smoke and sparks. There was nothing to do but lie there, bracing for one or the other, admiring the magnificent array of stars and the phosphorescence glowing in the wake.

With first light, despite the sleep deprivation, dehydration, seasickness, and filth, the asylum seekers were energized by the fact that, according to the Indonesians, we would likely reach Australian territory before nightfall. Although there was still no land in sight, the arrival of birds circling overhead was unanimously interpreted as a sign that we were getting close. The sea had also calmed: no more waves crashed upon the deck. Initially, this was an enormous relief. For the first time, the sun dried us out. As it crept higher, however, it proved to be far more powerful than during the past two days, and soon, without a single cloud in the sky to blunt the blistering rays, everyone was longing for the same frigid breakers we previously cursed.

The tarp was brought back out. While blocking the sun's glare, it also trapped its heat. A couple of people, desperate for fresh air, cut up the box of water cups, which was almost empty, and made visors from the cardboard. One of the fathers in the stern, wearing a Qatar Airways sleeping mask to protect his face, found a length of string and rigged up some sheets and scarves for shade. The bow—the only covered part of the boat—reeked dizzyingly of vomit and urine. None of the dozen Iranians who rushed to fill the space when we embarked had since dared to leave it. Now they were suffering. An argument arose between them and their comrades on the open deck. The tarp was obstructing the entrance to the bow, it seemed, and smothering its already rank and humid air.

"Please," one woman begged. "We can't breathe in here."

There was little desire among the deck dwellers, however, to endure direct exposure to the sun for the comfort of those who had thus far enjoyed comparatively plush accommodations.

Presently, the heat finished off anyone who might have been bearing up. The pregnant woman's condition bordered on critical. She was flushed and drenched in sweat and heaved dryly, with nothing left to give. Sami was weeping. Amir lay supine. His eyes drooped catatonically, and when I tried to make him drink some water, he weakly gripped my ankle.

"I need help," he said. "Call for help."

That decision seemed to be up to Siya. There was a satellite phone onboard: Siya said the plan was to contact the Australian authorities once we were well within their waters. The navy would then bring us ashore. In the past, asylum boats often made it all the way—but the landing can be treacherous (when one boat smashed on the cliffs in 2010, fifty people drowned), and now it's standard practice to request a "rescue" before reaching Christmas

Island. Although Australian rescuers, when responding to distress calls, venture much farther north than where we currently were, Siya wanted to be sure. I think it was Amir's pitiful entreaties that finally persuaded him to make the call.

An Iranian man who knew some English—the one who in Jakarta told me he was an engineer—spoke to the dispatch. The Indonesians had brought a hand-held GPS device; neither they nor the asylum seekers, however, knew how to work it. Eventually, someone offered his iPhone, and the engineer read out our coordinates.

While we waited to be rescued, the Iranians set about destroying their passports. "So they can't deport you," Farah told me. Clearly, though, the task also carried some symbolic weight. Rather than simply jettisoning them, the asylum seekers painstakingly ripped out each individual page, crumpled it into a ball, and tossed it to the wind. A pair of scissors was passed around. The burgundy covers, emblazoned with the Iranian coat of arms, were cut into tiny pieces. The work was accomplished with flair and relish. Only one man seemed hesitant. Moving closer, I saw that the passport he was disposing of was his son's. When the scissors came his way, he carefully cut out the photo on the first page and slipped it in his wallet.

Soon, on the horizon, a ship appeared. A government airplane buzzed above us, swooped low and made a second pass. The asylum seekers waved shirts in the air, crying out in jubilation. The younger Indonesian performed a dance atop the engine room; he seemed amazed we had made it. Some of the men emptied their pockets, thrusting on him all the cash they had. The Indonesian beamed. "Thank you, brothers!"

Two skiffs broke off from the battleship and motored our way. Each carried six Australians in gray fatigues, riot helmets and sidearms holstered on their thighs. The Indonesians cut the engine (and after three days of its unrelenting clamor, the silence that replaced it was startling). The skiffs maneuvered abreast of us, one on each side.

The Australian sailors all looked like fresh recruits. One of them held a manual of some kind. He read from it in a loud voice. "Are there any English speakers?"

The engineer stepped forward.

"Does anyone onboard require medical assistance?"

When the engineer translated this, nearly everyone raised his hand. The pregnant woman was helped to her feet and presented. Her head hung heavily. She was almost too weak to stand.

While the Australian with the manual recited more questions—including some in Indonesian addressed to the crew, who shook their heads dumbly, refusing to answer—his fellow sailors passed to the asylum seekers new life vests, a couple jerrycans of fresh water, some bags of frozen tortillas, bottles of honey, and a tub of strawberry jam. "We're going back to the ship now," one of them told the engineer. "You have to turn the engine back on and keep going. We'll be behind you."

This information was met with disbelief. Once again the pregnant woman was raised up and displayed. "Can you take her with you at least?" asked the engineer. The sailors exchanged embarrassed looks. Plainly, they wished they could.

We still couldn't see land—and not long after the skiffs left us for the battleship, it, too, was lost from view. The return of the empty and limitless ocean, not to mention the incessantly pounding sun, was incredibly demoralizing. To make matters worse, we no longer had any means of communication. When they first glimpsed the plane and ship, all the asylum seekers, following Siya's example, threw their cell phones overboard. For some reason, amid the exultation, the satellite phone and GPS system had also gone into the water.

There was nothing to do but heed the Australian's command and "keep going." It was four or five hours after we made contact with the first ship when a second, smaller patrol boat materialized. Two more skiffs of sailors came out to meet us. This time they immediately boarded the boat, moving people aside, herding everyone forward. The officer in charge announced that he was taking control of the vessel.

After the officer spotted Joel's camera, we were both summoned to the stern, at which point we identified ourselves as journalists. While a big Australian with a bushy beard worked the tiller, the officer went through a list of prewritten questions with the crew, each of whom either couldn't read or declined to. (Unless it's their second offense, or someone dies, the Indonesian fishermen who bring asylum boats across are often not prosecuted.) The officer was polite to Joel and me. He said we had been lucky with the weather. If we had left a few days earlier, the boat would have capsized.

·   ·   ·

It inspires a unique kind of joy, that first glimpse of land. The sun was low, and you could almost mistake it for some play of light and shadow. As rousing as it was to see, the presence of a fixed object against which to mark our progress also made you realize just how slowly we had been going. It was late at night by the time we reached Christmas Island. The Australians guided our boat into the shelter of a shallow cove, beneath sheer cliffs draped in vegetation. After tying up on a mooring, the officer revealed that we would stay the night here and disembark tomorrow. When the engineer relayed the complaints of the asylum seekers—who, consolidated in the bow, had even less space now than before—the officer responded: "Are you safe? Are your lives in danger anymore?" He seemed to be losing patience and, noticing a wrapper floating by the stern, angrily reproached the Iranians: "You're in a nice country now."

It rained fitfully throughout the night. The next day, we were all ferried by a push-barge from the mooring to a jetty around the point. The jetty was swarmed with customs and immigration officials, federal police, and employees of a private company that runs the island's detention centers. Joel and I were welcomed to Australia, given water, coffee, and a ride to a surprisingly luxurious hotel. Everyone else was interned. Later that afternoon, while walking into town, I saw our little boat being towed out to sea. There, the officer had told me, it would be lit on fire.

The families and minors were taken to a relatively comfortable facility, with access to an outdoor soccer field and recreational area. The single men went to a place resembling a maximum-security prison. None of the asylum seekers would stay at either location for long. While I was on the island, flights full of detainees were leaving almost every night for Papua New Guinea and the Republic of Nauru. By now, most if not all of the people from our boat have been transferred to one of the two island nations. If they were sent to the detention center on Papua New Guinea, they are probably living in the tent city that was erected there as part of its expansion. If they were sent to the detention center on Nauru, they are probably living in the tent city that was erected there after rioting asylum seekers in July burned the buildings down.

Because the governments of Nauru and Papua New Guinea lack the capability to process refugee claims—Australian officials are still training them to do so—the asylum seekers have a long wait ahead of them. Some might not be able to hold out: already, dozens of Iranians, after seeing the conditions at the Papua New Guinea facility, have asked to be sent back to their country. Among those who decide to tough it out, it's most likely that few will be found to have valid cases. Moreover, unlike with Afghanistan and Sri Lanka, no agreement exists between Iran and Australia allowing for the forcible repatriation of asylum seekers whose applications are unsuccessful. This means that the Iranians who are denied asylum by Nauru or Papua New Guinea, and who decline to voluntarily return to Iran, will enter a kind of limbo, in which they can neither be resettled on those islands nor sent to the Australian mainland nor sent home. Absent another solution, these people could be flown back to Christmas Island and detained indefinitely.

· · ·

We reached Australia one day after Tony Abbott was elected prime minister. In keeping with his Operation Sovereign Borders policy, Abbott has since directed the navy to send back to Indonesia, whenever possible, asylum boats intercepted at sea. So far this has happened twice, in late September, when two boatloads of asylum seekers were turned over, offshore, to Indonesian authorities. The second transfer took place the same day that a boat full of Lebanese asylum seekers broke apart less than a hundred yards off the Java coast near Sukabumi, the Indonesian city whose police station Joel and I briefly visited. More than twenty bodies, many of them children, washed ashore, and more remained missing.

According to a Lebanese community leader interviewed by the Australian Broadcasting Corporation, most of the dead came from a small village near the border with Syria. One asylum seeker, who managed to swim to safety, lost his sister-in-law, his brother-in-law, three of their children, his wife and all eight of his children. The community leader said there were many more Lebanese fleeing the Syrian border who had already paid smugglers and were on their way to Indonesia.

When I got back to Afghanistan, I met with several men preparing to go to Australia. One of them, Qais Khan, opened a small auto-parts shop in Kabul in 2005. Qais told me that for years, while Afghans from the provinces came regularly into the city, he did very well. Since 2010, however, the deteriorating security situation in the rural areas adjacent to the capital had stultified commerce and ruined many retailers. Last year, Qais's shop went out of business; now he was struggling to feed his wife and two children.

A couple of months ago, fifteen of Qais's friends paid a smuggler at Sarai Shahzada and left for Indonesia. Among them was Qais's next door neighbor, a driver for a member of parliament, who decided to flee after receiving three letters from the Taliban threatening to kill him. Qais told me he was waiting to hear whether his friends were successful—in which case, he would go as well.

"And if they're not?" I asked. "If they're sent to Papua New Guinea or the Republic of Nauru?"

Qais thought for a moment and then admitted he would probably go anyway. In fact, he had already taken out the necessary loans to pay the smuggler. "At least there you have a chance," he said. "At least there is a possibility."

I felt obligated to tell him he was wrong. "You won't get to Australia," I said.

Qais didn't seem to hear. The words simply didn't register. "Australia, Europe, America," he said. "They're not like here. You have a chance."

New York

FINALIST—FEATURE
WRITING

*Eleven months after the Sandy
Hook shooting, Lisa Miller visited
Newtown, Connecticut. There
she interviewed the parents of
murdered children, the daughter
of the school principal who died
trying to protect her students,
the Roman Catholic priest who
performed eight funerals in five
days, the regulars at My Place,
where the shooter's mother once
had a place at the bar. The result
was this portrait of a community
overwhelmed by sorrow but
divided by the attention—and
money—that December 14
brought to it. Lisa Miller is a
contributing editor at* New York
and the author of Heaven: Our
Enduring Fascination with the
Afterlife. *Widely considered one of
the best-edited magazines in the
country,* New York *received the
National Magazine Award for
Magazine of the Year in 2013.*

Lisa Miller

Orders of Grief

For weeks, nobody slept. On the first night after the shootings in December, Raul Arguello lay awake in his bed in Sandy Hook, Connecticut, listening to the sirens coming from the direction of his daughters' school. His children, thank God, were warm and breathing under his roof, but the sirens reminded him that bodies—twenty of them first-graders—were being taken from the building under the cover of darkness and brought somewhere, maybe the morgue. The next day, in their large, comfortable house on a high hill, Robert and Debora Accomando made meatballs and spaghetti sauce for all the families, feeling that it was the least they could do; one of the murdered boys had been on the same wrestling team as their son. Twenty minutes down the highway, in Waterbury, Lisa Brown was riveted to the cable news. Ten years earlier, her own daughter had died, suddenly, of an asthma attack, and now she felt the parents' pain like a hole in her own heart. Lisa heard her daughter that first night telling her what to do: Raise $15,000 to buy a bronze angel, and donate it to the town in honor of the dead.

It was ten days before Christmas; the gift-giving season was in full swing. And so the outpouring began. The governor and the news crews came at once; the president arrived on Sunday. By the following Thursday, the town assessor, Christopher Kelsey, had an additional job, which was to sort, catalogue, and store all the stuff that well-wishers were sending, unbidden. The quantity was astonishing: 63,780 teddy bears by Good Friday; 636 boxes of toys; 2,200 boxes of school supplies. Backpacks, bicycles, and paper products, much of it tissues from Walmart. "Tissues seemed to be popular. There was a lot of crying going on. Tissues made sense." Kelsey found a spare warehouse and, with the help of a crew from the Seventh-day Adventist church, led an army of sifters and sorters. Five hundred and eighty volunteers spent hour upon hour separating iTunes gift cards from Starbucks cards. Every item earmarked for the families went into huge, pallet-size boxes upon which victims' family names were printed. Soto, Lewis, Barden, Hubbard. Books, cards, angels, Christmas-tree ornaments. Charm bracelets bearing a particular name.

Children have not been to school at Sandy Hook Elementary since the morning of December 14. The community recently voted to raze the school and erect a new one in its place—the demolition has begun—but this past December, it was where everyone wanted to be, and an enormous shrine grew up in the grassy space by the road, spreading down the main street and into the central intersection of Sandy Hook, by the Subway shop and the hair-cutting place, a seemingly boundless jumble of flowers and cards and signs and votive candles and more stuffed animals and more Christmas trees and more ornaments and angels. "Someone would put a teddy bear down, and all of a sudden there would be, I don't know, twelve bouquets of flowers and a partridge in a pear tree," David Brooker, a local artist, told me. A crew from out of town appeared one day with tents to erect atop the offerings, and Kelsey strung utility lights, so the constant pilgrims could at least see their way.

The residents of Sandy Hook were both overwhelmed by the world's attention and infuriated by it. Shrines, news trucks, and tour buses filled with well-wishers clogged the town's arteries so much the place became virtually unrecognizable. You couldn't drive anywhere; you couldn't park. The writer Renata Adler, who has lived in Newtown for thirty-five years, told me she got lost on the way to the post office.

"You'd pick up the phone," says Patrick Kinney, a PR man on loan to manage the influx of offers, "and it might be a quilter in Appalachia" looking to donate a blanket she'd made with twenty-six appliquéd angels. "Or it might be Quincy Jones." On the night of the shooting, Harry Connick Jr. drove to Newtown from wherever he was to keep company with the family of Ana Grace Márquez-Greene; her father, Jimmy, had played in Harry's band. Giants receiver Victor Cruz paid a visit to the family of Jack Pinto, who had been buried in his Cruz jersey. James Taylor gave an invitation-only concert at a church in Bethel nearby; up front, as Taylor sang "Sweet Baby James," sat the Mattiolis. James was the name of their six-year-old son.

The goodwill of the world descended on Newtown, yet the people there received it in unequal measure. The Bethel church holds only 850, which in a town of 28,000 meant some who felt that the tragedy affected them were excluded from the concert. There were trips on Air Force One, but only for the family members who would lobby lawmakers for new gun laws; there were 4,000 free tickets to a July Yankees game, an amazing boon, but 4,000 is less than a fifth of the town. NASCAR memorialized the Sandy Hook victims with a special car at the Daytona 500, and the fire chief who had stayed outside Sandy Hook Elementary that morning had the honor of unveiling it, not the police chief, who had entered the school.

·   ·   ·

As grief settled on the town, so did money. Cash poured in from everywhere, arriving in envelopes addressed to no one. To Newtown. The town of Newtown. The families of Newtown. There were stories of cheerleaders, having sponsored fund-raisers, walking around with $30,000 in their pockets. A guidance counselor at Newtown High School reportedly opened the mail to find $1,000 in cash. Around the country, people sold ribbons, bracelets, cupcakes, and sent in the proceeds, five and ten dollars at a time. The Davenport West honor society in Iowa sent in a check for $226.69, and the parents of a three-year-old named Lillian sent $290.94, donations from her birthday party. According to the Connecticut attorney general, about $22 million has flooded the town since December 14, finding its way into about seventy different charities set up in the wake of the massacre. Very quickly, the matter of disbursing these funds became something else, a proxy fight over how to evaluate grief.

Foundations were created in the names of nearly every victim: an animal shelter for Catherine Hubbard; an autism fund in the name of Dylan Hockley. But there were other funds, started by others in town moved by the tragedy, whose priorities occasionally collided: A handful of gun-control groups were launched, each endeavoring to claim distinction, in a town where Democrats hunt for fun. Rob Cox and a group of friends who play Frisbee together launched Sandy Hook Promise, a moderate gun-control group that also provides family support; the Newtown Action Alliance is a political-advocacy group; and United Physicians of Newtown, started by doctors, focuses on public health. From their kitchen table, the Accomandos launched My Sandy Hook Family Fund to help the victims' families cope with the immediate aftermath; within the first month, they raised a million dollars to help parents pay the bills and organized volunteers to cook dinner, make airport runs, shovel driveways, iron shirts. The Rotary Club raised money, and so did the Lions Club. "We have become a town of activists," says Arguello, a pediatrician and a founder of the doctors' group.

The biggest fund by far was the one set up by nine p.m. the day of the attack, under the auspices of the United Way of Western Connecticut. By April, it held $11 million, and local psychiatrist Chuck Herrick was named president of the board of the fund, a position that has made him one of the most unpopular men in town. It was Herrick, along with a handful of others, who had to help calculate the disbursements to the parents of murdered children and who had to defend those calculations when the bereaved accused the United Way of being unfair, insensitive, condescending, elitist, paternalistic and, in a mantra recited by the grieving, of "raising money on the backs of our dead."

The tension between the families and the United Way reached its first peak in the spring. On April 9, in a letter sent to the families with a press release attached, Kim Morgan, the CEO of the United Way of Western Connecticut, explained that the board had decided to make an "initial" payout of $4 million. E-mails instantly flew among the families. How did they come up with the $4 million figure (less than half the full amount)? Why was it taking so long to decide what to do with the money? Why should they, the grieving and bereft, entrust this process to a disembodied board, comprising, as the Newtown Patch website said, "local dignitaries": Herrick; Monsignor Robert Weiss, the Catholic priest; a lawyer; a prominent business owner; and a former town finance officer. Didn't the money belong to them? "This is when it will get cutthroat," a commenter on the Patch predicted.

On April 11, Morgan, Herrick, and the rest of the board met with thirty or more family members in an auxiliary room at St. Rose of Lima Church, the enormous Catholic church in town. Chairs were arranged in a circle, remembers one participant, and in a tense exchange, families asked questions. It had been four months, one parent complained. The drawn-out process was adding pain to their pain. What about people who hadn't been able to get back to work and really needed money right now? asked another. Above all, some expressed fury that the board was making unilateral decisions regarding money they felt was intended for them. The board was less sure. The donations had not been made with a stated purpose, they said, and the fund had been designed from the outset to compensate the victims, yes, but also the community at large. That $11 million reflected a nation's sympathy, the parents answered; at whom was that sympathy directed if not at them? "Some people were shouting, and some people were crying. It was all pretty new," says that family member. A few mothers ran out of the room.

After the shooting, the media became enamored of Newtown's quaintness, but until that day, whatever "small town" feeling the town possessed was, the townspeople say, mythological. Sandy Hook is officially part of Newtown—governed by the same town council and part of the same school system—but it is a distinct and separate place. Newtown's center is picture-perfect New England, grand houses settled around a flag. Old-timers remember Sandy Hook as where the riffraff used to live—I heard a legend about a Hells Angels shooting where a guy got his face blown off in front of what's now Sandy Hook Wine & Liquor—and other than that, it was pasture, "more cows and horses than people," as Brian Mauriello, who grew up in Newtown, likes to say.

Over the past twenty years, though, Sandy Hook has grown into a very ordinary exurb: big houses, bigger lots, curvy roads, and cul-de-sacs. It's an appealing home for busy professionals, attracted by the real estate and public schools. They work in Hartford, Danbury, Armonk, Stamford, and Manhattan, and at the hedge funds in lower Fairfield County. Until "12/14," it was a place where busy people watched television after a long day, where parents sending their children to the same school might remain strangers for years. Over lunch at her dining-room table, Francine Wheeler told me she can't count the number of people who approached her after her six-year-old son, Ben, died in his first-grade classroom to say these kinds of things: "I've lived down the street from you for years; I've seen you playing outside with your boys; I've always been meaning to meet you."

The tragedy changed the tenor of Newtown, drawing people out of their cocoons and propelling them to something beyond neighborliness. It wasn't just the meals and the home visits, the endless prayers and letters and offers of help. And it wasn't just that people started to use their turn signals at the crazy intersection by the flagpole or that they continue to pay it forward at the local Starbucks. It was a kind of solidarity that you see among veterans: When a group of family members helped to draft legislation suppressing crime-scene photos, support in town was nearly unanimous. And when one of the murdered children has a birthday, word often gets around. On the day that Jack Pinto would have turned seven, all the kids in town went to school in their sports jerseys, having organized the tribute themselves.

Herrick and his fellow board members had initially faced two questions: first, how to calculate disbursements to the grieving, which meant drawing lines around groups of victims and prioritizing their grief. And second, how to weigh the immediate pain of the bereaved against the future (and unknown) needs of the town. The fund's steering committee spoke early on to Kenneth Feinberg, the attorney who after 9/11 found his calling advising municipalities and families on the best way to collect and distribute funds in the event of a mass shooting or terrorist event.

Feinberg's method is bloodlessly simple: Create one independent fund. Collect as much money as you can in a short period of time. Figure out who the victims are and develop an algorithm for distribution, stipulating that such a calculus will never be fair. Distribute the money quickly, and shut the fund down. Feinberg believes subjective measures of victimhood, like "need" or "entitlement," should never be part of any such accounting. "Don't send in your tax returns or tell us how much you have in the bank. We're not going to say Johnny's death is worth more than Mary's death," Feinberg told me. "Money is a poor substitute for loss. That's it."

But the situation in Newtown didn't subject itself to such cold, actuarial analysis, the board felt. When Adam Lanza opened fire, he hurt everyone in town. As Herrick said, "It's two degrees of separation." And unlike in Boston or Aurora or in New York City after the 9/11 attacks, where grief could dissipate over a large geographic area or among a great many people, the grief in Newtown was exponentially more concentrated. Here, if you were the relative of a victim, you had many comrades in grief. And your neighbors, who were grieving, too, often expressed their pain in conflicting ways.

Adam Lanza took forty victims, a number most—but not all—people in town agree on. He shot and killed twenty first-graders in two classrooms. Those are the victims most have focused on, often called, simply, "angels." Reports say Lanza made eye contact with the children; some of them nestled in their teachers' arms as he murdered them. Jesse Lewis yelled "run" before he was shot, his mother, Scarlett, says; reports say Noah Pozner was shot eleven times, losing his jaw and his left hand. There were also adult victims, whose deaths have received less attention: Lauren Rousseau and Victoria Soto, the first-grade teachers; two teacher's aides; the school psychologist; and the principal. In Newtown, the dead make up the first tier of victims: the twenty-six. Over time, that number came to describe not just the victims of Lanza's massacre but their immediate families, too. These and two people who were wounded would receive compensation under a Feinberg-type plan.

But there is another group that Herrick's committee also hoped to take into account. These are the twelve children in the two classrooms who survived—one little girl in Lauren Rousseau's class and eleven children in Victoria Soto's, six of whom survived by running as the shooter reloaded his gun. These kids have been called "survivors" and are also known as "the twelve." One person I spoke to heard the following version of that morning from a seven-year-old girl: *The bad man shot my friend. And then he shot my other friend. And then he stopped, and I took my friend's hand, and we slipped in blood, and we bumped into the bad man, and we ran and ran and ran and ran.* They found their way to a neighbor's house, where he discovered them, sitting in the driveway and crying and reportedly saying the most unbelievable things. "We can't go back to school." "He had a big gun and a little gun." And: "There was blood in her mouth and she fell to the ground."

The parents of the twelve were, with the two and the relatives of the twenty-six, initially part of "the forty," but they have since seceded, forming a separate and nearly impenetrable clan. They are estranged from the twenty-six; they rarely speak to the press. Their kids saw unimaginable things, and the parents are protective above all, worrying about nightmares now and PTSD and behavior problems down the road. But as the town began to weigh and measure degrees of grief, the parents of the twelve saw that in their plight was a horrible paradox and found themselves unable or unwilling to fight very hard for their share of the funds. Their children may have to cope forever with the memory of what they saw. But at least they can be kissed good night.

To describe the way grief afflicted the town, many people invoke the metaphor of concentric circles, the ripples created by a rock in a lake. At the center are the twenty-six, and then the two and the twelve. Beyond that are all the teachers and children who made it out alive, including the children of Robert Bazuro, who skipped school on the fourteenth in order to honor their uncle, who had recently died. "I feel that my brother saved the lives of my children," says Bazuro.

Then there are the cops and the firefighters and the EMTs. There are all the people connected to the people at the school that day: parents, grandparents, cousins, and friends. There are scoutmasters, camp counselors, coaches, pastors, and clerks: the lady at the checkout with a special fondness for a certain kid she'd been saying hi to since he learned to walk.

Herrick and his colleagues on the steering committee believed that the needs in Newtown would be great and that they would be unforeseen. They talked to folks in Columbine, Colorado. They talked to folks at Virginia Tech and in Oklahoma City. They learned about the slow unraveling that occurs in a community after an event like this, the rise in divorce, spousal abuse, alcoholism, teenage truancy and drug use. They thought that while some of the $11 million might go to the victims' families, to help them start to heal, some could be used as insurance against such outcomes, to pay for mental-health support and other kinds of preventive services. They saw themselves as the most conservative type of guardians, hoping "to prepare," as Herrick put it to me, "for the long term." In an audit this summer, the Connecticut attorney general acknowledged to Kim Morgan and Chuck Herrick that the foundation had not violated donor intent—of the 20,000 envelopes and cards the AG inspected, only 1,373 were addressed to the families. But he also slapped their wrists for mishandling the process: "I am, however, concerned," he wrote. Poor communication by the board "facilitated the misunderstandings about and inaccurate public information related to the fund."

·   ·   ·

Until June, families were allowed to schedule walks through Sandy Hook Elementary School with police escort, and, just before the school was shuttered for good, Cristina Lafferty-Hassinger, daughter of the slain principal, Dawn Hochsprung, took the police up on their standing offer. Cristina, who is twenty-nine and has four young children, lives in Oakville, a thirty-minute drive from Newtown, and had never seen her mother's workplace. Her mother was fierce, a fighter, and Cristina was having trouble getting a picture of that morning right in her mind; her stepfather, George, came along for moral support. Together, they stopped at the spot where Dawn was gunned down. "I *know* she didn't have time to think," George said later. "But if she did have time, she would have said, 'Look at you, you scrawny little shit. I could take you.'" On the edge of her bathroom sink on the day I visited Cristina, there was a green rubber bracelet of the Livestrong variety. It said WWDD: WHAT WOULD DAWN DO?

Among the families of the twenty-six, there are a few who became full-time warriors, and Lafferty-Hassinger is one of these. She believes that she has been freer than members of other families to agitate against the United Way because she does not live in Newtown and is thus protected from the judgment of her neighbors. In February, she had discovered that families were being asked to fill out paperwork to claim any emergency funds (held separately from the $11 million), a fact she found outrageous. Many of the twenty-six families had still not gone back to work; some were still not getting out of bed. "One of the families said they'd rather lose their house than go hat in hand and go begging," she told me. On February 25, she posted the following message to her Facebook page: "The United Way of Western Connecticut gallantly stepped up to manage the influx of donations, but who are they really helping? They offered their trusted name to evoke confidence from eager donors, but more than two months later the victims' families are being asked for proof of hardship before even the smallest disbursement is issued. Proof of hardship?"

Many in town found the public fights about money distasteful. One person told me the phrase "embarrassment of riches" came to mind. In March, Monsignor Weiss told a reporter for the *Hartford Courant* that the $11 million must not become a "perverted lottery" for the bereaved.

But Cristina doesn't really care what people think of her, and she doesn't believe that grieving people ought to face judgment for simply claiming what's theirs. She quotes Tom Teves, a new friend who lost his twenty-four-year-old son in the Aurora theater shooting: "If I want to gamble my $200,000 away at a Vegas casino, who cares? My son is dead—it's none of your business." A lot of the families agreed with her, Cristina told me, but felt inhibited to speak. "They don't want to walk into the grocery store and have someone whispering, 'They're asking for money because their kid died.'"

"The process of grieving is as individual as your fingerprint," Francine's husband, David Wheeler, told me. Many of the twenty-six will not speak to the press. Some of them are on TV all the time. Scarlett Lewis was on the *Today* show last week, and as she sat there waiting to talk to Matt Lauer, she thought, *This is so surreal that at times your brain just explodes.* The twenty-six may be a fractious group, but those I spoke to defend one another's right to be idiosyncratic—ugly, compassionate, silent, loving, selfish, spiritual, depressed—in their grief. There are also those who feel Sandy Hook Promise has claimed too large a role for itself. And there are those in town who discount Lafferty-Hassinger's persistent agitating as a symptom of her deeper, broader anger. "It is hard," Morgan says, "to argue with someone who is suffering."

After the April meeting, under pressure from the governor's office, the board announced that it would not disburse the funds a little bit at a time, as it had planned, but in one lump payment of $7.7 million. And Ken Feinberg was invited to Newtown to advise the board and meet with the families.

Still, the families were unsatisfied. At a meeting over the summer, when some of them queried the board how it arrived at the $7.7 figure, Second Selectman Will Rodgers pushed back. The families were lucky to be getting anything, Rodgers suggested, according to people who were there. (When asked about his comments, Rodgers says he was speaking about the possibility that other organizations less committed to victims' compensation could have taken control of the fund early on and that this recollection takes his comments out of context.) In August, each of the twenty-six received a check for $281,000. The two got $75,000 each. And the twelve got $20,000.

Some in town believe that the twelve were shortchanged. I raise the issue with Lafferty-Hassinger. Don't these kids, who have been through so much, deserve the benefit of a safety net? She responds with a quip she has heard among the twenty-six. "Okay, it sucks. You only got $20,000. Want to trade?"

•   •   •

Ben Wheeler appears to his mother in dreams. Recently, Francine says, "he just came and hugged and kissed me. I said, 'Oh, no, it's a dream. Is it going to turn into a nightmare?' But no, he just kept hugging and kissing me." Early on, in January, she had a dream that she rode an elevator all the way down, and when the door opened, Ben was there. "Mama," he told her. "I'm so happy. I'm loved. I'm okay. I'm so happy. I'm okay." And then, "Don't let them trademark you, Mama."

The Wheelers are among the most active of the Newtown families. In January, David Wheeler gave passionate testimony before the Connecticut State Legislature. In April, the Wheelers stood by the president in Hartford as he pressured Congress to pass gun-control legislation. Just before the vote, Obama handed his weekly video address to David and Francine, who wept as she remembered her son, who wanted to be an architect and also a paleontologist. In May, the Wheelers did a long interview with Bill Moyers, both of them breaking down when David mentioned December 13, the day before the day their lives became unrecognizable to them.

The Wheelers' very public displays of grief are incomprehensible to some, though Francine says their outspokenness is a way to make connections with others and continue being good parents to both of their sons—to Ben, who died, and to Nate, who is ten. If they can change the politics of gun violence by telling their story, she believes, they can save lives. But David, formerly an actor, now a graphic designer, always looks devastated, with basset-hound bags beneath his eyes. Francine's face is more motile, sparkling one minute, crumpled the next.

It's not so hard to be public in public, the Wheelers tell me. They're both performers; it's only natural, says David, that trauma would force them back into comfortable roles. It's much, much harder to have to be public all the time, Francine explains—in

Newtown, the families of the twenty-six carry the celebrity of all tragic figures. Everyone in town knows their names and the names and faces of their dead; they are perpetually exposed, even in their everyday routines. There are three groceries in town, but Francine likes Caraluzzi's best, and she has a hard time there, even now, because she visited so frequently with Benny. She would let him loose in the aisles, to the annoyance of the other shoppers. It is horrible, she says, to have to break down in a place where everyone knows exactly who you are and what, exactly, happened to your kid. "My greatest need of strangers is to treat me like a stranger."

Stories circulate among the twenty-six of those who, in stabs at empathy, have said entirely the wrong thing: "Move on," or "This too shall pass," or "Will you hug me for me?" The rest of the town, even those very close to the grieving, find themselves on eggshells, constantly worried they'll misspeak or misstep. Nelba Márquez-Greene can feel how much other people in town want her to be better. "We are the face of every parent's nightmare," she says. But nothing makes her feel better. "I feel terrible, and I'm giving myself permission to say I feel terrible." She is a tiny, neat person, with a dispassionate way of talking, and is working for Sandy Hook Promise now, busily giving keynote speeches and a TED talk, but the idea that her work life might console her or ease her pain is laughable. It's as if, she tells me evenly, you needed a liver transplant and someone came up and gave you a heart.

Every day, Francine Wheeler makes a list of the things she's grateful for, and she always includes her morning coffee. Around her neck, she wears a tiny picture of Ben in a tiny square frame and a silver pendant in the shape of a treble clef. When I admire it, she tells me that Ben's ashes are enclosed in the necklace. "He had perfect pitch," she says.

When I visit them at home, David shows me his amulets, too, more ashes in a pendant, a bracelet of green agate, another one, on a leather thong, strung by Ben's counselor at camp. But by three o'clock, the Wheelers are distracted. Nate is due home from school, and they're listening with all their nerve endings for the squeak of the bus. Nate was at Sandy Hook Elementary School on 12/14 as well. When he arrives, on time, he shows his parents the new *Guinness* book he got that day at school. He has his brother's ashes in a pendant, too.

．　　　．　　　．

In October, a coalition of gun groups announced that it was declaring the first anniversary of the shooting "Guns Save Lives Day." Pat Llodra, the first selectman, was flinty in her response. "We will not host a political rally of any stripe on that day and we hope that all such inclined persons understand that they and their agenda are not welcome. We ask for privacy and expect that all caring folks, including the media, will accommodate us." And then, like the schoolteacher she used to be, she added the unveiled threat of her own judgment: "Those persons . . . who choose not to accede to our request . . . show the world their own personal and ethical fiber."

This is the question before the town now: how to lay claim to an uncertain future, to move forward without moving on and build unity among the various factions. What is an acceptable tribute? What is too much? Some locals have told me that, when out in the world, they try not to say the name of the place they live; "Newtown" evokes in outsiders such horror. "This is a good town," says Arguello, the pediatrician. "We don't want to be remembered just for that day."

Monsignor Weiss has a hunch that the future of Newtown will not include him. Pastor of St. Rose for fourteen years, he is haunted, he says, by the memory of crunching glass under his shoes, for when he approached the school that day, a police officer asked if he cared to enter and give the children a blessing and he declined. "It gets me," he says, beginning to cry. "I said, 'You know what? These children don't need a blessing. They are with the Lord already.'" He turned around and went back to the fire-house, feeling that the living needed him more.

But that memory and the eight funerals he performed in five days and self-doubt over his leadership these past months continue to torment him. He never wanted to be the face of the town, he says, the small-town priest consoling his decimated flock. But walking away from the firehouse late that first day, he was mobbed by reporters, and "all of a sudden," he says, "you find yourself talking to Katie Couric." He's chronically ill now; his digestion is shot; he can barely control his emotions. "I feel like I'm a museum piece. Everywhere I go, people stare at me. I think I make people uncomfortable." Friends in the priesthood are counseling him to save his health and find another post or another parish, and he is taking their advice seriously. "Every time I stand at the pulpit, I wonder, *Am I a reminder of 12/14?*"

Llodra has taken a different approach. Petite, blonde, and seventy-one, she had been in her mayorlike position for three years and was getting ready to retire when Adam Lanza entered Sandy Hook Elementary. The events of 12/14 forced her into a role she could hardly have imagined and to which, by most accounts, she magnificently rose: She was the sensible, compassionate den mother to a collection of people screaming in pain and acting out, as people do, in anger and selfishness and love. It was Llodra's idea to ask the wrecking crews at the school to sign stringent nondisclosure agreements such that no photos of the interior ever appear online and that no souvenirs from the school ever show up on eBay. She redeployed her staff to cope with the influx of goods and visitors; she tried to smooth relations between the families and the board. In the waiting room to her office on the day I was there hung the green sign that has become the hopeful mantra of so many: WE ARE SANDY HOOK. WE CHOOSE LOVE. (Some I spoke to rolled their eyes at the phrase, knowing how fractious the town has been.) She introduced the metaphor "sacred soil" to describe the shrines she cleaned up last winter, a deft bit of wordsmithery that allowed the entire town to feel good about turning a nation's love into compost. Llodra is a pull-yourself-up, brush-yourself-off kind of person, and now, she feels, enough is enough.

"It's not all about the victims," she told me during an interview in her office. "It could have been any one of these children. By happenstance, he turned left instead of right." Newtown must not become absorbed in its own victimhood, she believes. It must "grow through that specialness and not become the thing that defines them." In July, Llodra announced on her blog that the town would no longer be hosting special events. And last month, as the anniversary approached, she asked well-wishers to keep their gift-giving impulses in check and to express their generosity through other means.

For many people in Newtown, the killing of those six- and seven-year-olds resurrected the pain of previous trauma or loss. In interviews, I heard about the death of a brother in a car crash; the near death of a child; an attempted rape; a gunshot wound. Llodra is one of these. Four years ago, she lost her forty-two-year-old daughter, Sharon, and Llodra believes that her own experience with grief helped her understand the incomparable suffering of losing a child. Many in Newtown, she believes, have been like families stuck in the initial phase after a death, when the women with casseroles are still coming by to stock the freezer. The next phase is harder and more personal but necessary. "I would give anything to have my daughter back," she told me, "but I like who I am now better than who I was then."

Llodra is no longer planning to retire. She has a lot of things to do: resolve the acrimony around Fairfield Hills, the campus of the dilapidated psychiatric hospital in town, which is now the focus of a development fight. Manage the issue of armed guards in the local schools, on which the town remains divided. And, of course, rebuild Sandy Hook Elementary School. The 400 Sandy Hook kids have taken over an empty school building in Monroe, ten miles away; parents are complaining about the length of the bus ride and the stress on their kids. Once again, Llodra is in the position of having to acknowledge generosity without bowing before it. Monroe has been great, but "these are our kids," she says. She wants Newtown to become again what she knows it can be: a place where there are great schools and playgrounds and where parents on the sidelines of sports events, she says, can be overheard "crabbing about taxes."

•   •   •

That jocular, suburban normalcy seems possible, even now, if only in glimmers. There are all kinds of places to eat and drink in town—pizza, passable Japanese, a bowl of chowder—but probably the most popular is My Place, a regular Italian joint of the vinyl-booths variety. The real draw is the pub, tucked in the back, where, in an amber haze, amid televisions and twinkling lights, the co-owner, Mark Tambascio, pulls the taps on a wide selection of microbrews. I went there during the first game of the World Series to meet Rob Cox of Sandy Hook Promise; he wanted to show me the bar stool dedicated to the Flatliners, the name of his Frisbee team, so called because all the players are approaching heart-attack age. When I arrived, every seat was taken. People stood in clumps, holding pints and greeting newcomers by name—high fives and backslaps for all.

Nancy Lanza, Adam's mother, whom he shot four times on the morning of December 14 before driving to the school, was a regular at My Place, and I had the strong feeling that everyone at the bar could tell me which stool had been hers: down near the end, by the entry to the restaurant. The Frisbee team regularly retires to My Place after its Tuesday-night game, and Cox recalls occasionally exchanging small talk with Nancy. Tambascio was friendly with her and is a neutral party in town—his bathrooms are marked YANKEES and RED SOX, because in Fairfield County, even tight-knit families can have split allegiances. For all these months, he hasn't spoken ill of her.

Cox arrived, on his way to a 10:40 p.m. hockey game in a neighboring town—it's hard to get ice time—and introduced me around. There was Terrence Ford, enormous, with a biker-guy look, who showed up out of nowhere to help direct traffic in Sandy Hook that day; cop cars were screaming so fast down the hill he could smell their brake pads burning. "That day was shit," he hollered, over the din. "It's still shit. It will always be shit." There was Scott Wolfman, who works pro bono at Sandy Hook Promise and was busy organizing a trip for a few of the dads to see Pearl Jam that weekend in Hartford. There was the girl Cox took to the sixth-grade dance, now standing in a posse of moms, all of whom had just been to a seminar at the library about how to handle teenagers' moods at home. Just shrug it off, the experts said. Laugh. Be goofy. Don't engage. It wasn't clear how much of this camaraderie was built in the aftermath of the shooting and how much survived it. But the atmosphere in My Place that night was very much the town's own idyllic picture of itself.

And on TV, the Red Sox were winning; the Cardinals had committed three errors in one game. Nelba Márquez-Greene came in to meet me, texting on her phone, having just finished taping a TED talk. Someone else had a picture on their phone of Márquez-Greene speaking, gazing up and smiling, but Nelba seemed embarrassed by the attention. The conversation turned to Wolfman's Halloween party: an annual event, a bawdy blowout, no kids allowed. Cox was teasing Márquez-Greene, encouraging her to come, but she said she probably wouldn't be in a party mood. In the meantime, though, right now, she thought she might be persuaded to have a drink.

Rolling Stone

FINALIST—REPORTING

You may not know this story, but you certainly remember the cover. When Rolling Stone *published a selfie of Dzhokhar Tsarnaev, one of the Boston Marathon bombers, on its cover, the magazine was quickly denounced for glamorizing someone even the editors called "a monster." Overlooked in the ensuing frenzy was the quality of Janet Reitman's reporting. Reitman would later admit being surprised by the reaction to the cover, but this was not the first time one of her stories had provoked controversy: her* Rolling Stone *piece "Inside Scientology" was also a Reporting finalist in 2007. Nor was it the first time* Rolling Stone *had put a monster on the cover. The magazine won its first National Magazine Award in 1971 for a story about Charles Manson.*

Janet Reitman

Jahar's World

Peter Payack awoke around four a.m. on April 19, 2013, and saw on his TV the grainy surveillance photo of the kid walking out of the minimart. The boy, identified as "Suspect #2" in the Boston bombing, looked familiar, thought Payack, a wrestling coach at the Cambridge Rindge and Latin School. On the other hand, there were a million skinny kids with vaguely ethnic features and light-gray hoodies in the Boston area, and half the city was probably thinking they recognized the suspect. Payack, who'd been near the marathon finish line on the day of the bombing and had lost half of his hearing from the blast, had hardly slept in four days. But he was too agitated to go back to bed. Later that morning, he received a telephone call from his son. The kid in the photo? "Dad, that's Jahar."

"I felt like a bullet went through my heart," the coach recalls. "To think that a kid we mentored and loved like a son could have been responsible for all this death. It was beyond shocking. It was like an alternative reality."

People in Cambridge thought of nineteen-year-old Dzhokhar Tsarnaev—"Jahar" to his friends—as a beautiful, tousle-haired boy with a gentle demeanor, soulful brown eyes, and the kind of shy, laid-back manner that "made him that dude you could always just vibe with," one friend says. He had been a captain of the Cambridge Rindge and Latin wrestling team for two years and a promising student. He was also "just a normal American kid," as his friends described him, who liked soccer, hip-hop, girls; obsessed over *The Walking Dead* and *Game of Thrones*; and smoked a copious amount of weed.

Payack stared at his TV, trying to reconcile Dzhokhar, the bomber accused of unspeakable acts of terrorism, with the teenage boy who had his American nickname "Jahar" inscribed on his wrestling jacket. He'd worn it all the time.

That afternoon, Payack spoke with CNN, where he issued a direct appeal. "Jahar," he said, "this is Coach Payack. There has been enough death, destruction. Please turn yourself in."

At that precise moment, just west of Cambridge, in suburban Watertown, Jahar Tsarnaev lay bleeding on the floor of a twenty-two-foot motorboat dry-docked behind a white clapboard house. He'd been wounded just after midnight in a violent confrontation with police that had killed his twenty-six-year-old brother, Tamerlan. For the next eighteen hours, he would lie quietly in the boat, as the dawn broke on a gray day and thousands of law-enforcement officials scoured a twenty-block area in search of him. He was found just after six p.m., though it would take nearly three more hours for FBI negotiators to persuade him to surrender.

The following morning, Payack received a text from one of the agents with the FBI's Crisis Negotiating Unit. He'd heard Payack's televised appeal, told him he'd invoked the coach's name while speaking with Jahar. "I think it helped," the agent said. Payack was relieved. "Maybe by telling Jahar that I was thinking about him, it gave him pause," Payack says. "Maybe he'd seen himself going out as a martyr for the cause. But all of a sudden, here's somebody from his past, a past that he liked, that he fit in with, and it hit a soft spot."

When investigators finally gained access to the boat, they discovered a jihadist screed scrawled on its walls. In it, according to a thirty-count indictment handed down in late June, Jahar appeared to take responsibility for the bombing, though he admitted he did not like killing innocent people. But "the U.S. government is killing our innocent civilians," he wrote, presumably referring to Muslims in Iraq and Afghanistan. "I can't stand to see such evil go unpunished. . . . We Muslims are one body, you hurt one, you hurt us all," he continued, echoing a sentiment that is cited so frequently by Islamic militants that it has become almost cliché. Then he veered slightly from the standard script, writing a statement that left no doubt as to his loyalties: "Fuck America."

•　　　•　　　•

In the twelve years since the attacks on the World Trade Center and the Pentagon, there have been more than twenty-five plots to strike the United States hatched by Americans, most of which were ill-conceived or helped along by undercover operatives who, in many cases, provided their targets with weapons or other materials. A few—including the plots to blow up the New York subway system and Times Square—were legitimate and would have been catastrophic had they come to fruition. Yet none did until that hazy afternoon of April 15, 2013, when two pressure-cooker bombs exploded near the marathon finish line on Boylston Street, killing three people, including an eight-year-old boy. Close to 300 more were injured by flying shrapnel, with many losing a leg or an arm or an eye: a scene of unbelievable carnage that conjured up images of Baghdad, Kabul, or Tel Aviv.

An uneasy panic settled over Boston when it was revealed that the Tsarnaev brothers were not, as many assumed, connected to a terrorist group, but young men seemingly affiliated with no one but themselves. Russian émigrés, they had lived in America for a decade—and in Cambridge, a city so progressive it had its own "peace commission" to promote social justice and diversity. Tamerlan, known to his American friends as "Tim," was a talented boxer who'd once aspired to represent the United States in the Olympics. His little brother, Jahar, had earned a scholarship to the University of Massachusetts Dartmouth and was thinking about becoming an engineer or a nurse or maybe a dentist—his focus changed all the time. They were Muslim, yes, but they were also *American*—especially Jahar, who became a naturalized U.S. citizen on September 11, 2012.

Since the bombing, friends and acquaintances of the Tsarnaevs, as well as the FBI and other law-enforcement officials, have tried to piece together a narrative of the brothers, most of which has focused on Tamerlan, whom we now know was on multiple U.S. and Russian watch lists prior to 2013, though neither the FBI nor the CIA could find a reason to investigate him further. Jahar, however, was on no one's watch list. To the contrary, after several months of interviews with friends, teachers, and coaches still reeling from the shock, what emerges is a portrait of a boy who glided through life, showing virtually no signs of anger, let alone radical political ideology or any kind of deeply felt religious beliefs.

At his arraignment at a federal courthouse in Boston on July 10, Jahar smiled, yawned, slouched in his chair, and generally seemed not to fully grasp the seriousness of the situation while pleading innocent to all charges. At times he seemed almost to smirk—which wasn't a "smirk," those who know him say. "He just seemed like the old Jahar, thinking, 'What the fuck's going on here?'" says Payack, who was at the courthouse that day.

It had been the coach who'd helped Jahar come up with his nickname, replacing the nearly impossible-to-decipher *Dzhokhar* with a simpler and cooler-sounding rendering. "If he had a hint of radical thoughts, then why would he change the spelling of his name so that more Americans in school could pronounce it?" asks one longtime friend, echoing many others. "I can't feel that my friend, the Jahar I knew, is a terrorist," adds another. "That Jahar isn't, to me."

"Listen," says Payack, "there are kids we don't catch who just fall through the cracks, but this guy was seamless, like a billiard ball. No cracks at all." And yet a deeply fractured boy lay under that facade; a witness to all of his family's attempts at a better life as well as to their deep bitterness when those efforts failed and their dreams proved unattainable. As each small disappointment wore on his family, ultimately ripping them apart, it also furthered Jahar's own disintegration—a series of quiet yet powerful body punches. No one saw a thing. "I knew this kid, and he was a good kid," Payack says, sadly. "And, apparently, he's also a monster."

. . .

Though Dzhokhar Tsarnaev was raised largely in America, his roots are in the restive North Caucasus, a region that has known centuries of political turmoil. Born on July 22, 1993, he spent the first seven years of his life in the mountainous Central Asian republic of Kyrgyzstan, where his father, Anzor, had grown up in exile. Anzor is from Chechnya, the most vilified of the former Soviet republics, whose people have been waging a near-continuous war since the eighteenth century against Russian rule. Dzhokhar's mother, Zubeidat, is an Avar, the predominantly Muslim ethnic group of Chechnya's eastern neighbor, Dagestan, which has been fighting its own struggle for independence against the Russians since the late 1700s. After the fall of the Soviet Union, Chechen nationalists declared their independence, which resulted in two brutal wars where the Russian army slaughtered tens of thousands of Chechens and leveled its capital city, Grozny. By 1999, the violence had spread throughout the region, including Dagestan.

Though Islam is the dominant religion of the North Caucasus, religion played virtually no role in the life of Anzor Tsarnaev, a tough, wiry man who'd grown up during Soviet times, when religious worship in Kyrgyzstan was mostly underground. In Dagestan, where Islam had somewhat stronger footing, many women wear hijabs; Zubeidat, though, wore her dark hair like Pat Benatar. The couple met while Anzor was studying law and were married on October 20, 1986. The next day, their first child,

Tamerlan, was born. Three more children would follow, all of them born in Kyrgyzstan, where Anzor secured a job as an investigator in the prosecutor's office in the nation's capital, Bishkek.

It was a prestigious position, especially for a Chechen, but Anzor had larger ambitions. He hoped to take his family to America, where his brother, Ruslan, an attorney, was building an upper-middle-class life. After Russia invaded Chechnya in 1999, setting off the second of the decade's bloody wars, Anzor was fired from his job as part of a large-scale purge of Chechens from the ranks of the Kyrgyz government. The Tsarnaevs then fled to Zubeidat's native Dagestan, but war followed close behind. In the spring of 2002, Anzor, Zubeidat, and Jahar, then eight, arrived in America on a tourist visa and quickly applied for political asylum. The three older children, Ailina, Bella, and Tamerlan, stayed behind with relatives.

During their first month in America, Jahar and his parents lived in the Boston-area home of Dr. Khassan Baiev, a Chechen physician and friend of Anzor's sister, who recalled Anzor speaking of discrimination in Kyrgyzstan that "went as far as beatings." This abuse would be the premise of the Tsarnaevs' claim for asylum, which they were granted a year later. In July 2003, the rest of the family joined them in Cambridge, where they'd moved into a small, three-bedroom apartment at 410 Norfolk St.; a weathered building with peeling paint on a block that otherwise screams gentrification.

There are just a handful of Chechen families in the Boston area, and the Tsarnaevs seemed a welcome addition. "They had wonderful children," recalls Anna Nikeava, a Chechen who befriended the Tsarnaevs shortly after they arrived. "They were very soft, like cuddly kittens, all four kids, always hugging and kissing each other." And the parents, too, seemed to adore each other, even while Anzor, who spoke broken English, worked as a mechanic, making just ten dollars an hour. For the first year, the Tsarnaevs received public assistance. But they never seemed to struggle, Anna says. "They were very much in love and enjoying life. They were fun."

Chechen families are very traditional—Anna, a warm and talkative woman in her late forties, tells me that in her country, "Ladies don't wear pants, you have to wear a skirt," and marrying outside the culture is taboo. The Tsarnaevs were atypical in that regard. Zubeidat was a "very open, modern lady" with a taste for stylish jeans, high heels, and short skirts. "She had the tattooed eyebrows, permanent makeup, very glamorous," says Anna. "And her children were always dressed up nicely too."

Zubeidat adored her children, particularly Tamerlan, a tall, muscular boy she compared to Hercules. Jahar, on the other hand, was the baby, his mother's "*dwog*," or "heart." "He looked like an angel," says Anna, and was called "Jo-Jo" or "Ho."

"He was always like, 'Mommy, Mommy, yes, Mommy'—even if his mom was yelling at him," says Anna's son Baudy Mazaev, who is a year and a half younger than Jahar. "He was just, like, this nice, calm, compliant, pillow-soft kid. My mom would always say, 'Why can't you talk to me the way Dzhokhar talks to his mother?'"

There were five or six Chechen boys of roughly the same age in their circle, but Baudy and Jahar were particularly close. Now a student at Boston University, Baudy remembers family get-to-gethers in the Tsarnaevs' cramped, top-floor apartment, where Jahar and Tamerlan shared a small room with a bunk bed; in an even smaller room, their sisters shared just a mattress. There was never room for everyone around the tiny kitchen table, so the boys would engage in epic games of manhunt or play video games on the giant TV in the living room while their parents ate and socialized. Anzor was famous for his booming laugh, which Jahar inherited—"It was so loud, the whole room would know if he was laughing," says Baudy.

Jahar idolized his older brother, Tamerlan—all the children appeared to—and as a child, he followed his brother's example and learned to box. But it was wrestling that became his primary sport, as was also true for Baudy, a squarely built kid who competed in a higher weight class than the slender, 130-pound Jahar. "It's a Chechen thing," says Baudy. "When I went to Chechnya to see my cousins, the first thing they ask is, 'You want to wrestle?'"

Baudy is fiercely proud of his heritage, and Jahar, who shares a name with Chechnya's first president, Dzhokhar Dudayev (one of Anzor's personal heroes), had similar "Chechen pride." He embraced the national Chechen symbol, the wolf; learned traditional dances; and could speak Chechen as well as Russian. He even talked about marrying a Chechen girl. "He would always talk about how pretty Chechen girls were," says Baudy, though, to his knowledge, Jahar had never met one, aside from the sisters of some of their friends.

There were many, many Jahars in Cambridge: children of immigrants with only the haziest, if idealized, notions of their ethnic homelands. One of the most liberal and intellectually sophisticated cities in the United States, Cambridge is also one of the most ethnically and economically diverse. There are at least fifty nationalities represented at the city's one public high school, Cambridge Rindge and Latin School, whose motto—written on walls, murals, and school-course catalogs and proclaimed over the PA system—is "Opportunity, Diversity, Respect." About 45 percent of its students live in public or subsidized housing, largely in the city's densely populated working-class neighborhoods. There are more affluent areas, and in them live the children of professors from nearby Harvard and MIT who also attend Rindge, "but not in tremendous numbers," says Cambridge schools superintendent Dr. Jeffrey M. Young. "What you do have is some actively engaged political families"—like those of the school's most famous alumni, Matt Damon and Ben Affleck—"and then there's the voiceless, who we try to encourage to have more of a voice."

All of the Tsarnaev children went to Rindge, as the school is known, but it was Jahar who assimilated best. Though he'd arrived in America speaking virtually no English, by high school he was fluent, with only a trace of an accent, and he was also fluent in the local patois. (Among his favorite words, his friends say, was "sherm," Cambridge slang for "slacker.") Jahar, or "Jizz," as his friends also called him, wore grungy Pumas, had a great three-point shot, and became a dedicated pot smoker—something a number of Cambridge teens tell me is relatively standard in their permissive community, where you can score weed in the high school bathrooms and smoke on the street without much of a problem. A diligent student, he was nominated to the National Honor Society in his sophomore year, which was also when he joined the wrestling team. "He was one of those kids who's just a natural," says Payack, his coach, who recalls Jahar as a supportive teammate who endured grueling workouts and runs without a single complaint. In his junior year, the team made him a captain. By then, everyone knew him as "Jahar," which his teammates would scream at matches to ensure the refs would never mispronounce his name.

"I could never quite get his name—Dokar? Jokar?" says Larry Aaronson, a retired Rindge history teacher (Jahar, he says, eventually told him to call him "Joe"). Aaronson, a longtime friend of the late historian Howard Zinn, also lives on Norfolk Street, down the block from the Tsarnaevs' home. "I asked him once where he was from, and he said Chechnya. And I'm like, 'Chechnya? Are you shitting me?'" says Aaronson. "I said, 'My God, how did you cope with all that stress?' And he said, 'Larry, that's how come we came to America, and how lucky that we came to Cambridge, of all places!' He just embraced the city, the school and the whole culture—he gratefully took advantage of it. And that's what endeared me to him: This was the quintessential kid from the war zone, who made total use of everything we offer so that he could remake his life. And he was gorgeous," he adds.

•   •   •

Jahar's friends were a diverse group of kids from both the wealthier and poorer sections of Cambridge; black, white, Jewish, Catholic, Puerto Rican, Bangladeshi, Cape Verdean. They were, as one Cambridge parent told me, "the good kids"—debate champs, varsity athletes, student-government types, a few brainiacs who'd go off to elite New England colleges. A diligent student, Jahar talked about attending Brandeis or Tufts, recalls a friend I'll call Sam, one of a tight-knit group of friends, who, using pseudonyms, agreed to speak exclusively to *Rolling Stone*. "He was one of the realest dudes I've ever met in my life," says Sam, who spent nearly every day with Jahar during their teens, shooting hoops or partying at a spot on the Charles River known as the "Riv." No matter what, "he was the first person I'd call if I needed a ride or a favor. He'd just go, 'I got you, dog'—even if you called him totally wasted at, like, two or three in the morning."

"He was just superchill," says another friend, Will, who recalls one New Year's Eve when Jahar packed eight or nine people—including one in the trunk—into his green Honda Civic. Of course, he adds, the police pulled them over, but Jahar was unfazed. "Even if somebody caught him drinking," says his buddy Jackson, "he was the calm, collected kid who always knew how to talk to police."

He had morals, they all agree. "He never picked on anybody," says Sam, adding that much like his brother, Jahar was a great boxer. "He was better at boxing than wrestling—he was a beast." But while he could probably knock out anyone he wanted, he never did. "He wasn't violent, though—that's the crazy thing. He was never violent," says Sam.

"He was smooth as fuck," says his friend Alyssa, who is a year younger than Jahar. Girls went a little crazy over him—though to Jahar's credit, his friends say, even when he had crushes, he never exploited them. "He'd always be like, 'Chill, chill, let's just hang out,'" says Sam, recalling Jahar's almost physical aversion to any kind of attention. "He was just really humble—that's the best way to describe him."

Cara, a vivacious, pretty blonde whom some believe Jahar had a secret crush on, insists they were just friends. "He was so sweet. He was too sweet, you know?" she says sadly. The two had driver's ed together, which led to lots of time getting high and hanging out. Jahar, she says, had a talent for moving between social groups and always seemed able to empathize with just about anyone's problems. "He is a golden person, really just a genuine good guy who was cool with everyone," she says. "It's hard to really explain Jahar. He was a Cambridge kid."

Cambridge kids, the group agrees, have a fairly nonchalant attitude about things that might make other people a little uptight. A few years ago, for instance, one of their mutual friends decided to convert to Islam, which some, like Cara, thought was really cool, and others, like Jackson, met with a shrug. "But that's the kind of high school we went to," Jackson says. "It's the type of thing where someone could say, 'I converted to Islam,' and you're like, 'OK, cool.'" And in fact, a number of kids they knew did convert, he adds. "It was kind of like a thing for a while."

Jahar never denied he was a Muslim, though he sometimes played it down. He fasted during Ramadan, which included giving up pot—an immense act of self-control, his friends say. "But the most religious thing he ever said was, 'Don't take God's name in vain,'" says Alyssa, who is Jewish. "Yeah," says Jackson, "he might have been religious, but it was the type of thing where unless he told you, you wouldn't know."

A few years ago, one Rindge wrestler, another Muslim, attended an informal lunchtime high school prayer group, where he spotted Jahar. "I didn't know he was Muslim until I saw him at that Friday prayer group," he says. "It wasn't something we ever talked about."

His friend Theo, who also wrestled with Jahar, thinks somewhat differently. "I actually think he had a real reverence for Islam," he says. There was one occasion in particular, a few years ago, when Jahar became visibly uncomfortable when James, the friend who'd converted, began speaking casually about the faith. "He didn't get mad, but he kind of shut him down," Theo recalls. "And it showed me that he took his religion really seriously. It wasn't conditional with him."

Yet he "never raised any red flags," says one of his history teachers, who, like many, requested anonymity, given the sensitivity of the case. Her class, a perennial favorite among Rindge students, fosters heated debates about contemporary political issues like globalization and the crises in the Middle East, but Jahar, she says, never gave her any sense of his personal politics, "even when he was asked to weigh in." Alyssa, who loved the class, agrees: "One of the questions we looked at was 'What is terrorism? How do we define it culturally as Americans? What is the motivation for it—can we ever justify it?' And I can say that Jahar never expressed to us that he was pro-terrorism at all, ever."

Except for once.

"He kind of did, one time to me, express that he thought acts of terrorism were justified," says Will. It was around their junior year; the boys had been eating at a neighborhood joint called Izzy's and talking about religion. With certain friends—Will and Sam among them—Jahar opened up about Islam, confiding his hatred of people whose "ignorance" equated Islam with terrorism, defending it as a religion of peace, and describing jihad as a personal struggle, nothing more. This time, says Will, "I remember telling him I thought certain aspects of religion were harmful, and I brought up the 9/11 attacks."

At which point Jahar, Will says, told him he didn't want to talk about it anymore. Will asked why. "He said, 'Well, you're not going to like my view.' So I pressed him on it, and he said he felt some of those acts were justified because of what the U.S. does in other countries, and that they do it so frequently, dropping bombs all the time."

To be fair, Will and others note, Jahar's perspective on U.S. foreign policy wasn't all that dissimilar from a lot of other people they knew. "In terms of politics, I'd say he's just as anti-American as the next guy in Cambridge," says Theo. Even so, Will decided not to push it. "I was like, 'Wow, this dude actually *supports* that? I can't have this conversation anymore.'"

They never brought it up again.

⋅   ⋅   ⋅

In retrospect, Jahar's comment about 9/11 could be seen in the context of what criminal profilers call "leakage": a tiny crack in an otherwise carefully crafted facade that, if recognized—it's often not—provides a key into the person's interior world. "On cases where I've interviewed these types of people, the key is looking past their exterior and getting access to that interior, which is very hard," says Tom Neer, a retired agent from the FBI's Behavioral Analysis Unit and now a senior associate with the Soufan Group, which advises the government on counterterrorism. "Most people have a public persona as well as a private persona, but for many people, there's a secret side, too. And the secret side is something that they labor really hard to protect."

There were many things about Jahar that his friends and teachers didn't know—something not altogether unusual for immigrant children, who can live highly bifurcated lives, toggling back and forth between their ethnic and American selves. "I never saw the parents, and didn't even know he had a brother," says Payack, who wondered why Jahar never had his family rooting for him on the sidelines, as his teammates did. "If you're a big brother and you love your little brother, why don't you come and watch him in sports?"

Theo wondered, too. "I asked him about that once, and he told me that he'd boxed when he was younger, and he'd never lost a boxing match, so he didn't want his dad to see him lose." It sounded plausible: Jahar had an innate ability as a wrestler, but he never put in the time to be truly great. "It wasn't really on his list," says Theo. On the other hand, losing didn't seem to bother him, either. "Other kids, when they lose they get angry—they think the ref made a bad call, and maybe they'll throw a chair. Or they'll cry, or sulk in a corner," says Payack. Jahar would simply walk off the mat with a shrug. "He'd just kind of have this face like, 'Oh, well, I tried.'"

On Senior Night, the last home match of the season, every Rindge senior wrestler is asked to bring a parent or relative to walk them onto the gym floor to receive a flower and have their picture taken. Jahar brought no one. "We had one of the coaches walk him out to get his flower," says Payack. This, too, didn't seem to bother Jahar—and even if it did, he never mentioned it. "With our friends, you don't need to confide in them to be close to them," says Jackson.

Jahar's family seemed to exist in a wholly separate sphere from the rest of his life. Jackson, who lived nearby, would occasionally see Anzor working on cars; several others knew of Jahar's sisters from their older siblings. And there were always stories about Tamerlan, who'd been a two-time Golden Gloves champion. But almost nobody met Tamerlan in person, and virtually no one from school ever went to the Tsarnaevs' house. "I mean never— not once," says Jackson. One friend of Jahar's older sister Bella would say that the apartment at 410 Norfolk "had a vibe that out- siders weren't too common."

·   ·   ·

There are a number of indications that the troubles in the Tsar- naev family went deeper than normal adjustment to American life. Anzor, who suffered from chronic arthritis, headaches, and stomach pain, had an erratic temperament—a residual, he'd say, of the abuse he'd suffered in Kyrgyzstan—and struck one neigh- bor on Norfolk Street as a "miserable guy," who'd bark at his neighbors over parking spaces and even grab the snow shovels out of their hands when he felt they weren't shoveling the walk properly. Despite his demeanor, he was an intensely hard worker. "I remember his hands," says Baudy. "He'd be working on cars in the Boston cold, no gloves, and he'd have these thick bumps on his knuckles from the arthritis. But he loved it. He saw his role as putting food on the table."

Zubeidat, an enterprising woman, worked as a home-health aide then switched to cosmetology, giving facials at a local salon and later opening a business in her home. "She never wanted to commit," says Baudy, who liked Jahar's mother but saw her as a typical striver. "She was trying to get rich faster—like, 'Oh, this is taking too long. We'll try something else.'"

But the money never came. By 2009, Anzor's health was deteriorating, and that August, the Tsarnaevs, who hadn't been on public assistance for the past five years, began receiving benefits again, in the form of food stamps and cash payouts. This inability to fully support his family may have contributed to what some who knew them refer to as Anzor's essential "weakness" as a father, deferring to Zubeidat, who could be highly controlling.

A doting mother, "she'd never take any advice about her kids," says Anna. "She thought they were the smartest, the most beautiful children in the world"—Tamerlan most of all. "He was the biggest deal in the family. In a way, he was like the father. Whatever he said, they had to do."

Tamerlan's experience in Cambridge was far less happy than Jahar's. Already a teenager when he arrived in America, Tamerlan spoke with a thick Russian accent, and though he enrolled in the English as a Second Language program at Rindge, he never quite assimilated. He had a unibrow, and found it hard to talk to girls. One former classmate recalls that prior to their senior prom, a few of Tamerlan's friends tried to find him a date. "He wasn't even around," she says, "it was just his friends asking girls to go with him." But everyone said no, and he attended the prom alone.

After graduating in 2006, he enrolled at Bunker Hill Community College to study accounting but attended for just three semesters before dropping out. A talented pianist and composer, he harbored a desire to become a musician, but his ultimate dream was to become an Olympic boxer, after which he'd turn pro. This was also his father's dream—a champion boxer himself back in Russia, Anzor reportedly pushed Tamerlan extremely hard, riding behind him on his bicycle while his son jogged to the local boxing gym. And Tamerlan did very well under his father's tutelage, rising in the ranks of New England fighters. One of the best in his weight class, Tamerlan once told a fighter to "practice punching a tree at home" if he wanted to be truly great. But his arrogance undermined his ambitions. In 2010, a rival trainer, claiming Tamerlan had broken boxing etiquette by taunting his fighter before a match, lodged a complaint with the national boxing authority that Tamerlan should be disqualified from nationwide competition as he was not an American citizen. The authorities, coincidentally, were just in the process of changing their policy to ban all non-U.S. citizens from competing for a national title.

This dashed any Olympic hopes, as Tamerlan was not yet eligible to become a U.S. citizen. His uncle Ruslan had urged him to join the army. It would give him structure, he said, and help him perfect his English. "I told him the best way to start your way in a new country—give something," Ruslan says. But Tamerlan laughed, his uncle recalls, for suggesting he kill "our brother Muslims."

Tamerlan had discovered religion, a passion that had begun in 2009. In interviews, Zubeidat has suggested it was her idea, a way to encourage Tamerlan, who spent his off-hours partying with his friends at local clubs, to become more serious. "I told Tamerlan that we are Muslim, and we are not practicing our religion, and how can we call ourselves Muslims?" she said. But Anna suspects there was something else factoring into the situation. Once,

Anna recalls, Zubeidat hinted that something might be wrong. "Tamerlan told me he feels like there's two people living in him," she confided in her friend. "It's weird, right?"

Anna, who wondered if Tamerlan might be developing a mental illness, suggested Zubeidat take him to a "doctor" ("If I said 'psychiatrist,' she'd just flip," she says), but Zubeidat seems to have believed that Islam would help calm Tamerlan's demons. Mother and son began reading the Koran—encouraged, Zubeidat said, by a friend of Tamerlan's named Mikhail Allakhverdov, or "Misha," a thirty-something Armenian convert to Islam whom family members believe Tamerlan met at a Boston-area mosque. Allakhverdov has denied any association with the attack. "I wasn't his teacher," he told the *New York Review of Books*. "If I had been his teacher, I would have made sure he never did anything like this." But family members have said Allakhverdov had a big influence on Tamerlan, coming to the house and often staying late into the night, talking with Tamerlan about Islam and the Koran. Uncle Ruslan would later tell the *Daily Mail* that Allakhverdov would "give one-on-one sermons to Tamerlan over the kitchen table, during which he claimed he could talk to demons and perform exorcisms."

Zubeidat was pleased. "Don't interrupt them," she told her husband one evening when Anzor questioned why Allakhverdov was still there around midnight. "Misha is teaching him to be good and nice."

.　　　.　　　.

Before long, Tamerlan had quit drinking and smoking pot and started to pray five times a day, even taking his prayer rug to the boxing gym. At home, he spent long hours on the Internet reading Islamic websites, as well as U.S. conspiracy sites, like Alex Jones's InfoWars. He told a photographer he met that he didn't understand Americans and complained about a lack of values.

He stopped listening to music. "It is not supported by Islam," Tamerlan said. "Misha says it's not really good to create or listen to music." Then, in 2011, he decided to quit boxing, claiming it was not permitted for a Muslim to hit another man.

Zubeidat, too, had become increasingly religious—something that would get in the way of her marriage as well as her job at an upscale Belmont salon, where she broke for daily prayers and refused to work on male clients. She was ultimately fired, after which she turned her living room into a minisalon. One of her former clients recalls her wearing "a head wrap" in the house and a hijab whenever she went outside. "She started to refuse to see boys who'd gone through puberty," recalls the client. "A religious figure had told her it was sacrilegious."

What really struck her client, beyond Zubeidat's zeal, were her politics. During one facial session, she says, Zubeidat told her she believed 9/11 was a government plot to make Americans hate Muslims. "It's real," she said. "My son knows all about it. You can read on the Internet."

It was during this period that Jahar told his friend Will that he felt terrorism could be justified, a sentiment that Tamerlan apparently shared. Whether or not Jahar truly agreed with his brother, their relationship was one where he couldn't really question him. In Chechen families, Baudy says, "Your big brother is not quite God, but more than a normal brother." When they were kids, Baudy recalls, Tamerlan used to turn off the TV and make them do pushups. Now he urged them to study the Koran.

"Jahar found it kind of a nuisance," says Baudy, and tried to shrug it off as best as he could. But he couldn't do much. "You're not going to get mad at your elders or tell them to stop doing something, especially if it's about being more religious." During one visit a few years ago, Baudy recalls, Tamerlan interrupted them on the computer to say that if they were going to be surfing the Internet, they should focus on their faith. He gave them a book—*Islam 101*—and instructed them to read. He gave the same book to James, the high school convert who, as a new Muslim, was one of the very few of Jahar's friends who came to the house. Tamerlan also taught James how to pray. "I guess they'd sit there for hours," says Sam, who would hear about it afterward. Sam couldn't figure it out. "It was crazy because back a few years ago, Timmy was so like us, a regular dude, boxing, going to school, hanging out, partying all the time. But then he changed and became anti-fun."

By 2011, all remnants of "Timmy" seemed to be gone. When his close friend and sparring partner Brendan Mess began dating a nonpracticing Muslim, Tamerlan criticized Mess's girlfriend for her lack of modesty. And he also reportedly criticized Mess for his "lifestyle"—he was a local pot dealer. On September 11, 2011—the tenth anniversary of 9/11—Mess and two of his friends were killed in a grisly triple murder that remains unsolved. Since the bombing, authorities have been vigorously investigating the crime, convinced that Tamerlan had something to do with it, though so far there's no hard evidence.

"All I know is Jahar was really wary of coming home high because of how his brother would react. He'd get really angry," says Will. "He was a really intense dude."

"And if you weren't Muslim, he was even more intense," says Sam, who notes that he never met Tamerlan in person, though he heard stories about him all the time from Jahar. "I was fascinated—this dude's, like, six-three, he's a boxer—I wanted to meet him," says Sam. "But Jahar was like, 'No, you *don't* want to meet him.'"

Jahar rarely spoke to his friends about his sisters, Ailina and Bella, who, just a few years older than he, kept to themselves but also had their own struggles. Attractive, dark-haired girls who were "very Americanized," as friends recall, they worshipped Tamerlan, whom one sister would later refer to as her "hero"—but they were also subject to his role as family policeman. When Bella was a junior in high school, her father, hearing that she'd been seen in the company of an American boy, pulled her out of school and dispatched Tamerlan to beat the boy up. Friends later spotted Bella wearing a hijab; not long afterward, she disappeared from Cambridge entirely. Some time later, Ailina would similarly vanish. Both girls were reportedly set up in arranged marriages.

Anna Nikeava was unaware the girls had even left Boston and suspects the parents never talked about it for fear of being judged. "Underneath it all, they were a screwed-up family," she says. "They weren't Chechen"—they had not come from Chechnya, as she and others had—"and I don't think the other families accepted them as Chechens. They could not define themselves or where they belonged. And poor Jahar was the silent survivor of all that dysfunction," she says. "He never said a word. But inside, he was very hurt, his world was crushed by what was going on with his family. He just learned not to show it."

Anzor, who'd been at first baffled and later "depressed" by his wife's and son's religiosity, moved back to Russia in 2011 and that summer was granted a divorce. Zubeidat was later arrested for attempting to shoplift $1,600 worth of clothes from a Lord & Taylor. Rather than face prosecution, she skipped bail and also returned to Russia, where she ultimately reconciled with her ex-husband. Jahar's sisters, both of whom seemed to have escaped their early marriages, were living in New Jersey and hadn't seen their family in some time.

And Tamerlan was now married, too. His new wife, Katherine Russell, was a Protestant from a well-off family in Rhode Island. After high school, she'd toyed with joining the Peace Corps but instead settled on college at Boston's Suffolk University. She'd met Tamerlan at a club during her freshman year, in 2007, and found him "tall and handsome and having some measure of worldliness," one friend would recall. But as their relationship progressed, Katherine's college roommates began to worry that Tamerlan was "controlling" and "manipulative." They became increasingly concerned when he demanded that she cover herself and convert to Islam.

Though Katherine has never spoken to the press, what is known is that she did convert to Islam, adopting the name "Karima," and soon got pregnant and dropped out of college. In June 2010, she and Tamerlan were married; not long afterward, she gave birth to their daughter, Zahira. Around this time, both her friends and family say, she "pulled away." She was seen in Boston, shopping at Whole Foods, cloaked and wearing a hijab. She rarely spoke around her husband, and when alone, recalls one neighbor, she spoke slowly with an accent. "I didn't even know she was an American," he says.

Jahar, meanwhile, was preparing for college. He had won a $2,500 city scholarship, which is awarded each year to about forty to fifty Cambridge students; he ended up being accepted at a number of schools, including Northeastern University and UMass Amherst. But UMass Dartmouth offered him a scholarship. "He didn't want to force his parents to pay a lot of money for school," says Sam, who recalls that Jahar never even bothered to apply to his fantasy schools, Brandeis and Tufts, due to their price tags. A number of his friends would go off to some of the country's better private colleges, "but Jizz rolled with the punches. He put into his head, 'I can't go to school for mad dough, so I'm just going to go wherever gives me the best deal.' Because, I mean, what's the point of going to a school that's going to cost $30,000 a year—for what? Pointless." His other friends agree.

A middling school an hour and a half south of Boston, UMass Dartmouth had one distinguishing feature—its utter lack of character. "It's beige," says Jackson. "It's, like, the most depressing campus I've ever seen." Annual costs are about $22,000.

Jahar arrived in the fall of 2011 and almost immediately wanted to go home. North Dartmouth, where the university is based, is a working-class community with virtually nothing to boast of except for a rather sad mall and a striking number of fast-food joints. It has a diverse student population, but their level of curiosity seemed to fall far below his friends' from Rindge. "Using my high-school essays for my english class #itsthateasy," Jahar tweeted in November 2011. "You know what i like to do? answer my own questions cuz no one else can."

"He was hating life," says Sam. "He used to always call and say it's mad wack and the people were corny." His one saving grace was that one of his best friends from Rindge had gone to UMass Dartmouth, too—though he would later transfer. "All they would do was sit in the car and get high—it was that boring," says Sam.

On the weekends, campus would empty out, and Jahar came home as often as he could. But home was no longer "home," as his parents were gone. Many of his closest friends were gone as well. Tamerlan, though, was always around. "Pray," the older brother told the younger. "You cannot call yourself a Muslim unless you thank Allah five times a day."

. . .

Much of what is known about the two years of Jahar's life leading up to the bombing comes from random press interviews with students at UMass Dartmouth, none of whom seemed to have been particularly close with Jahar, and from Jahar's tweets, which, like many eighteen- or nineteen-year-olds', were a mishmash of sophomoric jokes, complaints about his roommate, his perpetual lateness, some rap lyrics, the occasional deep thought ("Find your place and your purpose and make a plan for the future"), and, increasingly, some genuinely revealing statements. He was homesick. He suffered from insomnia. He had repeated zombie dreams. And he missed his dad. "I can see my face in my dad's pictures as a youngin, he even had a ridiculous amount of hair like me," he tweeted in June 2012.

Jahar had begun his studies to be an engineer but by last fall had found the courses too difficult. He switched to biology and, to make money, he dealt pot—one friend from his dorm says he always had big Tupperware containers of weed in his fridge.

As he had at Rindge, Jahar drifted between social groups, though he clung to friends from high school who also attended UMass Dartmouth. But he soon gravitated to a group of Kazakh students, wealthy boys with a taste for excellent pot, which Jahar, who spoke Russian with them, often helped to provide. By his sophomore year, even as he gained U.S. citizenship, he abandoned his American Facebook for the Russian version, Vkontakte, or VK, where he listed his world view as "Islam" and his interests as "career and money." He joined several Chechnya-related groups and posted Russian-language-joke videos. "He was always joking around, and often his jokes had a sarcastic character," says Diana Valeeva, a Russian student who befriended Jahar on VK. Jahar also told Diana that he missed his homeland and would happily come for a visit. "But he did not want to return forever," she says.

Tamerlan's journey the past two years is far easier to trace. Though no more Chechen than his brother, Tamerlan was also— as his resident green card reminded him—not really an American. Islam, or Tamerlan's interpretation of it, had become his identity. He devoured books on Chechnya's separatist struggle, a war that had taken on a notably fundamentalist tone since the late 1990s, thanks to a surge of Muslim fighters from outside of the Caucusus who flocked to Chechnya to wage "holy war" against the Russians. It is not uncommon for young Chechen men to romanticize jihad, and for those who are interested in that kind of thing, there are abundant Chechen jihadist videos online that reinforce this view. They tend to feature Caucasian fighters who, far from the lecturing sheikhs often found in al-Qaeda recruitment videos, look like grizzled navy SEALs, humping through the woods in camouflage and bandannas. Tamerlan would later post several of these videos on his YouTube page, as well as "The Emergence of Prophecy: The Black Flags from Khorasan," a central part of al-Qaeda and other jihadist mythology, which depicts fierce, supposedly end-times battles against the infidels across a region that includes parts of Afghanistan, Pakistan, and Iran.

But Brian Glyn Williams, a professor of Islamic studies at UMass Dartmouth and an expert on terrorism and the politics of Chechnya, believes that Tamerlan's journey—which he calls "jihadification"—was less a young man's quest to join al-Qaeda than to discover his own identity. "To me, this is classic diasporic reconstruction of identity: 'I'm a Chechen, and we're fighting for jihad, and what am I doing? Nothing.' It's not unlike the way some Irish Americans used to link Ireland and the IRA—they'd never been to Northern Ireland in their lives, but you'd go to certain parts of Southie in Boston, and all you see are donation cans for the IRA."

For Jahar, identity likely played into the mix as well, says Williams, who, though he never met Jahar at UMass Dartmouth, coincidentally corresponded with him during his senior year of high school. One of Williams's friends taught English at Rindge, and "he told me he had this Chechen kid in his class who wanted to do his research paper on Chechnya, a country he'd never lived in." Williams agreed to help Jahar. "The thing that struck me was how little he actually knew," he says. "He didn't know anything about Chechnya, and he wanted to know *everything*."

Whether Jahar gained much from his studies—or even did much of it—is unknown. Tamerlan, having devoured all the books he could find, was preparing to take the next step. In January 2012, he traveled to Dagestan, where he spent six months. Dagestan has been embroiled in a years-long civil war between Muslim guerrillas and the (also Muslim) police, as well as Russian forces. Bombs go off in the streets regularly, and young men, lured by the romance of the fight, often disappear to "go to the forest," a euphemism for joining the insurgency. Tamerlan, too, seemed to have wanted to join the rebellion, but he was dissuaded from this pursuit by, among others, a distant cousin named Magomed

Kartashov, who also happened to be a Dagestani Islamist. Kartashov's Western cousin, who came to Dagestan dressed in fancy American clothes and bragging of being a champion boxer, had no place in their country's civil war, he told Tamerlan. It was an internal struggle—in an interview with *Time* magazine, associates of Kartashov's referred to it as "banditry"—and had only resulted in Muslims killing other Muslims. Kartashov urged Tamerlan to embrace nonviolence and forget about Dagestan's troubles. By early summer, Tamerlan was talking about holy war "in a global context," one Dagestani Islamist recalls.

In July 2012, Tamerlan returned to Cambridge. He grew a five-inch beard and began to get in vocal debates about the virtues of Islam. He vociferously criticized U.S. policy in the Middle East. Twice over the next six or eight months, he upset services at a local mosque with a denunciation of Thanksgiving and also, in January 2013, of Martin Luther King Jr.

The boys' uncle Ruslan hoped that Jahar, away at school, would avoid Tamerlan's influence. Instead, Jahar began to echo his older brother's religious fervor. The Prophet Muhammad, he noted on Twitter, was now his role model. "For me to know that I am FREE from HYPOCRISY is more dear to me than the weight of the ENTIRE world in GOLD," he posted, quoting an early Islamic scholar. He began following Islamic Twitter accounts. "Never underestimate the rebel with a cause," he declared.

Though it seems as if Jahar had found a mission, his embrace of Islam also may have been driven by something more basic: a need to belong. "Look, he was totally abandoned," says Payack, who believes that the divorce of his parents and their subsequent move back to Russia was pivotal, as was the loss of the safety net he had at Rindge.

Theo, who goes to college in Vermont and is one of the few of Jahar's friends to not have any college loans, can't imagine the stress Jahar must have felt. "He had all of this stuff piled up on his shoulders, as well as college, which he's having to pay for himself. That's not easy. All of that just might make you say 'Fuck it' and give up and lose faith.

Wick Sloane, an education advocate and a local community-college professor, sees this as a widespread condition among many young immigrants who pass through his classrooms. "All of these kids are grateful to be in the United States. But it's the usual thing: Is this the land of opportunity or isn't it? When I look at what they've been through, and how they are screwed by federal policies from the moment they turn around, I don't understand why *all* of them aren't angrier. I'm actually kind of surprised it's taken so long for one of these kids to set off a bomb."

•   •   •

"A decade in America already," Jahar tweeted in March 2012. "I want out." He was looking forward to visiting his parents in Dagestan that summer, but then he learned he wouldn't receive his U.S. passport in time to make the trip. "#Imsad," he told his followers. Instead, he spent the summer lifeguarding at a Harvard pool. "I didn't become a lifeguard to just chill and get paid," Jahar tweeted. "I do it for the people, saving lives brings me joy." He was living with Tamerlan and his sister-in-law, who were going through their own troubles. Money was increasingly tight, and the family was on welfare. Tamerlan was now a stay-at-home dad; his wife worked night and day as a home-health aide to support the family.

Tamerlan had joined an increasing number of Cambridge's young adults who were being priced out due to skyrocketing real-estate prices. "It's really hard to stay in Cambridge because it's becoming so exclusive," says Tamerlan's former Rindge classmate Luis Vasquez, who is running for a seat on the Cambridge City Council. "We feel like we're being taken over."

In August, Jahar, acutely aware of the troubles all around him, commented that $15 billion was spent on the Summer Olympics. "Imagine if that money was used to feed those in need all over the world," he wrote. "The value of human life ain't shit nowadays that's #tragic." In the fall, he returned to North Dartmouth and college, where, with no Tamerlan to catch him, he picked up his life, partying in his dorm and letting his schoolwork slide.

"Idk why it's hard for many of you to accept that 9/11 was an inside job, I mean I guess fuck the facts y'all are some real #patriots #gethip," Jahar tweeted. This is not an uncommon belief. Payack, who also teaches writing at the Berklee College of Music, says that a fair amount of his students, notably those born in other countries, believe 9/11 was an "inside job." Aaronson tells me he's shocked by the number of kids he knows who believe the Jews were behind 9/11. "The problem with this demographic is that they do not know the basic narratives of their histories—or really any narratives," he says. "They're blazed on pot and searching the Internet for any 'factoids' that they believe fit their highly dehistoricized and decontextualized ideologies. And the adult world totally misunderstands them and dismisses them—and does so at our collective peril," he adds.

Last December, Jahar came home for Christmas break and stayed for several weeks. His friends noticed nothing different about him, except that he was desperately trying to grow a beard—with little success. In early February, he went back to Rindge to work with the wrestling team, where he confided in Theo, who'd also come back to help, that he wished he'd taken wrestling more seriously. He could have been really good had he applied himself a bit more.

At 410 Norfolk St., Tamerlan, once a flashy dresser, had taken to wearing a bathrobe and ratty sweatpants, day after day, while Jahar continued to explore Islam. "I meet the most amazing people," he tweeted. "My religion is the truth."

But he also seemed at times to be struggling, suggesting that even his beloved Cambridge had failed him in some way. "Cambridge got some real, genuinely good people, but at the same time this city can be fake as fuck," he said on January 15. Also that day: "I don't argue with fools who say Islam is terrorism it's not worth a thing, let an idiot remain an idiot."

According to a transcript from UMass Dartmouth, reviewed by the *New York Times*, Jahar was failing many of his classes his sophomore year. He was reportedly more than $20,000 in debt to the university. Also weighing on him was the fact that his family's welfare benefits had been cut in November 2012, and in January, Tamerlan and his wife reportedly lost the Section 8 housing subsidy that had enabled them to afford their apartment, leaving them with the prospect of a move.

Why a person with an extreme or "radical" ideology may decide to commit violence is an inexact science, but experts agree that there must be a cognitive opening of some sort. "A person is angry, and he needs an explanation for that angst," explains the Soufan Group's Tom Neer. "Projecting blame is a defense mechanism. Rather than say, 'I'm lost, I've got a problem,' it's much easier to find a convenient enemy or scapegoat. The justification comes later—say, U.S. imperialism, or whatever. It's the explanation that is key."

For Tamerlan Tsarnaev, the explanation for his anger was all around him. And so, dissuaded from his quest to wage jihad in Dagestan, he apparently turned his gaze upon America, the country that, in his estimation, had caused so much suffering, most of all his own.

In early February, soon after losing his housing subsidy, Tamerlan drove to New Hampshire, where, according to the indictment, he purchased "48 mortars containing approximately eight pounds of low-explosive powder." Also during this general period, Jahar began downloading Islamic militant tracts to his computer, like the first issue of the al-Qaeda magazine *Inspire*, which, in an article titled "Make a Bomb in the Kitchen of Your Mom," offered detailed instructions on how to construct an IED using a pressure cooker, explosive powder from fireworks, and shrapnel, among other readily available ingredients.

Jahar returned home for spring break in March and spent time hanging out with his regular crew. He brought his friend Dias Kadyrbayev home with him, driving Dias's flashy black BMW with the joke license plate TERRORISTA. He hung out with a few friends and went to the Riv, where they lit off fireworks; he met other friends at a local basketball court, one of his usual haunts. He looked happy and chill, as he always did, and was wearing a new, brown military-style jacket that his friends thought was "swag." "And that was the last time I saw him," says Will.

What went on in the apartment at 410 Norfolk during March and early April remains a mystery. "It's hard to understand how there could be such disassociation in that child," says Aaronson, who last saw Jahar in January, presumably before the brothers' plan was set. "They supposedly had an arsenal in that fucking house! In the house! I mean, he could have blown up my whole fucking block, for God's sakes."

According to the indictment, the brothers went to a firing range on March 20, where Jahar rented two 9mm handguns, purchased 200 rounds of ammunition, and engaged in target practice with Tamerlan. On April 5, Tamerlan went online to order electronic components that could be used in making IEDs. Friends of Jahar's would later tell the FBI that he'd once mentioned he knew how to build bombs. But no one seemed to really take it all that seriously.

"People come into your life to help you, hurt you, love you and leave you and that shapes your character and the person you were meant to be," Jahar tweeted on March 18. Two days later: "Evil triumphs when good men do nothing."

April 7: "If you have the knowledge and the inspiration all that's left is to take action."

April 11: "Most of you are conditioned by the media."

The bombs went off four days later.

•   •   •

On the afternoon of April 18, Robel Phillipos, a friend of Jahar's from Cambridge as well as from UMass Dartmouth, was watching the news on campus and talking on the phone with Dias. He told Dias, who was in his car, to turn on the TV when he got home. One of the bombers, he said, looked like Jahar. Like most of their friends, Dias thought it was a coincidence and texted Jahar that he looked like one of the suspects on television. "Lol," Jahar wrote back, casually. He told his friend not to text him anymore. "I'm about to leave," he wrote. "If you need something in my room, take it."

According to the FBI, Robel, Dias, and their friend Azamat met at Pine Dale Hall, Jahar's dorm, where his roommate informed them that he'd left campus several hours earlier. So they hung out in his room for a while, watching a movie. Then they spotted Jahar's backpack, which the boys noticed had some fireworks inside, emptied of powder. Not sure what to do, they grabbed the bag as well as Jahar's computer, and went back to Dias and Azamat's off-campus apartment, where they "started to freak out, because it became clear from a CNN report . . . that Jahar was one of the Boston Marathon bombers," Robel later told the FBI.

But no one wanted Jahar to get in trouble. Dias and Azamat began speaking to each other in Russian. Finally, Dias turned to Robel and asked in English if he should get rid of the stuff. "Do what you have to do," Robel said. Then he took a nap.

Dias later confessed that he'd grabbed a big black trash bag, filled it with trash and stuffed the backpack and fireworks in there. Then he threw it in a dumpster; the bag was later retrieved from the municipal dump by the FBI. The computer, too, was eventually recovered. Until recently, its contents were unknown.

The contents of Jahar's closely guarded psyche, meanwhile, may never be fully understood. Nor, most likely, will his motivations—which is quite common with accused terrorists. "There is no single precipitating event or stressor," says Neer. "Instead, what you see with most of these people is a gradual process of feeling alienated or listless or not connected. But what they all have in common is a whole constellation of things that aren't working right."

A month or so after the bombing, I am sitting on Alyssa's back deck with a group of Jahar's friends. It's a lazy Sunday in May, and the media onslaught has died down a bit; the FBI, though, is still searching for the source of the brothers' "radicalization," and al-Qaeda in the Arabian Peninsula, capitalizing on the situation, has put Tamerlan, dressed in his crisp, white *Saturday Night Fever* shirt and aviator shades, in the pages of its most recent *Inspire*. Jahar has a growing and surprisingly brazen fan club— #FreeJahar—and tens of thousands of new Twitter followers, despite the fact that he hasn't tweeted since before his arrest.

Like so many of his fans, some of Jahar's friends have latched onto conspiracy theories about the bombing, if only because "there are too many unanswered questions," says Cara, who points out that the backpack identified by the FBI was not the same color as Jahar's backpack. There's also a photo on the Internet of Jahar walking away from the scene, no pack, though if you look closely, you can see the outline of a black strap. "Photoshopped!" the caption reads.

Mostly, though, his friends are trying to move on. "We're concerned with not having this tied to us for the rest of our lives," says Alyssa, explaining why she and Sam and Jackson and Cara and Will and James and Theo have insisted I give them pseudonyms. Even as Jahar was on the run, his friends started hearing from the FBI, whose agents shortly descended upon their campuses—sometimes wearing bulletproof vests—looking for insight and phone numbers.

"You're so intimidated, and you think if you don't answer their questions, it looks suspicious," says Jackson, who admits he gave up a number of friends' phone numbers after being pressed by the FBI.

Sam says he thinks the feds tapped his phone. All of the kids were interviewed alone, without a lawyer. "I didn't even know I could have a lawyer," says Jackson. "And they didn't tell me that anything I said might be used against me, which was unfair, because, I mean, I'm only nineteen."

But the worst, they all agree, is Robel, who was interviewed four times by the FBI and denied he knew anything until, on the fourth interview, he came clean and told them he'd helped remove the backpack and computer from Jahar's dorm room. Robel is nineteen but looks twelve, and is unanimously viewed by his friends as the most innocent and sheltered of the group. He is now facing an eight-year prison sentence for lying to a federal officer.

"So you see why we don't want our names associated," says Sam. "It's not that we're trying to show that we're not Jahar's friends. He was a *very* good friend of mine."

•   •   •

Jahar is, of course, still alive—though it's tempting for everyone to refer to him in the past tense, as if he, too, were dead. He will likely go to prison for the rest of his life, which may be his best possible fate, given the other option, which is the death penalty. "I can't wrap my head around that," says Cara. "Or any of it."

Nor can anyone else. For all of their city's collective angst and community processing and resolutions of being "one Cambridge," the reality is that none of Jahar's friends had any idea he was unhappy, and they really didn't know he had any issues in his family other than, perhaps, his parents' divorce, which was kind of normal.

"I remember he was upset when his dad left the country," says Jackson. "I remember he was giving me a ride home and he mentioned it."

"Now that I think about that, it must have added a lot of pressure having both parents be gone," says Sam.

"But, I mean, that's the mystery," says Jackson. "I don't really know." It's weird, they all agree.

"His brother must have brainwashed him," says Sam. "It's the only explanation."

Someone mentions one of the surveillance videos of Jahar, which shows him impassively watching as people begin to run in response to the blast. "I mean, that's just the face I'd always see chilling, talking, smoking," says Jackson. He wishes Jahar had looked panicked. "At least then I'd be able to say, 'OK, something happened.' But . . . nothing."

That day's *Boston Globe* has run a story about the nurses at Beth Israel Deaconess Hospital who took care of Jahar those first few days after his capture. They were ambivalent, to say the least, about spending too much time with him, for fear of, well, liking him. One nurse said she had to stop herself from calling him "hon." The friends find this story disgusting. "People just have blood in their eyes," says Jackson.

One anecdote that wasn't in the article but that has been quietly making its way around town, via one of his former nurses, is that Jahar cried for two days straight after he woke up in the hospital. No one in the group has heard this yet, and when I mention it, Alyssa gives an anguished sigh of relief. "That's good to know," she says.

"I can definitely see him doing that," says Sam, gratefully. "I hope he's crying. I'd definitely hope . . ."

"I hope he'd wake up and go, 'What the fuck did I do the last forty-eight hours?'" says Jackson, who decides, along with the others, that this, the crying detail, sounds like Jahar.

But, then again, no one knows what he was crying about.

The New Yorker

WINNER—ESSAYS
AND CRITICISM

Ariel Levy was nineteen-weeks pregnant when she flew to Mongolia "to report a story on the country's impending transformation as money flooded in." On her second night in Ulaanbaatar, she miscarried. "And then there was another person on the floor in front of me," she would later write, "moving his arms and legs, alive." The National Magazine Award judges used phrases like "stark honesty," "precise timing," and "perfect pitch" to describe this story. Readers will certainly agree. Or they may simply remember the sentence "My baby was as pretty as a seashell." Levy is a New Yorker *staff writer and the author of* Female Chauvinist Pigs: Women and the Rise of Raunch Culture. *Her essay "The Lesbian's Brides' Handbook" was published in* The Best American Essays 2008.

Ariel Levy

Thanksgiving in Mongolia

My favorite game when I was a child was Mummy and Explorer. My father and I would trade off roles: one of us had to lie very still with eyes closed and arms crossed over the chest, and the other had to complain, "I've been searching these pyramids for so many years. When will I ever find the tomb of Tutankhamen?" (This was in the late seventies, when Tut was at the Met, and we came in from the suburbs to visit him frequently.) At the climax of the game, the explorer stumbles on the embalmed pharaoh and—brace yourself—the mummy opens his eyes and comes to life. The explorer has to express shock, and then says, "So, what's new?" To which the mummy replies, "*You.*"

I was not big on playing house. I preferred make-believe that revolved around adventure, featuring pirates and knights. I was also domineering, impatient, relentlessly verbal, and, as an only child, often baffled by the mores of other kids. I was not a popular little girl. I played Robinson Crusoe in a small wooden fort that my parents built for me in the back yard. In the fort, I was neither ostracized nor ill at ease—I was self-reliant, brave, ingeniously surviving, if lost.

The other natural habitat for a child who loves words and adventure is the page, and I was content when my parents read me *Moby-Dick*, *Pippi Longstocking*, or *The Hobbit*. I decided early that I would be a writer when I grew up. That, I thought, was the profession that went with the kind of woman I wanted to become: one who is free to do whatever she chooses. I started keeping a diary in third grade and, in solidarity with Anne Frank, gave it a name and made it my confidante. To this day, I feel comforted and relieved of loneliness, no matter how foreign my surroundings, if I have a pad and a pen with which to record my experiences.

I've spent the past twenty years putting myself in foreign surroundings as frequently as possible. There is nothing I love more than traveling to a place where I know nobody and where everything will be a surprise, and then writing about it. The first time I went to Africa for a story, I was so excited that I barely slept during the entire two-week trip. Everything was new: the taste of springbok meat, the pink haze over Cape Town, the noise and chaos of the corrugated-tin alleyways in Khayelitsha township. I could still feel spikes of adrenaline when I was back at my desk in New York, typing, while my spouse cooked a chicken in the kitchen.

But as my friends, one after another, made the journey from young woman to mother, it glared at me that I had not. I would often listen to a Lou Reed song called "Beginning of a Great Adventure," about the possibilities of imminent parenthood. "A little me or he or she to fill up with my dreams," Lou sings, with ragged hopefulness, "a way of saying life is not a loss." It became the soundtrack to my mulling on motherhood. I knew that a child would make life as a professional explorer largely impossible. But having a kid seemed in many ways like the wildest trip of all.

I always get terrified right before I travel. I become convinced that this time will be different: I won't be able to figure out the map or communicate with non-English speakers or find the people I need in order to write the story I've been sent in search of. I will be lost and incompetent and vulnerable. I know that my panic will turn to excitement once I'm there—it always does—but that doesn't make the fear before takeoff any less vivid. So it was with childbearing: I was afraid for ten years. I didn't like childhood, and I was afraid that I'd have a child who didn't either. I was afraid I would be an awful mother. And I was afraid of being grounded, sessile—stuck in one spot for eighteen years of oboe lessons and math homework that I couldn't finish the first time around.

I was on book tour in Athens when I decided that I would do it. My partner—who had always indicated that I would need to cast the deciding vote on parenthood—had come with me, and we were having one of those magical moments in a marriage when you find each other completely delightful. My Greek publisher and his wife took us out dancing and drinking and cooked for us one night in their little apartment, which was overrun with children, friends, moussaka, and cigarette smoke. "Americans are not relaxed," one of the other guests told me, holding his three-year-old and drinking an ouzo. Greece was falling apart. The streets of Athens were crawling with cats and dogs that people had abandoned because they could no longer afford pet food. But our hosts were jubilant. Their family didn't seem like a burden; it seemed like a party. The idea bloomed in my head that being governed by something other than my own wishes and wanderlust might be a pleasure, a release.

I got pregnant quickly, to my surprise and delight, shortly before my thirty-eighth birthday. It felt like making it onto a plane the moment before the gate closes—you can't help but thrill. After only two months, I could hear the heartbeat of the creature inside me at the doctor's office. It seemed like magic: a little eye of newt in my cauldron and suddenly I was a witch with the power to brew life into being. Even if you are not Robinson Crusoe in a solitary fort, as a human being you walk this world by yourself. But when you are pregnant you are never alone.

•　　　•　　　•

My doctor told me that it was fine to fly up until the third trimester, so when I was five months pregnant I decided to take one last big trip. It would be at least a year, maybe two, before I'd be able to leave home for weeks on end and feel the elation of a new place revealing itself. (It's like having a new lover—even the parts you aren't crazy about have the crackling fascination of the unfamiliar.) Just before Thanksgiving, I went to Mongolia.

People were alarmed when I told them where I was going, but I was pleased with myself. I liked the idea of being the kind of woman who'd go to the Gobi Desert pregnant, just as, at twenty-two, I'd liked the idea of being the kind of girl who'd go to India by herself. And I liked the idea of telling my kid, "When you were inside me, we went to see the edge of the earth." I wasn't truly scared of anything but the Mongolian winter. The tourist season winds down in October, and by late November, when I got on the plane, the nights drop to twenty degrees below zero. But I was prepared: I'd bought snow pants big enough to fit around my convex gut and long underwear two sizes larger than I usually wear.

To be pregnant is to be in some kind of discomfort pretty much all the time. For the first few months, it was like waking up with a bad hangover every single morning but never getting to drink—I was nauseated but hungry, afflicted with a perpetual headache, and really qualified only to watch television and moan. That passed, but a week before I left for Mongolia I started feeling an ache in my abdomen that was new. "Round-ligament pain" is what I heard from everyone I knew who'd been pregnant and what I read on every prenatal website: the uterus expanding to accommodate the baby, as he finally grew big enough to make me look actually pregnant, instead of just chunky. That thought comforted me on the fourteen-hour flight to Beijing while I shifted endlessly, trying to find a position that didn't hurt my round ligaments.

When my connecting flight landed in Mongolia, it was morning, but the gray haze made it look like dusk. Ulaanbaatar is among the most polluted capital cities in the world, as well as the coldest. The drive into town wound through frozen fields and clusters of felt tents—*gers*, they're called there—into a crowded city of stocky, Soviet-era municipal buildings, crisscrossing telephone and trolley lines, and old Tibetan Buddhist temples with pagoda roofs. The people on the streets moved quickly and clumsily, burdened with layers against the bitter weather.

I was there to report a story on the country's impending transformation as money flooded in through the mining industry. Mongolia has vast supplies of coal, gold, and copper ore; its wealth was expected to double in five years. But a third of the population still lives nomadically, herding animals and sleeping in *gers*, burning coal or garbage for heat. Until the boom, Mongolia's best-known export was cashmere. As Jackson Cox, a young consultant from Tennessee who'd lived in Ulaanbaatar for twelve years, told me, "You're talking about an economy based on yak meat and goat hair."

I got together with Cox on my first night in town. He sent a chauffeured car to pick me up—every Westerner I met in UB had a car and a driver—at the Blue Sky Hotel, a new and sharply pointed glass tower that split the cold sky like a shark fin. When I arrived at his apartment, he and a friend, a mining-industry lawyer from New Jersey, were listening to Beyoncé and pouring champagne. The place was clean and modern but modest: for expats in UB, it's far easier to accumulate wealth than it is to spend it. We went to dinner at a French restaurant, where we all ordered beef because seafood is generally terrible in Mongolia, which is separated from the sea by its hulking neighbors (and former occupiers) China and Russia. Then they took me to an underground gay bar called 100 Per Cent—which could have been in Brooklyn except that everyone in Mongolia still smoked indoors. I liked sitting in a booth in a dark room full of smoking, gay Mongolians, but my body was feeling strange. I ended the night early.

When I woke up the next morning, the pain in my abdomen was insistent; I wondered if the baby was starting to kick, which everyone said would be happening soon. I called home to complain, and my spouse told me to find a Western clinic. I e-mailed Cox to get his doctor's phone number, thinking that I'd call if the pain got any worse, and then I went out to interview people: the minister of the environment, the president of a mining concern, and, finally, a herdsman and conservationist named Tsetsegee Munkhbayar, who became a folk hero after he fired shots at mining operations that were diverting water from nomadic communities. I met him in the sleek lobby of the Blue Sky with Yondon Badral—a smart, sardonic man I'd hired to translate for me in UB and to accompany me a few days later to the Gobi, where we would drive a Land Rover across the cold sands to meet with miners and nomads. Badral wore jeans and a sweater; Munkhbayar was dressed in a long, traditional *deel* robe and a fur hat with a small metal falcon perched on top. It felt like having a latte with Genghis Khan.

In the middle of the interview, Badral stopped talking and looked at my face; I must have been showing my discomfort. He said that it was the same for his wife, who was pregnant, just a few weeks further along than I was, and he explained the situation to Munkhbayar. The nomad's skin was chapped pink from the wind; his nostrils, eyes, and ears all looked as if they had receded into his face to escape the cold. I felt a little surge of pride when he said that I was brave to travel so far in my condition. But I was also starting to worry.

I nearly canceled my second dinner with the Americans that evening, but I figured that I needed to eat and they offered to meet me at the Japanese restaurant in my hotel. Cox was leaving the next day to visit his family for Thanksgiving, and he was feeling guilty that he'd spent a fortune on a business-class ticket. I thought about my uncomfortable flight over and said that it was probably worth it. "You're being a princess," Cox's friend told him tartly, but I couldn't laugh. Something was happening inside me. I had to leave before the food came.

I ran back to my room, pulled off my pants, and squatted on the floor of the bathroom, just as I had in Cambodia when I had dysentery, a decade earlier. But the pain in that position was unbearable. I got on my knees and put my shoulders on the floor and pressed my cheek against the cool tile. I remember thinking, *This is going to be the craziest shit in history.*

I felt an unholy storm move through my body, and after that there is a brief lapse in my recollection; either I blacked out from the pain or I have blotted out the memory. And then there was another person on the floor in front of me, moving his arms and legs, alive. I heard myself say out loud, "This can't be good." But it *looked* good. My baby was as pretty as a seashell.

He was translucent and pink and very, very small, but he was flawless. His lovely lips were opening and closing, opening and closing, swallowing the new world. For a length of time I cannot delineate, I sat there, awestruck, transfixed. Every finger, every toenail, the golden shadow of his eyebrows coming in, the elegance of his shoulders—all of it was miraculous, astonishing. I held him up to my face, his head and shoulders filling my hand, his legs dangling almost to my elbow. I tried to think of something maternal I could do to convey to him that I was, in fact, his mother, and that I had the situation completely under control. I kissed his forehead and his skin felt like a silky frog's on my mouth.

I was vaguely aware that there was an enormous volume of blood rushing out of me, and eventually that seemed interesting, too. I looked back and forth between my offspring and the lake of blood consuming the bathroom floor and I wondered what to do about the umbilical cord connecting those two things. It was surprisingly thick and ghostly white, a twisted human rope. I felt sure that it needed to be severed—that's always the first thing that happens in the movies. I was afraid that if I didn't cut that cord my baby would somehow suffocate. I didn't have scissors. I yanked it out of myself with one swift, violent tug.

In my hand, his skin started to turn a soft shade of purple. I bled my way across the room to my phone and dialed the number for Cox's doctor. I told the voice that answered that I had given birth in the Blue Sky Hotel and that I had been pregnant for nineteen weeks. The voice said that the baby would not live. "He's alive now," I said, looking at the person in my left hand. The voice said that he understood, but that it wouldn't last, and that he would send an ambulance for us right away. I told him that if there was no chance the baby would make it I might as well take a cab. He said that that was not a good idea.

Before I put down my phone, I took a picture of my son. I worried that if I didn't I would never believe he had existed.

·   ·   ·

When the pair of Mongolian EMTs came through the door, I stopped feeling competent and numb. One offered me a tampon, which I knew not to accept, but the realization that of the two of us I had more information stirred a sickening panic in me and I said I needed to throw up. She asked if I was drunk, and I said, offended, No, I'm *upset*. "Cry," she said. "You just cry, cry, cry." Her partner bent to insert a thick needle in my forearm and I wondered if it would give me Mongolian AIDS, but I felt unable to do anything but cry, cry, cry. She tried to take the baby from me, and I had the urge to bite her hand. As I lay on a gurney in the back of the ambulance with his body wrapped in a towel on top of my chest, I watched the frozen city flash by the windows. It occurred to me that perhaps I was going to go mad.

In the clinic, there were very bright lights and more needles and IVs and I let go of the baby and that was the last I ever saw him. He was on one table and I was on another, far away, lying still under the screaming lights, and then, confusingly, the handsomest man in the world came through the door and said he was my doctor. His voice sounded nice, familiar. I asked if he was South African. He was surprised that I could tell, and I explained that I had spent time reporting in his country, and then we talked a bit about the future of the ANC and about how beautiful it is in Cape Town. I realized that I was covered in blood, sobbing, and flirting.

Soon, he said that he was going home and that I could not return to the Blue Sky Hotel, where I might bleed to death in my room without anyone knowing. I stayed in the clinic overnight, wearing a T-shirt and an adult diaper that a kind, fat, giggling young nurse gave me. After she dressed me, she asked, "You want toast and tea?" It was milky and sweet and reminded me of the chai I drank in Nepal, where I went backpacking in the Himalayas with a friend long before I was old enough to worry about the expiration of my fertility. It had been a trip spent pushing my young body up the mountains, past green-and-yellow terraced fields and villages full of goats, across rope bridges that hung tenuously over black ravines with death at the bottom. We consumed a steady diet of hashish and Snickers bars and ended up in a blizzard that killed several hikers but somehow left us only chilly.

I had been so lucky. Very little had ever truly gone wrong for me before that night on the bathroom floor. And I knew, as surely as I now knew that I wanted a child, that this change in fortune was my fault. I had boarded a plane out of vanity and selfishness, and the dark Mongolian sky had punished me. I was still a witch, but my powers were all gone.

That is not what the doctor said when he came back to the clinic in the morning. He told me that I'd had a placental abruption, a very rare problem that, I later read, usually befalls women who are heavy cocaine users or who have high blood pressure. But sometimes it happens just because you're old. It could have happened anywhere, the doctor told me, and he repeated what he'd said the night before: there is no correlation between air travel and miscarriage. I said that I suspected he was being a gentleman and that I needed to get out of the clinic in time for my eleven-o'clock meeting with the secretary of the interior, whose office I arrived at promptly, after I went back to the Blue Sky and showered in my room, which looked like the site of a murder.

I spent the next five days in that room. Slowly, it set in that it was probably best if I went home instead of to the Gobi, but at first I could not leave. Thanksgiving came and went. There were rolling brownouts when everything went dark and still. I lay in my bed and ate Snickers and drank little bottles of whiskey from the minibar while I watched television programs that seemed as strange and bleak as my new life. Someone had put a white bath mat on top of the biggest bloodstain, the one next to my bed, where I had crouched when I called for help, and little by little the white went red and then brown as the blood seeped through it and oxidized. I stared at it. I looked at the snow outside my window falling on the Soviet architecture. But mostly I looked at the picture of the baby.

•   •   •

When I got back from Mongolia, I was so sad I could barely breathe. On five or six occasions, I ran into mothers who had heard what had happened, and they took one look at me and burst into tears. (Once, this happened with a man.) Within a week, the apartment we were supposed to move into with the baby fell through. Within three, my marriage had shattered. I started lactating. I continued bleeding. I cried ferociously and without warning—in bed, in the middle of meetings, sitting on the subway. It seemed to me that grief was leaking out of me from every orifice.

I could not keep the story of what had happened in Mongolia inside my mouth. I went to buy clothes that would fit my big body but that didn't have bands of stretchy maternity elastic to accommodate a baby who wasn't there. I heard myself tell a horrified saleswoman, "I don't know what size I am, because I just had a baby. He died, but the good news is, now I'm fat." Well-meaning women would tell me, "I had a miscarriage, too," and I would reply, with unnerving intensity, "He was *alive*." I had given birth, however briefly, to another human being, and it seemed crucial that people understand this. Often, after I told them, I tried to get them to look at the picture of the baby on my phone.

After several weeks, I was looking at it only once a day. It was months before I got it down to once a week. I don't look at it much anymore, but people I haven't seen in a while will say, "I'm so sorry about what happened to you." And their compassion pleases me.

But the truth is, the ten or twenty minutes I was somebody's mother were black magic. There is no adventure I would trade them for; there is no place I would rather have seen. Sometimes, when I think about it, I still feel a dark hurt from some primal part of myself, and if I'm alone in my apartment when this happens I will hear myself making sounds that I never made before I went to Mongolia. I realize that I have turned back into a wounded witch, wailing in the forest, undone.

Most of the time it seems sort of OK, though, natural. *Nature.* Mother Nature. She is free to do whatever she chooses.

The New Yorker

WINNER—COLUMNS AND COMMENTARY

The National Magazine Awards judges described Emily Nussbaum as "discerning and authoritative" and likened her to New Yorker critics of the past, including Edmund Wilson and Pauline Kael. "She can zing with the best of them," the judges said (in "Shark Week," House of Cards is "handsome but sleazy, like a CEO in a hotel bar"; in "Private Practice," Master of Sex's Lizzy Caplan is "the swizzle stick in the show's erotic cocktail"). But what really sets Nussbaum apart is her understanding of how and why we watch television (we being Nielsen families, Twitter users, fan-fiction chroniclers, and even other critics). As she suggests in "Difficult Women," she's still the woman "argu[ing], often drunkenly, at cocktail parties" to get you to take Sex and the City seriously.

Emily Nussbaum

Shark Week *and* Difficult Women *and* Private Practice

Shark Week

House of Cards is an original release from Netflix, a DVD-distribution and streaming company that has decided, after several years of selling tickets to the circus, to jump into the ring. Adapted from a British political thriller and produced by David Fincher, the series stars Kevin Spacey as a mercenary Democratic House majority whip and Robin Wright as his wife. This prestigious résumé has turned *House of Cards* into big news—not least because Netflix has cleverly released all thirteen episodes at once. As a model of TV production, it's an exciting experiment, with the potential to liberate showrunners from the agony of weekly ratings. It suggests fresh possibilities for the medium, feeding an audience that has already been trained to binge on quality TV in DVD form.

As a television show, however, *House of Cards* is not so revolutionary. This isn't to say it's bad or not worth watching or unmemorable. (Certain lines, such as "Twitter twat, WTF?," might become catchphrases—for all its elegant contours, the show is marbled with camp.) Over a recent weekend, *House of Cards* acted something like a scotch bender, with definite highs and lows.

I found the first two episodes handsome but sleazy, like a CEO in a hotel bar. Yet by episode 5 I was hypnotized by the show's ensemble of two-faced sociopaths. Episode 8 was a thoughtful side trip into sympathy for Spacey's devilish main character, but by then I was exhausted, and only my compulsive streak kept me going until the finale—at which point I was critically destabilized and looking forward to season 2.

Sensually, visually, *House of Cards* is a pleasure. Its acrid view of political ambition is nothing new (that perspective is all over TV these days, on shows like HBO's *Veep* and Starz's *Boss*), but the series has some sharp twists, with an emphasis on corporate graft and media grandstanding. There's also one truly poignant plot about a working-class congressman hooked on drugs. Yet in the days after I watched the show, its bewitching spell grew fainter—and if *House of Cards* had been delivered weekly I might have given up earlier. Much of the problem is Spacey himself, as Francis (Frank) Underwood, a wheeler-dealer who is denied the job of secretary of state and then conspires, with his steely wife, to go even higher. Spacey's basilisk gaze seems ideal for the role, but he's miscast by being too well cast—there's no tension in seeing a shark play a shark. It's a lot easier to buy his opposite number, the investigative blogger Zoe Barnes (the awesomely hoydenish Kate Mara), who strikes up an affair with Underwood in return for access. Her hair slicked down like a seal, her eyes dead, and her T-shirt sexily V-necked, Barnes is like some millennial demon from the digital unconscious, catnip for condescending older men. You could criticize the show's portrayal of female reporters as venal sluts in black eyeliner, but it's hard to object too much since Mara's performance, which has a freaky, repressive verve, is the liveliest thing in the show. Robin Wright is regal as Claire, Underwood's charity-running wife, and Sakina Jaffrey makes a quiet impact as the president's chief of staff, a restrained professional who in this lurid context feels downright exotic.

Fincher's Washington is full of eerie imagery, such as a homeless man folding a twenty-dollar bill into an origami swan, and it's magnificently lit (although I don't understand why a sought-after journalist like Zoe lives in a flophouse full of spiders). But eventually the show's theatrical panache, along with Spacey's Shakespearean asides to the camera, starts to feel as gimmicky as a fashion-magazine shoot, with melancholic shots of Claire jogging in a graveyard. The show may be made of elegant material, but it's not built to last—it's a meditation on amorality that tells us mostly what we already know.

And, honestly, the more I watched, the more my mind kept wandering to Shonda Rhimes's *Scandal*—an ABC series that's soapy rather than noirish but much more fun and that, in its lunatic way, may have more to say about Washington ambition. *Scandal*, which is inspired by a real-life political "fixer," started slowly, as a legal procedural blended with a Rielle Hunter–flavored presidential affair. It took a season to shed its early conception of Kerry Washington's PR bigwig Olivia Pope as a "white hat." But, once it did—whoa, Nelly. Popping with colorful villains, vote-rigging conspiracies, waterboarding, assassinations, montages set to R&B songs, and the best gay couple on television (the president's chief of staff, Cyrus, and his husband, James, an investigative reporter), the series has become a giddy, paranoid fever dream, like *24* crossed with *The West Wing*, lit up in neon pink. Last week's episode was such a #GameChanger—that's the hashtag that the show's creator used to advertise the episode—that Twitter exploded with exclamation points.

Because *Scandal* is so playful and is unafraid to be ridiculous, it has access to emotional colors that rarely show up in Fincher's universe, whose aesthetics insist that we take it seriously. Like Underwood, Jeff Perry's Cyrus is a Machiavelli who cozies up to the president, but he's got rage, wit, and a capacity for passion, not just oleaginous asides. During last week's episode, he and his husband faced off, naked, in a fight about Cyrus's crimes. (They'd stripped to demonstrate that they weren't wearing wires.) The scene was absurd but also genuinely intimate, with all the daring that *House of Cards* lacks. Rhimes's show is made under the opposite circumstances from Fincher's: nearly twice as many episodes, ratings pressure, constant threat of cancellation, a ravenous tweeting audience. These forces wreck other network dramas, and Rhimes's previous shows have flown off the rails, but *Scandal* has only got stronger. It's become more opera than soap opera, as the critic Ryan McGee observed online. Like much genre fiction, *Scandal* uses its freedom to indulge in crazy what-ifs: What if everyone but the president knew that the election was fixed? What if the president tried to divorce his pregnant wife? What if—well, I don't want to spoil everything, but you might consider jumping in at the beginning of season 2. It's a different kind of binge watch.

· · ·

After nine seasons, NBC's once great mockumentary sitcom *The Office* is ending its run. Instead of going out like *30 Rock*—at the top of its game—*The Office* has had a more typical trajectory, staggering to the finish line in a weakened state. First, it was hobbled by the departure of Steve Carell as Michael Scott, the bad boss whose Pinocchio-like transformation concluded when he found real love. In the aftermath, the writers introduced new characters, but they never jelled; potential plots were set up, fiddled with, then abandoned.

Still, the biggest problem has been the relationship that used to be the show's heart: the one between Jim and Pam, work friends whose unspoken longing fueled the early seasons. Jim was a handsome prankster trapped in a soul-killing job; as an escape, he poured all his emotions into sweet, plain Pam, who was engaged to a neglectful man named Roy. That primal triangle went fractal, very effectively: the initial model flipped several times, as

Pam rejected Jim, then Jim, Pam, and it was mimicked in crueler forms (Angela, Dwight, and Andy), sillier forms (Kelly, Ryan, and Darryl), and more grownup forms (Michael, Jan, and Holly), until nearly every character had dealt with some form of unspoken longing or romantic betrayal.

Eventually, Pam and Jim married and had two children. They were soul mates, and the show had the sense not to throw any doubt into that mix—until this season. Now the showrunners have made the bold choice to threaten a perfect marriage, with Jim in Philadelphia, pursuing his dream job at a sports-marketing company. He's distracted, seduced by the free, fun-guy single life he never had, and, as a result, he's left Pam isolated, with two small kids, furious at the financial risk, her supportive smile cracking. The primal triangle has resurfaced, with a bizarre revelation—Brian, the soundman on the crew that has been filming the show's implicit documentary for years, has broken the fourth wall and fallen for Pam. And she has clearly, in her Pam-like way, nurtured this emotional affair.

Much of the show's audience has bridled at this development, but it works for me. I'm impressed by the daring of the writing staff, which has done the unthinkable: set up a realistic challenge to a marriage of soul mates. Pam may be a sweetie, but she has a history of passive-aggressive insecurity, fear of change, and, well, sneakiness. Under pressure, she triangulates. She flirted with Jim while engaged to Roy; when she briefly moved to New York to attend Pratt, she attracted a male friend whom Jim found so threatening that he proposed. (In contrast, Jim wasn't even tempted by a colleague who threw herself at him.) Jim's sexy new job is much like the one he dreamed of when he played the online game Second Life, in season 4. These compulsive flirtations are Pam's Second Life.

I have no idea if the show will be able to pull this off; on a beloved network sitcom, there's no way that Pam and Jim will divorce. Who would want them to? But I appreciate this return to the show's roots, which were always about complicating easy notions of human happiness. As Michael Scott once put it, "Would I rather be feared or loved? Easy. Both. I want people to be afraid of how much they love me."

Difficult Women

When people talk about the rise of great TV, they inevitably credit one show, *The Sopranos*. Even before James Gandolfini's death, the HBO drama's mystique was secure: novelistic and cinematic, David Chase's auteurist masterpiece cracked open the gangster genre like a rib cage, releasing the latent ambition of television, and launching us all into a golden age.

The Sopranos deserves the hype. Yet there's something screwy about the way that the show and its cable-drama blood brothers have come to dominate the conversation, elbowing other forms of greatness out of the frame. It's a bias that bubbles up early in Brett Martin's otherwise excellent new book, *Difficult Men: Behind the Scenes of a Creative Revolution: From* The Sopranos *and* The Wire *to* Mad Men *and* Breaking Bad, a deeply reported and dishy account of just how your prestige-cable sausage is made. I tore through the book, yet when I reached Martin's chronicle of the rise of HBO I felt a jolt. "It might as well have been a tourism campaign for a post-Rudolph Giuliani, de-ethnicized Gotham awash in money," Martin writes of one of my favorite shows. "Its characters were types as familiar as those in *The Golden Girls*: the Slut, the Prude, the Career Woman, the Heroine. But they talked more explicitly, certainly about their bodies, but also about their desires and discontents outside the bedroom, than women on TV ever had before."

Martin gives *Sex and the City* credit for jump-starting HBO, but the condescension is palpable, and the grudging praise is reserved for only one aspect of the series—the rawness of its subject matter. Martin hardly invented this attitude: he is simply reiterating what has become the reflexive consensus on the show, right down to the hackneyed *Golden Girls* gag. Even as *The Sopranos* has ascended to TV's Mt. Olympus, the reputation of *Sex and the City* has shrunk and faded, like some tragic dry-clean-only dress tossed into a decade-long hot cycle. By the show's fifteenth anniversary, this year, we fans had trained ourselves to downgrade the show to a "guilty pleasure," to mock its puns, to get into self-flagellating conversations about those blinkered and blinged-out movies. Whenever a new chick-centric series debuts, there are invidious comparisons: don't worry, it's no *Sex and the City*, they say. As if that were a good thing.

But *Sex and the City*, too, was once one of HBO's flagship shows. It was the peer of *The Sopranos*, albeit in a different tone and in a different milieu, deconstructing a different genre. Mob shows, cop shows, cowboy shows—those are formulas with gravitas. *Sex and the City*, in contrast, was pigeonholed as a sitcom. In fact, it was a bold riff on the romantic comedy: the show wrestled with the limits of that pink-tinted genre for almost its entire run. In the end, it gave in. Yet until that last-minute stumble it was sharp, iconoclastic television. High-feminine instead of fetishistically masculine, glittery rather than gritty, and daring in its conception of character, *Sex and the City* was a brilliant and, in certain ways, radical show. It also originated the unacknowledged first female antihero on television: ladies and gentlemen, Carrie Bradshaw.

·   ·   ·

Please, people, I can hear your objections from here. But first think back. Before *Sex and the City*, the vast majority of iconic "single girl" characters on television, from That Girl to Mary Tyler Moore and Molly Dodd, had been you-go-girl types—which is to say, actual role models. (Ally McBeal was a notable and problematic exception.) They were pioneers who offered many single women the representation they craved, and they were also, crucially, adorable to men: vulnerable and plucky and warm. However varied the layers they displayed over time, they flattered a specific pathology: the cultural requirement that women greet other women with the refrain "Oh, me, too! Me, too!"

In contrast, Carrie and her friends—Miranda, Samantha, and Charlotte—were odder birds by far, jagged, aggressive, and sometimes frightening figures, like a makeup mirror lit up in neon. They were simultaneously real and abstract, emotionally complex and philosophically stylized. Women identified with them— "I'm a Carrie!"—but then became furious when they showed flaws. And, with the exception of Charlotte (Kristin Davis), men didn't find them likable: there were endless cruel jokes about Samantha (Kim Cattrall), Miranda (Cynthia Nixon), and Carrie as sluts, man haters, or gold diggers. To me, as a single woman, it felt like a definite sign of progress: since the elemental representation of single life at the time was the comic strip "Cathy" (*ack! chocolate!*), better that one's life should be viewed as glamorously threatening than as sad and lonely.

Carrie Bradshaw herself began as a mirror for another woman: she was the avatar of the *New York Observer* columnist Candace Bushnell, a steely "sexual anthropologist" on the prowl for blind items. When the initial showrunner, Darren Star, and his mostly female writing staff adapted Bushnell's columns, they transformed that icy Carrie, pouring her into the warm body of Sarah Jessica Parker. Out popped a chatterbox with a schnoz, whose advanced fashion sense was not intended to lure men into matrimony. For a half dozen episodes, Carrie was a happy, curious explorer, out companionably smoking with modelizers. If she'd stayed that way, the show might have been another *Mary Tyler Moore*: a playful, empowering comedy about one woman's adventures in the big city.

Instead, Carrie fell under the thrall of Mr. Big, the sexy, emotionally withholding forty-three-year-old financier played by Chris Noth. From then on, pleasurable as *Sex and the City* remained, it also felt designed to push back at its audience's wish for identification, triggering as much anxiety as relief. It switched the romantic comedy's primal scene, from "Me, too!" to "Am I like *her*?" A man practically woven out of red flags, Big wasn't there to rescue Carrie; instead, his "great love" was a slow poisoning. She spun out, becoming anxious, obsessive, and, despite her charm, wildly self-centered—in her own words, "the frightening woman whose fear ate her sanity." Their relationship was viewed with concern by her friends, who were not, as Martin suggests, mere "types" but portrayals of a narrow slice of wealthy white thirty-something Manhattanites: the Waspy gallerina, the liberal-feminist lawyer, the decadent power publicist.

Although the show's first season is its slightest, it swiftly establishes a bold mixture of moods—fizzy and sour, blunt and arch—and shifts between satirical and sincere modes of storytelling. (It's not even especially dated: though the show has gained a reputation for over-the-top absurdity, I can tell you that these night clubs and fashion shows do exist—maybe even more so now that Manhattan has become a gated island for the wealthy.) There is already a melancholic undertow, full of foreshadowing. "What if he never calls and three weeks from now I pick up the *New York Times* and I read that he's married some perfect little woman who never passes gas under his five-hundred-dollar sheets?" Carrie frets in episode 11. In a moment of clarity, she tells Miranda that, when she's around Big, "I'm not like me. I'm, like, Together Carrie. I wear little outfits: Sexy Carrie and Casual Carrie. Sometimes I catch myself actually *posing*. It's just—it's exhausting."

That was the conundrum Carrie faced for the entire series: true love turned her into a fake. The season 1 neurotic Carrie didn't stick, though. She and Big fixed things; then they broke up again, harder. He moved to Paris. She met Aidan (John Corbett), the marrying type. In season 3, the writers upped the ante, having Carrie do something overtly antiheroic: she cheated on a decent man with a bad one (Big, of course), now married to that "perfect little woman," Natasha. They didn't paper over the repercussions: Natasha's humiliation and the way Carrie's betrayal hardened Aidan, even once he took her back. During six seasons, Carrie changed, as anyone might from thirty-two to thirty-eight, and not always in positive ways. She got more honest and more responsible; she became a saner girlfriend. But she also became scarred, prissier, strikingly gun-shy—and, finally, she panicked at the question of what it would mean to be an older single woman.

Her friends went through changes, too, often upon being confronted with their worst flaws—Charlotte's superficiality, Miranda's caustic tongue, Samantha's refusal to be vulnerable. In a departure from nearly all earlier half-hour comedies, the writers fully embraced the richness of serial storytelling. In a movie we go from glare to kiss in two hours. *Sex and the City* was liberated from closure, turning "once upon a time" into a wry mantra, treating its characters' struggles with a rare mixture of bluntness and compassion. It was one of the first television comedies to let its characters change in serious ways, several years before other half-hour comedies, like *The Office*, went and stole all the credit.

.   .   .

So why is the show so often portrayed as a set of empty, static cartoons, an embarrassment to womankind? It's a classic misunderstanding, I think, stemming from an unexamined hierarchy: the assumption that anything stylized (or formulaic or pleasurable or funny or feminine or explicit about sex rather than about violence or made collaboratively) must be inferior. Certainly, the show's formula was strict: usually four plots—two deep, two shallow—linked by Carrie's voice-over. The B plots generally involved one of the non-Carrie women getting laid; these slapstick sequences were crucial to the show's rude rhythms, interjecting energy and rupturing anything sentimental. (It's one reason those bowdlerized reruns on E! are such a crime: with the literal and figurative fucks edited out, the show *is* a rom-com.)

Most unusually, the characters themselves were symbolic. As I've written elsewhere—and argued, often drunkenly, at cocktail parties—the four friends operated as near-allegorical figures, pegged to contemporary debates about women's lives, mapped along three overlapping continuums. The first was emotional: Carrie and Charlotte were romantics; Miranda and Samantha were cynics. The second was ideological: Miranda and Carrie were second-wave feminists, who believed in egalitarianism; Charlotte and Samantha were third-wave feminists, focused on exploiting the power of femininity from opposing angles. The third concerned sex itself. At first, Miranda and Charlotte were prudes while Samantha and Carrie were libertines. Unsettlingly, as the show progressed, Carrie began to glide toward caution, away from freedom, out of fear.

Every conversation the friends had, at brunch or out shopping, amounted to a *Crossfire*-like debate. When Carrie sleeps with a dreamy French architect and he leaves a thousand dollars by her bed, she consults her friends. "Money is power. Sex is power," Samantha argues. "Therefore, getting money for sex is simply an exchange of power." "Don't listen to the dime-store Camille Paglia," Miranda shoots back. The most famous such conversation took place four episodes in, after Charlotte's boyfriend asked her to have anal sex. The friends pile into a cab for a raucous debate about whether her choice is about power-exchange (Miranda) or about finding a fun new hole (Samantha). "I'm not a hole!" Charlotte protests, and they hit a pothole. "What was that?" Charlotte asks. "A preview," Miranda and Samantha say in unison and burst out laughing.

The show's basic value system aligns with Carrie: romantic, second-wave, libertine. But *Sex and the City*'s real strength was its willingness not to stack the deck: it let every side make a case so that complexity carried the day. When Carrie and Aidan break up, they are both right. When Miranda and Carrie argue about her move to Paris, they are both right. The show's style could be brittle, but its substance was flexible, in a way that made the series feel peculiarly broad-ranging, covering so much ground, so fleetly, that it became easy to take it for granted.

·   ·   ·

Endings count in television, maybe too much. *The Sopranos* concluded with a black screen: it rejected easy satisfaction and pissed off its most devoted fans. (David Chase fled to the South of France.)

Three years earlier, in 2004, *Sex and the City* had other pressures to contend with: while a mob film ends in murder, we all know where a romantic comedy ends. I'll defend until my dying day the sixth-season plot in which Carrie seeks respite with a celebrity like her, the Russian artist Aleksandr (Mikhail Baryshnikov), a chilly genius she doesn't love but who offers her a dreamlike fairy tale, the one she has always longed for: Paris, safety, money, pleasure. It felt ugly and sad in a realistic way. In one of the season's, and the show's, best episodes, she saw other older women settling (Candice Bergen) or falling out of windows (the hilarious Kristen Johnston, who delivered one of *Sex and the City*'s best monologues: "When did everybody stop smoking? When did everybody pair off? . . . I'm so bored I could die"). The show always had a realpolitik directness about such social pressures; as another HBO series put it recently, winter was coming.

And then, in the final round, *Sex and the City* pulled its punches and let Big rescue Carrie. It honored the wishes of its heroine, and at least half of the audience, and it gave us a very memorable dress, too. But it also showed a failure of nerve, an inability of the writers to imagine or to trust themselves to portray any other kind of ending—happy or not. And I can't help but wonder: What would the show look like without that finale? What if it were the story of a woman who lost herself in her thirties, who was changed by a poisonous, powerful love affair, and who emerged, finally, surrounded by her friends? Who would Carrie be then? It's an interesting question, one that shouldn't erase the show's powerful legacy. We'll just have to wait for another show to answer it.

Private Practice

Masters of Sex, a new hour-long drama on Showtime, is a fizzy, ebullient quasi-historical romp about the team of scientific pioneers who transformed American attitudes toward sex. But let's not bury the lead: it's also a serious turn-on.

For many viewers, this will be reason enough to watch, and there's no shame in that game; this is adult cable television's bread and butter, after all. Luckily, the show has an appeal beyond solid date-night viewing. *Masters of Sex* is based on Thomas Maier's lively 2009 book of the same title, which tells the story of the rise of William Masters, a renegade who aimed to study sex in the lab, using human subjects. In 1950s St. Louis, where Masters was a prominent OB-GYN, this was an idea outrageous enough that he had to keep the project secret. Then, almost by chance, Masters found his soul mate. Virginia Johnson was a low-level secretary with no college degree, but she had social skills that the doctor lacked, in addition to a spitfire sexual iconoclasm. The two became intellectual partners and, later, lovers—though few knew about that part until many years afterward. Their best-selling 1966 study blasted through medical prudery and Freudian hornswoggle, explaining the physiology of orgasms, spreading the good word about healthy sexuality, and turning them into national celebrities.

This sounds like a romantic, upbeat story, and at times *Masters of Sex* does have a caper-plot element, as Johnson (Lizzy Caplan) flirts with doctors and nurses in the hospital, convincing them to "do it" for science. The sex scenes are graphic and often very funny, with classic Showtime panache, and they star people you definitely want to see having sex (or, in many cases, masturbating with sensors pasted to their skin, as the doctors murmur things like "turgidity of nipples"). In its stylish pilot, *Masters of Sex* initially comes off a bit like *Mad Men with Benefits*: fetishistic fun with a historical pedigree. But over the first six episodes, the show deepens by degrees, becoming more poignant and more surprising, too. It begins to acknowledge some of the unsettling implications of the doctor's work and lets characters who start as entertaining cartoons gain complexity, taking the plot in new directions.

When we first meet him, Masters (Michael Sheen) has begun his sex study without official permission: he's been paying a skeptical prostitute to let him watch through a keyhole while he takes notes on positions and duration. His interest seems fueled by equal parts radical scientific curiosity and radical innocence. "Is that a common practice amongst prostitutes?" he asks, astonished by the revelation that his subject has faked an orgasm to speed up a customer. "It's a common practice amongst anyone with a twat," she replies.

Masters is married to a lovely woman named Libby (the charming Caitlin FitzGerald), and they are struggling with infertility—he's made her believe it's her fault, when, in fact, he knows that he has a low sperm count. At the university hospital where he works, the doctor's kindness to his patients coexists with a peevish, shut-down air of arrogance, the native entitlement of a big-shot doctor of his era. Then Johnson arrives, a former night-club singer, twice divorced, a single mother of two kids—a worldly woman seeking a sense of purpose. As Masters's assistant, she handles all the administration and much of the design of the study, but her effect on him is stronger than those roles would suggest. Heterodox and bold in her manner, she's a destabilizing force whose charisma acts like a magnet, spinning every moral compass into a panic. And yet, despite her bravado, she's under society's thumb, too: she needs to keep this job.

.   .   .

The show departs in several key ways from the true story, blurring chronology and conflating characters and adding in one or two questionable twists for the sake of drama. In a few cases, it makes events *less* strange than they were in reality: in the actual experiments, anonymous couples mated with paper bags over their heads. (Later on, Masters's mother helpfully sewed silk masks.) These early episodes briskly sketch out a fraught fifties milieu, including the sub rosa doctor-nurse hookup scene; the lonely Masters marriage and its origins in Masters's unhappy childhood; and Johnson's struggles with her irresponsible ex (the hilarious Mather Zickel) and her son, who begins to hate her for neglecting him.

Along the way, we get a sense of the ebb and flow of Masters and Johnson's research, which began to bump up against charged social questions, like homosexuality and the then-accepted Freudian notion that vaginal climax was more "mature." There are satisfyingly silly comic set pieces, including a flirtation between a blond nurse and a doctor who are paired for study, as well as a few on-the-nose bits reminiscent of a conventional medical drama. The dialogue isn't always subtle, but it's often sharp. (When a chagrined cad deflowers a virgin, he moans, "It's like those signs you see in thrift shops. You break it, you buy it.") A few episodes in, Allison Janney shows up to give an affecting performance as the university provost's wife.

For all the show's appeal, none of this would work without Lizzy Caplan, the swizzle stick in the show's erotic cocktail. In previous roles, Caplan has stood out as a modern girl, all defensive postures and tomboy sarcasm. On the cult TV classic *Party Down*, she was a jittery cater-waiter; in the underestimated dark movie comedy *Bachelorette*, a self-destructive hipster; in *Mean Girls*, a furious goth. But in *Masters of Sex* she's chilled out and self-possessed, the type of woman who turns everything she says into an intelligent come-on, even when that's not her intent. With her elegant nose and amused eyes, black-slash eyebrows and warm mouth, she's like a pen-and-ink illo of herself. At times, the script can be a bit worshipful of the character—"that woman is magic," one voice-over coos—but Caplan is watchable enough to override that flaw. And it's a fascinating conception of a female superhero: her libido is a superpower, one she tries to use for good rather than evil, with mixed results.

Since the era when the Bada Bing girls writhed reliably, each Sunday night, in the background of Tony Soprano's business meetings, cable television has adopted, if not an actual Madonna/whore complex, something approaching a Gallant/Goofus one. The most artistically prestigious series, such as *The Wire*, *Breaking Bad*, and even *Mad Men*, might include sex or nudity, but they generally do so for some plot-based reason, not as keep-'em-watching titillation. The shows that deliver more graphic scenes, often at oddly predictable twenty-minute intervals—*Game of Thrones*, *Boardwalk Empire*, *True Blood*—share a slightly seamy quality, as if the boobs were contractually required product placement.

Masters of Sex threads this needle well. Sex is its subject, after all—and the show makes the case, beneath its cinematic lacquer, that it is not something merely exciting or trivial but a deep human necessity. Deprived of intimacy and true release, people shrivel up. "Once you've seen Oz, who wants to go back to Kansas?" one heartbroken character asks. In this way, *Masters of Sex* reminded me not of a few other Showtime series, with their mood of anomie and disdain, but of *Orange Is the New Black*, the Netflix series that, for all its comic bounce, takes sex seriously as pleasure, power, and escape. These stories are humanistic, not cynical, and although they go in for a level of prurience, the nudity isn't simply there to jump the needle on the viewer's electrocardiogram. *Masters of Sex* may not be revolutionary TV, but it's got something just as useful: good chemistry.

Architect

FINALIST—COLUMNS
AND COMMENTARY

In these three columns for
Architect—*the magazine of the*
American Institute of Architects—
Witold Rybczynski examines
significant building projects in
Boston, Seattle, and Poundbury,
England ("the town that Prince
Charles built"). As the National
Magazine Award judges said,
"Rybczynski's writing is engaging
for both veteran architects and
those who merely live and work in
the buildings they design." Born in
Scotland and raised in England
and Canada, Rybczynski has
taught at McGill and the
University of Pennsylvania; written
for The Atlantic, The New Yorker,
and Slate; *and is the author of*
several books, including Home:
A Short History of an Idea *and,*
most recently, How Architecture
Works: A Humanist's Toolkit.
"Oh, and by the way," his website
explains, "it's pronounced
Vee-told Rib-chin-ski."

Witold Rybczynski

Overexposed *and* Radical Revival *and* Behind the Façade

Overexposed

I recently visited two civic buildings in Seattle that are now almost a decade old: Central Library, designed by Rem Koolhaas and Joshua Prince-Ramus of OMA, and City Hall, designed by Peter Q. Bohlin of Bohlin Cywinski Jackson. Why bother to write about these buildings now? When the library opened in 2004, the *New York Times* critic Herbert Muschamp called it "the most exciting building it has been my honor to review." City Hall, just a few blocks away, earned no such acclaim when it opened the following year, and to this day it remains a well-kept secret.

Has the library lived up to its initial fanfare? And has a very good building in City Hall been overshadowed by its more celebrated neighbor? I came to find answers to those questions, believing that it's best to judge buildings in the fullness of time, when the rough edges have been worn smooth and it's possible to assess the durability—aesthetic as well as physical—of the design.

This flies in the face of our current obsession with the new-new thing. The mere announcement of a competition short list is "news." Buildings are given the thumbs-up—or -down—on opening day, prior to being put into use. Projects are rated "green" irrespective of actual performance. And design awards are bestowed on buildings even before they are built. Pause to consider how unusual that is—as if Oscars were awarded for unfilmed screenplays or the Pulitzers included a category called Best Book Proposal.

The architects for the library and City Hall were both selected in the summer of 1999. Library administrators narrowed a field of twenty-nine contestants to five—a balanced mix of two big names, two tyros, and an established regional firm. The process got off to a rocky start when the big names—Norman Foster and Cesar Pelli—dissatisfied with the selection process, withdrew and, following a lackluster presentation, Portland-based Zimmer Gunsul Frasca was eliminated.

That left the tyros. Both in their fifties, neither Steven Holl nor Rem Koolhaas had a large portfolio of built work, although both were favorites of what a Seattle journalist called "the black-turtleneck crowd." Following three days of well-attended public presentations, Koolhaas got the nod. The iconoclastic Dutchman did not disappoint, producing a design consisting of superimposed platforms in a huge prism-shaped greenhouse. The unusual "uniting of hip with pragmatic" as *Architectural Record* put it, was an immediate sensation.

The city hall project was overshadowed from the start. Public wrangling between Mayor Paul Schell and some members of the city council delayed the architect-selection process, and when the short list was announced, it seemed an anticlimax after the exciting head-to-head competition between Holl and Koolhaas. The closest on the list to a firebrand was Antoine Predock, an architectural maverick with a flamboyant style that was popular in the Southwest, although it seemed an odd fit for Seattle. John and Patricia Patkau were less well known but, being based in nearby Vancouver, British Columbia, were almost local.

The sleeper was Peter Bohlin. A seasoned practitioner like Predock, he was best known for exquisitely detailed houses, including a sprawling estate for Bill Gates on Lake Washington. The *Seattle Times*, which had called Koolhaas and Holl "sexy, jet-setting, international designers about whom civic boosters dream and major magazines write," referred to Bohlin's public presentation as "subdued"—which is also a pretty good description of his architecture.

The wrangling between the mayor and the council continued even after Bohlin was selected, which cast a pall over the project. Whereas the opening of the library was extensively covered by the world's media, led by Muschamp's rave review, City Hall was ignored. My search of the Avery Index did not turn up a single review of City Hall by the major architectural press, only a brief news clip in *Architectural Record* that referred to the proposed design as "transparent and pragmatic," which seems a step down from "hip and pragmatic."

That wasn't how the mayor saw it; Bohlin's unaffected approach is exactly what attracted him. Schell, who had served as dean of the University of Washington's College of Architecture and Urban Planning, followed architecture and was familiar with Bohlin's work. "I knew the Gates house as well as a recent building at the University of Washington, so I had a good feel for what Bohlin would bring to the table," he told me. "You really want someone who is a little old shoe, and will last on the shelf."

So, how has the old shoe worn? The quartzite floors, limestone and titanium walls, fir and maple paneling, glass railings, and stainless steel everything else look much as they must have on opening day eight years ago, as I discovered on my recent tour of the building. The "stream" that crosses the city hall lobby, and cascades beside a grand exterior stair to the lowest part of the steeply sloping site forty feet below, fills the interior with a pleasant gurgling sound. The sky-lit lobby has been described as a public agora, and I watched people wandering in and out of it at will. No one was opening bags or asking for IDs. Elevator access is unrestricted. City Hall was designed in the immediate aftermath of the 1999 WTO protests, the so-called Battle of Seattle, as well as 9/11. What must have been a difficult decision—to create a transparent, welcoming building rather than a bunker—is now fully vindicated.

Bohlin's design exhibits an old-fashioned sort of modernism, in which the plan explains itself as you move through it—the council chamber here, the offices over there. The structure is comprehensible, and care is lavished on construction. Bohlin belongs to the details-should-show-how-things-are-made school, but unlike Renzo Piano, he is a bit of a mannerist; planes slide by other planes, materials are layered upon each other, and odd junctions abound. This casual approach has been compared to that of Gunnar Asplund and Sigurd Lewerentz, early Swedish modernists whom Bohlin admires, and it serves to humanize the architecture.

Good buildings don't just fulfill existing functions, they suggest new ones. A large room designed for overflow crowds during council meetings has turned into a well-used public meeting space. The large plazas that step down the hill on the west side of the building, designed by landscape architect Kathryn Gustafson, have become a favored locale with free lunchtime concerts and a weekly farmers market in the summer. At the recent historic same-sex marriage ceremony performed in City Hall, the couples descended the grand exterior stair amid cheers, flowers, and confetti. One area that has yet to find a use is an empty "multipurpose space" at the base of the building. A long ruby-red glass wall that casts an eerie glow and creates a spooky atmosphere on the interior, and on the exterior, struck me as a feeble effort to inject glam into the design.

I asked my City Hall guide why he thought the building had received so little attention in the media. "When City Hall opened, the emphasis was put on its green features," he said, "which is not very sexy." The building, which received a LEED Gold rating, claims a 24 percent reduction in energy use; although a projected solar array was never installed, there is a large green roof as well as a monster water tank in the basement. It's true that reduction in storm-water runoff doesn't stir the imagination, but I think it's more than that. This low-key building, adjusted to its site and its surroundings, paying deference to the 2002 Justice Center across the street (designed by NBBJ), carefully stepping down the hill, and taking advantage of views of Elliott Bay, is the opposite of an icon. City Hall blends with its setting and does not photograph well, and I suspect that its subtle charms are appreciated only gradually, over time. This is slow architecture.

No one has ever described Rem Koolhaas as slow. The Seattle Central Library perches uncomfortably on its sloping site—no places for outdoor lunches here—although I suspect the awkwardness was intended. It's that sort of building: startling, in-your-face, challenging conventions, a prickly presence amid the downtown skyscrapers (and very photogenic). The library looks like a giant piece of urban infrastructure, an impression heightened at night, when the crisscrossing trusses of the bridgelike structure are apparent inside the faceted, glowing lantern.

Although the glass skin appeared grimy the day I visited, on the whole the library doesn't show its age—but for different reasons than City Hall. Koolhaas and Prince-Ramus had a smaller construction budget (less than $300 per square foot, compared to $363 per square foot for City Hall), and they opted to spend it on structure and space rather than on materials and detailing. The interior finishes are downright cheap: sheetrock; bare concrete; exposed, sprayed fireproofing; and an acoustic ceiling that looks like it's made from old sleeping bags. As for elegant details, well, there aren't any. This is a building where the reading room and the service basement are equally bare-bones.

This very roughness works to the building's advantage, however. Like all big-city libraries, and perhaps more than most, the

Seattle library is a hangout for the homeless and young down-towners—given Seattle's grungy dress code, it can be hard to tell them apart. Yet everyone looks at home—the tough, no-frills interior neither patronizes nor intimidates.

Last year, the library had 2 million visitors, which is remarkable for a city the size of Seattle (the mighty New York Public Library had 2.3 million). The wear doesn't show—there's not much that you can do to a polished concrete floor, nylon carpeting, and galvanized-metal balustrades that resemble floor grates. The unusual, stainless steel floor tiles in the reading room are scratched up, but that only enhances their industrial chic, although I thought that the sulfurous chartreuse escalators and elevators were starting to show their age. One feature that has fallen victim to intensive use is the trendy upholstered foam furniture that I remember from a previous visit; it has been replaced by PVC seating that resembles Adirondack chairs. As I sat making notes, it struck me that while the vertiginous, Escher-like interior was as stimulating as ever, it could also be overwhelming, which was not particularly conducive to concentration. A little calm would not have been out of place.

The ramped, spiraling bookstacks were widely heralded when the building opened, although none of the librarians I spoke to could think of a single library that has recently adopted this unusual feature, which now seems more like a gimmick than a real innovation. But there is no doubt that the striking, faceted glass building is a hit with the public. And not just library-goers; a quarter of the visitors are tourists, for the library has joined Pike Place Market and the Space Needle as one of Seattle's must-see sights. Although the librarians who showed me around boasted of their building's popularity, it's unclear that the experience of using a public library is actually enhanced when it doubles as a tourist attraction.

What difference does a decade make? Both buildings can now be appreciated in the fuller context of their architects' subsequent work. Koolhaas's hard-nosed interior takes its place with the Porto concert hall and Milstein Hall at Cornell, and his pursuit of eye-catching building forms has continued with the CCTV headquarters in Beijing. Bohlin's self-styled "soft modernism" has found further expression in several campus buildings, a federal courthouse, and a studio for Pixar, although he has also produced unexpectedly iconic designs for Apple stores in New York and Shanghai.

In many ways, the library and City Hall represent two different faces of modernism. Koolhaas's design is a freely structured, contemporary version of a civic monument, a modern counterpart to Carrère & Hastings's New York Public Library. Much like that landmark, the Seattle library is a building of its time—although of a different time. It's rough and chic, glamorously gritty, and fashionably unconcerned with hierarchies and traditional architectural virtues.

Bohlin's City Hall is different; it doesn't put on airs. After spending a day in the building my chief impression was of craftsmanship, unruffled calm, and an even-handed sense of balance—a veritable civics lesson in glass, maple, and natural light. In a culture that is intrigued by novelty and glamour, it is perhaps inevitable that chic would trump craft. But given several more decades, I'm not so sure. I wouldn't discount the staying power of well-made old shoes.

Radical Revival

Although Americans regularly pay lip service to the value of diversity, the truth is that people of different incomes generally choose—for a variety of reasons—to live apart. Nevertheless, since 1992, the federal government has spent more than $5 billion to encourage the rich and poor to live side by side. The so-called Hope VI program has awarded several hundred block grants to scores of cities around the country to replace the barracklike public housing projects of the 1950s with a blend of subsidized and market housing.

Replacing the projects, which concentrate the poor in isolated enclaves, with mixed-income neighborhoods certainly sounds like a great idea. But what does it take to make a successful socially engineered community that departs so radically from the American mainstream? The model for the Hope VI program was a pioneering housing experiment in Boston called Harbor Point, the nation's first attempt to transform a large dysfunctional federal public housing project into a mixed-income planned community. Now twenty-five years old, Harbor Point, perhaps more than other projects, can help answer that difficult question.

Harbor Point occupies fifty acres on Columbia Point, a peninsula jutting into Dorchester Bay, just south of downtown Boston. Today, Columbia Point is best known for I. M. Pei's John F. Kennedy Presidential Library and Museum, but for three decades it was the site of the city's largest—and most notorious—public housing project. In 1954, M. A. Dyer, a local firm, designed twenty-seven nearly identical three- and seven-story apartment buildings, deployed on super-blocks à la Ville Radieuse. The architecture followed the no-frills style of public housing of that era: utilitarian, flat-roof boxes. Although the project functioned reasonably well at first, by the 1970s, thanks to the absence of screening, lax management, and general neglect, it had become a no-man's land of crack houses, street crime, and lawlessness. By 1979, things were so bad that three-quarters of the 1,504 housing units were boarded up and vacant. In 1980, the Boston Housing Authority, which had been successfully sued for dereliction by the remaining tenants, was placed in receivership.

Two years later, the city of Boston did something unexpected. With federal approval, it leased the whole project to a real estate developer to rebuild as a privately managed residential community. Two-thirds of the new units would be market rate, but the remainder would be subsidized social housing. Simply put, the idea was that the former would cross-subsidize—and stabilize—the latter. This was, in many ways, a desperate gamble: Blending public housing into a commercial development had never been tried before on this scale; in addition, it was unclear if middle-class tenants would want to live in an isolated site in a distinctly unfashionable part of the city. On the other hand, the waterfront location was attractive and only ten minutes from downtown on the T.

Harbor Point is the brainchild of a developer named Joe Corcoran, who founded Corcoran Jennison Companies in 1971. As Jane Roessner recounts in *A Decent Place to Live*, a history of the project published in 2000, it was Corcoran who first approached the U.S. Department of Housing and Urban Development with the idea of turning Columbia Point public housing into a mixed-income community. The son of Irish immigrants, Corcoran had grown up in Dorchester, attended Boston College High School at Columbia Point, and watched the construction—and eventual decay—of the public housing project there. "I hated public housing," he told me when we met in his Columbia Point office. "Warehousing low-income families all in one place was a formula for social disaster."

He and his partners, Joe Mullins and Gary Jennison, developed an unusual solution for integrating public housing into a market-oriented residential community: They made the public housing tenants partners in the project. Corcoran admits that there were practical advantages to this arrangement. "When you show up at a meeting with a group of poor people on your side, it's hard for the politicians to turn you down," he says. But more important, sharing responsibility was a way of ensuring the continued success of a mixed-income community.

The unprecedented tenant control that Corcoran advocates includes full and equal partnership during the design phase—both sides must agree on all decisions—active participation in day-today management, as well as a stake in the financial success of the development. "The tenants' council gets 10 percent of the cash flow to finance its operations," he says.

The council has twelve elected members, seven from the subsidized tenants and five from the market tenants—the disparity reflecting that subsidized tenants tend to be long-time residents (eight years on average at Harbor Point), compared to market tenants (less than two years). Every month, representatives from the council and from the developer meet to discuss ongoing problems such as tenant complaints, maintenance issues, and evictions. "After our experience, we won't do a mixed-income project unless the tenants are partners," Corcoran says.

Corcoran Jennison today owns and manages more than 24,000 residential units, mostly affordable and mixed-income rentals. Like all of the company's properties, Harbor Point has rules of behavior: no pets, no repairing or washing cars on site, no consumption of alcoholic beverages in public areas, no loud noises after eleven p.m., and so on. In addition, car access is restricted to residents and guests (while the streets are publicly owned, they are maintained—and patrolled—privately). "We are able to relax some rules as the property matures, and in other properties we make them more strict as the resident population evolves," says Miles Byrne, who managed Harbor Point for seven years. "There is so much distrust in the early years of any mixed-income community, in large part because we inherit a resident population that has only known the public housing universe, where promises were broken, properties were neglected, and decisions were reached without resident input."

Corcoran Jennison is strict about enforcement, but Byrne emphasizes that, in the case of subsidized tenants, eviction is a last resort. "Guns and drugs are the third rail, but on everything else, we—the developer and the council—try to make it work. After all, subsidized tenants have many fewer housing options than market tenants." He emphasizes that managing low-income housing is more demanding than managing simple market housing and that many municipal housing bureaucracies are bad at it. "They're not very entrepreneurial," he says. "And they often develop an adversarial relationship with their tenants."

Sound management and tenant control are crucial, but urban design is important, too. The plan for Harbor Point was the work of the late Joan E. Goody of Boston-based Goody, Clancy & Associates. She sympathized with the demands of the public housing occupants. "They wanted to live in a 'normal' neighborhood," she wrote in a 1993 article in *Places* magazine, "one that didn't look or work like a project, one that felt safe for walking around and letting their children out to play."

To achieve normality, the Ville Radieuse plan was converted into a street grid with sidewalks, on-street parking, and no cul-de-sacs. Seventeen of the original buildings were replaced by new five-, six-, and seven-story brick apartment blocks oriented to the street; the rest of the structures were renovated and given pitched roofs and bay windows. Among the apartment buildings, Goody placed groups of two- and three-story townhouses—modest, New England–style buildings of painted clapboard with stoops and picket fences. All the ground floor apartments were given their own front doors—a simple feature "that nurtures pride and identity," as the architecture critic of the *Boston Globe*, Robert Campbell, wrote in a 1990 article.

Although this sounds a lot like what would later become known as New Urbanism, the first designs for Harbor Point predate Seaside and call for none of the decorative charm of that seminal project; this is New Urbanism on a diet. In any case, Goody, a Harvard-trained modernist, did not consider herself a New Urbanist. "Joan was a humanist rather than a traditionalist," says David Dixon, FAIA, principal in charge of urban design at Goody Clancy. "She was more interested in how people live today than in how they wanted to live in the past. That's why she looked to nearby Boston neighborhoods such as Dorchester, rather than to old New England towns."

In his 1990 article, Campbell concluded that "Harbor Point will flourish if it begins to grow at its edges and mesh with its surroundings." The ten lanes of Interstate 93 are a formidable barrier between the site and the rest of Dorchester, but the immediate surroundings are being filled in, and Harbor Point itself is flourishing. There are two schools and a church across the street, the adjacent University of Massachusetts campus has expanded, and the projected Edward M. Kennedy Institute, next to the JFK Library, is in the works. Corcoran Jennison has built an apartment building, an office building, and a hotel next to the housing development, and although its plans for a new residential community were scotched by the recession—the university acquired the land—a $60 million apartment complex is on the boards for another neighboring site.

On a recent warm and sunny day in June, I walked over to Harbor Point from the nearby MBTA station and discovered a surprising number of people on the street. "Surprising" because a typical planned community of nine-to-five white-collar workers is usually empty at noon on a weekday. Since many of the subsidized tenants at Harbor Point work at nontraditional jobs—night-shift cleaners, taxi drivers, security guards—they are around during the day. Another result of the mixed-income community is greater heterogeneity. There are mothers with strollers (a third of the subsidized residents are children), and elderly bench sitters from the seniors' residence. A large number of the market tenants at Harbor Point are college students, and while there are fewer of them today than when regular classes are in session, they are a presence, too.

Harbor Point is a walkable community: The buildings are close to the sidewalks and the mature trees offer plenty of shade. It's leafy green, but at thirty units per acre, the impression is urban. Goody, whose sensible, low-key architecture has stood the test of time, oriented the streets so that they terminate in views of either the harbor or the Boston skyline. Along the water's edge is a public promenade with a spectacular vista of downtown across the bay. The other major landscape feature of Harbor Point is a 1,000-foot-long mall modeled on Boston's Commonwealth Avenue in Back Bay. This kind of mimicry doesn't always work—many neotraditional developments have "boulevards" weakly defined by single-family houses—but here the apartment buildings, barely visible behind a line of street trees, are exactly the right scale for the long green space.

The base of one of the apartment buildings facing the mall houses a small commercial strip containing a convenience store, dry cleaner, hair salon, daycare center, and Fiskie's Café, whose tables and chairs spill out onto the sidewalk. I ordered a Buffalo chicken wrap at the café for lunch. At the table next to me, three East Asian kids were having a snack; another table was occupied by a group of Hispanic men.

Harbor Point is as ethnically diverse as Boston itself. Although the one-to-two ratio between subsidized and market units remains, the last twenty-five years have seen changes in the population. The majority of the subsidized residents today are Hispanics, rather than African Americans as in the past; family size has dropped, leading Corcoran Jennison to convert some of the four- and five-bedroom apartments into smaller units. Less than half of the market tenants are white, and there is a large Asian population. There are also more college students sharing apartments, as well as retirees and young professionals.

"We attract out-of-towners who like coming here because of the racial mix," Corcoran told me. In a Yelp review, a University of Massachusetts student from the Bay Area who identified herself as Katy H. wrote that she enjoyed her year living in Harbor

Point: "Lots of residents were students, but in addition to that, there were families, single adults, elderly couples, you name it—they lived here." She added, "If you consider yourself to be close-minded or intolerant of different cultures and people—this is NOT the neighborhood for you."

Most of the Yelp reviewers seemed unaware that many of their neighbors were low-income families. This is not surprising, since the units occupied by subsidized tenants are indistinguishable from the rest, inside and out. But reading between the lines, I sense occasional tensions: complaints about scratched cars, noisy parties, teenagers acting up. This might dismay social activists who imagine mixed-income housing to be some sort of happy melting pot. On the other hand, the market rents that Corcoran Jennison is able to charge (a one-bedroom apartment is currently about $2,400 a month, up from $800 fifteen years ago) and the satisfaction expressed by most of the Yelp reviewers lays to rest skeptics' fears that rich and poor can't live together. At Harbor Point, the two groups share amenities, exercise in the same fitness center, swim in the same pool, shop in the same convenience store, serve as building captains, and deliberate together on the tenants' council. Given the disparity among different income groups today, a degree of social distance would hardly be surprising. But with American society economically polarized as never before, creating an environment in which rich and poor live amicably side by side is no mean accomplishment.

So, what did it take to make Harbor Point a success? A visionary and committed developer + a responsive architect + the active participation of low-income residents + an experienced property-management team. Not a simple formula. But to paraphrase Winston Churchill: It could be said that Harbor Point is the least likely model for public housing, except for all the others that have been tried.

Behind the Façade

Poundbury is "the town that Prince Charles built." Not surprisingly, given his royal highness's vocal campaign against modern architecture, British critics have been merciless in their ridicule of Poundbury's perceived shortcomings. "An embarrassing anachronism as the new century dawns," wrote Hugh Aldersey-Williams in the *New Statesman* in 1999, when the project was still in its infancy. More recently, writing in the *Observer*, Stephen Bayley found Poundbury "fake, heartless, authoritarian and grimly cute," and Andy Spain, blogging on *ArchDaily*, characterized it as "an over sanitised middle-class ghetto that has a whiff of resignation that there is nothing positive to live for so we must retreat to the past." Snide judgments made on the basis of seemingly fleeting visits.

What's the town really like? I spent six days there in September, frequenting its eateries, wandering its streets, and generally trying to experience the place as a resident might. Construction started twenty years ago, and while two decades is a short time in the life of a town, it's long enough for the newness to start to rub off. As I discovered, there is a lot more to Poundbury than meets the modernist critic's jaundiced eye. The place is neither anachronistic nor utopian nor elitist. Nor is it a middle-class ghetto. In fact, Poundbury embodies social, economic, and planning innovations that can only be called radical.

What struck me first was the unusual layout, a rabbit warren of dog-legged streets and crooked lanes, interspersed with many small squares—none of them actually square. Although confusing at first, after a day or two it's easy enough to find one's way around—much like navigating the center of a medieval town. Instead of a main street, shops, cafés, and a pub are scattered here and there. I had a beer at The Poet Laureate, which is named in honor of Ted Hughes. The outdoor tables spill out onto a square dominated by a market hall with fat columns shaped like milk bottles.

This particular village square is part of the first phase of Poundbury's construction, which was completed in 2001. The scale becomes larger and denser in the newer sections, which have rows of terrace houses, small apartment buildings, and office blocks. Poundbury is built on a hill, and the highest spot is occupied by Queen Mother Square, named in honor of the prince's grandmother. The partially complete plaza is lined by four- and five-story office and residential buildings, and will soon have a 120-foot-tall campanile-like tower. But the impression of a small market town is maintained in the higgledy-piggledy street layout and in the resolutely traditional—that is to say, not-modernist—architecture.

The bright blue electric bus that swings by the square, on the other hand, is very modern indeed. POUNDBURY VIA TOWN CENTRE reads its destination board, a reminder that Poundbury is not a stand-alone community—this is not Celebration or Seaside—but an extension of Dorchester, a small county town of 20,000, set among the gently rolling hills of Dorset in southwest England.

For Dorchester residents, Poundbury is a new appendage on the edge of town, but for designers it is a demonstration of Prince Charles's ideas about architecture, which he first detailed in a 1988 BBC documentary, *A Vision of Britain*. That film, which was followed by a book of the same name, came four years after he had delivered the first of his antimodernist broadsides, characterizing a proposed extension to London's National Gallery as a "monstrous carbuncle on the face of a much-loved and elegant friend." In his book, Charles threw down the gauntlet: "We *can* build new developments which echo the familiar, attractive features of our regional vernacular styles," he wrote. "There *are* architects who can design with sensitivity and imagination so that people can live in more pleasant surroundings." Whence Poundbury.

.   .   .

How did the heir apparent become a real estate developer? You can blame Edward III. In the fourteenth century, the king established the Duchy of Cornwall, a land trust to benefit his eldest son, Edward, known as the Black Prince. The king cannily prevented the prince and his successors from touching the capital, and over the centuries the duchy has done well, with a current worth of more than $1 billion. In 1987, Dorchester's local planning authority determined that the only open land that could accommodate the future growth needs of the town was 400 acres belonging to the duchy. Under ordinary circumstances, as it had done in the past, the duchy would have sold the land to be developed in a conventional manner. But because Charles, the twenty-fourth duke of Cornwall, had such an interest in urbanism, with the town's consent, the duchy took a more active role.

In 1988, after several false starts, Charles appointed the urban theorist and planner Léon Krier to prepare a master plan for an "urban village," a dense (fifteen to twenty dwellings per acre, instead of the usual ten to twelve), walkable, sustainable model for suburban development. Following a public consultation process, the local planning authority approved the concept, and five years later construction began.

The work is being carried out by a variety of regional builders working with local and London-based architects, each of whom has been given a restricted number of dwellings in any one contract to promote architectural variety. Peterjohn Smyth was the coordinating architect for the project's first phase, and Ben Pentreath is managing the current phase. Architecturally, there is nothing here that would be out of place in the prewar center of any provincial British town: Brick and stucco boxes with slate or clay-tile roofs and occasional flint panels, a scattering of Georgian and Regency revival townhouses, the occasional larger classical pile, and many buildings that are what one can only call "generic traditional."

The market hall with the milk bottle columns was designed by the prominent classicist John Simpson; the office blocks on Queen Mother Square are the work of Quinlan and Francis Terry; and an Arts & Crafts nursing home is designed by James Gorst. I liked Simpson's market hall; and the Terrys' classical office building, while a little standoffish, has a marvelous cupola. On the other hand, the fire station struck me as particularly heavy-handed; Mey House, designed by Barbara Weiss Architects, is altogether too self-important for an office building; and some of the larger residences veer dangerously close to McMansion territory.

Of course, the last is a relative judgment: The largest house at Poundbury is smaller than the *median* size of new houses in America (2,400 square feet), and an upscale Georgian revival terrace house in Woodlands Crescent squeezes four bedrooms into only 1,400 square feet. This particular crescent of thirty-eight virtually identical houses, designed by Pentreath, merely hints at its eighteenth-century roots and seems to me to strike exactly the right architectural note.

•   •   •

Despite the picturesque street layout, Krier's approach is not simply scenographic: It embodies the theories of the nineteenth-century Viennese architect and planner Camillo Sitte. Sitte believed that the old cities that people admired were not happy accidents but were in fact designed according to principles no less specific than in the other arts. In *Der Städtebau nach seinen künstlerischen Grundsätzen* (1889), translated into English as

The Art of Building Cities, Sitte provided a detailed urban design analysis of streets and squares in old Italian and northern European cities. "Modern city planning completely reverses the proper relationship between built-up area and open space," Sitte wrote. "In former times the open spaces—streets and plazas—were designed to have an enclosed character for a definite effect. Today we normally begin by parcelling out building sites, and whatever is left over is turned into streets and plazas."

Poundbury's Sitte-esqe roots are visible in its compact plan. Only 250 of the 400 acres are to be urbanized; the unbuilt space is concentrated at the edges, a green swathe of playing fields, allotment gardens, and pastures with grazing sheep. Krier has learned another lesson from Sitte: the value of accidental events. "We set up rigid systems, and then grow fearful of deviating from them by as much as a hair's breadth," Sitte wrote, bemoaning that city planning had become a branch of engineering in which formulaic solutions were rigorously applied. For Sitte—and Krier—planning is an art, and in art rules may be broken.

For example, in Poundbury, buildings generally come up to the sidewalk, but some have projecting stoops. Occasionally there are planting beds between the building and the sidewalk; sometimes a narrow garden, occasionally a deep garden. In a few cases, a building projects over the sidewalk to form an arcade. Simon Conibear, Poundbury's development manager, characterized Krier's planning to me as "80 percent harmony and 20 percent discord."

In Poundbury, the layout of the buildings predetermines the road pattern, not vice versa. Roads are merely a way of getting around, not an armature within which buildings must tightly fit, as is the case with most planned communities. The first time I heard Krier lecture, many years ago, he talked mainly about parking. Krier's point was that whereas the principles of sound urban design were all known long ago—and did not need to be reinvented—the great challenge for the modern city planner was how to accommodate the automobile.

This is as true in Britain as elsewhere: More than 77 percent of households currently own at least one car, and the ownership rate continues to increase. Krier's solution is not to banish cars to the periphery or to separate them from pedestrians. In Poundbury, automobiles are everywhere: The interiors of the blocks have parking courts with open-air stalls, car ports, and garages; there is parallel and head-in street parking, and some of the apartment buildings integrate on-grade protected parking. But it didn't feel as if the cars had taken over. For example, although several cars were parked in front of The Poet Laureate, the little square didn't resemble a parking lot. There were no white lines, no signage—people parked willy-nilly, where they wanted. On Saturday night the square was full of cars, but on Monday morning it turned back into an empty plaza.

Poundbury may not have a "pedestrian zone," but in a real sense the entire town is a pedestrian zone. It's up to the drivers to adjust to the built realm, not vice versa, for Poundbury calms traffic with a vengeance. In fact, there have yet to be any accidents, Conibear told me. "The street layout is deliberately chaotic," he said. "There are blind bends, no signage, not even stop signs. We also use the 'seventy-meter event' rule—that is, every seventy meters something happens to slow the cars down."

•   •   •

Poundbury is less than half-finished, with a current population of about 2,000 residents. Forty percent are retirees, typical for this area since southwest England is Britain's Arizona. Flats and small houses sell for £100,000 to £200,000 ($160,000 to $320,000), while large freestanding houses command in excess of £500,000 ($800,000). These are high prices in a region where the median gross annual pay is £25,000 ($40,000).

Yet Poundbury is not a middle-class ghetto: more than a third of the dwellings qualify as affordable housing. The majority is social housing, owned by charitable trusts and rented to low-income tenants, but there is also shared-equity housing, which allows qualifying buyers to purchase a share in a home, even if they cannot afford a mortgage on the full market value. What is unusual in Poundbury is that the affordable housing is "pepper potted"—that is, scattered, and it is similar in appearance to its neighbors. It's hard to get a complete picture of how well this works during a brief visit, although by all accounts, there is little social mixing between the two groups.

Another innovation at Poundbury is the embrace of mixed use, which is more extensive here than in most planned communities I've visited. Not only are the ground floors of many residential and office buildings devoted to commercial uses such as shops and cafés, there are medical clinics, professional offices for lawyers and accountants, garden centers, veterinarians, travel agents, and even a funeral home. There is also light industry: a large shed-like building at the bottom of a village green is a chocolate factory; a breakfast cereal manufacturing plant stands across the street from elegant townhouses; a low brick building with arched windows was until recently occupied by an electronics factory. The key to introducing industrial buildings on residential streets, says Conibear, is to make sure that they are built before the housing; residents accept a fait accompli, but they strongly resist the introduction of nonresidential uses after the fact. In all, Poundbury currently has an impressive 136 businesses generating 1,600 jobs—nearly one per resident.

·　　·　　·

I asked my landlady what her neighbors thought about Poundbury. "Not everyone likes it," she said. "Some people think it looks like a movie set." Although Poundbury is a commercial project—the duchy is emphatically not a charity—the execution is of high quality: tight graphic control over signage, crunchy pea gravel instead of expanses of bare asphalt, granite blocks not paint stripes to denote parking stalls. Walking about town, I am also struck by what is missing: intrusive commercial signs, gimcrack construction, and the plastic vulgarity that pervades even the historic center of Dorchester. I suppose to some that makes it a movie set. But the allusion is surely also prompted by the revivalist styles of the architecture, the very thing that sets off the critics.

In an article in *Building Design* in which he excoriated the traditional appearance of the architecture, Crispin Kelly asked: "If Poundbury's 1759 date stamp is not to our taste, do we have better pattern books of our own to promote to the punters . . . ?" I think the date stamp is more like 1940, but it's a good question. What would be a modernist pattern book?

The stylistic free-for-all that has produced Dubai and Doha is surely not the answer. On the strength of 1920s-era neighborhoods I've seen in Oslo and Tel Aviv, I can almost imagine an International Style–revival Poundbury, although, as Los Angeles's Getty Center decisively shows, white walls and pipe railings only get you so far. Individual modernist buildings have always looked good in the natural landscape—Fallingwater, the Glass House, the Sydney Opera House—or when surrounded by traditional buildings—think of Paris's Pompidou Centre, Lloyd's of London, the Bilbao Guggenheim Museum. But modernism has been notably deficient in creating an urban fabric. The modernist palette is simply too restricted—or perhaps not restricted enough. There is either too much repetition or too much variety, too much standardization or too little.

It seems to me that Poundbury could quite happily absorb a wider stylistic range, although neither Krier nor any of the architects I spoke to mentioned this possibility. But for the moment the imposition of an architectural code that favors tradition is understandable. The reason for "leaning on the past" is not nostalgia or lack of imagination but rather the recognition that the established vernacular offers the best chance for creating the nuanced variety and shadings of difference that produce a coherent urban environment and a recognizable sense of place.

Harper's Magazine

FINALIST—ESSAYS AND
CRITICISM

"Brave, powerful, painfully honest," said the National Magazine Award judges about "Sliver of Sky," Barry Lopez's account of the sexual abuse he suffered as a boy. "Eschewing self-pity or sentimentality," the judges continued, "Lopez describes how these experiences marked his life and how he finally made an uneasy peace with his past." Well known to readers for his essays, short stories, and books, Lopez has been described as "arguably the nation's premier nature writer" by the San Francisco Chronicle. His book Arctic Dreams: Imagination and Desire in a Northern Landscape won the National Book Award in 1986. Founded in 1850, Harper's is the oldest general-interest magazine in the country. It has won twenty-one National Magazine Awards, including awards in recent years for fiction, photography, and reporting.

Barry Lopez

Sliver of Sky

One day in the fall of 1938, a man named Harry Shier entered the operating room of a Toronto hospital and began an appendectomy procedure on a prepubescent boy. He was not a trained surgeon; he nearly botched the operation, and the boy's parents reacted angrily. Suspicions about Shier's medical credentials had already surfaced among operating-room nurses, and the hospital, aware of other complaints related to Shier's groin-area operations on young boys, opened a formal investigation. By the time the hospital board determined that both his medical degree, from a European university, and his European letters of reference were fraudulent, Harry Shier had departed for the United States.

A few years later, a police officer in Denver caught Shier raping a boy in the front seat of his automobile. Shier spent a year in prison and then slipped out of Colorado. In the late 1940s, he surfaced in North Hollywood, California, as the director of a sanitarium where he supervised the treatment of people with addictions, primarily alcoholics. In the summer of 1952, at the age of seven, I was introduced to him when I visited the sanitarium with my mother.

At the time, I lived with her and my younger brother in nearby Reseda, a town in the San Fernando Valley. My parents had recently divorced, and my father had moved across the country to Florida. To support the three of us, my mother had taken a day job teaching home economics at a junior high school in the city of San Fernando and also a job teaching dressmaking two evenings a week at Pierce Junior College in Woodland Hills, on the far western edge of the Valley.

Early that summer, my mother had somewhat reluctantly agreed to take in a houseguest, her first cousin Evelyn Carrothers. Evelyn, who was my mother's age, lived an hour away in Long Beach and was struggling with a drinking problem. Her marriage was also in trouble. Mother couldn't accommodate Evelyn for long in our one-bedroom house, so she began inquiring among her friends about other arrangements. People advised her to call Alcoholics Anonymous. Someone in the organization's Los Angeles office suggested that she contact the North Hollywood Lodge and Sanitarium.

One morning, Mother drove us all to the facility at 12003 Riverside Drive, known then around the Valley, I would later learn, as "Shier's dryer." In those years, Shier was renowned as someone who could "cure" alcoholism. He was also able to relate sympathetically to the families of alcoholics. When we arrived at the clinic, Mother introduced my four-year-old brother and me to "Dr." Shier. We shook hands with him, and he escorted the two of us to the sanitarium's kitchen, where we each selected a fresh doughnut from an array laid out on trays for the patients— frosted, sugared, glazed, covered with sprinkles. A nice man. I remember the building's corridors reeked that morning of something other than disinfectant. Paraldehyde, I was later informed, which Shier used liberally to sedate his patients.

Shortly after Evelyn had, in Shier's estimation, recovered enough to return to Long Beach—she would begin drinking again and, a year later, would return to his facility—he started dropping by our home in Reseda. He had gotten to know something of Mother's marital and financial situation from Evelyn, and during one of his early visits he told Mother that he was concerned: her income was not, in his view, commensurate with her capabilities. He said he might be able to do something about that. (Mother's divorce settlement required my father to send her ten dollars a month in child support—an obligation he rarely met, according to correspondence I would later find.) Shier said that one of his former patients was in a position to speak with the school board about Mother's value to the school system. This appeal was apparently made, and a short while later she received a small increase in salary.

She was grateful. Harry was pleased to help. Shier conducted himself around Mother like someone considering serious courtship. She was a handsome woman of thirty-nine, he a short, abrasively self-confident, balding man of fifty-six. He complimented her on the way she was single-handedly raising her two polite, neatly dressed sons. He complimented her on her figure. Occasionally he'd take her hand or caress her lightly on the shoulder. After a while, Shier began dropping by the house in the evening, just as my brother and I were getting into our pajamas. He'd bring a tub of ice cream along, and the four of us would have dessert together. One evening he arrived without the ice cream. He'd forgotten. He suggested I accompany him to the grocery store, where I could pick out a different dessert for each of us.

A few minutes after we left the house, he pulled his car up alongside a tall hedge on an unlit residential street off Lindley Avenue. He turned me to the side, put me facedown on the seat, pulled down my pajama bottoms, and pushed his erect penis into my anus. As he built toward his climax he told me, calmly but emphatically, that he was a doctor, that I needed treatment, and that we were not going to be adding to Mother's worries by telling her about my problem.

.   .   .

Shier followed this pattern of sexual assault with me for almost four years. He came by the house several times a month and continued to successfully direct Mother's attention away from what he was doing. It is hard to imagine, now, that no one suspected what was going on. It is equally difficult, even for therapists, to explain how this type of sexual violence can be perpetuated between two human beings for years without the victim successfully objecting. Why, people wonder, does the evidence for a child's resistance in these circumstances usually seem so meager? I believe it's because the child is too innocent to plan effectively and because, from the very start, the child faces a labyrinth of confused allegiances. I asked myself questions I couldn't answer: Do I actually need protection in this situation? From what, precisely? I was bewildered by what was happening. How could I explain to my mother what I was doing? Physical resistance, of course, is virtually impossible for most children. The child's alternatives, as I understand them, never get much beyond endurance and avoidance—and speculation about how to encourage intervention.

An additional source of confusion for me was the belief that I had been chosen as a special patient by Harry Shier, an esteemed doctor and the director of a prestigious institution. A weird sense of privilege was attached to Shier's interest in me, and to the existence of an unspecified medical condition too serious or exotic to share with Mother. Also, being the elder son in a lower-middle-class and fatherless family, I came to feel—or he encouraged me to feel—that I was shouldering an important responsibility for my family.

I understood that I was helping my family, and he complimented me on my maturity.

·   ·   ·

When Shier came to our house he would inform Mother that we were just going out to get some ice cream together or, on a Saturday afternoon, that he was going to take me to an early movie, and then maybe out to dinner at the Sportsmen's Lodge on Ventura Boulevard in Studio City. We would say goodbye and he would walk me to his car and we would drive off. If it was dark, he'd pull over soon in a secluded spot and rape me in the front seat; or we'd go to the movie and he'd force my head into his lap for a while, pushing at me through his trousers; or it would be dinner at the restaurant, where we'd hook our trout in a small pool for the chef to cook, and then he'd drive on to the sanitarium, where he'd park behind the single-story building. He'd direct me up an outside staircase to a series of rotting duckboards that led across the clinic's flat roof to a locked door, the outside entrance to a rooftop apartment, where I was to wait. He'd enter the front of the building, check on his patients, say good night to the nurses, and ascend an inside staircase to reach the interior door of his studio-size quarters. I'd see the lights go on inside. A moment later he'd open the door to the roof and pull me in.

One night in these chambers, after he was through with me, he took a medical text from a bookshelf. He sat me down beside him on the edge of the bed and showed me black-and-white photographs of men's genitals ravaged by syphilis. This, he said, was what came from physical intimacy with women.

In bed with him, I would try to maneuver myself so I could focus on the horizontal sliver of sky visible between the lower edge of the drawn blinds and the white sill of the partially open window. Passing clouds, a bird, the stars.

From time to time, often on the drive back to my home, Shier would remind me that if I were ever to tell anyone, if the treatments were to stop, he would have no choice but to have me committed to an institution. And then, if I were no longer around for my family . . . I'd seen how he occasionally slipped Mother a few folded bills in my presence. It would be best, I thought, if I just continued to be the brave boy he said I was.

I know the questions I initially asked myself afterward about these events were not very sophisticated. For example: Why hadn't Shier also molested my younger brother? My brother, I conjectured, had been too young in 1952, only four years old; later, with one brother firmly in hand, Shier had probably considered pursuing the other too much of a risk. (When we were older, my brother told me that Shier had molested him, several times, in the mid-1950s. I went numb with grief. After the four years of sexual violence with Shier were over, what sense of self-worth I still retained rested mainly with a conviction that, however I might have debased myself with Shier, I had at least protected my brother—and also probably saved my family from significant financial hardship. Further shame would come after I discovered that our family had never been in serious financial danger, that Mother's earnings had covered our every necessity, and more.)

.   .   .

My mother remarried in 1956. We moved to New York City, where my stepfather lived, and I never again saw the malachite-green-and-cream-colored Pontiac Chieftain pulling up in front of our house on Calvert Street. After we moved into my stepfather's apartment, I felt a great sense of freedom. I was so very far away now from Harry Shier. A new school, a new neighborhood, new friends. I had surfaced in another ocean. This discovery of fresh opportunity, however, which sometimes gave way to palpable euphoria, I nevertheless experienced as unreliable. I couldn't keep a hold on it. And then, two years after we moved east, when I was thirteen, Harry Shier flew into New York and my sense of safety collapsed. He arrived with my stepfather at our vacation home on the Jersey Shore one summer evening in 1958. He was my parents' guest for the weekend. A surprise for the boys.

Weren't we pleased?

The next morning, a Saturday, while my parents were preparing breakfast in the kitchen, Shier eased open the door of my attic bedroom and closed it quietly behind him. He walked wordlessly to the edge of my bed, his lips twitching in a characteristic pucker, his eyes fixed on mine. When he reached under the sheet

I kicked at him and sprang from the bed, grabbing a baseball bat that was leaning against the headboard. Naked, cursing, swinging at him with the bat, I drove him from the room and slammed the door.

While I dressed, he began a conversation downstairs with my parents.

Eavesdropping on them from the hallway next to the kitchen door, I heard Shier explain that I needed to be committed. He described—in grave tones, which gave his voice a kind of Delphic weight—how I was prone to delusions, a dangerous, potentially violent boy. Trouble ahead. Through the hinge gap in the doorway, I studied my mother and stepfather seated with him at the breakfast table. Their hands were folded squarely on the oilcloth. They took in Shier's measured, professional characterization with consternation and grief. In that moment, I couldn't bring myself to describe for them what he had done. The thought of the change it would bring to our lives was overwhelming, and, regardless, my own situation felt far too precarious. Having abruptly gained the security of a family with a devoted father, I could now abruptly lose it.

I left the house without delay, to play pickup baseball with my friends. In the afternoon I rode off alone on my bicycle to the next town inland. When I returned that evening, I learned that Shier had asked my stepfather to drive him straight back to New York that morning so that he could catch a plane west from Idlewild. I had insulted the doctor, my mother told me, and embarrassed the family. She presented his analysis of my behavior. When I tried to object, her response was, "But he's a *doctor!*"

Shier, she said, would confer with her and my stepfather in a few days by telephone, about accommodations for me in Los Angeles.

I was not, finally, sent to California, though the reason for this was never discussed with me. If my parents harbored any misgivings about Shier, I didn't hear them. I studied hard, came home on time, did my chores: I continued to behave as a dutiful son, a boy neither parent would willingly give up.

The trauma stayed with me, however, and in the spring of 1962, when I was seventeen, I gave in to a state of depression. I had become confused about my sexual identity and was haunted by a sense of contamination, a feeling that I had been rendered worthless as a man because of what I had done.

When I was immobilized in the elaborate web of Shier's appetites and undone by his ploys to ensure his own safety, I had assumed I was the only boy he was involved with. It was the sudden realization that there might have been—probably were—others and that he might still be raping boys in California that compelled me to break my silence and risk, I believed, disastrous humiliation. I phoned my stepfather at his office. He agreed to meet me in the lobby of the New York Athletic Club on Central Park South, where I thought he would feel comfortable.

He strode impatiently into his club that afternoon and took a seat opposite me in one of the lobby's large leather chairs. He was a busy man, but he was prepared to listen. I gave him a brief account of Shier's behavior and of my history with him, and I made two requests of him. First, that he never tell anyone what had happened; if he ever came to believe that Mother had to know, he was to let *me* tell her. Second, that he help me stop Shier. He listened with rising interest and increasing ire. He was especially angry, I later realized, at the idea that he had been duped by Shier that summer in New Jersey.

Early the next morning, he took a plane to Los Angeles, and late that same afternoon he met with two LAPD detectives. When he returned to New York three days later, my stepfather told me that the detectives he'd spoken with were going to scrutinize everything—the North Hollywood Lodge and Sanitarium, Shier's criminal record, his network of acquaintances. They were going to gather all the evidence. I only needed to be patient. The detectives would contact us.

That week gave way to another. My stepfather waved off my anxious inquiries. He was in touch with the detectives, he said. They were working on it. When I finally confronted him, he admitted that, in consultation with the detectives, he had decided it would be too great an undertaking for me to go up against such a clever deviant, to endure cross-examination in a trial. So he was choosing not to press charges. Besides, he said, Shier had bolted as soon as he had suspected an investigation was under way.

A week or so later, my stepfather told me that he had just heard from the LAPD detectives that Harry Shier had been killed—an automobile accident in Arizona. This was, I now believe, my stepfather's preemptive effort to force closure.

·   ·   ·

In 2003, forty-one years after these conversations with my stepfather and some years into my own effort to comprehend the psychological effects of what had happened to me, I phoned the LAPD. An officer there, an intermediary, was able to locate one of the two long-retired detectives who had begun the investigation of Shier in 1962. The detective did not want to speak with me directly, but he authorized the intermediary to pass on his recollections. (Because this information is at best thirdhand, I cannot be certain about either the dates or the circumstances surrounding Shier's early criminal history. The police department's official records of the case, including the detectives' notes from their conversations with my stepfather, were destroyed, along with other inactive records from that time.) The officer informed me about the botched operations at the hospital in Toronto and the sodomy charge in Colorado, gave me the approximate dates, and confirmed that the investigation had ended soon after it began because Shier had fled the state. The detective also recalled that Shier might have been killed shortly after he left California, possibly in South America, but he could not remember precisely.

In 1989, years before this conversation with the LAPD officer took place, I interviewed Evelyn Carrothers at her home in Studio City about her experiences with Shier. She said that "behind a façade of solicitous concern," Shier was a "mean man." A bully. She had never liked him, she said, but he had been very successful treating alcoholics in the Los Angeles area in the 1950s, and she herself had referred many people to him over the years. At the time I spoke with her, Evelyn had not only been sober a long while but had become a prominent member of Alcoholics Anonymous in southern California. She was upset, I thought, by my revelation that Shier was a pedophile, but she wouldn't give me the names of anyone who might have known him. She said she never knew what became of him, but she was sure he was dead. She even argued a case for Shier: Whatever wrong he might have done in his private life, he had been of great value to the larger community.

I've never been able to comprehend Evelyn's sense of the larger good, though her point of view is a position people commonly take when confronted with evidence of sexual crimes committed by people they respect. (A reputation for valued service and magnanimous gestures often forms part of the protective cover pedophiles create.)

A more obvious question I asked myself as I grew older was: How could my mother not have known? Perhaps she did, although she died, a few years after she was told, unwilling to discuss her feelings about what had gone on in California. I've made some measure of peace with her stance. When certain individuals feel severely threatened—emotionally, financially, physically— the lights on the horizon they use to orient themselves in the world might easily wink out. Life can then become a series of fear-driven decisions and compulsive acts of self-protection. People start to separate what is deeply troubling in their lives from what they see as good. To use the usual metaphor, they isolate the events from one another by storing them in different rooms in a large hotel. While these rooms share a corridor, they do not communicate directly with one another.

I'm not able, today, to put the image I have of my mother as her children's attentive guardian together with the idea of her as an innocent, a person blinded by the blandishments of a persistent pedophile. But for whatever reason, she was not able, back then, to consider what might be happening in the hours after she saw Shier drive away, her son's head, from her point of view on the porch, not quite clearing the sill of the car window as the two of them departed.

In June 1970, my stepfather related to my mother, without my knowledge, a distorted and incomplete version of what her friend Harry Shier had done, breaking the promise he had made to me that day eight years before when I'd spoken to him. They were having lunch together in Midtown Manhattan; she became hysterical and was taken from the restaurant by ambulance to a hospital. When she called me that evening, all she could bring herself to say, in a voice resigned and defeated, was, "I know what happened. I know what happened to you."

And then she never spoke of it again.

Six years later, in July 1976, as my mother was dying of lung cancer. I asked her whether she wanted to speak to me about California. She lay on her bed in a private room at Manhattan's Lenox Hill Hospital, rocking her head slowly back and forth like a metronome. Her face averted, she wept silently while I sat mute in a chair by the bed. She would not take my hand.

Some of the pathways of a debilitating sexual history are simply destined never to be mapped.

· · ·

The reasons monstrously abusive relationships persist between people are as complex, I think, as the mathematics of turbulence. The explanation I gave myself for decades, partly to avoid having to address any question of my own complicity, was that I had done this in order to keep our family safe and intact. After my father abandoned us, my mother told me that I would now be the man of the house. I took her remark literally. I began to double-check the locks on the doors at night. I mowed and weeded the lawn and took the trash out to the incinerator in the back yard to burn. I got the day's mail from the box on the street. Whenever Shier showed up at the door, I would bear down on myself: Just see the business with Shier through, I said to myself. Maybe another man, one of the more likable men Mother dated, would come and stay with us. And this one wouldn't walk out. Standing in the shower in Shier's filthy apartment, washing the blood and semen off my legs, I hammered this thought into my mind: You cannot quit.

I bottled the anger. I hid the blood. I adamantly focused anywhere else.

.   .   .

What my stepfather actually did when he went to California in 1962, and how he presented Shier's crimes to the detectives, I will never know. And though I know he saw Evelyn at that time, I don't know what he discussed with her. Over the years, right up to his death, whenever I asked him about what he'd done, he became evasive. In an effort to seem sincere, he would occasionally recall a forgotten detail from one of his conversations with the detectives. This additional fact would sometimes shift my basic understanding of the longer story he had already told, raising new questions. Or, alternatively, trying to demonstrate compassion, he might suddenly recall a fact meant to soothe me but that made no sense. He told me once, for example, that during his 1962 visit Evelyn had taken him to see Shier's grave at the Forest Lawn Memorial-Park in Glendale—several weeks before Shier was supposedly killed in an out-of-state automobile accident.

My stepfather, a recovering alcoholic, became, like Evelyn, a regionally prominent figure in Alcoholics Anonymous in the late 1960s. Whenever I inquired, in those early weeks of the investigation, about what sort of progress the detectives were making, he would find a way to mention how many alcoholics Shier had helped. Alcoholism, he said, was a "terrible disease," a more pervasive and serious issue, he wanted me to understand, than pedophilia. He suggested I would benefit from a slightly different perspective on all this. Shier, he conceded, was an awful man—but he had done a lot of good. I should consider, instead, how well I was doing. At seventeen I was student-body president at my Jesuit prep school. I had the highest academic average in my class senior year; I was lettering in two sports; I was escorting debutantes to balls at the Plaza, the Sherry-Netherland, the Pierre. Whatever might have occurred in California, he said, things had actually worked out all right. I should let it go.

For thirty years this was exactly the path I chose. Silence. I believed that in spite of Shier's brutalizations I could develop a stable, productive life, that I could simply walk away from everything that had happened.

.   .   .

The conclusion I eventually reached about my stepfather's refusal to pursue charges against Shier was that he did not want the family to be embarrassed by a trial. He was unable to understand that the decision to face cross-examination in a courtroom was not his to make. He could not appreciate that the opportunity to stand up in a public forum and describe, with Shier present, what he had done, and what he had forced me to do, was as important to me as any form of legal justice. Not to be allowed to speak or, worse, to have someone else relate my story and write its ending was to extend the original, infuriating experience of helplessness, to underscore the humiliation of being powerless. My stepfather's ultimate dismissal of my request for help was an instance, chilling for me, of an observation that victims of child molestation often make: If you tell them, they won't believe you. Believing you entails too much disruption.

From what I have read over the years in newspapers and magazines about scandals involving serial pedophiles, I have gathered that people seem to think that what victims most desire in the way of retribution is money and justice, apparently in that order. My own guess would be that what they most want is something quite different: they want to be believed, to have a foundation on which they can rebuild a sense of dignity. Reclaiming self-respect is more important than winning money, more important than exacting vengeance.

Victims do not want someone else's public wrath, the umbrage of an attorney or an editorial writer or a politician, to stand in for the articulation of their own anger. When a pedophile is exposed by a grand-jury indictment today, the tenor of public indignation often seems ephemeral to me, a response generated by "civic" emotion. Considering the number of children who continue to be abused in America—something like one in seven boys and one in three girls—these expressions of condemnation seem naïve. Without a deeper commitment to vigilance, society's outrage begins to take on the look of another broken promise.

. . .

Up until the time I interviewed Evelyn in the late 1980s, I had grown to more or less accept my stepfather's views about what had happened in California—which was, of course, my own form of denial. Whatever had been done to me, I held to the belief that things had actually turned out fairly well. By the time I was forty I had experienced some national success as a writer. I was friends with a large, if geographically scattered, group of people. And I was living happily in a rural, forested area in western Oregon with my wife of twenty years. Significantly, since I had moved to this mountainous place in 1970, the emotional attachment I felt to my home had become essential to any ongoing sense of well-being I had. My almost daily contact there with wild animals, the physical separation of the house from the homes of my neighbors, the flow of a large white-water river past the property, the undo-mesticated land unfolding for miles around, the rawness of the weather at the back door—all of it fed a feeling of security.

During the years of "traumatic sexual abuse," the term psychologists use for serial sexual abuse, the deepest and sometimes only relief I had was when I was confronted with the local, elementary forces of nature: hot Santa Ana winds blowing west into the San Fernando Valley from the Mojave Desert; Pacific storm surf crashing at Zuma and the other beaches west of Malibu; winter floods inundating our neighborhood when Caballero Creek breached its banks on its way to the Los Angeles River. I took from each of these encounters a sense of what it might feel like to become fully alive. When I gazed up beneath a flock of homing birds or listened as big winds swirled the dry leaves of eucalyptus trees or sat alone somewhere in a rarely traversed part of the Santa Monica Mountains, waiting for a glimpse of a coyote or a brush rabbit, I would feel exhilaration. Encouragement.

But deep inside, I knew things remained awry. (It is relatively easy today—it wasn't then—to find pertinent and explicit information about childhood sexual trauma. How one interprets that information or chooses to act on it remains a perilous second step.) I could not, for example, shake the old thought that by not having acted sooner I was somehow responsible for what happened to other boys after I left California. According to my stepfather, one of the investigating detectives said I had been lucky to walk away in 1956. Continuing their investigation after Shier disappeared, my stepfather told me, the detectives had located three other boys, "none of whom had fared well." The detectives' advice to my stepfather had been that neither he nor I should inquire further into what Harry Shier had been doing with young boys during his years in North Hollywood.

When I began a deliberate inquiry into my past, starting in 1989, I thought of myself as a man walking around with shrapnel sealed in his flesh, and I wanted to get the fragments out. The doubts and images I had put aside for years were now starting to fester. I felt more or less continually seasick, confronting every day a harrowing absence within myself. I imagined it as a mine shaft of bleak, empty space, which neither the love of a spouse nor the companionship of friends nor professional success could efface. The thought began to work on me that a single, bold step, however, some sort of confrontation with the past, might sufficiently jar this frame of mind and change it. I could, I thought, dramatically cure myself in this way.

I phoned Forest Lawn Memorial-Park. No, there was no Harry Shier buried in any of their cemeteries. I couldn't find an obituary for him in any of the southern California papers either. I called Evelyn and asked whether I could come to California and interview her. I would begin my healing, my ablution, by speaking with someone who had known him well. And on that same trip, I decided, I'd drive the rental car to 12003 Riverside Drive in North Hollywood. If the sanitarium was still there, I'd walk through the front door.

·　　·　　·

Shier's rooftop apartment, nearly hidden behind the branches of several Norfolk Island pines, remained just visible from the sidewalk. I parked in the shade of a pepper tree on Ben Street and walked through the main entrance of the white stucco building, which now housed a private secondary school, a yeshiva. No one took any notice of me standing in the foyer. If someone had come up to inquire about my business, I was prepared to say that I had been a patient in this place thirty years earlier, when it had been a hospital. But I seemed to be invisible.

I walked down the main corridor. In rooms to my right, where I'd once seen the bedridden lying in dim shadow, lights now blazed. Attentive students sat at desks, avidly scribbling while someone lectured. I arrived at an intersection and suddenly found myself staring at the foot of an interior staircase. The door to the stairs, slightly ajar, revealed steps winding upward to the left. My throat clenched like a fist in my neck.

I left the building as soon as I was able to turn around. I ran across Riverside Drive into an outdoor nursery with a fence around it. I went down a pea-gravel path, past potted camellias and olean-ders, past blooming primroses and azaleas. After a few minutes, breathing easily once more, the rigidity gone out of my back mus-cles, I crossed back to where I'd parked the car and drove away.

Later that afternoon, at the Central Library on West Fifth Street in downtown Los Angeles, I gathered several San Fernando Valley phone books from the 1950s, trying to remember the names of my mother's friends, guessing at the spellings—Emery, Falotico, Ling, Murray—hoping to dislodge a memory, to find a thread to follow. When my right index finger came to Shier's name, it halted there below the stark typeface. My bowels burst into my trousers.

In the men's room, I threw my undershorts into a waste bin and washed my pants in the sink, trying to keep the wet spot small. I was in my stocking feet, putting my pants back on, when a guard entered abruptly and stood alert and suspicious in the doorway. He informed me that the library was closing. I'll be only another moment, I assured him.

A few minutes later, shielding the wet seat of my pants with my briefcase, I met a friend for dinner nearby. When the maître d' asked whether we preferred eating outdoors or in, I suggested we sit outside. I didn't tell my friend where I'd been that day.

Over the years, I'd spoken to very few people about Shier—my brother, serious girlfriends, my wife, a few close friends. I didn't feel any need to be heard, and the chance of being misunderstood, of being taken for no more than the innocent victim, long ago, of a criminal's heinous acts seemed great. Pity, I thought, would take things in the wrong direction for me. What I wanted to know now was: *What happened to me?*

·   ·   ·

In the months following my visit to the building on Riverside, I placed an occasional call to state and county agencies in California, trying to track down some of the details that might have framed my story. Doing this, I came to suspect that I was missing the memory of certain events. I could recall many scenes from my childhood in the Valley, even remember some vividly, but I also became aware of gaps in that period of time from which nothing surfaced.

In the fall of 1996, I visited a therapist for the first time. I'd briefly seen a psychiatrist when I was in college, but we were not able to get anywhere. Years later, I understood it was because I hadn't been capable at the time of doing the required work. My expectation was that she would somehow simply fix me, get me over the anxiety, over the humiliation.

I chose therapy because my own efforts to clarify my past seemed dramatically unproductive, and because I was now, once again, of a mind that something was wrong with me. I had begun to recognize patterns in my behavior. If I sensed, for example, that I was being manipulated by someone, or disrespected, I quickly became furious out of all proportion. And I'd freeze sometimes when faced with a serious threat instead of calmly moving toward some sort of resolution. I suspected that these habits—no great insight—were rooted in my childhood experience.

Also, a persistent, anxiety-induced muscular tension across my shoulders had by now become so severe that I'd ruptured a cervical disc. When a regimen of steroids brought only limited relief, my doctor recommended surgery. After a second doctor said I had no option but surgery, I reluctantly agreed—until the surgical procedure was drawn up for me on a piece of paper: I'd be placed facedown and unconscious on an operating table, and a one-inch vertical slit would be opened in the nape of my neck. I said no, absolutely not. I'd live with the pain.

From the beginning, the therapist encouraged me to move at my own pace through the memories I was able to retrieve, and to resist the urge to fit any of these events into a pattern. I remember him saying in one of our first sessions, with regard to my apparent inability to protect myself in complex emotional situations such as my stepfather's betrayal, that I did "not even understand the concept of self-protection." I resented the statement. It made me feel stupid—but it also seemed like a start.

We worked together for four years. I described for him the particulars of the abuse: the sandpaper burn of Shier's evening stubble on my skin; his antic chihuahua, which defecated on the floor of the apartment and raced around on the bed when we were in it; Shier's tongue jammed into my mouth. I described the time he forced me to perform fellatio in my home while my mother and brother were away. Shier lay back on Mother's sleeping couch, self-absorbed, palming my head like a melon, supremely at ease. I told the therapist about my inability to break off the relationship with Shier and about my mother's apparent intention to look the other way.

At the start of therapy, I speculated that the real horror of those years would prove to be the actual acts of abuse—my choking on his semen, the towel forced over my face to silence me, the rectal bleeding. After a while, I began to see that the horror was more elusive, that it included more than just betrayals and denials and being yanked around in Shier's bed like a rag doll. The enduring horror was that I had learned to accommodate brutalization. This part of the experience remained with me long after I walked out of Shier's apartment for the last time.

Caught up in someone else's psychosis, overmatched at every turn, I had concentrated on only one thing: survival. To survive I needed to placate. My response to emotional confrontation in the years following that time, I came to see, was almost always to acquiesce or to overreact angrily, with no option in between. Therapy led me to comprehend that I had not, as I wanted to believe, been able to tough out the trauma. I had succumbed, and others besides me had experienced the consequences of my attempt to endure. I had ahead of me now a chance to do better, to be a person less given to anger.

I visited the therapist twice a week to start with, occasionally for double sessions; then it was once a week or less frequently until we decided we'd come to a resting place. In our final sessions, I fitted the pieces of my story together differently, creating "another narrative," as therapists are wont to say, of the early years in California, a broader context for the physical and emotional damage. After that, long-term sexual abuse no longer organized the meaning of my life as it had during the years I believed that I'd simply walked away from it.

One night in 1998, driving from the town where I had been seeing the therapist forty miles upriver to my home, I suddenly felt flooded with relief. The sensation was so strong I pulled over and got out of the truck. I walked to the edge of what I knew to be an unfenced, cultivated field. At first I thought I was experiencing physical relief, the breakdown of the last bit of tension in my upper back, which, after many weeks of physical therapy, no longer required surgery. But it was something else. A stony, overbearing presence I'd been fearful of nearly all my life wasn't there anymore. I stood in the dark by the side of the road for a long while, savoring the reprieve, the sudden disappearance of this tyranny. I recalled a dream I'd had midway through my therapy. I burst through a heavy cellar door and surprised an ogre devouring the entrails of a gutted infant, alive but impassive in the grip of his hand. The ogre was enraged at being discovered. What seemed significant was that I had broken down the door. It didn't matter whether it was the door into something or the door out.

Therapy's success for me was not so much my coming to understand that I had learned as a child to tolerate acts of abuse. It was discovering a greater capacity within myself to empathize with another person's nightmare. Most of the unresolved fear and anger I once held on to has now metamorphosed into compassion, an understanding of the predicaments nearly everyone encounters, at some level, at some time, in their lives.

·   ·   ·

A commonplace about trauma, one buried deep in the psyches of American men, is that it is noble to heal alone. What I've learned in recent years, however, is that this choice sometimes becomes a path to further isolation and trouble, especially for the family and friends of the one who has been wounded. I took exactly this path, intending to bother no one with my determined effort to recalibrate my life. It took a long while for me to understand that a crucial component of recovery from trauma is learning to comprehend and accept the embrace of someone who has no specific knowledge of what happened to you, who is disinterested.

We need others to bring us back into the comity of human life. This appears to have been the final lesson for me—to appreciate someone's embrace not as forgiveness or as an amicable judgment but as an acknowledgment that, from time to time, private life becomes brutally hard for every one of us, and that without one another, without some sort of community, the nightmare is prone to lurk, waiting for an opening.

I'm not interested any longer in tracking down the details of Harry Shier's death, or in wondering how, if it is still there, I might reenter his apartment above the building on Riverside Drive to gaze out at the sky through the corner window. I'm on the alert, now, though, for an often innocuous moment, the one in which an adult man begins to show an unusual interest in the welfare of someone's young son—especially if it's my grandson. He still, at the age of nine, reaches out for my hand when we start to cross a dangerous street.

Time

WINNER—PUBLIC
INTEREST

There was little surprise this year when Time *won the National Magazine Award for Public Interest for Steven Brill's "Bitter Pill," a 24,000-word piece that clearly explains the inordinately complicated business that is American health care. The reporting is thorough, even obsessive; the analysis, both dispassionate and damning; the sympathy for health-care consumers suffering financial distress, strongly felt yet never disabling. Brill was the founder of* American Lawyer—*which won four National Magazine Awards while he was editor in chief—and later CourtTV and Journalism Online, a company that helps publications charge for content.* Time *won the National Magazine Awards for Public Interest in 1999 and 2001, when Walter Isaacson was editor, and Magazine of the Year in 2012, while Rick Stengel was in charge.*

Steven Brill

Bitter Pill: Why Medical Bills Are Killing Us

1. Routine Care, Unforgettable Bills

When Sean Recchi, a forty-two-year-old from Lancaster, Ohio, was told last March that he had non-Hodgkin's lymphoma, his wife Stephanie knew she had to get him to MD Anderson Cancer Center in Houston. Stephanie's father had been treated there ten years earlier, and she and her family credited the doctors and nurses at MD Anderson with extending his life by at least eight years.

Because Stephanie and her husband had recently started their own small technology business, they were unable to buy comprehensive health insurance. For $469 a month, or about 20 percent of their income, they had been able to get only a policy that covered just $2,000 per day of any hospital costs. "We don't take that kind of discount insurance," said the woman at MD Anderson when Stephanie called to make an appointment for Sean.

Stephanie was then told by a billing clerk that the estimated cost of Sean's visit—just to be examined for six days so a treatment plan could be devised—would be $48,900, due in advance. Stephanie got her mother to write her a check. "You do anything you can in a situation like that," she says. The Recchis flew to Houston, leaving Stephanie's mother to care for their two teenage children.

About a week later, Stephanie had to ask her mother for $35,000 more so Sean could begin the treatment the doctors had decided was urgent. His condition had worsened rapidly since he had arrived in Houston. He was "sweating and shaking with chills and pains," Stephanie recalls. "He had a large mass in his chest that was . . . growing. He was panicked."

Nonetheless, Sean was held for about ninety minutes in a reception area, she says, because the hospital could not confirm that the check had cleared. Sean was allowed to see the doctor only after he advanced MD Anderson $7,500 from his credit card. The hospital says there was nothing unusual about how Sean was kept waiting. According to MD Anderson communications manager Julie Penne, "Asking for advance payment for services is a common, if unfortunate, situation that confronts hospitals all over the United States."

The total cost, in advance, for Sean to get his treatment plan and initial doses of chemotherapy was $83,900.

Why?

The first of the 344 lines printed out across eight pages of his hospital bill—filled with indecipherable numerical codes and acronyms—seemed innocuous. But it set the tone for all that followed. It read, "1 ACETAMINOPHE TABS 325 MG." The charge was only $1.50, but it was for a generic version of a Tylenol pill. You can buy a hundred of them on Amazon for $1.49 even without a hospital's purchasing power.

Dozens of midpriced items were embedded with similarly aggressive markups, like $283.00 for a "CHEST, PA AND LAT 71020." That's a simple chest X-ray, for which MD Anderson is routinely paid $20.44 when it treats a patient on Medicare, the government health-care program for the elderly.

Every time a nurse drew blood, a "ROUTINE VENIPUNCTURE" charge of $36.00 appeared, accompanied by charges of $23 to $78 for each of a dozen or more lab analyses performed on the blood sample. In all, the charges for blood and other lab tests done on Recchi amounted to more than $15,000. Had Recchi been old enough for Medicare, MD Anderson would have been paid a few hundred dollars for all those tests. By law, Medicare's payments approximate a hospital's cost of providing a service, including overhead, equipment, and salaries.

On the second page of the bill, the markups got bolder. Recchi was charged $13,702 for "1 RITUXIMAB INJ 660 MG." That's an injection of 660 mg of a cancer wonder drug called Rituxan. The average price paid by all hospitals for this dose is about $4,000, but MD Anderson probably gets a volume discount that would make its cost $3,000 to $3,500. That means the nonprofit cancer center's paid-in-advance markup on Recchi's lifesaving shot would be about 400 percent.

When I asked MD Anderson to comment on the charges on Recchi's bill, the cancer center released a written statement that said in part, "The issues related to health care finance are complex for patients, health care providers, payers and government entities alike. . . . MD Anderson's clinical billing and collection practices are similar to those of other major hospitals and academic medical centers."

The hospital's hard-nosed approach pays off. Although it is officially a nonprofit unit of the University of Texas, MD Anderson has revenue that exceeds the cost of the world-class care it provides by so much that its operating profit for the fiscal year 2010, the most recent annual report it filed with the U.S. Department of Health and Human Services, was $531 million. That's a profit margin of 26 percent on revenue of $2.05 billion, an astounding result for such a service-intensive enterprise.[1]

1. Here and elsewhere I define operating profit as the hospital's excess of revenue over expenses, plus the amount it lists on its tax return for depreciation of assets—because depreciation is an accounting expense, not a cash expense. John Gunn, chief operating officer of Memorial Sloan-Kettering Cancer Center, calls this the "fairest way" of judging a hospital's financial performance.

The president of MD Anderson is paid like someone running a prosperous business. Ronald DePinho's total compensation last year was $1,845,000. That does not count outside earnings derived from a much publicized waiver he received from the university that, according to the *Houston Chronicle*, allows him to maintain unspecified "financial ties with his three principal pharmaceutical companies."

DePinho's salary is nearly two and a half times the $750,000 paid to Francisco Cigarroa, the chancellor of entire University of Texas system, of which MD Anderson is a part. This pay structure is emblematic of American medical economics and is reflected on campuses across the United States, where the president of a hospital or hospital system associated with a university—whether it's Texas, Stanford, Duke, or Yale—is invariably paid much more than the person in charge of the university.

I got the idea for this article when I was visiting Rice University last year. As I was leaving the campus, which is just outside the central business district of Houston, I noticed a group of glass skyscrapers about a mile away lighting up the evening sky. The scene looked like Dubai. I was looking at the Texas Medical Center, a nearly 1,300-acre, 280-building complex of hospitals and related medical facilities, of which MD Anderson is the lead brand name. Medicine had obviously become a huge business. In fact, of Houston's top ten employers, five are hospitals, including MD Anderson with 19,000 employees; three, led by ExxonMobil with 14,000 employees, are energy companies. How did that happen, I wondered. Where's all that money coming from? And where is it going? I have spent the past seven months trying to find out by analyzing a variety of bills from hospitals like MD Anderson, doctors, drug companies, and every other player in the American health-care ecosystem.

When you look behind the bills that Sean Recchi and other patients receive, you see nothing rational—no rhyme or reason—about the costs they faced in a marketplace they enter through no choice of their own. The only constant is the sticker shock for the patients who are asked to pay.

Yet those who work in the health-care industry and those who argue over health-care policy seem inured to the shock. When we debate health-care policy, we seem to jump right to the issue of who should pay the bills, blowing past what should be the first question: Why exactly are the bills so high?

What are the reasons, good or bad, that cancer means a half-million- or million-dollar tab? Why should a trip to the emergency room for chest pains that turn out to be indigestion bring a bill that can exceed the cost of a semester of college? What makes a single dose of even the most wonderful wonder drug cost thousands of dollars? Why does simple lab work done during a few days in a hospital cost more than a car? And what is so different about the medical ecosystem that causes technology advances to drive bills up instead of down?

Recchi's bill and six others examined line by line for this article offer a close-up window into what happens when powerless buyers—whether they are people like Recchi or big health-insurance companies—meet sellers in what is the ultimate seller's market.

The result is a uniquely American gold rush for those who provide everything from wonder drugs to canes to high-tech implants to CT scans to hospital bill-coding and collection services. In hundreds of small and midsize cities across the country—from Stamford, Conn., to Marlton, N.J., to Oklahoma City—the American health-care market has transformed tax-exempt "nonprofit" hospitals into the towns' most profitable businesses and largest employers, often presided over by the regions' most richly compensated executives. And in our largest cities, the system offers lavish paychecks even to midlevel hospital managers, like the fourteen administrators at New York City's Memorial Sloan-Kettering Cancer Center who are paid over $500,000 a year, including six who make over $1 million.

Taken as a whole, these powerful institutions and the bills they churn out dominate the nation's economy and put demands on taxpayers to a degree unequaled anywhere else on earth. In the United States, people spend almost 20 percent of the gross domestic product on health care, compared with about half that in most developed countries. Yet in every measurable way, the results our health-care system produces are no better and often worse than the outcomes in those countries.

According to one of a series of exhaustive studies done by the McKinsey & Co. consulting firm, we spend more on health care than the next ten biggest spenders combined: Japan, Germany, France, China, the U.K., Italy, Canada, Brazil, Spain, and Australia. We may be shocked at the $60 billion price tag for cleaning up after Hurricane Sandy. We spent almost that much last week on health care. We spend more every year on artificial knees and hips than what Hollywood collects at the box office. We spend two or three times that much on durable medical devices like canes and wheelchairs, in part because a heavily lobbied Congress forces Medicare to pay 25 percent to 75 percent more for this equipment than it would cost at Walmart.

The Bureau of Labor Statistics projects that ten of the twenty occupations that will grow the fastest in the United States by 2020 are related to health care. America's largest city may be commonly thought of as the world's financial-services capital, but of New York's eighteen largest private employers, eight are hospitals and four are banks. Employing all those people in the cause of curing the sick is, of course, not anything to be ashamed of. But the drag on our overall economy that comes with taxpayers, employers, and consumers spending so much more than is spent in any other country for the same product is unsustainable. Health care is eating away at our economy and our treasury.

The health-care industry seems to have the will and the means to keep it that way. According to the Center for Responsive Politics, the pharmaceutical and health-care-product industries, combined with organizations representing doctors, hospitals, nursing homes, health services, and HMOs, have spent $5.36 billion since 1998 on lobbying in Washington. That dwarfs the $1.53 billion spent by the defense and aerospace industries and the $1.3 billion spent by oil and gas interests over the same period. That's right: the health-care-industrial complex spends more than three times what the military-industrial complex spends in Washington.

When you crunch data compiled by McKinsey and other researchers, the big picture looks like this: We're likely to spend $2.8 trillion this year on health care. That $2.8 trillion is likely to be $750 billion, or 27 percent, more than we would spend if we spent the same per capita as other developed countries, even after adjusting for the relatively high per capita income in the United States vs. those other countries. Of the total $2.8 trillion that will be spent on health care, about $800 billion will be paid by the federal government through the Medicare insurance program for the disabled and those sixty-five and older and the Medicaid program, which provides care for the poor. That $800 billion, which keeps rising far faster than inflation and the gross domestic product, is what's driving the federal deficit. The other $2 trillion will be paid mostly by private health-insurance companies and individuals who have no insurance or who will pay some portion of the bills covered by their insurance. This is what's increasingly burdening businesses that pay for their employees' health insurance and forcing individuals to pay so much in out-of-pocket expenses.

Breaking these trillions down into real bills going to real patients cuts through the ideological debate over health-care policy. By dissecting the bills that people like Sean Recchi face, we can see exactly how and why we are overspending, where the money is going, and how to get it back. We just have to follow the money.

The $21,000 Heartburn Bill

One night last summer at her home near Stamford, Conn., a sixty-four-year-old former sales clerk whom I'll call Janice S. felt chest pains. She was taken four miles by ambulance to the emergency room at Stamford Hospital, officially a nonprofit institution. After about three hours of tests and some brief encounters with a doctor, she was told she had indigestion and sent home. That was the good news.

The bad news was the bill: $995 for the ambulance ride, $3,000 for the doctors and $17,000 for the hospital—in sum, $21,000 for a false alarm.

Out of work for a year, Janice S. had no insurance. Among the hospital's charges were three "TROPONIN I" tests for $199.50 each. According to a National Institutes of Health website, a troponin test "measures the levels of certain proteins in the blood" whose release from the heart is a strong indicator of a heart attack. Some labs like to have the test done at intervals, so the fact that Janice S. got three of them is not necessarily an issue. The price is the problem. Stamford Hospital spokesman Scott Orstad told me that the $199.50 figure for the troponin test was taken from what he called the hospital's chargemaster. The chargemaster, I learned, is every hospital's internal price list. Decades ago it was a document the size of a phone book; now it's a massive computer file, thousands of items long, maintained by every hospital.

Stamford Hospital's chargemaster assigns prices to everything, including Janice S.'s blood tests. It would seem to be an important document. However, I quickly found that although every hospital has a chargemaster, officials treat it as if it were an eccentric uncle living in the attic. Whenever I asked, they deflected all conversation away from it. They even argued that it is irrelevant. I soon found that they have good reason to hope that outsiders pay no attention to the chargemaster or the process that produces it. For there seems to be no process, no rationale, behind the core document that is the basis for hundreds of billions of dollars in health-care bills.

Because she was sixty-four, not sixty-five, Janice S. was not on Medicare. But seeing what Medicare would have paid Stamford Hospital for the troponin test if she had been a year older shines a bright light on the role the chargemaster plays in our national medical crisis—and helps us understand the illegitimacy of that $199.50 charge. That's because Medicare collects troves of data on what every type of treatment, test, and other service costs hospitals to deliver. Medicare takes seriously the notion that nonprofit hospitals should be paid for all their costs but actually be nonprofit after their calculation. Thus, under the law, Medicare is supposed to reimburse hospitals for any given service, factoring in not only direct costs but also allocated expenses such as overhead, capital expenses, executive salaries, insurance, differences in regional costs of living, and even the education of medical students.

It turns out that Medicare would have paid Stamford $13.94 for each troponin test rather than the $199.50 Janice S. was charged.

Janice S. was also charged $157.61 for a CBC—the complete blood count that those of us who are *ER* aficionados remember George Clooney ordering several times a night. Medicare pays $11.02 for a CBC in Connecticut. Hospital finance people argue vehemently that Medicare doesn't pay enough and that they lose as much as 10 on an average Medicare patient. But even if the Medicare price should be, say, 10 percent higher, it's a long way from $11.02 plus 10 percent to $157.61. Yes, every hospital administrator grouses about Medicare's payment rates—rates that are supervised by a Congress that is heavily lobbied by the American Hospital Association, which spent $1,859,041 on lobbyists in 2012. But an annual expense report that Stamford Hospital is required to file with the federal Department of Health and Human Services offers evidence that Medicare's rates for the services Janice S. received are on the mark. According to the hospital's latest filing (covering 2010), its total expenses for laboratory work (like Janice S.'s blood tests) in the twelve months covered by the report were $27.5 million. Its total charges were $293.2 million. That means it charged about eleven times its costs. As we examine other bills, we'll see that like Medicare patients, the large portion of hospital patients who have private health insurance also get discounts off the listed chargemaster figures, assuming the hospital and insurance company have negotiated to include the hospital in the insurer's network of providers that its customers can use. The insurance discounts are not nearly as steep as the Medicare markdowns, which means that even the discounted insurance-company rates fuel profits at these officially nonprofit hospitals. Those profits are further boosted by payments from the tens of millions of patients who, like the unemployed Janice S., have no insurance or whose insurance does not apply because the patient has exceeded the coverage limits. These patients are asked to pay the chargemaster list prices.

If you are confused by the notion that those least able to pay are the ones singled out to pay the highest rates, welcome to the American medical marketplace.

Pay No Attention to the Chargemaster

No hospital's chargemaster prices are consistent with those of any other hospital, nor do they seem to be based on anything objective—like cost—that any hospital executive I spoke with was able to explain. "They were set in cement a long time ago and just keep going up almost automatically," says one hospital chief financial officer with a shrug.

At Stamford Hospital I got the first of many brush-offs when I asked about the chargemaster rates on Janice S.'s bill. "Those are not our real rates," protested hospital spokesman Orstad when I asked him to make hospital CEO Brian Grissler available to explain Janice S.'s bill, in particular the blood-test charges. "It's a list we use internally in certain cases, but most people never pay those prices. I doubt that Brian [Grissler] has even seen the list in years. So I'm not sure why you care."

Orstad also refused to comment on any of the specifics in Janice S.'s bill, including the seemingly inflated charges for all the lab work. "I've told you I don't think a bill like this is relevant," he explained. "Very few people actually pay those rates."

But Janice S. was asked to pay them. Moreover, the chargemaster rates are relevant, even for those unlike her who have insurance. Insurers with the most leverage, because they have the most customers to offer a hospital that needs patients, will try to negotiate prices 30 percent to 50 percent above the Medicare rates rather than discounts off the sky-high chargemaster rates. But insurers are increasingly losing leverage because hospitals are consolidating by buying doctors' practices and even rival hospitals. In that situation—in which the insurer needs the hospital more than the hospital needs the insurer—the pricing negotiation will be over discounts that work down from the chargemaster prices rather than up from what Medicare would pay. Getting a 50 percent or even 60 percent discount off the chargemaster price of an item that costs $13 and lists for $199.50 is still no bargain. "We hate to negotiate off of the chargemaster, but we have to do it a lot now," says Edward Wardell, a lawyer for the giant health-insurance provider Aetna Inc.

That so few consumers seem to be aware of the chargemaster demonstrates how well the health-care industry has steered the debate from why bills are so high to who should pay them.

The expensive technology deployed on Janice S. was a bigger factor in her bill than the lab tests. An "NM MYO REST/SPEC EJCT MOT MUL" was billed at $7,997.54. That's a stress test using a radioactive dye that is tracked by an X-ray computed tomography, or CT, scan. Medicare would have paid Stamford $554 for that test.

Janice S. was charged an additional $872.44 just for the dye used in the test. The regular stress test patients are more familiar with, in which arteries are monitored electronically with an electro-cardiograph, would have cost far less—$1,200 even at the hospital's chargemaster price. (Medicare would have paid $96 for it.) And although many doctors view the version using the CT scan as more thorough, others consider it unnecessary in most cases.

According to Jack Lewin, a cardiologist and former CEO of the American College of Cardiology, "It depends on the patient, of course, but in most cases you would start with a standard stress test. We are doing too many of these nuclear tests. It is not being used appropriately.... Sometimes a cardiogram is enough, and you don't even need the simpler test. But it usually makes sense to give the patient the simpler one first and then use nuclear for a closer look if there seem to be problems."

We don't know the particulars of Janice S.'s condition, so we cannot know why the doctors who treated her ordered the more expensive test. But the incentives are clear. On the basis of market prices, Stamford probably paid about $250,000 for the CT equipment in its operating room. It costs little to operate, so the more it can be used and billed, the quicker the hospital recovers its costs and begins profiting from its purchase. In addition, the cardiologist in the emergency room gave Janice S. a separate bill for $600 to read the test results on top of the $342 he charged for examining her.

According to a McKinsey study of the medical marketplace, a typical piece of equipment will pay for itself in one year if it carries out just ten to fifteen procedures a day. That's a terrific return on capital equipment that has an expected life span of seven to ten years. And it means that after a year, every scan ordered by a doctor in the Stamford Hospital emergency room would mean pure profit, less maintenance costs, for the hospital. Plus an extra fee for the doctor.

Another McKinsey report found that health care providers in the United States conduct far more CT tests per capita than those in any other country—71 percent more than in Germany, for example, where the government-run health-care system offers none of those incentives for overtesting. We also pay a lot more for each test, even when it's Medicare doing the paying. Medicare reimburses hospitals and clinics an average of four times as much as Germany does for CT scans, according to the data gathered by McKinsey.

Medicare's reimbursement formulas for these tests are regulated by Congress. So, too, are restrictions on what Medicare can do to limit the use of CT and magnetic resonance imaging (MRI) scans when they might not be medically necessary. Standing at the ready to make sure Congress keeps Medicare at bay is, among other groups, the American College of Radiology, which on November 14 ran a full-page ad in the Capitol Hill–centric newspaper *Politico* urging Congress to pass the Diagnostic Imaging Services Access Protection Act. It's a bill that would block efforts by Medicare to discourage doctors from ordering multiple CT scans on the same patient by paying them less per test to read multiple tests of the same patient. (In fact, six of *Politico*'s twelve pages of ads that day were bought by medical interests urging Congress to spend or not cut back on one of their products.)

The costs associated with high-tech tests are likely to accelerate. McKinsey found that the more CT and MRI scanners are out there, the more doctors use them. In 1997 there were fewer than 3,000 machines available, and they completed an average of 3,800 scans per year. By 2006 there were more than 10,000 in use, and they completed an average of 6,100 per year. According to a study in the *Annals of Emergency Medicine*, the use of CT scans in America's emergency rooms "has more than quadrupled in recent decades." As one former emergency-room doctor puts it, "Giving out CT scans like candy in the ER is the equivalent of putting a ninety-year-old grandmother through a patdown at the airport: Hey, you never know."

Selling this equipment to hospitals—which has become a key profit center for industrial conglomerates like General Electric and Siemens—is one of the U.S. economy's bright spots. I recently subscribed to an online headhunter's listings for medical-equipment salesmen and quickly found an opening in Connecticut that would pay a salary of $85,000 and sales commissions of up to $95,000 more, plus a car allowance. The only requirement was that applicants have "at least one year of experience selling some form of capital equipment."

In all, on the day I signed up for that jobs website, it carried 186 listings for medical-equipment salespeople just in Connecticut.

2. Medical Technology's Perverse Economics

Unlike those of almost any other area we can think of, the dynamics of the medical marketplace seem to be such that the advance of technology has made medical care more expensive, not less. First, it appears to encourage more procedures and treatment by making them easier and more convenient. (This is especially true for procedures like arthroscopic surgery.) Second, there is little patient pushback against higher costs because it seems to (and often does) result in safer, better care and because the customer getting the treatment is either not going to pay for it or not going to know the price until after the fact.

Beyond the hospitals' and doctors' obvious economic incentives to use the equipment and the manufacturers' equally obvious incentives to sell it, there's a legal incentive at work. Giving Janice S. a nuclear-imaging test instead of the lower-tech, less expensive stress test was the safer thing to do—a belt-and-suspenders approach that would let the hospital and doctor say they pulled out all the stops in case Janice S. died of a heart attack after she was sent home.

"We use the CT scan because it's a great defense," says the CEO of another hospital not far from Stamford. "For example, if anyone has fallen or done anything around their head—hell, if they even say the word *head*—we do it to be safe. We can't be sued for doing too much."

His rationale speaks to the real cost issue associated with medical-malpractice litigation. It's not as much about the verdicts or settlements (or considerable malpractice-insurance premiums) that hospitals and doctors pay as it is about what they do to avoid being sued. And some no doubt claim they are ordering more tests to avoid being sued when it is actually an excuse for hiking profits. The most practical malpractice-reform proposals would not limit awards for victims but would allow doctors to use what's called a safe-harbor defense. Under safe harbor, a defendant doctor or hospital could argue that the care provided was within the bounds of what peers have established as reasonable under the circumstances. The typical plaintiff argument that doing something more, like a nuclear-imaging test, might have saved the patient would then be less likely to prevail.

When Obamacare was being debated, Republicans pushed this kind of commonsense malpractice-tort reform. But the stranglehold that plaintiffs' lawyers have traditionally had on Democrats prevailed, and neither a safe-harbor provision nor any other malpractice reform was included.

Nonprofit Profit Makers

To the extent that they defend the chargemaster rates at all, the defense that hospital executives offer has to do with charity. As John Gunn, chief operating officer of Sloan-Kettering, puts it, "We charge those rates so that when we get paid by a [wealthy] uninsured person from overseas, it allows us to serve the poor."

A closer look at hospital finance suggests two holes in that argument. First, while Sloan-Kettering does have an aggressive financial-assistance program (something Stamford Hospital lacks), at most hospitals it's not a Saudi sheik but the *almost* poor—those who don't qualify for Medicaid and don't have insurance—who are most often asked to pay those exorbitant chargemaster prices. Second, there is the jaw-dropping difference between those list prices and the hospitals' costs, which enables these ostensibly nonprofit institutions to produce high profits even after all the discounts. True, when the discounts to Medicare and private insurers are applied, hospitals end up being paid a lot less overall than what is itemized on the original bills. Stamford ends up receiving about 35 percent of what it bills, which is the yield for most hospitals. (Sloan-Kettering and MD Anderson, whose great brand names make them tough negotiators with insurance companies, get about 50 percent). However, no matter how steep the discounts, the chargemaster prices are so high and so devoid of any calculation related to cost that the result is uniquely American: thousands of nonprofit institutions have morphed into high-profit, high-profile businesses that have the best of both worlds. They have become entities akin to low-risk, must-have public utilities that nonetheless pay their operators as if they were high-risk entrepreneurs. As with the local electric company, customers must have the product and can't go elsewhere to buy it. They are steered to a hospital by their insurance companies or doctors (whose practices may have a business alliance with the hospital or even be owned by it). Or they end up there because there isn't any local competition. But unlike with the electric company, no regulator caps hospital profits.

Yet hospitals are also beloved local charities.

The result is that in small towns and cities across the country, the local nonprofit hospital may be the community's strongest business, typically making tens of millions of dollars a year and paying its nondoctor administrators six or seven figures. As nonprofits, such hospitals solicit contributions, and their annual charity dinner, a showcase for their good works, is typically a major civic event. But charitable gifts are a minor part of their base; Stamford Hospital raised just over 1 percent of its revenue from contributions last year. Even after discounts, those $199.50 blood tests and multi-thousand-dollar CT scans are what really count.

Thus, according to the latest publicly available tax return it filed with the IRS, for the fiscal year ending September 2011, Stamford Hospital—in a midsize city serving an unusually high 50 percent share of highly discounted Medicare and Medicaid patients—managed an operating profit of $63 million on revenue actually received (after all the discounts off the chargemaster) of $495 million. That's a 12.7 percent operating profit margin, which would be the envy of shareholders of high-service businesses across other sectors of the economy.

Its nearly half-billion dollars in revenue also makes Stamford Hospital by far the city's largest business serving only local residents. In fact, the hospital's revenue exceeded all money paid to the city of Stamford in taxes and fees. The hospital is a bigger business than its host city.

There is nothing special about the hospital's fortunes. Its operating profit margin is about the same as the average for all nonprofit hospitals, 11.7 percent, even when those that lose money are included. And Stamford's 12.7 percent was tallied after the hospital paid a slew of high salaries to its management, including $744,000 to its chief financial officer and $1,860,000 to CEO Grissler.

In fact, when McKinsey, aided by a Bank of America survey, pulled together all hospital financial reports, it found that the 2,900 nonprofit hospitals across the country, which are exempt from income taxes, actually end up averaging higher operating profit margins than the 1,000 for-profit hospitals after the for-profits' income-tax obligations are deducted. In health care, being nonprofit produces more profit.

Nonetheless, hospitals like Stamford are able to use their sympathetic nonprofit status to push their interests. As the debate over deficit-cutting ideas related to health care has heated up, the American Hospital Association has run daily ads on Mike Allen's

Playbook, a popular Washington tip sheet, urging that Congress not be allowed to cut hospital payments because that would endanger the "$39.3 billion" in uncompensated care for the poor that hospitals now provide either through charity programs or because of patients failing to pay their debts. Based on the formula hospitals use to calculate the cost of this charity care, that amounts to approximately 5 percent of their total revenue for 2010.

Under Internal Revenue Service rules, nonprofits are not prohibited from taking in more money than they spend. They just can't distribute the overage to shareholders—because they don't have any shareholders.

So, what do these wealthy nonprofits do with all the profit? In a trend similar to what we've seen in nonprofit colleges and universities—where there has been an arms race of sorts to use rising tuition to construct buildings and add courses of study—the hospitals improve and expand facilities (despite the fact that the United States has more hospital beds than it can fill), buy more equipment, hire more people, offer more services, buy rival hospitals, and then raise executive salaries because their operations have gotten so much larger. They keep the upward spiral going by marketing for more patients, raising price,s and pushing harder to collect bill payments. Only with health care, the upward spiral is easier to sustain. Health care is seen as even more of a necessity than higher education. And unlike in higher education, in health care there is little price transparency—and far less competition in any given locale even if there were transparency. Besides, a hospital is typically one of the community's larger employers if not the largest, so there is unlikely to be much local complaining about its burgeoning economic fortunes.

In December, when the *New York Times* ran a story about how a deficit deal might threaten hospital payments, Steven Safyer, chief executive of Montefiore Medical Center, a large nonprofit hospital system in the Bronx, complained, "There is no such thing as a cut to a provider that isn't a cut to a beneficiary. . . . This is not crying wolf."

Actually, Safyer seems to be crying wolf to the tune of about $196.8 million, according to the hospital's latest publicly available tax return. That was his hospital's operating profit, according to its 2010 return. With $2.586 billion in revenue—of which 99.4 percent came from patient bills and 0.6 percent from fundraising events and other charitable contributions—Safyer's business is more than six times as large as that of the Bronx's most famous enterprise, the New York Yankees. Surely, without cutting services to beneficiaries, Safyer could cut what have to be some of the Bronx's better non-Yankee salaries: his own, which was $4,065,000, or those of his chief financial officer ($3,243,000), his executive vice president ($2,220,000), or the head of his dental department ($1,798,000).

Shocked by her bill from Stamford hospital and unable to pay it, Janice S. found a local woman on the Internet who is part of a growing cottage industry of people who call themselves medical-billing advocates. They help people read and understand their bills and try to reduce them. "The hospitals all know the bills are fiction, or at least only a place to start the discussion, so you bargain with them," says Katalin Goencz, a former appeals coordinator in a hospital billing department who negotiated Janice S.'s bills from a home office in Stamford.

Goencz is part of a trade group called the Alliance of Claim Assistant Professionals, which has about forty members across the country. Another group, Medical Billing Advocates of America, has about fifty members. Each advocate seems to handle forty to seventy cases a year for the uninsured and those disputing insurance claims. That would be about 5,000 patients a year out of what must be tens of millions of Americans facing these issues—which may help explain why 60 percent of the personal bankruptcy filings each year are related to medical bills.

"I can pretty much always get it down 30 percent to 5 percent simply by saying the patient is ready to pay but will not pay $300 for a blood test or an X ray," says Goencz. "They hand out blood tests and X rays in hospitals like bottled water, and they know it."

After weeks of back-and-forth phone calls, for which Goencz charged Janice S. $97 an hour, Stamford Hospital cut its bill in half. Most of the doctors did about the same, reducing Janice S.'s overall tab from $21,000 to about $11,000.

But the best the ambulance company would offer Goencz was to let Janice S. pay off its $995 ride in $25-a-month installments. "The ambulances never negotiate the amount," says Goencz.

A manager at Stamford Emergency Medical Services, which charged Janice S. $958 for the pickup plus $9.38 per mile, says that "our rates are all set by the state on a regional basis" and that the company is independently owned. That's at odds with a trend toward consolidation that has seen several private-equity firms making investments in what Wall Street analysts have identified as an increasingly high-margin business. Overall, ambulance revenues were more than $12 billion last year, or about 10 percent higher than Hollywood's box-office take. It's not a great deal to pay off $1,000 for a four-mile ambulance ride on the layaway plan or receive a 50 percent discount on a $199.50 blood test that should cost $15, nor is getting half off on a $7,997.54 stress test that was probably all profit and may not have been necessary. But, says Goencz, "I don't go over it line by line. I just go for a deal. The patient usually is shocked by the bill, doesn't understand any of the language, and has bill collectors all over her by the time they call me. So they're grateful. Why give them heartache by telling them they still paid too much for some test or pill?"

A Slip, a Fall, and a $9,400 Bill

The billing advocates aren't always successful. Just ask Emilia Gilbert, a school-bus driver who got into a fight with a hospital associated with Connecticut's most venerable nonprofit institution, which racked up quick profits on multiple CT scans then refused to compromise at all on its chargemaster prices. Gilbert, now sixty-six, is still making weekly payments on the bill she got in June 2008 after she slipped and fell on her face one summer evening in the small yard behind her house in Fairfield, Conn. Her nose bleeding heavily, she was taken to the emergency room at Bridgeport Hospital.

Along with Greenwich Hospital and the Hospital of St. Raphael in New Haven, Bridgeport Hospital is now owned by the Yale New Haven Health System, which boasts a variety of gleaming new facilities. Although Yale University and Yale New Haven are separate entities, Yale–New Haven Hospital is the teaching hospital for the Yale Medical School, and university representatives, including Yale president Richard Levin, sit on the Yale New Haven Health System board.

"I was there for maybe six hours, until midnight," Gilbert recalls, "and most of it was spent waiting. I saw the resident for maybe fifteen minutes, but I got a lot of tests."

In fact, Gilbert got three CT scans—of her head, her chest, and her face. The last one showed a hairline fracture of her nose. The CT bills alone were $6,538. (Medicare would have paid about $825 for all three.) A doctor charged $261 to read the scans.

Gilbert got the same troponin blood test that Janice S. got—the one Medicare pays $13.94 for and for which Janice S. was billed $199.50 at Stamford. Gilbert got just one. Bridgeport Hospital charged 20 percent more than its downstate neighbor: $239.

Also on the bill were items that neither Medicare nor any insurance company would pay anything at all for: basic instruments and bandages and even the tubing for an IV setup. Under Medicare regulations and the terms of most insurance contracts, these are supposed to be part of the hospital's facility charge, which in this case was $908 for the emergency room.

Gilbert's total bill was $9,418.

"We think the chargemaster is totally fair," says William Gedge, senior vice president of payer relations at Yale New Haven Health System. "It's fair because everyone gets the same bill. Even Medicare gets exactly the same charges that this patient got. Of course, we will have different arrangements for how Medicare or an insurance company will not pay some of the charges or discount the charges, but everyone starts from the same place." Asked how the chargemaster charge for an item like the troponin test was calculated, Gedge said he "didn't know exactly" but would try to find out. He subsequently reported back that "it's an historical charge, which takes into account all of our costs for running the hospital."

Bridgeport Hospital had $420 million in revenue and an operating profit of $52 million in 2010, the most recent year covered by its federal financial reports. CEO Robert Trefry, who has since left his post, was listed as having been paid $1.8 million. The CEO of the parent Yale New Haven Health System, Marna Borgstrom, was paid $2.5 million, which is 58 percent more than the $1.6 million paid to Levin, Yale University's president.

"You really can't compare the two jobs," says Yale–New Haven Hospital senior vice president Vincent Petrini. "Comparing hospitals to universities is like apples and oranges. Running a hospital organization is much more complicated." Actually, the four-hospital chain and the university have about the same operating budget. And it would seem that Levin deals with what most would consider complicated challenges in overseeing 3,900 faculty members, corralling (and complying with the terms of) hundreds of millions of dollars in government research grants, and presiding over a $19 billion endowment, not to mention admitting and educating 14,000 students spread across Yale College and a variety of graduate schools, professional schools, and foreign-study outposts. And surely Levin's responsibilities are as complicated as those of the CEO of Yale New Haven Health's smallest unit—the 184-bed Greenwich Hospital, whose CEO was paid $112,000 more than Levin.

"When I got the bill, I almost had to go back to the hospital," Gilbert recalls. "I was hyperventilating." Contributing to her shock was the fact that although her employer supplied insurance from Cigna, one of the country's leading health insurers, Gilbert's policy was from a Cigna subsidiary called Starbridge that insures mostly low-wage earners. That made Gilbert one of millions of Americans like Sean Recchi who are routinely categorized as having health insurance but really don't have anything approaching meaningful coverage.

Starbridge covered Gilbert for just $2,500 per hospital visit, leaving her on the hook for about $7,000 of a $9,400 bill. Under Connecticut's rules (states set their own guidelines for Medicaid, the federal-state program for the poor), Gilbert's $1,800 a month in earnings was too high for her to qualify for Medicaid assistance. She was also turned down, she says, when she requested financial assistance from the hospital. Yale New Haven's Gedge insists that she never applied to the hospital for aid, and Gilbert could not supply me with copies of any applications.

In September 2009, after a series of fruitless letters and phone calls from its bill collectors to Gilbert, the hospital sued her. Gilbert found a medical-billing advocate, Beth Morgan, who analyzed the charges on the bill and compared them with the discounted rates insurance companies would pay. During two court-required mediation sessions, Bridgeport Hospital's attorney wouldn't budge; his client wanted the bill paid in full, Gilbert and Morgan recall. At the third and final mediation, Gilbert was offered a 20 percent discount off the chargemaster fees if she would pay immediately, but she says she responded that according to what Morgan told her about the bill, it was still too much to pay. "We probably could have offered more," Gedge acknowledges. "But in these situations, our bill-collection attorneys only know

the amount we are saying is owed, not whether it is a chargemaster amount or an amount that is already discounted."

On July 11, 2011, with the school-bus driver representing herself in Bridgeport superior court, a judge ruled that Gilbert had
to pay all but about $500 of the original charges. (He deducted
the superfluous bills for the basic equipment.) The judge put her
on a payment schedule of $20 a week for six years. For her, the
chargemaster prices were all too real.

The One-Day, $87,000 Outpatient Bill

Getting a patient in and out of a hospital the same day seems like
a logical way to cut costs. Outpatients don't take up hospital rooms
or require the expensive 24/7 observation and care that come with
them. That's why in the 1990s Medicare pushed payment formulas on hospitals that paid them for whatever ailment they
were treating (with more added for documented complications),
not according to the number of days the patient spent in a bed.
Insurance companies also pushed incentives on hospitals to move
patients out faster or not admit them for overnight stays in the
first place. Meanwhile, the introduction of procedures like non-
invasive laparoscopic surgery helped speed the shift from inpatient to outpatient.

By 2010, average days spent in the hospital per patient had declined significantly, while outpatient services had increased even
more dramatically. However, the result was not the savings that
reformers had envisioned. It was just the opposite.

Experts estimate that outpatient services are now packed
with so much hidden profit that about two-thirds of the $750
billion annual U.S. overspending identified by the McKinsey research on health care comes in payments for outpatient services.
That includes work done by physicians, laboratories, and clinics
(including diagnostic clinics for CT scans or blood tests) and
same-day surgeries and other hospital treatments like cancer

chemotherapy. According to a McKinsey survey, outpatient emergency-room care averages an operating profit margin of 15 percent and nonemergency outpatient care averages 35 percent. On the other hand, inpatient care has a margin of just 2 percent. Put simply, inpatient care at nonprofit hospitals is, in fact, almost nonprofit. Outpatient care is wildly profitable.

"An operating room has fixed costs," explains one hospital economist. "You get 10 percent or 20 percent more patients in there every day who you don't have to board overnight, and that goes straight to the bottom line."

The 2011 outpatient visit of someone I'll call Steve H. to Mercy Hospital in Oklahoma City illustrates those economics. Steve H. had the kind of relatively routine care that patients might expect would be no big deal: he spent the day at Mercy getting his aching back fixed.

A blue-collar worker who was in his thirties at the time and worked at a local retail store, Steve H. had consulted a specialist at Mercy in the summer of 2011 and was told that a stimulator would have to be surgically implanted in his back. The good news was that with all the advances of modern technology, the whole process could be done in a day. (The latest federal filing shows that 63 percent of surgeries at Mercy were performed on outpatients.)

Steve H.'s doctor intended to use a RestoreUltra neurostimulator manufactured by Medtronic, a Minneapolis-based company with $16 billion in annual sales that bills itself as the world's largest stand-alone medical-technology company. "RestoreUltra delivers spinal-cord stimulation through one or more leads selected from a broad portfolio for greater customization of therapy," Medtronic's website promises. I was not able to interview Steve H., but according to Pat Palmer, a medical-billing specialist based in Salem, Va., who consults for the union that provides Steve H.'s health insurance, Steve H. didn't ask how much the stimulator would cost because he had $45,181 remaining on the $60,000 annual payout limit his union-sponsored health-insurance plan imposed. "He figured, How much could a day at Mercy cost?" Palmer says. "Five thousand? Maybe ten?"

Steve H. was about to run up against a seemingly irrelevant footnote in millions of Americans' insurance policies: the limit, sometimes annual or sometimes over a lifetime, on what the insurer has to pay out for a patient's claims. Under Obamacare, those limits will not be allowed in most health-insurance policies after 2013. That might help people like Steve H. but is also one of the reasons premiums are going to skyrocket under Obamacare.

Steve H.'s bill for his day at Mercy contained all the usual and customary overcharges. One item was "MARKER SKIN REG TIP RULER" for $3. That's the marking pen, presumably reusable, that marked the place on Steve H.'s back where the incision was to go. Six lines down, there was "STRAP OR TABLE 8X27 IN" for $31. That's the strap used to hold Steve H. onto the operating table. Just below that was "BLNKT WARM UPPER BDY 42268" for $32. That's a blanket used to keep surgery patients warm. It is, of course, reusable, and it's available new on eBay for $13. Four lines down there's "GOWN SURG ULTRA XLG 95121" for $39, which is the gown the surgeon wore. Thirty of them can be bought online for $180. Neither Medicare nor any large insurance company would pay a hospital separately for those straps or the surgeon's gown; that's all supposed to come with the facility fee paid to the hospital, which in this case was $6,289.

In all, Steve H.'s bill for these basic medical and surgical supplies was $7,882. On top of that was $1,837 under a category called "Pharmacy General Classification" for items like bacitracin ($108). But that was the least of Steve H.'s problems.

The big-ticket item for Steve H.'s day at Mercy was the Medtronic stimulator, and that's where most of Mercy's profit was collected during his brief visit. The bill for that was $49,237.

According to the chief financial officer of another hospital, the wholesale list price of the Medtronic stimulator is "about $19,000." Because Mercy is part of a major hospital chain, it might pay 5–15 percent less than that. Even assuming Mercy paid $19,000, it would make more than $30,000 selling it to Steve H., a profit margin of more than 150 percent. To the extent that I found any consistency among hospital chargemaster practices, this is one of them: hospitals routinely seem to charge two and a half times what these expensive implantable devices cost them, which produces that 150 percent profit margin.

As Steve H. found out when he got his bill, he had exceeded the $45,000 that was left on his insurance policy's annual payout limit just with the neurostimulator. And his total bill was $86,951. After his insurance paid that first $45,000, he still owed more than $40,000, not counting doctors' bills. (I did not see Steve H.'s doctors' bills.)

Mercy Hospital is owned by an organization under the umbrella of the Catholic Church called Sisters of Mercy. Its mission, as described in its latest filing with the IRS as a tax-exempt charity, is "to carry out the healing ministry of Jesus by promoting health and wellness." With a chain of 31 hospitals and 300 clinics across the Midwest, Sisters of Mercy uses a bill-collection firm based in Topeka, Kans., called Berlin-Wheeler Inc. Suits against Mercy patients are on file in courts across Oklahoma listing Berlin-Wheeler as the plaintiff. According to its most recent tax return, the Oklahoma City unit of the Sisters of Mercy hospital chain collected $337 million in revenue for the fiscal year ending June 30, 2011. It had an operating profit of $34 million. And that was after paying ten executives more than $300,000 each, including $784,000 to a regional president and $438,000 to the hospital president.

That report doesn't cover the executives overseeing the chain, called Mercy Health, of which Mercy in Oklahoma City is a part. The overall chain had $4.28 billion in revenue that year. Its hospital in Springfield, Mo. (pop. 160,660), had $880.7 million in revenue and an operating profit of $115 million, according to its federal filing. The incomes of the parent company's executives appear on other IRS filings covering various interlocking Mercy nonprofit corporate entities. Mercy president and CEO Lynn Britton made $1,930,000, and an executive vice president, Myra Aubuchon, was paid $3.7 million, according to the Mercy filing. In all, seven Mercy Health executives were paid more than $1 million each. A note at the end of an Ernst & Young audit that is attached to Mercy's IRS filing reported that the chain provided charity care worth 3.2 percent of its revenue in the previous year. However, the auditors state that the value of that care is based on the charges on all the bills, not the actual cost to Mercy of providing those services—in other words, the chargemaster value. Assuming that Mercy's actual costs are a tenth of these chargemaster values—they're probably less—all of this charity care actually cost Mercy about three-tenths of 1 percent of its revenue, or about $13 million out of $4.28 billion.

Mercy's website lists an eighteen-member media team; one member, Rachel Wright, told me that neither CEO Britton nor anyone else would be available to answer questions about compensation, the hospital's bill-collecting activities through Berlin-Wheeler, or Steve H.'s bill, which I had sent her (with his name and the date of his visit to the hospital redacted to protect his privacy).

Wright said the hospital's lawyers had decided that discussing Steve H.'s bill would violate the federal HIPAA law protecting the privacy of patient medical records. I pointed out that I wanted to ask questions only about the hospital's charges for standard items—such as surgical gowns, basic blood tests, blanket warmers, and even medical devices—that had nothing to do with individual patients. "Everything is particular to an individual patient's needs," she replied. Even a surgical gown? "Yes, even a surgical gown. We cannot discuss this with you. It's against the law." She declined to put me in touch with the hospital's lawyers to discuss their legal analysis.

Hiding behind a privacy statute to avoid talking about how it prices surgeons' gowns may be a stretch, but Mercy might have a valid legal reason not to discuss what it paid for the Medtronic device before selling it to Steve H. for $49,237. Pharmaceutical and medical-device companies routinely insert clauses in their sales contracts prohibiting hospitals from sharing information about what they pay and the discounts they receive. In January 2012, a report by the federal Government Accountability Office found that "the lack of price transparency and the substantial variation in amounts hospitals pay for some IMD [implantable medical devices] raise questions about whether hospitals are achieving the best prices possible."

A lack of price transparency was not the only potential market inefficiency the GAO found. "Although physicians are not involved in price negotiations, they often express strong preferences for certain manufacturers and models of IMD," the GAO reported. "To the extent that physicians in the same hospitals have different preferences for IMDs, it may be difficult for the hospital to obtain volume discounts from particular manufacturers."

"Doctors have no incentive to buy one kind of hip or other implantable device as a group," explains Ezekiel Emanuel, an oncologist and a vice provost of the University of Pennsylvania who was a key White House adviser when Obamacare was created. "Even in the most innocent of circumstances, it kills the chance for market efficiencies."

The circumstances are not always innocent. In 2008, Gregory Demske, an assistant inspector general at the Department of Health and Human Services, told a Senate committee that "physicians routinely receive substantial compensation from medical-device companies through stock options, royalty agreements, consulting agreements, research grants, and fellowships."

The assistant inspector general then revealed startling numbers about the extent of those payments: "We found that during the years 2002 through 2006, four manufacturers, which controlled almost 75 percent of the hip- and knee-replacement market, paid physician consultants over $800 million under the terms of roughly 6,500 consulting agreements."

Other doctors, Demske noted, had stretched the conflict of interest beyond consulting fees: "Additionally, physician ownership of medical-device manufacturers and related businesses appears to be a growing trend in the medical-device sector. . . . In some cases, physicians could receive substantial returns while contributing little to the venture beyond the ability to generate business for the venture." In 2010, Medtronic, along with several other members of a medical-technology trade group, began to make the potential conflicts transparent by posting all payments to physicians on a section of its website called Physician Collaboration. The voluntary move came just before a similar disclosure regulation promulgated by the Obama administration went into effect governing any doctor who receives funds from Medicare or the National Institutes of Health (which would include most doctors). And the nonprofit public-interest-journalism organization ProPublica has smartly organized data on doctor payments on its website. The conflicts have not been eliminated, but they are being aired, albeit on searchable websites rather than through a requirement that doctors disclose them to patients directly.

But conflicts that may encourage devices to be overprescribed or that lead doctors to prescribe a more expensive one instead of another are not the core problem in this marketplace. The more fundamental disconnect is that there is little reason to believe that what Mercy Hospital paid Medtronic for Steve H.'s device would have had any bearing on what the hospital decided to charge Steve H. Why would it? He did not know the price in advance.

Besides, studies delving into the economics of the medical marketplace consistently find that a moderately higher or lower price doesn't change consumer purchasing decisions much, if at all, because in health care there is little of the price sensitivity found in conventional marketplaces, even on the rare occasion that patients know the cost in advance. If you were in pain or in danger of dying, would you turn down treatment at a price 5 percent or 20 percent higher than the price you might have expected—that is, if you'd had any informed way to know what to expect in the first place, which you didn't?

The question of how sensitive patients will be to increased prices for medical devices recently came up in a different context. Aware of the huge profits being accumulated by device makers, Obama administration officials decided to recapture some of the money by imposing a 2.39 percent federal excise tax on the sales of these devices as well as other medical technology such as CT-scan equipment. The rationale was that getting back some of these generous profits was a fair way to cover some of the cost of the subsidized, broader insurance coverage provided by Obamacare—insurance that in some cases will pay for more of the devices. The industry has since geared up in Washington and is pushing legislation that would repeal the tax. Its main argument is that a 2.39 percent increase in prices would so reduce sales that it would wipe out a substantial portion of what the industry claims are the 422,000 jobs it supports in a $136 billion industry.

That prediction of doom brought on by this small tax contradicts the reams of studies documenting consumer price insensitivity in the health-care marketplace. It also ignores profit-margin data collected by McKinsey that demonstrates that device makers have an open field in the current medical ecosystem. A 2011 McKinsey survey for medical-industry clients reported that device makers are superstar performers in a booming medical economy. Medtronic, which performed in the middle of the group, delivered an amazing compounded annual return of 14.95 percent to shareholders from 1990 to 2010. That means $100 invested in the company in 1990 was worth $1,622 twenty years later. So if the extra 2.39 percent would be so disruptive to the market for products like Medtronic's that it would kill sales, why would the industry pass it along as a price increase to consumers? It hardly has to, given its profit margins.

Medtronic spokeswoman Donna Marquad says that for competitive reasons, her company will not discuss sales figures or the profit on Steve H.'s neurostimulator. But Medtronic's October 2012 quarterly SEC filing reported that its spine "products and therapies," which presumably include Steve H.'s device, "continue to gain broad surgeon acceptance" and that its cost to make all of its products was 24.9 percent of what it sells them for.

That's an unusually high gross profit margin—75.1 percent—for a company that manufactures real physical products. Apple also produces high-end, high-tech products, and its gross margin is 40 percent. If the neurostimulator enjoys that company-wide profit margin, it would mean that if Medtronic was paid $19,000 by Mercy Hospital, Medtronic's cost was about $4,500 and it made a gross profit of about $14,500 before expenses for sales, overhead, and management—including CEO Omar Ishrak's compensation, which was $25 million for the 2012 fiscal year.

Mercy's Bargain

When Pat Palmer, the medical-billing specialist who advises Steve H.'s union, was given the Mercy bill to deal with, she prepared a tally of about $4,000 worth of line items that she thought represented the most egregious charges, such as the surgical gown, the blanket warmer, and the marking pen. She restricted her list to those she thought were plainly not allowable. "I didn't dispute nearly all of them," she says. "Because then they get their backs up."

The hospital quickly conceded those items. For the remaining $83,000, Palmer invoked a 40 percent discount off chargemaster rates that Mercy allows for smaller insurance providers like the union. That cut the bill to about $50,000, for which the insurance company owed 80 percent, or about $40,000. That left Steve H. with a $10,000 bill.

Sean Recchi wasn't as fortunate. His bill—which included not only the aggressively marked-up charge of $13,702 for the Rituxan cancer drug but also the usual array of chargemaster fees for basics like generic Tylenol, blood tests, and simple supplies—had one item not found on any other bill I examined: MD Anderson's charge of $7 each for "ALCOHOL PREP PAD." This is a little square of cotton used to apply alcohol to an injection. A box of 200 can be bought online for $1.91.

We have seen that to the extent that most hospital administrators defend such chargemaster rates at all, they maintain that they are just starting points for a negotiation. But patients don't typically know they are in a negotiation when they enter the hospital, nor do hospitals let them know that. And in any case, at MD Anderson, the Recchis were made to pay every penny of the chargemaster bill up front because their insurance was deemed inadequate. That left Penne, the hospital spokeswoman, with only this defense for the most blatantly abusive charges for items like the alcohol squares: "It is difficult to compare a retail store charge for a common product with a cancer center that provides the item as part of its highly specialized and personalized care," she wrote in an e-mail. Yet the hospital also charges for that "specialized and personalized" care through, among other items, its $1,791-a-day room charge.

Before MD Anderson marked up Recchi's Rituxan to $13,702, the profit taking was equally aggressive, and equally routine, at the beginning of the supply chain—at the drug company. Rituxan is a prime product of Biogen Idec, a company with $5.5 billion in annual sales. Its CEO, George Scangos, was paid $11,331,441 in 2011, a 20 percent boost over his 2010 income. Rituxan is made and sold by Biogen Idec in partnership with Genentech, a South San Francisco–based biotechnology pioneer. Genentech brags about Rituxan on its website, as did Roche, Genentech's $45 billion parent, in its latest annual report. And in an Investor Day presentation last September, Roche CEO Severin Schwann stressed that his company is able to keep prices and margins high because of its focus on "medically differentiated therapies." Rituxan, a cancer wonder drug, certainly meets that test.

A spokesman at Genentech for the Biogen Idec–Genentech partnership would not say what the drug cost the companies to make, but according to its latest annual report, Biogen Idec's cost of sales—the incremental expense of producing and shipping each of its products compared with what it sells them for—was only 10 percent. That's lower than the incremental cost of sales for most software companies, and the software companies usually don't produce anything physical or have to pay to ship anything.

This would mean that Sean Recchi's dose of Rituxan cost the Biogen Idec–Genentech partnership as little as $300 to make, test, package, and ship to MD Anderson for $3,000 to $3,500, whereupon the hospital sold it to Recchi for $13,702.

As 2013 began, Recchi was being treated back in Ohio because he could not pay MD Anderson for more than his initial treatment. As for the $13,702-a-dose Rituxan, it turns out that Biogen Idec's partner Genentech has a charity-access program that Recchi's Ohio doctor told him about that enabled him to get those treatments free. "MD Anderson never said a word to us about the Genentech program," says Stephanie Recchi. "They just took our money up front."

Genentech spokeswoman Charlotte Arnold would not disclose how much free Rituxan had been dispensed to patients like Recchi in the past year, saying only that Genentech has "donated $2.85 billion in free medicine to uninsured patients in the U.S." since 1985. That seems like a lot until the numbers are broken down. Arnold says the $2.85 billion is based on what the drug maker sells the product for, not what it costs Genentech to make. On the basis of Genentech's historic costs and revenue since 1985, that would make the cost of these donations less than 1 percent of Genentech's sales—not something likely to take the sizzle out of CEO Severin's Investor Day.

Nonetheless, the company provided more financial support than MD Anderson did to Recchi, whose wife reports that he "is doing great. He's in remission."

Penne of MD Anderson stressed that the hospital provides its own financial aid to patients but that the state legislature restricts the assistance to Texas residents. She also said MD Anderson "makes every attempt" to inform patients of drug-company charity programs and that fifty of the hospital's 24,000 inpatients and outpatients, one of whom was from outside Texas, received charitable aid for Rituxan treatments in 2012.

3. Catastrophic Illness—and the Bills to Match

When medical care becomes a matter of life and death, the money demanded by the health-care ecosystem reaches a wholly different order of magnitude, churning out reams of bills to people who can't focus on them, let alone pay them. Soon after he was diagnosed with lung cancer in January 2011, a patient whom I will call Steven D. and his wife, Alice, knew that they were only buying time. The crushing question was, How much is time really worth? As Alice, who makes about $40,000 a year running a child-care center in her home, explained, "[Steven] kept saying he wanted every last minute he could get, no matter what. But I had to be thinking about the cost and how all this debt would leave me and my daughter." By the time Steven D. died at his home in northern California the following November, he had lived for an additional eleven months. And Alice had collected bills totaling $902,452. The family's first bill—for $348,000—which arrived when Steven got home from the Seton Medical Center in Daly City, Calif., was full of all the usual chargemaster profit grabs: $18 each for 88 diabetes-test strips that Amazon sells in boxes of 50 for $27.85; $24 each for 19 niacin pills that are sold in drugstores for about a nickel apiece. There were also four boxes of sterile gauze pads for $77 each. None of that was considered part of what was provided in return for Seton's facility charge for the intensive-care unit for two days at $13,225 a day, twelve days in the critical unit at $7,315 a day, and one day in a standard room (all of which totaled $120,116 over fifteen days). There was also $20,886 for CT scans and $24,251 for lab work. Alice responded to my question about the obvious overcharges on the bill for items like the diabetes-test strips or the gauze pads much as Mrs. Lincoln, according to the famous joke, might have had she been asked what she thought of the play. "Are you kidding?" she said. "I'm dealing with a husband who had just been told he has Stage IV cancer. That's all I can focus on. . . . You think I looked at the items on the bills? I just looked at the total."

Steven and Alice didn't know that hospital billing people consider the chargemaster to be an opening bid. That's because no medical bill ever says, "Give us your best offer." The couple knew only that the bill said they had maxed out on the $50,000 payout limit on a UnitedHealthcare policy they had bought through a community college where Steven had briefly enrolled a year before. "We were in shock," Alice recalls. "We looked at the total and couldn't deal with it. So we just started putting all the bills in a box. We couldn't bear to look at them."

The $50,000 that UnitedHealthcare paid to Seton Medical Center was worth about $80,000 in credits because any charges covered by the insurer were subject to the discount it had negotiated with Seton. After that $80,000, Steven and Alice were on their own, not eligible for any more discounts. Four months into her husband's illness, Alice by chance got the name of Patricia Stone, a billing advocate based in Menlo Park, Calif. Stone's typical clients are middle-class people having trouble with insurance claims. Stone felt so bad for Steven and Alice—she saw the blizzard of bills Alice was going to have to sort through—that, says Alice, she "gave us many of her hours," for which she usually charges $100, "for free." Stone was soon able to persuade Seton to write off $297,000 of its $348,000 bill. Her argument was simple: There was no way the D.'s could pay it now or in the future, though they would scrape together $3,000 as a show of good faith. With the couple's $3,000 on top of the $50,000 paid by the UnitedHealthcare insurance, that $297,000 write-off amounted to an 85 percent discount. According to its latest financial report, Seton applies so many discounts and write-offs to its chargemaster bills that it ends up with only about 18 percent of the revenue it bills for. That's an average 82 percent discount, compared with an average discount of about 65 percent that I saw at the other hospitals whose bills were examined—except for the MD Anderson and Sloan-Kettering cancer centers, which collect about 50 percent of their chargemaster charges. Seton's discounting practices may explain why it is the only hospital whose bills I looked at that actually reported a small operating loss—$5 million—on its last financial report.

Of course, had the D.'s not come across Stone, the incomprehensible but terrifying bills would have piled up in a box, and the Seton Medical Center bill collectors would not have been kept at bay. Robert Issai, the CEO of the Daughters of Charity Health System, which owns and runs Seton, refused through an e-mail from a public relations assistant to respond to requests for a comment on any aspect of his hospital's billing or collections policies. Nor would he respond to repeated requests for a specific comment on the $24 charge for niacin pills, the $18 charge for the diabetes-test strips, or the $77 charge for gauze pads. He also declined to respond when asked, via a follow-up e-mail, if the hospital thinks that sending patients who have just been told they are terminally ill bills that reflect chargemaster rates that the hospital doesn't actually expect to be paid might unduly upset them during a particularly sensitive time. To begin to deal with all the other bills that kept coming after Steven's first stay at Seton, Stone was also able to get him into a special high-risk insurance pool set up by the state of California. It helped but not much. The insurance premium was $1,000 a month, quite a burden on a family whose income was maybe $3,500 a month. And it had an annual payout limit of $75,000. The D.'s blew through that in about two months. The bills kept piling up. Sequoia Hospital—where Steven was an inpatient as well as an outpatient between the end of January and November following his initial stay at Seton—weighed in with twenty-eight bills, all at chargemaster prices, including invoices for $99,000, $61,000, and $29,000. Doctor-run outpatient chemotherapy clinics wanted more than $85,000. One outside lab wanted $11,900.

Stone organized these and other bills into an elaborate spreadsheet—a ledger documenting how catastrophic illness in America unleashes its own mini-GDP.

In July, Stone figured out that Steven and Alice should qualify for Medicaid, which is called Medi-Cal in California. But there was a catch: Medicaid is the joint federal-state program directed at the poor that is often spoken of in the same breath as Medicare. Although most of the current national debate on entitlements is focused on Medicare, when Medicaid's subsidiary program called Children's Health Insurance, or CHIP, is counted, Medicaid actually covers more people: 56.2 million compared with 50.2 million. As Steven and Alice found out, Medicaid is also more vulnerable to cuts and conditions that limit coverage, probably for the same reason that most politicians and the press don't pay the same attention to it that they do to Medicare: its constituents are the poor. The major difference in the two programs is that while Medicare's rules are pretty much uniform across state lines, the states set the key rules for Medicaid because the state finances a big portion of the claims. According to Stone, Steven and Alice immediately ran into one of those rules. For people even with their modest income, the D.'s would have to pay $3,000 a month in medical bills before Medi-Cal would kick in. That amounted to most of Alice's monthly take-home pay.

Medi-Cal was even willing to go back five months, to February, to cover the couple's mountain of bills, but first they had to come up with $15,000. "We didn't have anything close to that," recalls Alice.

Stone then convinced Sequoia that if the hospital wanted to see any of the Medi-Cal money necessary to pay its bills (albeit at the big discount Medi-Cal would take), it should give Steven a "credit" for $15,000—in other words, write it off. Sequoia agreed to do that for most of the bills. This was clearly a maneuver that Steven and Alice never could have navigated on their own. Covering most of the Sequoia debt was a huge relief, but there were still hundreds of thousands of dollars in bills left unpaid as Steven approached his end in the fall of 2011. Meantime, the bills kept coming. "We started talking about the cost of the chemo," Alice recalls. "It was a source of tension between us. . . . Finally," she says, "the doctor told us that the next one scheduled might prolong his life a month, but it would be really painful. So he gave up."

By the one-year anniversary of Steven's death, late last year, Stone had made a slew of deals with his doctors, clinics, and other providers whose services Medi-Cal did not cover. Some, like Seton, were generous. The home health-care nurse ended up working for free in the final days of Steven's life, which were over the Thanksgiving weekend. "He was a saint," says Alice. "He said he was doing it to become accredited, so he didn't charge us."

Others, including some of the doctors, were more hardnosed, insisting on full payment or offering minimal discounts. Still others had long since sold the bills to professional debt collectors, who, by definition, are bounty hunters. Alice and Stone were still hoping Medi-Cal would end up covering some or most of the debt.

As 2012 closed, Alice had paid out about $30,000 of her own money (including the $3,000 to Seton) and still owed $142,000—her losses from the fixed poker game that she was forced to play in the worst of times with the worst of cards. She was still getting letters and calls from bill collectors. "I think about the $142,000 all the time. It just hangs over my head," she said in December.

One lesson she has learned, she adds: "I'm never going to re-marry. I can't risk the liability."[2]

$132,303: The Lab-Test Cash Machine

As 2012 began, a couple I'll call Rebecca and Scott S., both in their fifties, seemed to have carved out a comfortable semiretirement in a suburb near Dallas. Scott had successfully sold his small industrial business and was working part time advising other industrial companies. Rebecca was running a small marketing company. On March 4, Scott started having trouble breathing. By dinnertime he was gasping violently as Rebecca raced him to the emergency room at the University of Texas Southwestern Medical Center. Both Rebecca and her husband thought he was about to die, Rebecca recalls. It was not the time to think about the bills that were going to change their lives if Scott survived, and certainly not the time to imagine, much less worry about, the piles of charges for daily routine lab tests that would be incurred by any patient in the middle of a long hospital stay. Scott was in the hospital for thirty-two days before his pneumonia was brought under control. Rebecca recalls that "on about the fourth or fifth day, I was sitting around the hospital and bored, so I went down to the business office just to check that they had all the insurance information." She remembered that there was, she says, "some kind of limit on it."

"Even by then, the bill was over $80,000," she recalls. "I couldn't believe it."

The woman in the business office matter-of-factly gave Rebecca more bad news: Her insurance policy, from a company called

2. In early February, Alice told *Time* that she had recently eliminated "most of" the debt through proceeds from the sale of a small farm in Oklahoma her husband had inherited and after further payments from Medi-Cal and a small life-insurance policy.

Assurant Health, had an annual payout limit of $200,000. Because of some prior claims Assurant had processed, the S.'s were well on their way to exceeding the limit. Just the room-and-board charge at Southwestern was $2,293 a day. And that was before all the real charges were added. When Scott checked out, his 161-page bill was $474,064. Scott and Rebecca were told they owed $402,955 after the payment from their insurance policy was deducted. The top billing categories were $73,376 for Scott's room; $94,799 for "RESP SERVICES," which mostly meant supplying Scott with oxygen and testing his breathing and included multiple charges per day of $134 for supervising oxygen inhalation, for which Medicare would have paid $17.94; and $108,663 for "SPECIAL DRUGS," which included mostly not-so-special drugs such as "SODIUM CHLORIDE .9%." That's a standard saline solution probably used intravenously in this case to maintain Scott's water and salt levels. (It is also used to wet contact lenses.) You can buy a liter of the hospital version (bagged for intravenous use) online for $5.16. Scott was charged $84 to $134 for dozens of these saline solutions.

Then there was the $132,303 charge for "LABORATORY," which included hundreds of blood and urine tests ranging from $30 to $333 each, for which Medicare either pays nothing because it is part of the room fee or pays $7 to $30. Hospital spokesman Russell Rian said that neither Daniel Podolsky, Texas Southwestern Medical Center's $1,244,000-a-year president, nor any other executive would be available to discuss billing practices. "The law does not allow us to talk about how we bill," he explained. Through a friend of a friend, Rebecca found Patricia Palmer, the same billing advocate based in Salem, Va., who worked on Steve H.'s bill in Oklahoma City. Palmer—whose firm, Medical Recovery Services, now includes her two adult daughters—was a claims processor for Blue Cross Blue Shield. She got into her current business after she was stunned by the bill her local hospital sent after one of her daughters had to go to the emergency room after an accident. She says it included items like the shade attached to an examining lamp. She then began looking at bills for friends as kind of a hobby before deciding to make it a business.

The best Palmer could do was get Texas Southwestern Medical to provide a credit that still left Scott and Rebecca owing $313,000. Palmer claimed in a detailed appeal that there were also overcharges totaling $113,000—not because the prices were too high but because the items she singled out should not have been charged for at all. These included $5,890 for all of that saline solution and $65,600 for the management of Scott's oxygen. These items are supposed to be part of the hospital's general room-and-services charge, she argued, so they should not be billed twice.

In fact, Palmer—echoing a constant and convincing refrain I heard from billing advocates across the country—alleged that the hospital triple-billed for some items used in Scott's care in the intensive-care unit. "First they charge more than $2,000 a day for the ICU, because it's an ICU and it has all this special equipment and personnel," she says. "Then they charge $1,000 for some kit used in the ICU to give someone a transfusion or oxygen. . . . And then they charge $50 or $100 for each tool or bandage or whatever that there is in the kit. That's triple billing." Palmer and Rebecca are still fighting, but the hospital insists that the S.'s owe the $313,000 balance. That doesn't include what Rebecca says were "thousands" in doctors' bills and $70,000 owed to a second hospital after Scott suffered a relapse. The only offer the hospital has made so far is to cut the bill to $200,000 if it is paid immediately, or for the full $313,000 to be paid in twenty-four monthly payments. "How am I supposed to write a check right now for $200,000?" Rebecca asks. "I have boxes full of notices from bill collectors. . . . We can't apply for charity, because we're kind of well off in terms of assets," she adds. "We thought we were set, but now we're pretty much on the edge."

Insurance That Isn't

"People, especially relatively wealthy people, always think they have good insurance until they see they don't," says Palmer. "Most of my clients are middle- or upper-middle-class people with insurance."

Scott and Rebecca bought their plan from Assurant, which sells health insurance to small businesses that will pay only for limited coverage for their employees or to individuals who cannot get insurance through employers and are not eligible for Medicare or Medicaid. Assurant also sold the Recchis their plan that paid only $2,000 a day for Sean Recchi's treatment at MD Anderson. Although the tight limits on what their policies cover are clearly spelled out in Assurant's marketing materials and in the policy documents themselves, it seems that for its customers the appeal of having something called health insurance for a few hundred dollars a month is far more compelling than comprehending the details. "Yes, we knew there were some limits," says Rebecca. "But when you see the limits expressed in the thousands of dollars, it looks OK, I guess. Until you have an event."

Millions of plans have annual payout limits, though the more typical plans purchased by employers usually set those limits at $500,000 or $750,000—which can also quickly be consumed by a catastrophic illness. For that reason, Obamacare prohibited lifetime limits on any policies sold after the law passed and phases out all annual dollar limits by 2014. That will protect people like Scott and Rebecca, but it will also make everyone's premiums dramatically higher, because insurance companies risk much more when there is no cap on their exposure.

But Obamacare does little to attack the costs that overwhelmed Scott and Rebecca. There is nothing, for example, that addresses what may be the most surprising sinkhole—the seemingly routine blood, urine, and other laboratory tests for which Scott was charged $132,000, or more than $4,000 a day. By my estimates, about $70 billion will be spent in the United States on about 7 billion lab tests in 2013. That's about $223 a person for sixteen tests per person. Cutting the overordering and overpricing could easily take $25 billion out of that bill. Much of that overordering involves patients like Scott S. who require prolonged hospital stays. Their tests become a routine, daily cash generator. "When you're getting trained as a doctor," says a physician who was involved in framing health-care policy early in the Obama administration, "you're taught to order what's called 'morning labs.' Every day you have a variety of blood tests and other tests done, not because it's necessary but because it gives you something to talk about with the others when you go on rounds. It's like your version of a news hook ... I bet 60 percent of the labs are not necessary."

The country's largest lab tester is Quest Diagnostics, which reported revenues in 2012 of $7.4 billion. Quest's operating income in 2012 was $1.2 billion, about 16.2 percent of sales.

But that's hardly the spectacular profit margin we have seen in other sectors of the medical marketplace. The reason is that the outside companies like Quest, which mostly pick up specimens from doctors and clinics and deliver test results back to them, are not where the big profits are. The real money is in health-care settings that cut out the middleman—the in-house venues, like the hospital testing lab run by Southwestern Medical that billed Scott and Rebecca $132,000. In-house labs account for about 60 percent of all testing revenue. Which means that for hospitals, they are vital profit centers. Labs are also increasingly being maintained by doctors who, as they form group practices with other doctors in their field, finance their own testing and diagnostic clinics. These labs account for a rapidly growing share of the testing revenue, and their share is growing rapidly. These in-house labs have no selling costs, and as pricing surveys repeatedly find, they can charge more because they have a captive consumer base in the hospitals or group practices. They also have an incentive to order more tests because they're the ones profiting from the tests. The *Wall Street Journal* reported last April that a study in the medical journal *Health Affairs* had found that doctors' urology groups with their own labs "bill the federal Medicare program for analyzing 72% more prostate tissue samples per biopsy while detecting fewer cases of cancer than counterparts who send specimens to outside labs."

If anything, the move toward in-house testing, and with it the incentive to do more of it, is accelerating the move by doctors to consolidate into practice groups. As one Bronx urologist explains, "The economics of having your own lab are so alluring." More important, hospitals are aligning with these practice groups, in many cases even getting them to sign noncompete clauses requiring that they steer all patients to the partner hospital. Some hospitals are buying physicians' practices outright; 54 percent of physician practices were owned by hospitals in 2012, according to a McKinsey survey, up from 22 percent ten years before. This is primarily a move to increase the hospitals' leverage in negotiating with insurers. An expensive by-product is that it brings testing into the hospitals' high-profit labs.

4. When Taxpayers Pick Up the Tab

Whether it was Emilia Gilbert trying to get out from under $9,418 in bills after her slip and fall or Alice D. vowing never to marry again because of the $142,000 debt from her husband's losing battle with cancer, we've seen how the medical marketplace misfires when private parties get the bills.

When the taxpayers pick up the tab, most of the dynamics of the marketplace shift dramatically.

In July 2011, an eighty-eight-year-old man whom I'll call Alan A. collapsed from a massive heart attack at his home outside Philadelphia. He survived, after two weeks in the intensive-care unit of the Virtua Marlton hospital. Virtua Marlton is part of a four-hospital chain that, in its 2010 federal filing, reported paying its CEO $3,073,000 and two other executives $1.4 million and $1.7 million from gross revenue of $633.7 million and an operating profit of $91 million. Alan A. then spent three weeks at a nearby convalescent-care center.

Medicare made quick work of the $268,227 in bills from the two hospitals, paying just $43,320. Except for $100 in incidental expenses, Alan A. paid nothing because 100 percent of inpatient hospital care is covered by Medicare.

The ManorCare convalescent center, which Alan A. says gave him "good care" in an "OK but not luxurious room," got paid $11,982 by Medicare for his three-week stay. That is about $571 a day for all the physical therapy, tests, and other services. As with all hospitals in nonemergency situations, ManorCare does not have to accept Medicare patients and their discounted rates. But it does accept them. In fact, it welcomes them and encourages doctors to refer them.

Health-care providers may grouse about Medicare's fee schedules, but Medicare's payments must be producing profits for ManorCare. It is part of a for-profit chain owned by Carlyle Group, a blue-chip private-equity firm.

About a decade ago, Alan A. was diagnosed with non-Hodgkin's lymphoma. He was seventy-eight, and his doctors in southern New Jersey told him there was little they could do. Through a family friend, he got an appointment with one of the lymphoma specialists at Sloan-Kettering. That doctor told Alan A. he was willing to try a new chemotherapy regimen on him. The doctor warned, however, that he hadn't ever tried the treatment on a man of Alan A.'s age.

The treatment worked. A decade later, Alan A. is still in remission. He now travels to Sloan-Kettering every six weeks to be examined by the doctor who saved his life and to get a transfusion of Flebogamma, a drug that bucks up his immune system.

With some minor variations each time, Sloan-Kettering's typical bill for each visit is the same as or similar to the $7,346 bill he received during the summer of 2011, which included $340 for a session with the doctor.

Assuming eight visits (but only four with the doctor), that makes the annual bill $57,408 a year to keep Alan A. alive. His actual out-of-pocket cost for each session is a fraction of that. For that $7,346 visit, it was about $50.

In some ways, the set of transactions around Alan A.'s Sloan-Kettering care represent the best the American medical marketplace has to offer. First, obviously, there's the fact that he is alive after other doctors gave him up for dead. And then there's the fact that Alan A., a retired chemist of average means, was able to get care that might otherwise be reserved for the rich but was available to him because he had the right insurance.

Medicare is the core of that insurance, although Alan A.—as do 90 percent of those on Medicare—has a supplemental-insurance policy that kicks in and generally pays 90 percent of the 20 percent of costs for doctors and outpatient care that Medicare does not cover.

Here's how it all computes for him using that summer 2011 bill as an example.

Not counting the doctor's separate $340 bill, Sloan-Kettering's bill for the transfusion is about $7,006.

In addition to a few hundred dollars in miscellaneous items, the two basic Sloan-Kettering charges are $414 per hour for five hours of nurse time for administering the Flebogamma and a $4,615 charge for the Flebogamma.

According to Alan A., the nurse generally handles three or four patients at a time. That would mean Sloan-Kettering is billing more than $1,200 an hour for that nurse. When I asked Paul Nelson, Sloan-Kettering's director of financial planning, about the $414-per-hour charge, he explained that 15 percent of these charges is meant to cover overhead and indirect expenses, 20 percent is meant to be profit that will cover discounts for Medicare or Medicaid patients, and 65 percent covers direct expenses. That would still leave the nurse's time being valued at about $800 an hour (65 percent of $1,200), again assuming that just three patients were billed for the same hour at $414 each. Pressed on that, Nelson conceded that the profit is higher and is meant to cover other hospital costs like research and capital equipment.

Whatever Sloan-Kettering's calculations may be, Medicare—whose patients, including Alan A., are about a third of all Sloan-Kettering patients—buys into none of that math. Its cost-based pricing formulas yield a price of $302 for everything other than the drug, including those hourly charges for the nurse and the miscellaneous charges. Medicare pays 80% of that, or $241, leaving Alan A. and his private insurance company together to pay about $60 more to Sloan-Kettering. Alan A. pays $6, and his supplemental insurer, Aetna, pays $54.

Bottom line: Sloan-Kettering gets paid $302 by Medicare for about $2,400 worth of its chargemaster charges, and Alan A. ends up paying $6.

The Cancer Drug Profit Chain

It's with the bill for the transfusion that the peculiar economics of American medicine take a different turn, even when Medicare is involved. We have seen that even with big discounts for insurance companies and bigger discounts for Medicare, the chargemaster prices on everything from room and board to Tylenol to CT scans are high enough to make hospital costs a leading cause of the $750 billion Americans overspend each year on health care. We're now going to see how drug pricing is a major contributor to the way Americans overpay for medical care.

By law, Medicare has to pay hospitals 6 percent above what Congress calls the drug company's "average sales price," which is supposedly the average price at which the drug maker sells the drug to hospitals and clinics. But Congress does not control what drug makers charge. The drug companies are free to set their own prices. This seems fair in a free-market economy, but when the drug is a one-of-a-kind lifesaving serum, the result is anything but fair.

Applying that formula of average sales price plus the 6 percent premium, Medicare cuts Sloan-Kettering's $4,615 charge for Alan A.'s Flebogamma to $2,123. That's what the drug maker tells Medicare the average sales price is plus 6 percent. Medicare again pays 80 percent of that, and Alan A. and his insurer split the other 20 percent, 10 percent for him and 90 percent for the insurer, which makes Alan A.'s cost $42.50.

In practice, the average sales price does not appear to be a real average. Two other hospitals I asked reported that after taking into account rebates given by the drug company, they paid an average of $1,650 for the same dose of Flebogamma, and neither hospital had nearly the leverage in the cancer-care marketplace that Sloan-Kettering does. One doctor at Sloan-Kettering guessed that it pays $1,400. "The drug companies give the rebates so that the hospitals will make more on the drug and therefore be encouraged to dispense it," the doctor explained. (A spokesperson for Medicare would say only that the average sales price is based "on manufacturers' data submitted to Medicare and is meant to include rebates.")

Nelson, the Sloan-Kettering head of financial planning, said the price his hospital pays for Alan A.'s dose of Flebogamma is "somewhat higher" than $1,400, but he wasn't specific, adding that "the difference between the cost and the charge represents the cost of running our pharmacy—which includes overhead cost—plus a markup." Even assuming Sloan-Kettering's real price for Flebogamma is "somewhat higher" than $1,400, the hospital would be making about 50 percent profit from Medicare's $2,123 payment. So even Medicare contributes mightily to hospital profit—and drug-company profit—when it buys drugs.

Flebogamma's Profit Margin

The Spanish business at the beginning of the Flebogamma supply chain does even better than Sloan-Kettering.

Made from human plasma, Flebogamma is a sterilized solution that is intended to boost the immune system. Sloan-Kettering buys it from either Baxter International in the United States or, as is more likely in Alan A.'s case, a Barcelona-based company called Grifols.

In its half-year 2012 shareholders report, Grifols featured a picture of the Flebogamma plasma serum and its packaging— "produced at the Clayton facility, North Carolina," according to the caption. Worldwide sales of all Grifols products were reported as up 15.2 percent, to $1.62 billion, in the first half of 2012. In the United States and Canada, sales were up 20.5 percent. "Growth in the sales . . . of the main plasma derivatives" was highlighted in the report, as was the fact that "the cost per liter of plasma has fallen." (Grifols operates 150 donation centers across the United States where it pays plasma donors twenty-five dollars apiece.)

Grifols spokesman Christopher Healey would not discuss what it cost Grifols to produce and ship Alan A.'s dose, but he did say that the company's average cost to produce its bioscience products, Flebogamma included, was approximately 55 percent of what it sells them for. However, a doctor familiar with the economics of cancer-care drugs said that plasma products typically have some of the industry's higher profit margins. He estimated that the Flebogamma dose for Alan A.—which Sloan-Kettering bought from Grifols for $1,400 or $1,500 and sold to Medicare for $2,135—"can't cost them more than $200 or $300 to collect, process, test, and ship."

In Spain, as in the rest of the developed world, Grifols' profit margins on sales are much lower than they are in the United States, where it can charge much higher prices. Aware of the leverage that drug companies—especially those with unique lifesaving products—have on the market, most developed countries regulate what drug makers can charge, limiting them to certain profit margins. In fact, the drug makers' securities filings repeatedly warn investors of tighter price controls that could threaten their high margins—though not in the United States.

The difference between the regulatory environment in the United States and the environment abroad is so dramatic that McKinsey & Co. researchers reported that overall prescription-drug prices in the United States are "50% higher for comparable products" than in other developed countries. Yet those regulated profit margins outside the United States remain high enough that Grifols, Baxter, and other drug companies still aggressively sell their products there. For example, 37 percent of Grifols's sales come from outside North America.

More than $280 billion will be spent this year on prescription drugs in the United States. If we paid what other countries did for the same products, we would save about $94 billion a year. The pharmaceutical industry's common explanation for the price difference is that U.S. profits subsidize the research and development of trailblazing drugs that are developed in the United States and then marketed around the world. Apart from the question of whether a country with a health-care-spending crisis should subsidize the rest of the developed world—not to mention the question of who signed Americans up for that mission—there's the fact that the companies' math doesn't add up.

According to securities filings of major drug companies, their R&D expenses are generally 15 percent to 20 percent of gross revenue. In fact, Grifols spent only 5 percent on R&D for the first nine months of 2012. Neither 5 percent nor 20 percent is enough to have cut deeply into the pharmaceutical companies' stellar bottom-line net profits. This is not *gross* profit, which counts only the cost of producing the drug, but the profit *after* those R&D expenses are taken into account. Grifols made a 32.3 percent net operating profit after all its R&D expenses—as well as sales, management, and other expenses—were tallied. In other words, even counting all the R&D across the entire company, including research for drugs that did not pan out, Grifols made healthy profits. All the numbers tell one consistent story: Regulating drug prices the way other countries do would save tens of billions of dollars while still offering profit margins that would keep encouraging the pharmaceutical companies' quest for the next great drug.

Handcuffs on Medicare

Our laws do more than prevent the government from restraining prices for drugs the way other countries do. Federal law also restricts the biggest single buyer—Medicare—from even trying to negotiate drug prices. As a perpetual gift to the pharmaceutical companies (and an acceptance of their argument that completely unrestrained prices and profit are necessary to fund the risk taking of research and development), Congress has continually prohibited the Centers for Medicare and Medicaid Services (CMS) of the Department of Health and Human Services from negotiating prices with drug makers. Instead, Medicare simply has to determine that average sales price and add 6 percent to it.

Similarly, when Congress passed Part D of Medicare in 2003, giving seniors coverage for prescription drugs, Congress prohibited Medicare from negotiating.

Nor can Medicare get involved in deciding that a drug may be a waste of money. In medical circles, this is known as the comparative-effectiveness debate, which nearly derailed the entire Obamacare effort in 2009.

Doctors and other health-care reformers behind the comparative-effectiveness movement make a simple argument: Suppose that after exhaustive research, cancer drug A, which costs $300 a dose, is found to be just as effective as or more effective than drug B, which costs $3,000. Shouldn't the person or entity paying the bill, e.g., Medicare, be able to decide that it will pay for drug A but not drug B? Not according to a law passed by Congress in 2003 that requires Medicare to reimburse patients (again, at average sales price plus 6 percent) for any cancer drug approved for use by the Food and Drug Administration. Most states require insurance companies to do the same thing.

Peter Bach, an epidemiologist at Sloan-Kettering who has also advised several health-policy organizations, reported in a 2009 *New England Journal of Medicine* article that Medicare's spending on the category dominated by cancer drugs ballooned from $3 billion in 1997 to $11 billion in 2004. Bach says costs have continued to increase rapidly and must now be more than $20 billion.

With that escalating bill in mind, Bach was among the policy experts pushing for provisions in Obamacare to establish a Patient-Centered Outcomes Research Institute to expand comparative-effectiveness research efforts. Through painstaking research, doctors would try to determine the comparative effectiveness not only of drugs but also of procedures like CT scans.

However, after all the provisions spelling out elaborate research and review processes were embedded in the draft law, Congress jumped in and added eight provisions that restrict how the research can be used. The prime restriction: Findings shall "not be construed as mandates for practice guidelines, coverage recommendations, payment, or policy recommendations."

With those fourteen words, the work of Bach and his colleagues was undone. And costs remain unchecked.

"Medicare could see the research and say, Ah, this drug works better and costs the same or is even cheaper," says Gunn,

Sloan-Kettering's chief operating officer. "But they are not allowed to do anything about it."

Along with another doomed provision that would have allowed Medicare to pay a fee for doctors' time spent counseling terminal patients on end-of-life care (but not on euthanasia), the Obama administration's push for comparative effectiveness is what brought opponents' cries that the bill was creating "death panels." Washington bureaucrats would now be dictating which drugs were worth giving to which patients and even which patients deserved to live or die, the critics charged.

The loudest voice sounding the death-panel alarm belonged to Betsy McCaughey, former New York State lieutenant governor and a conservative health-policy advocate. McCaughey, who now runs a foundation called the Committee to Reduce Infection Deaths, is still fiercely opposed to Medicare's making comparative-effectiveness decisions. "There is comparative-effectiveness research being done in the medical journals all the time, which is fine," she says. "But it should be used by doctors to make decisions—not by the Obama bureaucrats at Medicare to make decisions for doctors."

Bach, the Sloan-Kettering doctor and policy wonk, has become so frustrated with the rising cost of the drugs he uses that he and some colleagues recently took matters into their own hands. They reported in an October op-ed in the *New York Times* that they had decided on their own that they were no longer going to dispense a colorectal-cancer drug called Zaltrap, which cost an average of $11,063 per month for treatment. All the research shows, they wrote, that a drug called Avastin, which cost $5,000 a month, is just as effective. They were taking this stand, they added, because "the typical new cancer drug coming on the market a decade ago cost about $4,500 per month (in 2012 dollars); since 2010, the median price has been around $10,000. Two of the new cancer drugs cost more than $35,000 each per month of treatment. The burden of this cost is borne, increasingly, by patients themselves—and the effects can be devastating."

The CEO of Sanofi, the company that makes Zaltrap, initially dismissed the article by Bach and his Sloan-Kettering colleagues, saying they had taken the price of the drug out of context because of variations in the required dosage. But four weeks later, Sanofi cut its price in half.

Bureaucrats You Can Admire

By the numbers, Medicare looks like a government program run amok. After President Lyndon B. Johnson signed Medicare into law in 1965, the House Ways and Means Committee predicted that the program would cost $12 billion in 1990. Its actual cost by then was $110 billion. It is likely to be nearly $600 billion this year. That's due to the aging U.S. population and the popular program's expansion to cover more services, as well as the skyrocketing costs of medical services generally. It's also because Medicare's hands are tied when it comes to negotiating the prices for drugs or durable medical equipment. But Medicare's growth is not a matter of those "bureaucrats" that Betsy McCaughey complains about having gone off the rails in how they operate it.

In fact, seeing the way Alan A.'s bills from Sloan-Kettering were vetted and processed is one of the more eye-opening and least discouraging aspects of a look inside the world of medical economics.

The process is fast, accurate, customer-friendly, and impressively high tech. And it's all done quietly by a team of nonpolitical civil servants in close partnership with the private sector. In fact, despite calls to privatize Medicare by creating a voucher system under which the Medicare population would get money from the government to buy insurance from private companies, the current Medicare system is staffed with more people employed by private contractors (8,500) than government workers (700).

$1.5 Billion a Day

Sloan-Kettering sends Alan A.'s bills to Medicare electronically, all elaborately coded according to Medicare's rules.

There are two basic kinds of codes for the services billed. The first is a number identifying which of the 7,000 procedures were performed by a doctor, such as examining a chest X ray, performing a heart transplant, or conducting an office consultation for a new patient (which costs more than a consultation with a continuing patient—coded differently—because it typically takes more time). If a patient presents more complicated challenges, then these basic procedures will be coded differently; for example, there are two varieties of emergency-room consultations. Adjustments are also made for variations in the cost of living where the doctor works and for other factors, like whether doctors used their own office (they'll get paid more for that) or the hospital. A panel of doctors set up by the American Medical Association reviews the codes annually and recommends updates to Medicare. The process can get messy as the doctors fight over which procedures in which specialties take more time and expertise or are worth relatively more. Medicare typically accepts most of the panel's recommendations.

The second kind of code is used to pay the hospital for its services. Again, there are thousands of codes based on whether the person checked in for brain surgery, an appendectomy, or a fainting spell. To come up with these numbers, Medicare takes the cost reports—including allocations for everything from overhead to nursing staff to operating-room equipment—that hospitals across the country are required to file for each type of service and pays an amount equal to the composite average costs.

The hospital has little incentive to overstate its costs because it's against the law and because each hospital gets paid not on the basis of its own claimed costs but on the basis of the average of every hospital's costs, with adjustments made for regional cost differences and other local factors. Except for emergency services, no hospital has to accept Medicare patients and these prices, but they all do.

Similar codes are calculated for laboratory and diagnostic tests like CT scans, ambulance services, and, as we saw with Alan A.'s bill, drugs dispensed.

"When I tell my friends what I do here, it sounds boring, but it's exciting," says Diane Kovach, who works at Medicare's Maryland campus and whose title is deputy director of the provider billing group. "We are implementing a program that helps millions and millions of people, and we're doing it in a way that makes every one of us proud," she adds.

Kovach, who has been at Medicare for twenty-one years, operates some of the gears of a machine that reviews the more than 3 million bills that come into Medicare every day, figures out the right payments for each, and churns out more than $1.5 billion a day in wire transfers.

The part of that process that Kovach and three colleagues, with whom I spent a morning recently, are responsible for involves overseeing the writing and vetting of thousands of instructions for coders, who are also private contractors, employed by HP, General Dynamics, and other major technology companies. The codes they write are supposed to ensure that Medicare pays what it is supposed to pay and catches anything in a bill that should not be paid.

For example, hundreds of instructions for code changes were needed to address Obamacare's requirement that certain preventive-care visits, such as those for colonoscopies or contraceptive services, no longer be subject to Medicare's usual outpatient copay of 20 percent. Adding to the complexity, the benefit is limited to one visit per year for some services, meaning instructions had to be written to track patient timelines for the codes assigned to those services.

When performing correctly, the codes produce "edits" whenever a bill is submitted with something awry on it—if a doctor submits two preventive-care colonoscopies for the same patient in the same year, for example. Depending on the code, an edit will result in the bill's being sent back with questions or being rejected with an explanation. It all typically happens without a human being reading it. "Our goal at the first stage is that no one has to touch the bill," says Leslie Trazzi, who focuses on instructions and edits for doctors' claims.

Alan A.'s bills from Sloan-Kettering are wired to a data center in Shelbyville, Ky., run by a private company (owned by Well-Point, the insurance company that operates under the Blue Cross and Blue Shield names in more than a dozen states) that has the contract to process claims originating from New York and Connecticut. Medicare is paying the company about $323 million over five years—which, as with the fees of other contractors serving other regions, works out to an average of $0.84 per claim.

In Shelbyville, Alan A.'s status as a beneficiary is verified, and then the bill is sent electronically to a data center in Columbia, S.C., operated by another contractor, also a subsidiary of an insurance company. There, the codes are checked for edits, after which Alan A.'s Sloan-Kettering bill goes electronically to a data center in Denver, where the payment instructions are prepared and entered into what Karen Jackson, who supervises Medicare's outside contractors, says is the largest accounting ledger in the world. The whole process takes three days—and that long only because the data is sent in batches.

There are multiple backups to make sure this ruthlessly efficient system isn't just ruthless. Medicare keeps track of and publicly reports the percentage of bills processed "clean"—i.e., with no rejected items—within thirty days. Even the speed with which the contractors answer the widely publicized consumer phone lines is monitored and reported. The average time to answer a call from a doctor or other provider is 57.6 seconds, according to Medicare's records, and the average time to answer one of the millions of calls from patients is two minutes forty-one seconds, down from more than eight minutes in 2007. These times might come as a surprise to people who have tried to call a private insurer. That monitoring process is, in turn, backstopped by a separate ombudsman's office, which has regional and national layers.

Beyond that, the members of the House of Representatives and the Senate loom as an additional 535 ombudsmen. "We get calls every day from congressional offices about complaints that a beneficiary's claim has been denied," says Jonathan Blum, the deputy administrator of CMS. As a result, Blum's agency has an unusually large congressional liaison staff of fifty-two, most of whom act as caseworkers trying to resolve these complaints.

All the customer-friendliness adds up to only about 10 percent of initial Medicare claims' being denied, according to Medicare's latest published *Composite Benchmark Metric Report*. Of those initial Medicare denials, only about 20 percent (2 percent of total claims) result in complaints or appeals, and the decisions in only about half of those (or 1 percent of the total) end up being reversed, with the claim being paid.

The astonishing efficiency, of course, raises the question of whether Medicare is simply funneling money out the door as fast as it can. Some fraud is inevitable—even a rate of 0.1 percent is enough to make headlines when $600 billion is being spent. It's also possible that people can game the system without committing outright fraud. But Medicare has multiple layers of protection against fraud that the insurance companies don't and perhaps can't match because they lack Medicare's scale.

According to Medicare's Jackson, the contractors are "vigorously monitored for all kinds of metrics" and required every quarter "to do a lot of data analysis and submit review plans and error-rate-reduction plans."

And then there are the RACs—a wholly separate group of private "recovery audit contractors." Established by Congress during the George W. Bush administration, the RACs, says one hospital administrator, "drive the doctors and the hospitals and even the Medicare claims processors crazy." The RACs' only job is to review provider bills after they have been paid by Medicare claims processors and look for system errors, like faulty processing, or errors in the bills as reflected in doctor or hospital medical records that the RACs have the authority to audit.

The RACs have an incentive that any champion of the private sector would love. They get no up-front fees but instead are paid a percentage of the money they retrieve. They eat what they kill. According to Medicare spokeswoman Emma Sandoe, the RAC bounty hunters retrieved $797 million in the 2011 fiscal year, for which they were paid 9 percent to 12.5 percent of what they brought in, depending on the region where they were operating.

This process can "get quite anal," says the doctor who recently treated me for an ear infection. Although my doctor is on Park Avenue, she, like 96 percent of all specialists, accepts Medicare patients despite the discounted rates it pays, because, she says, "they pay quickly." However, she recalls getting bills from Medicare for $0.21 or $0.85 for supposed overpayments.

The DHHS's inspector general is also on the prowl to protect the Medicare checkbook. It reported recovering $1.2 billion last year through Medicare and Medicaid audits and investigations (though the recovered funds had probably been doled out over several fiscal years). The inspector general's work is supplemented by a separate, multiagency federal health-care-fraud task force, which brings criminal charges against fraudsters and issues regular press releases claiming billions more in recoveries.

This does not mean the system is airtight. If anything, all that recovery activity suggests fallibility, even as it suggests more buttoned-up operations than those run by private insurers, whose payment systems are notoriously erratic.

Too Much Health Care?

In a review of other bills of those enrolled in Medicare, a pattern of deep, deep discounting of chargemaster charges emerged that mirrored how Alan A.'s bills were shrunk down to reality. A $121,414 Stanford Hospital bill for a ninety-year-old California woman who fell and broke her wrist became $16,949. A $51,445 bill for the three days an ailing ninety-one-year-old spent getting tests and being sedated in the hospital before dying of old age became $19,242. Before Medicare went to work, the bill was chock-full of creative chargemaster charges from the California Pacific Medical Center—part of Sutter Health, a dominant non-profit northern California chain whose CEO made $5,241,305 in 2011.

Another pattern emerged from a look at these bills: some seniors apparently visit doctors almost weekly or even daily, for all varieties of ailments. Sure, as patients age they are increasingly in need of medical care. But at least some of the time, the fact that they pay almost nothing to spend their days in doctors' offices must also be a factor, especially if they have the supplemental insurance that covers most of the 20 percent not covered by Medicare.

Alan A. is now eighty-nine, and the mound of bills and Medicare statements he showed me for 2011—when he had his heart attack and continued his treatments at Sloan-Kettering—seemed to add up to about $350,000, although I could not tell for sure because a few of the smaller ones may have been duplicates. What is certain—because his insurance company tallied it for him in a year-end statement—was that his total out-of-pocket expense was

$1,139, or less than 0.2 percent of his overall medical bills. Those bills included what seemed to be thirty-three visits in one year to eleven doctors who had nothing to do with his recovery from the heart attack or his cancer. In all cases, he was routinely asked to pay almost nothing: $2.20 for a check of a sinus problem, $1.70 for an eye exam, $0.33 to deal with a bunion. When he showed me those bills he chuckled.

A comfortable member of the middle class, Alan A. could easily afford the burden of higher copays that would encourage him to use doctors less casually or would at least stick taxpayers with less of the bill if he wants to get that bunion treated. AARP (formerly the American Association of Retired Persons) and other liberal entitlement lobbies oppose these types of changes and consistently distort the arithmetic around them. But it seems clear that Medicare could save billions of dollars if it required that no Medicare supplemental-insurance plan for people with certain income or asset levels could result in their paying less than, say, 10 percent of a doctor's bill until they had paid $2,000 or $3,000 out of their pockets in total bills in a year. (The AARP might oppose this idea for another reason: it gets royalties from UnitedHealthcare for endorsing United's supplemental-insurance product.)

Medicare spent more than $6.5 billion last year to pay doctors (even at the discounted Medicare rates) for the service codes that denote the most basic categories of office visits. By asking people like Alan A. to pay more than a negligible share, Medicare could recoup $1 billion to $2 billion of those costs yearly.

Too Much Doctoring?

Another doctor's bill, for which Alan A.'s share was $0.19, suggests a second apparent flaw in the system. This was one of fifty bills from twenty-six doctors who saw Alan A. at Virtua Marlton hospital or at the ManorCare convalescent center after his heart attack or read one of his diagnostic tests at the two facilities. "They paraded in once a day or once every other day, looked at me, and poked around a bit and left," Alan A. recalls. Other than the doctor in charge of his heart-attack recovery, "I had no idea who they were until I got these bills. But for a dollar or two, so what?"

The "so what," of course, is that although Medicare deeply discounted the bills, it—meaning taxpayers—still paid from $7.48 (for a chest X-ray reading) to $164 for each encounter.

"One of the benefits attending physicians get from many hospitals is the opportunity to cruise the halls and go into a Medicare patient's room and rack up a few dollars," says a doctor who has worked at several hospitals across the country. "In some places it's a Monday-morning tradition. You go see the people who came in over the weekend. There's always an ostensible reason, but there's also a lot of abuse."

When health-care wonks focus on this kind of overdoctoring, they complain (and write endless essays) about what they call the fee-for-service mode, meaning that doctors mostly get paid for the time they spend treating patients or ordering and reading tests. Alan A. didn't care how much time his cancer or heart doctor spent with him or how many tests he got. He cared only that he got better.

Some private care organizations have made progress in avoiding this overdoctoring by paying salaries to their physicians and giving them incentives based on patient outcomes. Medicare and private insurers have yet to find a way to do that with doctors, nor are they likely to, given the current structure that involves hundreds of thousands of private providers billing them for their services.

In passing Obamacare, Congress enabled Medicare to drive efficiencies in hospital care based on the notion that good care should be rewarded and the opposite penalized. The primary lever is a system of penalties Obamacare imposes on hospitals for bad care—a term defined as unacceptable rates of adverse events, such as infections or injuries during a patient's hospital stay or re-admissions within a month after discharge. Both kinds of adverse events are more common than you might think: one in five Medicare patients is readmitted within thirty days, for example. One Medicare report asserts that "Medicare spent an estimated $4.4 billion in 2009 to care for patients who had been harmed in the hospital, and readmissions cost Medicare another $26 billion." The anticipated savings that will be produced by the threat of these new penalties are what has allowed the Obama administration to claim that Obamacare can cut hundreds of billions of dollars from Medicare over the next ten years without short-changing beneficiaries. "These payment penalties are sending a shock through the system that will drive costs down," says Blum, the deputy administrator of the Centers for Medicare and Medicaid Services.

There are lots of other shocks Blum and his colleagues would like to send. However, Congress won't allow him to. Chief among them, as we have seen, would be allowing Medicare, the world's largest buyer of prescription drugs, to negotiate the prices that it pays for them and to make purchasing decisions on the basis of comparative effectiveness. But there's also the cane that Alan A. got after his heart attack. Medicare paid $21.97 for it. Alan A. could have bought it on Amazon for about $12. Other than in a few pilot regions that Congress designated in 2011 after a push by the Obama administration, Congress has not allowed Medicare to drive down the price of any so-called durable medical equipment through competitive bidding.

This is more than a matter of the 124,000 canes Medicare reports that it buys every year. It's about mail-order diabetic supplies, wheelchairs, home medical beds, and personal oxygen supplies, too. Medicare spends about $15 billion annually for these goods.

In the areas of the country where Medicare has been allowed by Congress to conduct a competitive-bidding pilot program, the process has produced savings of 40 percent. But so far, the pilot programs cover only about 3 percent of the medical goods seniors typically use. Taking the program nationwide and saving 40 percent of the entire $15 billion would mean saving $6 billion a year for taxpayers.

The Way Out of the Sinkhole

"I was driving through central Florida a year or two ago," says Medicare's Blum. "And it seemed like every billboard I saw advertised some hospital with these big shiny buildings or showed some new wing of a hospital being constructed. . . . So when you tell me that the hospitals say they are losing money on Medicare and shifting costs from Medicare patients to other patients, my reaction is that central Florida is overflowing with Medicare patients and all those hospitals are expanding and advertising for Medicare patients. So you can't tell me they're losing money. . . . Hospitals don't lose money when they serve Medicare patients."

If that's the case, I asked, why not just extend the program to everyone and pay for it all by charging people under sixty-five the kinds of premiums they would pay to private insurance companies? "That's not for me to say," Blum replied.

In the debate over controlling Medicare costs, politicians from both parties continue to suggest that Congress raise the age of eligibility for Medicare from sixty-five to 67. Doing so, they argue, would save the government tens of billions of dollars a year. So it's worth noting another detail about the case of Janice S., which we examined earlier. Had she felt those chest pains and gone to the Stamford Hospital emergency room a month later, she would have been on Medicare, because she would have just celebrated her sixty-fifth birthday.

If covered by Medicare, Janice S.'s $21,000 bill would have been deeply discounted and, as is standard, Medicare would have picked up 80 percent of the reduced cost. The bottom line is that Janice S. would probably have ended up paying $500 to $600 for her 20 percent share of her heart-attack scare. And she would have paid only a fraction of that—maybe $100—if, like most Medicare beneficiaries, she had paid for supplemental insurance to cover most of that 20 percent.

In fact, those numbers would seem to argue for lowering the Medicare age, not raising it—and not just from Janice S.'s standpoint but also from the taxpayers' side of the equation. That's not a liberal argument for protecting entitlements while the deficit balloons. It's just a matter of hardheaded arithmetic.

As currently constituted, Obamacare is going to require people like Janice S. to get private insurance coverage and will subsidize those who can't afford it. But the cost of that private insurance—and therefore those subsidies—will be much higher than if the same people were enrolled in Medicare at an earlier age. That's because Medicare buys health-care services at much lower rates than any insurance company. Thus the best way both to lower the deficit and to help save money for people like Janice S. would seem to be to bring her and other near seniors into the Medicare system before they reach sixty-five. They could be required to pay premiums based on their incomes, with the poor paying low premiums and the better off paying what they might have paid a private insurer. Those who can afford it might also be required to pay a higher proportion of their bills—say, 25 percent or 30 percent—rather than the 20 percent they're now required to pay for outpatient bills.

Meanwhile, adding younger people like Janice S. would lower the overall cost per beneficiary to Medicare and help cut its deficit still more, because younger members are likelier to be healthier.

From Janice S.'s standpoint, whatever premium she would pay for this age-sixty-four Medicare protection would still be less than what she had been paying under the COBRA plan that she wished she could have kept after the rules dictated that she be cut off after she lost her job.

The only way this would not work is if sixty-four-year-olds started using health care services they didn't need. They might be tempted to because, as we saw with Alan A., Medicare's protection is so broad and supplemental private insurance costs so little that it all but eliminates patients' obligation to pay the 20 percent of outpatient-care costs that Medicare doesn't cover. To deal with that, a provision could be added requiring that sixty-four-year-olds taking advantage of Medicare could not buy insurance freeing them from more than, say, 5 percent or 10 percent of their responsibility for the bills, with the percentage set according to their wealth. It would be a similar, though more stringent, provision of the kind I've already suggested for current Medicare beneficiaries as a way to cut the cost of people overusing benefits.

If that logic applies to sixty-four-year-olds, then it would seem to apply even more readily to healthier forty-year-olds or eighteen-year-olds. This is the single-payer approach favored by liberals and used by most developed countries.

Then again, however much hospitals might survive or struggle under that scenario, no doctor could hope for anything approaching the income he or she deserves (and that will make future doctors want to practice) if 100 percent of their patients yielded anything close to the low rates Medicare pays.

"If you could figure out a way to pay doctors better and separately fund research . . . adequately, I could see where a single-payer approach would be the most logical solution," says Gunn, Sloan-Kettering's chief operating officer. "It would certainly be a lot more efficient than hospitals like ours having hundreds of people sitting around filling out dozens of different kinds of bills for dozens of insurance companies." Maybe, but the prospect of overhauling our system this way, displacing all the private insurers and other infrastructure after all these decades, isn't likely. For there would be one group of losers—and these losers have lots of clout. They're the health-care providers like hospitals and CT-scan-equipment makers whose profits—embedded in the bills we have examined—would be sacrificed. They would suffer because of the lower prices Medicare would pay them when the patient is sixty-four, compared with what they are able to charge when that patient is either covered by private insurance or has no insurance at all.

That kind of systemic overhaul not only seems unrealistic but is also packed with all kinds of risk related to the microproblems of execution and the macro-issue of giving government all that power.

Yet while Medicare may not be a realistic systemwide model for reform, the way Medicare works does demonstrate, by comparison, how the overall health-care market doesn't work.

Unless you are protected by Medicare, the health-care market is not a market at all. It's a crapshoot. People fare differently according to circumstances they can neither control nor predict. They may have no insurance. They may have insurance, but their employer chooses their insurance plan and it may have a payout limit or not cover a drug or treatment they need. They may or may not be old enough to be on Medicare or, given the different standards of the fifty states, be poor enough to be on Medicaid. If they're not protected by Medicare or they're protected only partly by private insurance with high copays, they have little visibility into pricing, let alone control of it. They have little choice of hospitals or the services they are billed for, even if they somehow know the prices before they get billed for the services. They have no idea what their bills mean, and those who maintain the charge-masters couldn't explain them if they wanted to. How much of the bills they end up paying may depend on the generosity of the hospital or on whether they happen to get the help of a billing advocate. They have no choice of the drugs that they have to buy or the lab tests or CT scans that they have to get, and they would not know what to do if they did have a choice. They are powerless buyers in a seller's market where the only sure thing is the profit of the sellers.

Indeed, the only player in the system that seems to have to balance countervailing interests the way market players in a real market usually do is Medicare. It has to answer to Congress and the taxpayers for wasting money, and it has to answer to portions of the same groups for trying to hold on to money it shouldn't. Hospitals, drug companies, and other suppliers, even the insurance companies, don't have those worries.

Moreover, the only players in the private sector who seem to operate efficiently are the private contractors working—dare I say it?—under the government's supervision. They're the Medicare claims processors that handle claims like Alan A.'s for $0.84 each. With these and all other Medicare costs added together, Medicare's total management, administrative, and processing expenses are about $3.8 billion for processing more than a billion claims a year worth $550 billion. That's an overall administrative and management cost of about two-thirds of 1 percent of the amount of the claims, or less than $3.80 per claim. According to its latest SEC filing, Aetna spent $6.9 billion on operating expenses (including claims processing, accounting, sales, and executive management) in 2012. That's about $30 for each of the 229 million claims Aetna processed, and it amounts to about 29 percent of the $23.7 billion Aetna pays out in claims.

The real issue isn't whether we have a single payer or multiple payers. It's whether whoever pays has a fair chance in a fair market. Congress has given Medicare that power when it comes to dealing with hospitals and doctors, and we have seen how that works to drive down the prices Medicare pays just as we've seen what happens when Congress handcuffs Medicare when it comes to evaluating and buying drugs, medical devices, and equipment. Stripping away what is now the sellers' overwhelming leverage in dealing with Medicare in those areas and with private payers in all aspects of the market would inject fairness into the market. We don't have to scrap our system and aren't likely to. But we can reduce the $750 billion that we overspend on health care in the United States in part by acknowledging what other countries have: because the health-care market deals in a life-or-death product, it cannot be left to its own devices.

Put simply, the bills tell us that this is not about interfering in a free market. It's about facing the reality that our largest consumer product by far—one-fifth of our economy—does not operate in a free market.

So how can we fix it?

Changing Our Choices

We should tighten antitrust laws related to hospitals to keep them from becoming so dominant in a region that insurance companies are helpless in negotiating prices with them. The hospitals' continuing consolidation of both lab work and doctors' practices is one reason that trying to cut the deficit by simply lowering the fees Medicare and Medicaid pay to hospitals will not work. It will only cause the hospitals to shift the costs to non-Medicare patients in order to maintain profits—which they will be able to do because of their increasing leverage in their markets over insurers. Insurance premiums will therefore go up—which in turn will drive the deficit back up because the subsidies on insurance premiums that Obamacare will soon offer to those who cannot afford them will have to go up.

Similarly, we should tax hospital profits at 75 percent and have a tax surcharge on all nondoctor hospital salaries that exceed, say,

$750,000. Why are high profits at hospitals regarded as a given that we have to work around? Why shouldn't those who are profiting the most from a market whose costs are victimizing everyone else chip in to help? If we recouped 75 percent of all hospital profits (from nonprofit as well as for-profit institutions), that would save over $80 billion a year before counting what we would save on tests that hospitals might not perform if their profit incentives were shaved.

To be sure, this too seems unlikely to happen. Hospitals may be the most politically powerful institution in any congressional district. They're usually admired as their community's most important charitable institution, and their influential stakeholders run the gamut from equipment makers to drug companies to doctors to thousands of rank-and-file employees. Then again, if every community paid more attention to those administrator salaries, to those nonprofits' profit margins, and to charges like $77 for gauze pads, perhaps the political balance would shift.

We should outlaw the chargemaster. Everyone involved, except a patient who gets a bill based on one (or worse, gets sued on the basis of one), shrugs off chargemasters as a fiction. So why not require that they be rewritten to reflect a process that considers actual and thoroughly transparent costs? After all, hospitals are supposed to be government-sanctioned institutions accountable to the public. Hospitals love the chargemaster because it gives them a big number to put in front of rich uninsured patients (typically from outside the United States) or, as is more likely, to attach to lawsuits or give to bill collectors, establishing a place from which they can negotiate settlements. It's also a great place from which to start negotiations with insurance companies, which also love the chargemaster because they can then make their customers feel good when they get an Explanation of Benefits that shows the terrific discounts their insurance company won for them.

But for patients, the chargemasters are both the real and the metaphoric essence of the broken market. They are anything but irrelevant. They're the source of the poison coursing through the health care ecosystem.

We should amend patent laws so that makers of wonder drugs would be limited in how they can exploit the monopoly our patent laws give them. Or we could simply set price limits or profit-margin caps on these drugs. Why are the drug profit margins treated as another given that we have to work around to get out of the $750 billion annual overspend, rather than a problem to be solved?

Just bringing these overall profits down to those of the software industry would save billions of dollars. Reducing drug makers' prices to what they get in other developed countries would save over $90 billion a year. It could save Medicare—meaning the taxpayers—more than $25 billion a year, or $250 billion over ten years. Depending on whether that $250 billion is compared with the Republican or Democratic deficit-cutting proposals, that's a third or a half of the Medicare cuts now being talked about.

Similarly, we should tighten what Medicare pays for CT or MRI tests a lot more and even cap what insurance companies can pay for them. This is a huge contributor to our massive overspending on outpatient costs. And we should cap profits on lab tests done in-house by hospitals or doctors.

Finally, we should embarrass Democrats into stopping their fight against medical-malpractice reform and instead provide safe-harbor defenses for doctors so they don't have to order a CT scan whenever, as one hospital administrator put it, someone in the emergency room says the word "head." Trial lawyers who make their bread and butter from civil suits have been the Democrats' biggest financial backer for decades. Republicans are right when they argue that tort reform is overdue. Eliminating the rationale or excuse for all the extra doctor exams, lab tests, and use of CT scans and MRIs could cut tens of billions of dollars a year while drastically cutting what hospitals and doctors spend on malpractice insurance and pass along to patients.

Other options are more tongue in cheek, though they illustrate the absurdity of the hole we have fallen into. We could limit administrator salaries at hospitals to five or six times what the lowest-paid licensed physician gets for caring for patients there. That might take care of the self-fulfilling peer dynamic that Gunn of Sloan-Kettering cited when he explained, "We all use the same compensation consultants." Then again, it might unleash a wave of salary increases for junior doctors.

Or we could require drug companies to include a prominent, plain-English notice of the gross profit margin on the packaging of each drug, as well as the salary of the parent company's CEO. The same would have to be posted on the company's website. If nothing else, it would be a good test of embarrassment thresholds.

None of these suggestions will come as a revelation to the policy experts who put together Obamacare or to those before them who pushed health-care reform for decades. They know what the core problem is—lopsided pricing and outsize profits in a market that doesn't work. Yet there is little in Obamacare that addresses that core issue or jeopardizes the paydays of those thriving in that marketplace. In fact, by bringing so many new customers into that market by mandating that they get health insurance and then providing taxpayer support to pay their insurance premiums, Obamacare enriches them. That, of course, is why the bill was able to get through Congress.

Obamacare does some good work around the edges of the core problem. It restricts abusive hospital-bill collecting. It forces insurers to provide explanations of their policies in plain English. It requires a more rigorous appeal process conducted by independent entities when insurance coverage is denied. These are all positive changes, as is putting the insurance umbrella over tens of millions more Americans—a historic breakthrough. But none of it is a path to bending the health-care cost curve. Indeed, while Obamacare's promotion of statewide insurance exchanges may help distribute health-insurance policies to individuals now frozen out of the market, those exchanges could raise costs, not lower them. With hospitals consolidating by buying doctors' practices and competing hospitals, their leverage over insurance companies is increasing. That's a trend that will only be accelerated if there are more insurance companies with less market share competing in a new exchange market trying to negotiate with a dominant hospital and its doctors. Similarly, higher insurance premiums—much of them paid by taxpayers through Obamacare's subsidies for those who can't afford insurance but now must buy it—will certainly be the result of three of Obamacare's best provisions: the prohibitions on exclusions for preexisting conditions, the restrictions on copays for preventive care, and the end of annual or lifetime payout caps.

Put simply, with Obamacare we've changed the rules related to who pays for what, but we haven't done much to change the prices we pay.

When you follow the money, you see the choices we've made, knowingly or unknowingly.

Over the past few decades, we've enriched the labs, drug companies, medical-device makers, hospital administrators, and purveyors of CT scans, MRIs, canes, and wheelchairs. Meanwhile, we've squeezed the doctors who don't own their own clinics, don't work as drug or device consultants, or don't otherwise game a system that is so gameable. And of course, we've squeezed everyone outside the system who gets stuck with the bills.

We've created a secure, prosperous island in an economy that is suffering under the weight of the riches those on the island extract.

And we've allowed those on the island and their lobbyists and allies to control the debate, diverting us from what Gerard Anderson, a health-care economist at the Johns Hopkins Bloomberg School of Public Health, says is the obvious and only issue: "All the prices are too damn high."

The Atlantic

FINALIST—PUBLIC
INTEREST

The National Magazine Award for Public Interest celebrates stories that make a difference. Jean M. Twenge's article addresses the widely shared fear—fostered in part, truth be told, by magazines—that older women are doomed to childlessness without medical intervention. Twenge's own experience—three children born after her thirty-fifth birthday—belies this "baby panic." But Twenge's piece relies on more than mere anecdote. Instead it looks at the evidence, examines the dangers, and offers solutions. Now 157 years old, The Atlantic *continues to flourish both in print and online. The National Magazine Award nomination for this piece—the judges called it "solid science reporting combined with compelling personal narrative"—was* The Atlantic*'s twenty-eighth in the last five years.*

Jean M. Twenge

How Long Can You Wait to Have a Baby?

In the tentative, post-9/11 spring of 2002, I was, at thirty, in the midst of extricating myself from my first marriage. My husband and I had met in graduate school but couldn't find two academic jobs in the same place, so we spent the three years of our marriage living in different states. After I accepted a tenure-track position in California and he turned down a postdoctoral research position nearby—the job wasn't good enough, he said—it seemed clear that our living situation was not going to change.

I put off telling my parents about the split for weeks, hesitant to disappoint them. When I finally broke the news, they were, to my relief, supportive and understanding. Then my mother said, "Have you read *Time* magazine this week? I know you want to have kids."

Time's cover that week had a baby on it. "Listen to a successful woman discuss her failure to bear a child, and the grief comes in layers of bitterness and regret," the story inside began. A generation of women who had waited to start a family was beginning to grapple with that decision, and one media outlet after another was wringing its hands about the steep decline in women's fertility with age: "When It's Too Late to Have a Baby," lamented the U.K.'s *Observer*; "Baby Panic," *New York* magazine announced on its cover.

The panic stemmed from the April 2002 publication of Sylvia Ann Hewlett's headline-grabbing book, *Creating a Life*, which counseled that women should have their children while they're young or risk having none at all. Within corporate America, 42 percent of the professional women interviewed by Hewlett had no children at age forty, and most said they deeply regretted it. Just as you plan for a corner office, Hewlett advised her readers, you should plan for grandchildren.

The previous fall, an ad campaign sponsored by the American Society for Reproductive Medicine (ASRM) had warned, "Advancing age decreases your ability to have children." One ad was illustrated with a baby bottle shaped like an hourglass that was—just to make the point glaringly obvious—running out of milk. Female fertility, the group announced, begins to decline at twenty-seven. "Should you have your baby now?" asked *Newsweek* in response.

For me, that was no longer a viable option.

I had always wanted children. Even when I was busy with my postdoctoral research, I volunteered to baby-sit a friend's pre-schooler. I frequently passed the time in airports by chatting up frazzled mothers and babbling toddlers—a two-year-old, quite to my surprise, once crawled into my lap. At a wedding I attended in my late twenties, I played with the groom's preschool-age nephews, often on the floor, during the entire rehearsal and most of the reception. ("Do you fart?" one of them asked me in an overly loud voice during the rehearsal. "Everyone does," I replied solemnly, as his grandfather laughed quietly in the next pew.)

But, suddenly single at thirty, I seemed destined to remain childless until at least my midthirties, and perhaps always. Flying to a friend's wedding in May 2002, I finally forced myself to read the *Time* article. It upset me so much that I began doubting my divorce for the first time. "And God, what if I want to have two?" I wrote in my journal as the cold plane sped over the Rockies. "First at 35, and if you wait until the kid is 2 to try, more than likely you have the second at 38 or 39. If at all." To reassure myself about the divorce, I wrote, "Nothing I did would have changed the situation." I underlined that.

I was lucky: within a few years, I married again, and this time the match was much better. But my new husband and I seemed to face frightening odds against having children. Most books and websites I read said that one in three women ages thirty-five to thirty-nine would not get pregnant within a year of starting to try. The first page of the ASRM's 2003 guide for patients noted that women in their late thirties had a 30 percent chance of remaining childless altogether. The guide also included statistics that I'd seen repeated in many other places: a woman's chance of pregnancy was 20 percent each month at age thirty, dwindling to 5 percent by age forty.

Every time I read these statistics, my stomach dropped like a stone, heavy and foreboding. Had I already missed my chance to be a mother?

•　　　•　　　•

As a psychology researcher who'd published articles in scientific journals, some covered in the popular press, I knew that many scientific findings differ significantly from what the public hears about them. Soon after my second wedding, I decided to go to the source: I scoured medical-research databases and quickly learned that the statistics on women's age and fertility—used by many to make decisions about relationships, careers, and when to have children—were one of the more spectacular examples of the mainstream media's failure to correctly report on and interpret scientific research.

The widely cited statistic that one in three women ages thirty-five to thirty-nine will not be pregnant after a year of trying, for instance, is based on an article published in 2004 in the journal *Human Reproduction*. Rarely mentioned is the source of the data:

French birth records from 1670 to 1830. The chance of remaining childless—30 percent—was also calculated based on historical populations.

In other words, millions of women are being told when to get pregnant based on statistics from a time before electricity, antibiotics, or fertility treatment. Most people assume these numbers are based on large, well-conducted studies of modern women, but they are not. When I mention this to friends and associates, by far the most common reaction is: "No . . . No way. *Really?*"

Surprisingly few well-designed studies of female age and natural fertility include women born in the twentieth century—but those that do tend to paint a more optimistic picture. One study, published in *Obstetrics and Gynecology* in 2004 and headed by David Dunson (now of Duke University), examined the chances of pregnancy among 770 European women. It found that with sex at least twice a week, 82 percent of thirty-five-to-thirty-nine-year-old women conceive within a year, compared with 86 percent of twenty-seven-to-thirty-four-year-olds. (The fertility of women in their late twenties and early thirties was almost identical—news in and of itself.) Another study, released this March in *Fertility and Sterility* and led by Kenneth Rothman of Boston University, followed 2,820 Danish women as they tried to get pregnant. Among women having sex during their fertile times, 78 percent of thirty-five-to-forty-year-olds got pregnant within a year, compared with 84 percent of twenty-to-thirty-four-year-olds. A study headed by Anne Steiner, an associate professor at the University of North Carolina School of Medicine, the results of which were presented in June, found that among thirty-eight- and thirty-nine-year-olds who had been pregnant before, 80 percent of white women of normal weight got pregnant naturally within six months (although that percentage was lower among other races and among the overweight). "In our data, we're not seeing huge drops until age forty," she told me.

Even some studies based on historical birth records are more optimistic than what the press normally reports: One found that, in the days before birth control, 89 percent of thirty-eight-year-old women were still fertile. Another concluded that the typical woman was able to get pregnant until somewhere between ages forty and forty-five. Yet these more encouraging numbers are rarely mentioned—none of these figures appear in the American Society for Reproductive Medicine's 2008 committee opinion on female age and fertility, which instead relies on the most-ominous historical data.

In short, the "baby panic"—which has by no means abated since it hit me personally—is based largely on questionable data. We've rearranged our lives, worried endlessly, and forgone countless career opportunities based on a few statistics about women who resided in thatched-roof huts and never saw a light bulb. In Dunson's study of modern women, the difference in pregnancy rates at age twenty-eight versus thirty-seven is only about 4 percentage points. Fertility does decrease with age, but the decline is not steep enough to keep the vast majority of women in their late thirties from having a child. And that, after all, is the whole point.

·　　·　　·

I am now the mother of three children, all born after I turned thirty-five. My oldest started kindergarten on my fortieth birthday; my youngest was born five months later. All were conceived naturally within a few months. The toddler in my lap at the airport is now mine.

Instead of worrying about my fertility, I now worry about paying for child care and getting three children to bed on time. These are good problems to have.

Yet the memory of my abject terror about age-related infertility still lingers. Every time I tried to get pregnant, I was consumed by anxiety that my age meant doom. I was not alone. Women on Internet message boards write of scaling back their careers or having fewer children than they'd like to because they can't bear the thought of trying to get pregnant after thirty-five. Those who have already passed the dreaded birthday ask for tips on how to stay calm when trying to get pregnant, constantly worrying—just as I did—that they will never have a child. "I'm scared because I am 35 and everyone keeps reminding me that my 'clock is ticking.' My grandmother even reminded me of this at my wedding reception," one newly married woman wrote to me after reading my 2012 advice book, *The Impatient Woman's Guide to Getting Pregnant*, based in part on my own experience. It's not just grandmothers sounding this note. "What science tells us about the aging parental body should alarm us more than it does," wrote the journalist Judith Shulevitz in a *New Republic* cover story late last year that focused, laserlike, on the downsides of delayed parenthood.

How did the baby panic happen in the first place? And why hasn't there been more public pushback from fertility experts?

One possibility is the "availability heuristic": when making judgments, people rely on what's right in front of them. Fertility doctors see the effects of age on the success rate of fertility treatment every day. That's particularly true for in vitro fertilization, which relies on the extraction of a large number of eggs from the ovaries because some eggs are lost at every stage of the difficult process. Younger women's ovaries respond better to the drugs used to extract the eggs, and younger women's eggs are more likely to be chromosomally normal. As a result, younger women's IVF success rates are indeed much higher—about 42 percent of those younger than thirty-five will give birth to a live baby after one IVF cycle, versus 27 percent for those ages thirty-five to forty, and just 12 percent for those ages forty-one to forty-two. Many studies have examined how IVF success declines with age, and these statistics are cited in many research articles and on-line forums.

Yet only about 1 percent of babies born each year in the United States are a result of IVF, and most of their mothers used the technique not because of their age but to overcome blocked fallopian tubes, male infertility, or other issues: about 80 percent of IVF patients are forty or younger. And the IVF statistics tell us very little about natural conception, which requires just one egg rather than a dozen or more, among other differences.

Studies of natural conception are surprisingly difficult to conduct—that's one reason both IVF statistics and historical records play an outsize role in fertility reporting. Modern birth records are uninformative because most women have their children in their twenties and then use birth control or sterilization surgery to prevent pregnancy during their thirties and forties. Studies asking couples how long it took them to conceive or how long they have been trying to get pregnant are as unreliable as human memory. And finding and studying women who are trying to get pregnant is challenging as there's such a narrow window between when they start trying and when some will succeed.

Another problem looms even larger: women who are actively trying to get pregnant at age thirty-five or later might be less fertile than the average over-thirty-five woman. Some highly fertile women will get pregnant accidentally when they are younger, and others will get pregnant quickly whenever they try, completing their families at a younger age. Those who are left are, disproportionately, the less fertile. Thus, "the observed lower fertility rates among older women presumably overestimate the effect of biological aging," says Dr. Allen Wilcox, who leads the Reproductive Epidemiology Group at the National Institute of Environmental Health Sciences. "If we're overestimating the biological decline of fertility with age, this will only be good news to women who have been most fastidious in their birth-control use, and may be more fertile at older ages, on average, than our data would lead them to expect."

These modern-day research problems help explain why historical data from an age before birth control are so tempting. However, the downsides of a historical approach are numerous. Advanced medical care, antibiotics, and even a reliable food supply were unavailable hundreds of years ago. And the decline in fertility in the historical data may also stem from older couples' having sex less often than younger ones. Less-frequent sex might have been especially likely if couples had been married for a long time or had many children or both. (Having more children of course makes it more difficult to fit in sex, and some couples surely realized—*eureka!*—that they could avoid having another mouth to feed by scaling back their nocturnal activities.) Some historical studies try to control for these problems in various ways—such as looking only at just-married couples—but many of the same issues remain.

· · ·

The best way to assess fertility might be to measure "cycle viability," or the chance of getting pregnant if a couple has sex on the most fertile day of the woman's cycle. Studies based on cycle viability use a prospective rather than retrospective design—monitoring couples as they attempt to get pregnant instead of asking couples to recall how long it took them to get pregnant or how long they tried. Cycle-viability studies also eliminate the need to account for older couples' less active sex lives. David Dunson's analysis revealed that intercourse two days before ovulation resulted in pregnancy 29 percent of the time for thirty-five-to-thirty-nine-year-old women, compared with about 42 percent for twenty-seven-to-twenty-nine-year-olds. So, by this measure, fertility falls by about a third from a woman's late twenties to her late thirties. However, a thirty-five-to-thirty-nine-year-old's fertility two days before ovulation was the same as a nineteen-to-twenty-six-year-old's fertility three days before ovulation: according to Dunson's data, older couples who time sex just one day better than younger ones will effectively eliminate the age difference.

Don't these numbers contradict the statistics you sometimes see in the popular press that only 20 percent of thirty-year-old women and 5 percent of forty-year-old women get pregnant per cycle? They do, but no journal article I could locate contained these numbers, and none of the experts I contacted could tell me what data set they were based on. The American Society for Reproductive Medicine's guide provides no citation for these statistics; when I contacted the association's press office asking where they came from, a representative said they were simplified for a popular audience and did not provide a specific citation.

Dunson, a biostatistics professor, thought the lower numbers might be averages across many cycles rather than the chances of getting pregnant during the first cycle of trying. More women will get pregnant during the first cycle than in each subsequent one because the most fertile will conceive quickly and those left will have lower fertility on average.

Most fertility problems are not the result of female age. Blocked tubes and endometriosis (a condition in which the cells lining the uterus also grow outside it) strike both younger and older women. Almost half of infertility problems trace back to the man, and these seem to be more common among older men, although research suggests that men's fertility declines only gradually with age.

Fertility problems unrelated to female age may also explain why, in many studies, fertility at older ages is considerably higher among women who have been pregnant before. Among couples who haven't had an accidental pregnancy—who, as Dr. Steiner put it, "have never had an 'oops'"—sperm issues and blocked tubes may be more likely. Thus, the data from women who already have a child may give a more accurate picture of the fertility decline due to "ovarian aging." In Kenneth Rothman's study of the Danish women, among those who'd given birth at least once previously, the chance of getting pregnant at age forty was similar to that at age twenty.

·   ·   ·

Older women's fears, of course, extend beyond the ability to get pregnant. The rates of miscarriages and birth defects rise with age, and worries over both have been well ventilated in the popular press. But how much do these risks actually rise? Many miscarriage statistics come from—you guessed it—women who undergo IVF or other fertility treatment, who may have a higher miscarriage risk regardless of age. Nonetheless, the *National Vital Statistics Reports*, which draw data from the general population, find that 15 percent of women ages twenty to thirty-four, 27 percent of women thirty-five to thirty-nine, and 26 percent of women forty to forty-four report having had a miscarriage. These increases are hardly insignificant, and the true rate of miscarriages is higher, since many miscarriages occur extremely early in a pregnancy—before a missed period or pregnancy test. Yet it should be noted that even for older women, the likelihood of a pregnancy's continuing is nearly three times that of having a known miscarriage.

What about birth defects? The risk of chromosomal abnormalities such as Down syndrome does rise with a woman's age—such abnormalities are the source of many of those very early, undetected miscarriages. However, the probability of having a child with a chromosomal abnormality remains extremely low. Even at early fetal testing (known as chorionic villus sampling), 99 percent of fetuses are chromosomally normal among thirty-five-year-old pregnant women, and 97 percent among forty-year-olds. At forty-five, when most women can no longer get pregnant, 87 percent of fetuses are still normal. (Many of those that are not will later be miscarried.) In the near future, fetal genetic testing will be done with a simple blood test, making it even easier than it is today for women to get early information about possible genetic issues.

•　　　•　　　•

What does all this mean for a woman trying to decide when to have children? More specifically, how long can she safely wait?

This question can't be answered with absolutely certainty for two big reasons. First, while the data on natural fertility among modern women are proliferating, they are still sparse. Collectively, the three modern studies by Dunson, Rothman, and Steiner included only about 400 women thirty-five or older, and they might not be representative of all such women trying to conceive.

Second, statistics, of course, can tell us only about probabilities and averages—they offer no guarantees to any particular person. "Even if we had good estimates for the average biological decline in fertility with age, that is still of relatively limited use to individuals, given the large range of fertility found in healthy women," says Allen Wilcox of the NIH.

So what is a woman—and her partner—to do?

The data, imperfect as they are, suggest two conclusions. No. 1: fertility declines with age. No. 2, and much more relevant: the vast majority of women in their late thirties will be able to get pregnant on their own. The bottom line for women, in my view, is: plan to have your last child by the time you turn forty. Beyond that, you're rolling the dice, though they may still come up in your favor. "Fertility is relatively stable until the late thirties, with the inflection point somewhere around thirty-eight or thirty-nine," Steiner told me. "Women in their early thirties can think about years, but in their late thirties, they need to be thinking about months." That's also why many experts advise that women older than thirty-five should see a fertility specialist if they haven't conceived after six months—particularly if it's been six months of sex during fertile times.

There is no single best time to have a child. Some women and couples will find that starting—and finishing—their families in their twenties is what's best for them, all things considered. They just shouldn't let alarmist rhetoric push them to become parents before they're ready. Having children at a young age slightly lowers the risks of infertility and chromosomal abnormalities and moderately lowers the risk of miscarriage. But it also carries costs for relationships and careers. Literally: an analysis by one economist found that, on average, every year a woman postpones having children leads to a 10 percent increase in career earnings.

For women who aren't ready for children in their early thirties but are still worried about waiting, new technologies—albeit imperfect ones—offer a third option. Some women choose to freeze their eggs, having a fertility doctor extract eggs when they are still young (say, early thirties) and cryogenically preserve them. Then, if they haven't had children by their self-imposed deadline, they can thaw the eggs, fertilize them, and implant the embryos using IVF. Because the eggs will be younger, success rates are theoretically higher. The downsides are the expense—perhaps $10,000 for the egg freezing and an average of more than $12,000 per cycle for IVF—and having to use IVF to get pregnant. Women who already have a partner can, alternatively, freeze embryos, a more common procedure that also uses IVF technology.

At home, couples should recognize that having sex at the most fertile time of the cycle matters enormously, potentially making the difference between an easy conception in the bedroom and expensive fertility treatment in a clinic. Rothman's study found that timing sex around ovulation narrowed the fertility gap between younger and older women. Women older than thirty-five who want to get pregnant should consider recapturing the glory of their twenty-something sex lives or learning to predict ovulation by charting their cycles or using a fertility monitor.

.   .   .

I wish I had known all this back in the spring of 2002, when the media coverage of age and infertility was deafening. I did, though, find some relief from the smart women of *Saturday Night Live.*

"According to author Sylvia Hewlett, career women shouldn't wait to have babies, because our fertility takes a steep drop-off after age twenty-seven," Tina Fey said during a "Weekend Update" sketch. "And Sylvia's right; I *definitely* should have had a baby when I was twenty-seven, living in Chicago over a biker bar, pulling down a cool $12,000 a year. That would have worked out great." Rachel Dratch said, "Yeah. Sylvia, um, thanks for reminding me that I have to hurry up and have a baby. Uh, me and my four cats will get *right* on that."

"My neighbor has this adorable, cute little Chinese baby that speaks Italian," noted Amy Poehler. "So, you know, I'll just buy one of those." Maya Rudolph rounded out the rant: "Yeah, Sylvia, maybe your next book should tell men our age to stop playing Grand Theft Auto III and holding out for the chick from *Alias.*" ("You're *not* gonna get the chick from *Alias,*" Fey advised.)

Eleven years later, these four women have eight children among them, all but one born when they were older than thirty-five. It's good to be right.

ESPN the Magazine

FINALIST—FEATURE
WRITING

The portrait of Michael Jordan that emerges from this story is that of a great athlete consumed by his own legend, a generous friend who can also be "self-centered, bullying, and cruel." The National Magazine Award judges called it simply "one of the year's most poignant and memorable stories." Born and raised in the Mississippi Delta, Wright Thompson was a reporter for the New Orleans Times-Picayune *and the* Kansas City Star *before joining ESPN.com in 2006. Writing for both ESPN.com and* ESPN the Magazine, *he has covered baseball, football, basketball, NASCAR, boxing, cricket, and, yes, bullfighting. Thompson now lives in Oxford, Mississippi.* ESPN the Magazine *won its first National Magazine Award in 1999. Since then the magazine has been nominated for eighteen more awards and won three.*

Wright Thompson

Michael Jordan Has Not Left the Building

F ive weeks before his fiftieth birthday, Michael Jordan sits behind his desk, overlooking a parking garage in downtown Charlotte. The cell phone in front of him buzzes with potential trades and league proposals about placing ads on jerseys. A rival wants his best players and wants to give him nothing in return. Jordan bristles. He holds a Cuban cigar in his hand. Smoking is allowed.

"Well, s———, being as I own the building," he says, laughing.

Back in the office after his vacation on a 154-foot rented yacht named *Mister Terrible*, he feels that relaxation slipping away. He feels pulled inward, toward his own most valuable and destructive traits. Slights roll through his mind, eating at him: *worst record ever, can't build a team, absentee landlord.* Jordan reads the things written about him, the fuel arriving in a packet of clips his staff prepares. He knows what people say. He needs to know, a needle for a hungry vein. There's a palpable simmering whenever you're around Jordan, as if Air Jordan is still in there, churning, trying to escape. It must be strange to be locked in combat with the ghost of your former self.

Smoke curls off the cigar. He wears slacks and a plain white dress shirt, monogrammed on the sleeve in white, understated. An ID badge hangs from one of those zip line cords on his belt, with his name on the bottom: Michael Jordan, just in case anyone didn't recognize the owner of a struggling franchise who in another life was the touchstone for a generation. There's a shudder in every child of the eighties and nineties who does the math and realizes that Michael Jordan is turning fifty. Where did the years go? Jordan has trouble believing it, difficulty admitting it to himself. But he's in the mood for admissions today, and there's a look on his face, a half-smile, as he considers how far to go.

"I . . . I always thought I would die young," he says, leaning up to rap his knuckles on the rich, dark wood of his desk.

He has kept this fact a secret from most people. A fatalist obsession didn't go with his public image and, well, it's sort of strange. His mother would get angry with him when he'd talk to her about it. He just could never imagine being old. He seemed too powerful, too young, and death was more likely than a slow decline. The universe might take him, but it would not permit him to suffer the graceless loss and failure of aging. A tragic flaw could undo him but never anything as common as bad knees or failing eyesight.

Later that night, standing in his kitchen, he squints across his loft at the television. His friend Quinn Buckner catches him.

"You gonna need to get some glasses," Buckner says.

"I can see," Jordan says.

"Don't be bulls——ing me," Buckner says. "I can see you struggling."

"I can see," Jordan insists.

The television is built into the modern stone fireplace in his sprawling downtown condo, the windows around them overlooking Tryon Street. An open bottle of Pahlmeyer merlot sits on an end table. Buckner, a former NBA guard from near Chicago and a Pacers broadcaster, is in town for an upcoming game. They've been talking, about Jordan's birthday and about the changes in his life, all seeming to happen at once. Jordan feels in transition. He moved out of his house in Chicago and is moving into a new one in Florida in three weeks. He's engaged. Inside he's dealing, finally, with the cost of his own competitive urges, asking himself difficult questions. To what must he say goodbye? What is there to look forward to? Catching an introspective Jordan is like finding a spotted owl, but here he is, considering himself. His fiancée, Yvette Prieto, and her friend Laura laugh over near the kitchen island. Jordan relights his cigar. It keeps going out.

"Listen," Buckner says, "Father Time ain't lost yet."

The idea hangs in the air.

"Damn," Buckner continues. "Fifty."

He shakes his head.

"Can you believe it?" Jordan says quietly, and it sounds like he's talking to himself.

•   •   •

A day before, Jordan had flown to Charlotte from Chicago, a trip he's made many times. This flight was different from all the others. When his Gulfstream IV, which is painted to look like a sneaker, took off and turned south, he no longer lived in the city where he had moved in 1984. The past months had been consumed with a final flurry of packing, putting the first half of his life in boxes. He has felt many emotions in his fifty years: hope and anger, disappointment, joy and despair. But lately there's been a feeling that would have disgusted the thirty-year-old version of himself: nostalgia.

The packing and cataloging started several years ago, after his divorce. One night at his suburban Chicago mansion, he sat on the floor of his closet with Estee Portnoy. She manages his business enterprises and, since the divorce, much of his personal life—his consigliere. It was one in the morning. They were flummoxed by a safe. Jordan hadn't opened it in years, and he couldn't remember the combination. Everything else stopped as this consumed him. After ten failed attempts, the safe would go into a security shutdown and need to be blown open. None of the usual numbers worked. Nine different combinations failed; they had one try left. Jordan focused. He decided it had to be a combination of his birthday, February 17, and old basketball numbers. He typed in six digits: 9, 2, 1, 7, 4, 5. *Click.* The heavy door swung open and he reached in, rediscovering his gold medal from the 1984 Olympics. It wasn't really gold anymore. It looked tarnished, changed—a duller version of itself.

The memories came to him, how he felt then. "It was very pure, if I can say it right," he'd explain later. "It was pure in 1984 . . . I was still dreaming." During the Olympics, he was deep in negotiations with Nike for his first shoe contract. He traded pins with other athletes. Eight years later, when he was the most famous person in the world and the Dream Team was forced to stay outside the Olympic Village, he'd be disappointed when that separation kept him from swapping pins again.

Jordan tried on an old pair of shorts and didn't fit in them. He found first-edition Air Jordans. In his cavernous Nike closet, he counted nearly 5,000 boxes of shoes, some of which he marked to keep, others to give to friends. There was his uniform for the Dream Team. An employee found a stack of letters he'd written his parents as a college student at North Carolina, and what struck her as she flipped through the pages was how *normal* he seemed. Despite all the things that had been gained in the years since, that person had been lost. The kid in the letters hadn't yet been hardened by wealth and fame and pressure. He told his parents about grades and practice and the food in the dining hall. He always needed money. One letter ended: *P.S. Please send stamps.*

For a rage-filled day and a half, he thought he'd lost two of his Bulls championship rings, No. 3 and No. 5. He tore the house apart screaming, "Who stole my rings? Who stole No. 5?"

"You talk about a mad f———ing panic," he says.

Following the final title, the Bulls presented him a case with room for all six rings, but Jordan had never put them together. Now as he found them spread around the house, he slipped each one into its slot. He began plotting amendments to his will that if the missing rings emerged for sale after his death, they should be returned immediately to his estate. Buying a duplicate wouldn't be worth it because even if he didn't tell anyone, *he'd* know. Finally the missing rings were found in a memorabilia room, and the set of six was complete. He could exhale and continue packing.

He discovered old home movies and watched them, seeing his young kids. They're all in or out of college now. Warmups had collected dust alongside his baseball cleats and a collection of bats and gloves. The astonishing thing to him was how much he enjoyed this. "At thirty I was moving so fast," he says. "I never had time to think about all the things I was encountering, all the things I was touching. Now when I go back and find these things, it triggers so many different thoughts: *God, I forgot about that.* That's how fast we were moving. Now I can slow it down and hopefully remember what that meant. That's when I know I'm getting old."

He laughs, knowing how this sounds, like a man in a midlife crisis, looking fondly at something that's never coming back.

"I value that," he says. "I like reminiscing. I do it more now watching basketball than anything. Man, I wish I was playing right now. I would give up everything now to go back and play the game of basketball."

"How do you replace it?" he's asked.

"You don't. You learn to live with it."

"How?"

"It's a process," he says.

·   ·   ·

The remembering continues in Charlotte, with Jordan and his best friend, George Koehler, crowding around an iPad map, trying to find Jordan's first house in Chicago.

There's circular poetry about George being here. When Jordan first landed in Chicago in 1984, he stepped out of O'Hare and found that the Bulls had neglected to send anyone to get him. Still a country boy, Jordan was nervous and uncertain. A young limo driver saw him and gave him a ride. That was George, and he's been with Jordan ever since. They're together much of the time. Jordan trusts Koehler completely. Koehler might have more famous athletes programmed into his phone than anyone on the planet since one of the best ways to find Jordan is to call George.

"Where you looking at?" George asks, pointing.

"Essex Drive," Jordan says, finding his old street. "I remember going up to that McDonald's and getting my damn McRib. When I first got there."

There was a finished basement in that place. Charles Oakley lived behind him. So did another Bulls forward, Rod Higgins, who runs the Bobcats' basketball operations. The basement had a hot tub and a pool table that could be converted for ping-pong. They'd play for hours, listening over and over to the first Whitney Houston album. Last year Jordan was sitting on the Bobcats bench with Curtis Polk, his lawyer and a team executive, when Polk received a text saying Houston had died. Her death really affected Jordan, not because he and Houston were close friends, but because it made him aware of his own mortality. It made him measure the distance between fifty and ping-pong on Essex Drive.

"They had some battles down there," George says, laughing.

"Me and Oak," Jordan says.

Higgins is standing with them and is looking at the map too.

"I used to kill him in pool," Jordan says, nodding toward Rod.

"I got a different version," Higgins cracks.

"Kill or be killed," Jordan woofs. "Losing is killing."

There's an unspoken shadow over the stories about that town house on Essex Drive. James Jordan remodeled the basement for his son. Did all the work himself because he'd never let Michael pay for something he could do on his own. The first winter, while Michael was out of town for the All-Star Game, his pipes froze. His dad ripped out the walls, replacing the pipes himself, patching and repainting when he finished. He spent two weeks fixing his son's home. James and Mike—that's where all this nostalgia has been headed, from the moment it began.

Dear Mama and Pops . . . Please send stamps.

.   .   .

George Koehler looks down at the ring on his finger. It's from the Bulls' first championship. Jordan gave replicas to family and close friends.

"I don't know if I ever told you the story why I wear this ring," George says.

"Nope," Jordan says.

"I made a promise to your dad," George says.

George was always scared he'd get robbed, so he kept the ring at home. James, known to everyone as Pops, busted him: "Where's your ring? My son didn't spend his money to have you put that s—— in a drawer."

"I can hear him saying it," Jordan says, smiling.

Pops told George that if someone stole his ring, "we'll get you another one."

Jordan roars over the word "we."

"I like that," he says, his shoulders heaving. "That sounds like him too."

"After what happened to him," George says, "I wear the ring."

Memories come back. The day Pops was killed, he was scheduled to fly to Chicago. He'd called George the night before to ask for a ride. George waited at O'Hare, but Pops never came out. A half hour passed, and George called Mama J, his name for Deloris Jordan. Just wait, she said. Pops probably missed his plane. Two or three hours later, the next flight from Charlotte landed. Pops didn't get off the plane. George dialed Mama J again, and she said that something must have come up and that Pops would call. Pops never called.

"F———er," George finally says, clearing his throat, "made me cry."

George tries to change the subject. He is attuned to Jordan's moods and knows that when Michael gets sad, he becomes quiet, withdrawn, turning inward.

"You know how many jump shots I took to get this thing?" George jokes.

"Played your ass off, George," Jordan shoots back.

But the ghost of Pops is in the room now. "He never met my fiancée," Jordan says. "He never got to see my kids grow up. He died in ninety-three. Jasmine was a year old. Marcus was three years old. Jeffrey was five years old."

"Where do you most feel your dad's presence?" he's asked.

Five seconds pass, then ten. Silence. He leans back into his chair, limp, his paunch noticeable for the first time. The sky outside is gray. He scrunches his mouth, rubs his neck. Suddenly he looks older, his eyes glassy, and even twenty years after his father was murdered—robbed of a Lexus and two championship rings given to him by his son—it's clear that Jordan still needs his dad. He finally answers.

"Probably with him," Jordan says, nodding toward George.

On the floor, leaning against the wall, waiting to be hung, is a framed print Jordan moved here from Chicago. It's of an empty arena, dark and quiet, with a bright white light coming out of the open tunnel doors, beckoning. Really, it's about dealing with losses: with aging, with retirement, with death. In it, Jordan is walking toward the light and there's a ghost walking next to him, with a hand on his shoulder. It's his dad.

"The thing we'd do," he says, "we'd stay up all night and watch cowboy movies. Westerns."

Jordan still watches them obsessively, and it's easy to imagine he does it to feel the presence of his father. One of his employees joked that she'd rather fly commercial than on Jordan's Gulfstream because a passenger on his plane is subjected to hours of shootouts and showdowns.

"Name a Western," George says. "He'll tell you the beginning, middle, and end."

"I watch 'em all the time," Jordan says. "I watch Marshal Dillon. I watch all of 'em."

"I think his favorite Western is my favorite Western," George says.

"You and I have three we really like," Jordan says.

"*Outlaw Josey Wales*," George says.

"That's my favorite," Jordan says.

"*Two Mules . . . ,*" George begins.

". . . *for Sister Sara*," Jordan finishes.

"The other one I like is *Unforgiven*," George says.

"My father loved that," Jordan says.

·   ·   ·

The opposite of this creeping nostalgia is the way Jordan has always collected slights, inventing them—nurturing them. He can be a breathtaking asshole: self-centered, bullying, and cruel. That's the ugly side of greatness. He's a killer, in the Darwinian sense of the word, immediately sensing and attacking someone's weakest spot. He'd moo like a cow when the overweight general manager of the Bulls, Jerry Krause, would get onto the team bus. When the Bulls signed the injury-prone Bill Cartwright, Jordan teased him as Medical Bill, and he once punched Will Perdue during practice. He punched Steve Kerr, too, and who knows how many other people.

This started at an early age. Jordan genuinely believed his father loved his older brother, Larry, more than he loved him, and he used that insecurity as motivation. He burned and thought if he succeeded he would demand an equal share of love. His whole life has been about proving things to the people around him, to strangers, to himself. This has been successful and spectacularly unhealthy. If the boy in those letters from Chapel Hill is gone, it is this appetite to prove—to attack and to dominate and to win— that killed him. In the many biographies written about Jordan, most notably in David Halberstam's *Playing for Keeps*, a common word used to describe Jordan is "rage." Jordan might have stopped playing basketball, but the rage is still there. The fire remains, which is why he searches for release, on the golf course or at a blackjack table, why he spends so much time and energy on his basketball team and why he dreams of returning to play.

He's in his suite at the Bobcats arena, just before tip-off of another loss, annoyed that one of his players is talking to the opponents. Tonight he's going to sit on the bench to send a message that the boss is watching. He used to sit there a lot, but he got a few phone calls from NBA commissioner David Stern telling him to chill with the screaming at officials. Mostly he watches in private, for good reason. Once, when he was an executive with the Wizards, mad at how the team was playing, he hurled a beer can at his office TV, then launched nearly everything on his desk after it, a fusillade of workplace missiles. Now, ten years later, he mostly just yells.

"I'm going downstairs," he says.

"Be nice," someone in the suite says.

"I'll try," he says, and he's out the door.

•　　　•　　　•

The inner circle stays behind, gathered in suite 27, just across the concourse from the executive offices. They've all been around for years, some from the very beginning. Estee Portnoy is here, and George. Rod Higgins and Bobcats president Fred Whitfield, an old friend from North Carolina, come and go. They're waiting on Jordan to return after the game, killing time, handling work stuff, telling stories.

Back when they used to shoot a lot of commercials, Jordan's security team would wait for him in his trailer while he was on set. A woman named Linda cooked Michael's meals, and he loved cinnamon rolls. She'd bake a tray and bring it to him. When it came time to film, he'd see the guards eyeing the cinnamon rolls and he'd walk over and spit on each one, to make sure nobody took his food.

In the late eighties, Jordan looked in Whitfield's closet and saw that half of it was filled with Nike and the other half filled with Puma. Jordan bundled the Puma gear in his arms, tossing it onto the living room floor. He took a knife from the kitchen and cut it to shreds. Call Howard White, his contact at Nike, he told Fred, and tell him to replace it all. Same thing happened with George. He bought a pair of New Balance shoes he loved, and Jordan saw them one day and insisted he hand them over. *Call Howard White at Nike.*

"He demands that loyalty," Whitfield says.

"Anywhere we go," Portnoy says, "he looks at people's feet."

"First thing he looks at," Whitfield says. "He looks down all the time."

"You know what's funny?" Portnoy says. "I do the same thing now."

"I do too!" Whitfield says, laughing.

A group from Nike comes into the suite, along with a team from the ad agency Wieden & Kennedy. Around these people, you see most clearly that Jordan is at the center of several overlapping universes, at the top of the billion-dollar Jordan Brand at Nike, of the Bobcats, of his own company, with dozens of employees and contractors on the payroll. In case anyone in the inner circle forgets who's in charge, they only have to recall the code names given to them by the private security team assigned to overseas trips. Estee is Venom. George is Butler. Yvette is Harmony. Jordan is called Yahweh—a Hebrew word for God.

Jordan is used to being the most important person in every room he enters and, going a step further, in the lives of everyone he meets. The Gulfstream takes off when he steps onboard. He has left a friend in Las Vegas who was late and recently left two security guards behind. He has been trying to leave George for years but can never beat him to the plane. He does what he wants, when he wants. On a long trip to China in the Nike plane, he woke up just as everyone else was taking an Ambien and settling in to sleep. Didn't matter. He turned on the lights and jammed the plane's stereo. If Michael is up, the unwritten rule goes, everybody is up. People cater to his every whim, making sure a car is waiting when he lands, smoothing out any inconvenience. In Chicago there was someone who kept gas in his cars. Not long ago he called his office from Florida, fuming, stuck at a gas station, unable to fill up.

"What's my billing zip code?" he asked.

It was down in Florida, where he was spending time with Yvette's Cuban family, that he got a taste of the life he'd traded for the jet-set circus of modern celebrity. They weren't fawning—her grandparents, who speak little English, aren't basketball fans—and as he sat at a dinner table, with people laughing and eating home-cooked food, he remembered growing up in Wilmington. "It's gone," he says. "I can't get it back. My ego is so big now that I expect certain things. Back then, you didn't."

The people in the suite know about his ego and his moods and his anger. They know better than most. George jokes a lot about the bite marks on his ass. But they also know Jordan, and if they're being honest, they love him. They know how kind he can be, having roses sent on Mother's Day to every mom who works for him. They see him gutted after meeting with another Make-a-Wish child. They see him swell with pride over any success of his children. They've been inside the machine, seeing firsthand the siege of fame, the hardness and cynicism it demands. So they think all the stories of Michael being Michael are funny, even endearing, while someone from the outside can hear the same story and be horrified, seeing a permanent adolescent spitting on food or cutting up clothes.

His friends, for instance, watched the Hall of Fame speech and laughed.

      •   •   •

In the three and a half years since Jordan built his induction remarks around all the slights that pushed him toward greatness, the speech has become exhibit A for those who believe Jordan is, as one basketball writer put it, "strangely bitter" and "lost, wandering." They're not wrong, not exactly, but something was obscured when the speech became a metaphor for swollen ego and lack of self-awareness.

The speech itself, if you watch it again, is an open window into what Jordan is like in private: funny, caustic, confident, sarcastic, competitive. He sees himself not as a gifted athlete but as someone who refused to lose. So standing at the podium—after he composed himself, wiping away tears nine times before he even began, sniffling well into the first section—he said that he had a fire inside and that "people added wood to that fire." Then he listed every doubter, cataloging all their actions, small and large. He started with his brothers and worked through high school to college to the NBA. He took a shot at longtime nemesis Jerry Krause: "I don't know who invited him . . . I didn't." It was petty but also startlingly honest.

The unspoken thread that runs through the criticism is that Jordan didn't understand what was required of a retired athlete, a mixture of nostalgia and reflection. The five-year wait is supposed to give those emotions time to sprout and grow. People wanted the Jordan on the floor of his closet, not the one who did whatever it took to win. That's the allure of a Hall of Fame speech. It reveals that these icons were sort of like us all along. Jordan didn't give that speech, and the reason is both simple and obvious. He didn't see himself as part of the past or as someone who'd found perspective. He wasn't nostalgic that night. The anger that drove his career hadn't gone away, and he didn't know what to do with it. So at the end of the speech, he said perhaps the most telling and important thing in it, which has been mostly forgotten.

He described what the game meant to him. He called it his "refuge" and the "place where I've gone when I needed to find comfort and peace." Basketball made him feel complete, and it was gone.

"One day," he said, "you might look up and see me playing the game at fifty."

Chuckles rippled through the room. His head jerked to the side, and he cut his eyes the way he does when challenged, and he said, "Oh, don't laugh."

Everyone laughed harder.

"Never say never," he said.

•   •   •

He's trying to change, taking small steps. For the past few years, he's gone on sailing trips because Yvette loves them, even though he hates the water. The first time, he went stir-crazy on the boat. This most recent trip, he felt his rage dissolve. It was a victory. He didn't watch basketball. Every morning he'd wake with the sun and plant himself in the fishing chair, popping his first Corona by eight with his friends, reeling in big yellowfin tuna, which hit a trolling bait like a submarine. They make great sushi. Four other couples came along, and they celebrated New Year's Eve. Jordan was happy. "Drinking and eating and drinking and eating and drinking and eating" is how he described the vacation to a friend, going through cases of his favorite tequila, fully unplugged, which lasted until he flew home. Then he was around the game again, and the old urges began to eat at him.

In Charlotte, he starts thinking about 218.

Every morning since returning from the islands, he's been in the gym. At mealtime he texts his nutritionist to find out what he can and can't eat. Ostensibly, the reason is that he stepped on a scale after leaving the excess palace of *Mister Terrible* and saw this number staring back: 261. Nine days later, sitting in his office and surrounded by basketball, he's down to 248. He'll claim it's about health or looking good for his fiftieth birthday party. But in his mind, there's a target: 218, a familiar and dangerous number in Jordan's world.

That's his playing weight.

When he mentions that Yvette never saw him play basketball, he says, "She never saw me at 218." On the wall of his office there's a framed photograph of him as a young man, rising toward the rim, legs pulled up near his chest, seeming to fly. He smiles at it wistfully.

"I was 218," he says.

The chasm between what his mind wants and what his body can give grows every year. If Jordan watches old video of Bulls games and then hits the gym, he says he'll go "berserk" on the exercise machines. It's frightening. A while back, his brother, Larry, who works for the team, noticed a commotion on the practice court. He looked out the window of his office and saw his brother dominating one of the best players on the Bobcats in one-on-one. The next morning, Larry says with a smile, Jordan never made it into his office. He got as far as the team's training room, where he received treatment.

"You paying the price, aren't you?" Larry asked.

"I couldn't hardly move," Jordan said.

There's no way to measure these things, but there's a strong case to be made that Jordan is the most intense competitor on the planet. He's in the conversation, at the very least, and now he has been reduced to grasping for outlets for this competitive rage. He's in the middle of an epic game of Bejeweled on his iPad, and he's moved past level 100, where he won the title Bejeweled Demigod. He mastered sudoku and won $500 beating Portnoy at it. In the Bahamas, he sent someone down to the Atlantis hotel's gift shop to buy a book of word-search puzzles. In the hotel room, he raced Portnoy and Polk, his lawyer, beating them both. He can see all the words at once, as he used to see a basketball court. "I can't help myself," he says. "It's an addiction. You ask for this special power to achieve these heights, and now you got it and you want to give it back, but you can't. If I could, then I could breathe."

Once, the whole world watched him compete and win—game 6, the Delta Center—and now it's a small group of friends in a hotel room playing a silly kid's game. The desire remains the same, but the venues, and the stakes, keep shrinking. For years he was beloved for his urges when they manifested on the basketball court, and now he's ridiculed when they show up in a speech.

His self-esteem has always been, as he says, "tied directly to the game." Without it, he feels adrift. Who am I? What am I doing? For the past ten years, since retiring for the third time, he has been running, moving as fast as he could, creating distractions, distance. When the schedule clears, he'll call his office and tell them not to bother him for a month, to let him relax and play golf. Three days later they'll get another call, asking if the plane can pick him up and take him someplace. He's restless. So he owns the Bobcats, does his endorsements, plays hours of golf, hoping to block out thoughts of 218. But then he gets off a boat, comes home to a struggling team. He feels his competitiveness kick in, almost a chemical thing, and he starts working out, and he wonders: Could he play at fifty? What would he do against LeBron?

What if?

"It's consumed me so much," he says. "I'm my own worst enemy. I drove myself so much that I'm still living with some of those drives. I'm living with that. I don't know how to get rid of it. I don't know if I could. And here I am, still connected to the game."

He thinks about the things Phil Jackson taught him. Jackson always understood him and wasn't afraid to poke around inside Jordan. Once during his ritual of handing out books for his players to read, he gave Jordan a book about gambling. It's a Zen koan Jordan needs now, in this new challenge: To find himself, he must lose himself. Whenever he obsesses about returning to play, he tries to sleep, knowing that when he wakes up, things will be better. He knows he won't get to 218. He knows he won't ever play pro basketball again. He knows he's got to quiet these drives, to find a way to live the life he worked so hard to create, *to be still.*

"How can I enjoy the next twenty years without so much of this consuming me?" he asks, sitting behind his desk as his cell phone buzzes with trade offers. "How can I find peace away from the game of basketball?"

•   •   •

He's home.

Jordan steps into his loft, which is dark and modern, with exposed ductwork and a sparkling backsplash in the kitchen. The design feels masculine, vaguely Asian. A pool table with tan felt is to the left, cigar ashtrays scattered around the place. There's an hour until the Bobcats-Celtics tip-off in Boston, which he'll watch from his favorite chair, a rich brown, low-slung lounger.

"Where you at?" he calls toward the rear of the condo.

Yvette's voice sounds bright and cheerful.

"Hey, honey," she says, "I'm back here."

She's thirty-four years old, has worked in a hospital and in real estate, and is happiest with the domestic life that Jordan lost long ago. This past year, Portnoy got a birthday present from her boss, as usual, but for the first time in sixteen years, she also got a card. It was from the store Papyrus. She recognized it and inside, Jordan had signed his name. Estee laughed, mostly at her own surprise over such ordinary behavior. Yvette had done what any person would do when a birthday approached. She'd bought a card on her own. She didn't staff it out.

Whatever changes he's made are because of her, and she offers him the best hope to rediscover pieces of the boy who wrote those letters from college. Two Easters ago, Yvette went with him to North Carolina to visit family, which is spread around the state. She'd been bugging him about taking her to Wilmington, to show her where he grew up. Like most people, she sometimes struggled to imagine him before. She wanted to meet the Mike Jordan who needed his mom and dad to send stamps. This required about seven hours of driving, which he didn't want to do. Finally, he gave in. "It's amazing what women can talk you into doing," he says. "Make you change. Ten years ago, we'd have been arguing all f———ing day. I would've won. This time, this stage where I am, you win. That's progress."

Tonight, the guys are ordering Ruth's Chris to go, and Yvette and Laura are making salads. Friends gather around the kitchen island, and the place is filled with laughter. They're washing lettuce. It's easy and loose. Jordan is killing Buckner about drinking all his wine, everyone erupting at the volleyed barbs, and later, when George hands Quinn an expensive bottle of merlot with a bendy straw in it, Yvette falls into hysterics. It was a joint George-Yvette operation, from the sound of her giddy cackling.

She pushes Jordan, making him try new things. The home in Florida is almost finished, and it will be theirs together. In conversation among his staff, the golf club estate has been called a "retirement home," and Jordan's friends like to imagine him in the huge outdoor living area, lounging on a big couch, relaxing. Their wish for him is peace.

He seems to have it tonight, at least for a moment.

"Baby," Yvette says, "can you get us some wine?"

Jordan ducks into the climate-controlled wine room and comes out with one of his favorites. The cork pops softly. Glasses line the counter, and he pours wine into each one, handing them off as he finishes.

"Here ya go, ladies," he says.

.   .   .

Over the next seven hours, all of it spent watching one basketball game after another, he's again pulled inward, on a Tilt-a-Whirl of emotion, mostly shades of anger, from active screaming to a slow, silent burn. He transforms from a businessman returning from the office—*Honey, I'm home!*—to a man on fire. The first sparks come from a *SportsCenter* debate, one of those impossible, vaguely ridiculous arguments that can, of course, never be won: Who's a better quarterback, Joe Montana or Tom Brady?

"I can't wait to hear this conversation," he says.

He stretches his legs out on the ottoman, wearing sweats and socks, and as one of the guys on television argues for Brady, Jordan laughs.

"They're gonna say Brady because they don't remember Montana," he says. "Isn't that amazing?"

Aging means losing things, and not just eyesight and flexibility. It means watching the accomplishments of your youth be diminished, maybe in your own eyes through perspective, maybe in the eyes of others through cultural amnesia. Most people live anonymous lives, and when they grow old and die, any record of their existence is blown away. They're forgotten, some more slowly than others, but eventually it happens to virtually everyone. Yet for the few people in each generation who reach the very pinnacle of fame and achievement, a mirage flickers: immortality. They come to believe in it. Even after Jordan is gone, he knows people will remember him. *Here lies the greatest basketball player of all time.* That's his epitaph. When he walked off the court for the last time, he must have believed that nothing could ever diminish what he'd done. That knowledge would be his shield against aging.

There's a fable about returning Roman generals who rode in victory parades through the streets of the capital; a slave stood behind them, whispering in their ears, "All glory is fleeting." Nobody does that for professional athletes. Jordan couldn't have known that the closest he'd get to immortality was during that final walk off the court, the one symbolically preserved in the print in his office. All that can happen in the days and years that follow is for the shining monument he built to be chipped away, eroded. Maybe he realizes that now. Maybe he doesn't. But when he sees Joe Montana joined on the mountaintop by the next generation, he has to realize that someday his picture will be on a screen next to LeBron James as people argue about who was better.

The debaters announce the results of an Internet poll, and 925,000 people voted. There was a tie: 50 percent said Montana and 50 percent said Brady. It doesn't matter that Montana never lost a Super Bowl or that, unlike Brady, he never faded on the biggest stage. Questions of legacy, of greatness, are weighted in favor of youth. Time itself is on Brady's side, for now.

Jordan shakes his head.

"That doesn't make any sense," he says.

•   •   •

Jordan plays his new favorite trivia game, asking which current players could be nearly as successful in his era. "Our era," he says over and over again, calling modern players soft, coddled, and ill-prepared for the highest level of the game. This is personal to him since he'll be compared to this generation and since he has to build a franchise with this generation's players.

"I'll give you a hint," he says. "I can only come up with four."

He lists them: *LeBron, Kobe, Tim Duncan, Dirk Nowitzki.* As he's making his point, Yvette walks into the living room area and, in a tone of voice familiar to every husband who argues sports with his buddies, asks, "You guys need anything?"

When someone on TV compares LeBron to Oscar Robertson, Jordan fumes. He rolls his eyes, stretches his neck, frustrated. "It's absolutely . . ." he says, catching himself. "The point is, no one is critiquing the personnel that he's playing against. Their knowledge of how to play the game . . . that's not a fair comparison. That's not right . . . Could LeBron be successful in our era? Yes. Would he be as successful? No."

The Bobcats game starts and the Celtics jump all over them. The officials aren't helping, and Jordan sits up, livid, certain that the Celtics are getting all the calls because they have the stars.

"COME ON, MAN!" he screams.

"You ain't getting that one," Buckner says. "But you used to get away with s—— other people couldn't get away with."

There's a hard silence in the room. Jordan's voice lowers.

"I don't believe that," he growls.

"Bull. S——," Buckner says. "Let's not get carried away now. You and Larry."

Jordan ignores him: He's locked in.

"That's a foul!" he yells. "See what I mean? THAT'S A FOUL!"

It's a nice night, and Jordan moves out to his balcony, on the seventh floor, looking down the barrel of Tryon Street. The TV is up in the right corner. He smokes a cigar. The Bobcats tie the game, then fall behind again.

"Getbackgetbackgetback," Jordan yells at the TV. "Matchup, MATCHUP. Where you GOING? DIVE FOR THE BALL!"

They're going to lose—he's going to lose—and he is quiet on the couch. It's over. He doesn't talk for a minute, then mutters something, then is silent for another half a minute.

He changes the channel to the Heat-Jazz game. During the broadcast, he is the answer to a trivia question. This is the court where he made his most famous shot, and he points to the place where he took it. He remembers how tired he felt at the end of that game. A cell phone rests on Jordan's chest. His legs stretch out on a tree-trunk coffee table.

"What's Bird up to?" Jordan asks.

"Down in Naples," Buckner says.

"Playing golf every day?" Jordan asks.

"Bored," Buckner says.

"Think he'll ever get back in?" Jordan asks.

"He'll damn sure get back in it," Buckner says. "He didn't say it, but I just know him."

The announcers gush about LeBron, mentioning him in the same sentence with Jordan, who hears every word. Those words have an effect on him. He stares at the TV and points out a flaw in LeBron's game.

"I study him," he says.

When LeBron goes right, he usually drives; when he goes left, he usually shoots a jumper. It has to do with his mechanics and how he loads the ball for release. "So if I have to guard him," Jordan says, "I'm gonna push him left so nine times out of ten, he's gonna shoot a jump shot. If he goes right, he's going to the hole and I can't stop him. So I ain't letting him go right."

For the rest of the game, when LeBron gets the ball and starts his move, Jordan will call out some variation of "drive" or "shoot." It's not just LeBron. He sees fouls the officials miss, and the replays prove him right. When someone shoots, he knows immediately whether it's going in. He calls out what guys are going to do before they do it, more plugged into the flow of the game than some of the players on the court. He's answering texts, buried in his phone, when the play-by-play guy announces a LeBron jump shot. Without looking up, Jordan says, "Left?"

The outdoor heater makes the porch warm. Hours pass, creating distance from the Bobcats loss. Nobody says much. George plays Bejeweled on an iPad. The air is filled with the sounds of basketball: horns, squeaking sneakers, the metallic clang of the rim. These are the sounds of Jordan's youth.

He holds a cigar and relights it every now and then, the whoosh of the butane torch breaking the silence. The heater's flame is reflected on three different windows, shadows flickering on Jordan's face. He never says it, but it seems as though he's playing the game in his head, using his rage for its intended purpose. He still knows how to play. He could shut down LeBron, if his body wouldn't betray him, if he could hold off time, if he could get to 218.

•   •   •

George goes to bed. An hour later, the last game of the night ends. Buckner says goodbye and rides the elevator down. Yvette and her friend Laura headed toward the back of the condo long ago.

Jordan is alone.

He hates being alone because that means it's quiet, and he doesn't like silence. He can't sleep without noise. Sleep has always been a struggle for him. All the late-night card games, the trips to the casino during the playoffs, they've been misunderstood. They weren't the disease, they were the cure. They provided noise, distraction, a line of defense. He didn't even start drinking until he was twenty-seven and complained of insomnia to a doctor. Have a few beers after the game, he was advised. That would knock off the edge.

The house is dark. It's almost one a.m., and he opens the iPad app that controls the loft's audio-visual system. Every night he does the same thing, and he does it now: turn the bedroom television to the Western channel. The cowboy movies will break the darkness, break the silence, allow him to rest. It's just like the old days, him and Pops. Jordan climbs into bed. The film on the screen is *Unforgiven*. He knows every scene, and sometime before the shootout in the saloon, he falls asleep.

Runner's World

FINALIST—FEATURE
WRITING

At the age of six, Bret Dunlap was hit by a pickup truck and thrown more than fifty feet, incurring brain damage so severe that doctors said he would never walk again—and would be dead by thirteen. In what the National Magazine Award judges described as "measured, unsentimental prose," Steve Friedman portrays Dunlap, now forty-five, as a lonely but determined man who runs marathons despite his injuries. Friedman is the author of seven books, including a memoir, Lost on Treasure Island, about his sometimes inglorious career as a magazine editor. With a monthly audience of more than 3 million, Runner's World was widely praised for its coverage of the 2013 Boston Marathon—a race the magazine was covering live when the bombs exploded near the finish line.

Steve Friedman

Bret, Unbroken

You know what people think. They see jeans too short and winter coat too shiny, too grimy, and think, *homeless*. They watch a credit card emerge from those jeans and think, *grifter*. They behold a frozen grin, hear a string of strangled, tortured pauses, and think, *slow. Stupid.*

You learned too young about cruelty and pity. You learned too young that explaining yourself didn't help, that it made things worse. People laughed. Made remarks. Backed away. So you stopped explaining. You got a job, got a cat, got an apartment, and people can think what they want to think. You built a life without explanation and it was enough.

What people see now, this moment, is a solitary man leaning into the wind, trudging down snow-dusted streets toward a faint, watery dawn.

It's December 20, 2012, almost the shortest day of the year. You have been up since four-thirty a.m. You have eaten your oatmeal and cranberries, and you have fed Taffy the cat and packed your lunch of canned chicken and coleslaw, and you are alone on the streets of Rhinelander, Wisconsin, an industrial town of 7,800 that squats at the confluence of the Wisconsin and Pelican rivers, deep in the woods of the Northern Highlands. It's 2.5 miles, at least part of which you usually run, to Drs. Foster and Smith, the mail-order and online pet-supply colossus where you have worked for almost eighteen years. (*Warehouse dummy*, people think, and they don't know about your college credits or your study of military history or that you speak German, understand a little Russian, and can say "How are you?" and "Thank you, goodbye," in Romanian.)

When you crest a hill half a mile from the warehouse, you pause, turn, and notice the quality of the light, how even in the hard, cold days before Christmas, the weak morning sun turns the smokestacks and factories of downtown Rhinelander into friendly things, peaceful and benign. You think about the most beautiful light in the world, the sunrise behind the barn due east of your mother's house, sixty-five miles away. No one knows what you think about the quality of light. Few know that you love horses or that you have plans to breed chickens or that you long for love or that you have hardened yourself to never receiving it.

That's fine by you. It used to be fine, in any case. It was fine before the day two years ago, when your brother Eric asked you to run a 5K race. He was running a 10K, and he thought it would be nice to have company. You refused—you didn't want to make anyone uncomfortable. You didn't want to deal with people looking at you, with them thinking things.

But he was insistent. That was the day you started running. Since then, you haven't been so sure about things. You're forty-five now, and you're not so sure you know what people think. You're not so sure about the life you have spent so much energy constructing.

You're not so sure it's enough.

You don't remember anything from before the accident, and you know that's a blessing, a small one in a life filled with blessings that are too small for most to see. You don't remember the chicken coop behind your house, or how Eric played the saxophone, or how the family's black Labrador, Snowball, howled along.

You were six, a kindergartner, and it was October, and you were running across the street in Mukwonago, Wisconsin, on the outskirts of Milwaukee, to see your best friend's new toy truck.

His grandmother had been visiting from North Dakota and he was hollering for you to come see it, so you broke from your older brothers, Eric and Mark, and darted into the street. Approaching from behind a curve at the bottom of a hill, the driver of a pickup truck happened into the worst moment of his life. On one side, a little boy and his grandmother and his toy truck and five other children, all waiting for the school bus. On the other side, your brothers. All of them gaping at you, in the middle of the road.

You were wearing a hooded nylon Packers jacket and a piece of the pickup truck's grillwork stuck to it. Your shoes came off—still tied, with the socks still in them—as your body skidded down the road. It skidded fifty or sixty feet before a man in a VW Beetle jumped out and stopped you. There wasn't a visible mark on you.

The driver who hit you slammed on his pickup's brakes, jumped out, and ran to the nearest house, pounded on the door. The woman who answered said, "Calm down. It's one of Barb's. She'll have already called an ambulance." And she had. Your mother had seen everything.

The ambulance took you, unconscious, to Waukesha Memorial Hospital. Your pelvis had cracked in two places, and your large intestine was torn open. Doctors removed your teeth, which had been broken and loosened by the impact. They performed a colostomy, put a brace on your left leg and a cast on your right one, which they put in traction. Your mother arrived with your kindergarten class photo, taken a few weeks earlier. She shoved it at one of the doctors. "This is what you got," she said. "I don't care what you do, just get him back to me alive."

With the cast and brace and all the bandages, the only part of you anyone could see was one foot, so your mother stroked that foot. She called her mother, who lived next door, and told her to take care of your brothers, to get them to school, to make everything as normal as possible, and when doctors told her you had suffered a terrible blow to your head, that your brain was severely damaged, that you would never walk or talk again, that your intellect would never progress beyond that of an eight-year-old, that you would die by the time you were thirteen, she said nothing, kept petting your foot.

Nothing happened for days—or a week or two weeks, no one remembers—and when your grandfather was visiting, doctors told him they'd have to perform an operation to relieve the swelling in your brain, and the procedure was risky, it might kill you, but that if they did nothing, you would certainly die. They told him that everyone should prepare for your death, and he asked the doctors if they had told your mother, and when they said they had, he told them he was sure your mother was taking care of everything, and he was right. Your mother had called the funeral parlor.

She brought in a tape recorder and the tape she had made. The chickens and Snowball. Eric wailing on his saxophone. She strung ornaments from the wires above your hospital bed. You were still unconscious, but she talked to you. She brought in the teenagers from the YMCA who had taught you and your brothers music and judo and swimming. Eric and Mark kept going to school and every day their teachers asked, "Has he talked yet?" and every day they had to say no.

You needed blood, more than your mother and her family could provide. She told a neighbor and the neighbor said not to worry, her dad was a foreman at the Waukesha Motor Company, he could do something. He told all the shifts, "Okay, there's a little guy in the hospital, and he needs blood, and need I remind you, all your vacation vouchers go through me?"

You awoke from the coma, but you didn't speak, and then one day you did. You don't remember what you said, but your mother does. You said, "No!"

The doctors told your mother you should be moved to a rehab facility, where you could live out your days. If living was the right word.

Your mother was a hard woman, who by her own admission liked horses better than dogs, and dogs better than most people.

She was poor—your mother didn't believe in euphemisms—working for her brother, who owned a greenhouse. Your father had been gone for a while. ("Oh, he was a loving man," says your mother. "He loved tall and short. He loved blond and brunette and redhead.") Your mother was under no illusions about the comforts you'd receive at home. But she grabbed a nurse and together they wrestled you onto an air mattress and they shoved the air mattress into the back of your mother's green Pinto station wagon, and for what doctors thought would be a few miserable years, you went home.

She wouldn't let you have a wheelchair. Your mother was a hard woman, and she knew she would die one day, and if by some miracle—some great, undeserved blessing—it happened before you were gone, she knew you would have to be hard, too. She wrestled you onto that air mattress six days a week for months, slid you into that Pinto, and drove you to the physical therapist and the occupational therapist and the speech therapist.

It was the left side of your brain that had been injured. (Hemiparesis was the technical diagnosis.) Because of that, you had trouble with balance, and weakness and nerve damage in the right side of your body—right-handed before the accident, you would have to become a lefty. The left side of your face was partially paralyzed. Your speech was impaired. You needed medication to prevent seizures, medication you would take for years. To the doctors' surprise, your brain started growing again, but it didn't work like it used to.

So you learned to read, then you forgot. You learned arithmetic, then forgot. You learned to talk, then forgot. You had to learn things over and over again.

Your mother loved musicals, and trying to sing along with her was sometimes easier than trying to talk. She and your grandmother also read you stories from baby books, showed you how to add two plus two. Even today, your mother can quote pages from *If I Ran the Circus*. If asked, she said you had problems. She refused to use the word "handicapped."

Whenever visitors came over, they brought you toys, and your brothers were delighted, because they're the ones who got to play with the toys. GI Joes were the best of all. Eric, ten, was unfailingly kind, solicitous. He had always been that way. Serious, quiet, he had announced when he was five that he wanted to be an ichthyologist and asked for a bathyscaphe for Christmas. He would go on to become a high school physics teacher before making the suggestion that would change your life. Mark, eight, wasn't unfailingly anything. Wild, unpredictable, impulsive, he would spend his teenage years running a high school loan-shark operation, employing teenage muscle to keep the enterprise efficient, joining the army right out of high school, then, after that, becoming a long-haul trucker. Mark teased you, commandeered your GI Joes. But woe to any other child who picked on you— and there were a few, before Mark and his gang got hold of them.

A blizzard came that first winter home, cutting power, closing the roads. Eric nailed blankets over the windows, spread blankets over the living room floor. One of your mother's girlfriends had a husband with a snowmobile, and he brought you your antiseizure pills.

Your mother was poor, but she knew that education was important, and she knew what a comfort music could be, and she made your brothers take piano lessons, so she made you take them, too. Your right hand didn't work? Big deal, her brother had a boy with Down's syndrome, and when he was over, your mother gave him a saw and told him to go outside and get some wood for the fireplace.

If your cousin with Down's syndrome could saw wood, you could learn to play the piano. Your mother explained the situation to your brothers' music teacher, told her what she wanted. What she needed. And your brothers' music teacher found a composer—a veteran of the Crimean War who'd had his right hand blown off. He had composed music for the left hand only. You learned how to play the piano left-handed.

You would grow into a man who built a life alone, a safe strategy that could keep out teachers who thought you were slow, doctors who called you stupid, children who teased you. You remember most of them. But you don't remember everyone.

At Clarendon Avenue Elementary School, there was a foot race, and you had trouble walking, never mind running, but all the kids had to compete. One of the fastest kids in your class was also one of the most rotten. A mean lowlife destined for a bad end. That's what your mom remembers hearing about him. But she also remembers him finishing the race, and then looking back, and seeing how far you had to go, and jumping back on the course, and finishing the race again, right behind you, not making fun of you, but keeping you company.

There were the pills and the one-handed music lessons and everything else, but your mother had refused to sue the man who had hit you. He hadn't been drinking. It was an accident. He had kids, too. That's the way she saw it. She had fired her lawyer because he had decided to research the assets of that man. She had yelled at that lawyer, too. *How dare he?!* And she had yelled at the judge, the judge who told her to sit down and shut up, and who told her lawyer she should sue or be reprimanded for being financially irresponsible. "That man didn't get up that morning and decide, 'I'm going to wipe out a six-year-old!'" she yelled at the judge.

Your mother got by. Your uncle paid her every week you were in the hospital, but not long after you got out, she returned to the greenhouse, and she got into a squabble with your uncle's wife, so she took other jobs—waitressing, wrapping meat at one deli, taking orders at another.

If you were pouring milk into your cereal bowl and you spilled it all over, your mother grabbed a towel and cleaned it up, but she left it to you to make yourself another bowl. You fell down a lot and when that happened, she wouldn't even stop talking, she'd just reach down and put you on your feet and if you fell again, she would pick you up again.

Your broken bones healed. Doctors reversed the colostomy. Because of the brain damage, you still walked awkwardly, but you fell less. You talked more. And to others, it might have looked like a happy fable: Little boy suffers grievous injury, through tough love and support finds his place in the world. But you hadn't found your place.

If your mother didn't know it then, she would soon enough. You were in second grade. It was a spring afternoon, and your mother had come to the school. She might have been hard, but she could also be fun. Every so often she'd stop by school and gather you and your brothers, and maybe a few other kids, and take all of you to go feed the ducks, or to go fishing, or to just sit by a lake and play.

She was on her way to your classroom when she saw you in the hall. You were throwing books and ripping paper. You had reasons, you knew that, and she did, too. The right side of your body didn't work well. Neither did your mouth. You knew answers and couldn't say them fast enough and you knew that people thought you were stupid, and you weren't. Your mother knew how frustrated you were, and if she had been someone else, she might have held you, stroked your head, comforted you.

She snatched you up and she paddled you, right in the school hallway, and people were watching by now, they had heard the commotion and they were shocked, but they didn't know what she knew, they didn't know what she told you that day, dragging you out to her car.

"You can't do all the things the other kids do?" she said. "Tough. You are going to have to deal with it." She was not religious—she had her reasons, generations old and having nothing to do with you—but now, to her sobbing, raging second-grader, she invoked God.

"God never said anything about fair," she said. "He said you got a chance."

After that, she grabbed a marker at home and she scrawled this onto your school bag: "Failure is not falling down. Failure is not getting back up." She wrote the same thing on the refrigerator.

She read to you every day. She did math problems with you. She paid you and Mark a penny each for every fly you killed. She let you play horseshoes, and didn't let you see how that terrified her, and everyone else in the vicinity. And she might have softened, might have let you slide when things were toughest, might have given you a break. But she didn't.

The doctors had told her to make sure your clothes had Velcro fasteners, so that you'd be able to get in and out of them yourself. But she knew the easy cruelty of children, knew the taunts you would easily incite without pasting Velcro targets all over yourself. So she made you shirts with giant buttonholes, and she bought big buttons and she sewed those on and she told you that you were going to learn how to button your clothes.

That first night she and her mother—your grandmother—stood in your room and watched you. When you got to the last button you—and they—realized you had miscalculated, that the two sides were misaligned by one buttonhole. Your grandmother moved to help you. "Get back! If you can't keep your hands off, you should go home," your mother snapped. "He needs to learn to do it himself."

And as you unbuttoned your shirt, with your good left hand and your claw of a right hand, your grandmother stood with her own hands clenched behind her back, to keep them from reaching out to you, and she wept.

Your mother watched, dry-eyed.

Your mother took you to a support group for people who had suffered brain injuries and their families. When one of the mothers of another young man, also brain-damaged, said, "I'm a survivor, too," your mother snapped, "Oh, no, you're not. You're a parent. This is your job!"

You were put in special classes in high school, and hated them. Other kids would frown and whimper if they couldn't answer a question and then an advisor would do the work for them. You didn't want anyone doing your work. You studied Latin because rolling those strange words around your tongue seemed to strengthen it and German because thinking sentences through in that language helped you express them in English.

By the time you were a sophomore in high school, Eric had left for college and Mark's loan-sharking business was booming and his friends—Speedy and Ben and Rich—were your friends. One of them was gay, and your mom was worried that he was a bad influence on you. Not because he was gay. Because he was sneaky. If you were gay, that was fine, but she wanted you to be gay because you were gay, not because you were lonely and one of your loan-sharking brother's sneaky friends was a predator.

When you were a senior, six weeks before you were due to graduate, your mother got a call from your school. You had walked out of a class and nobody knew where you were. She found you on State Highway 83, headed north. She asked where you were going and you said you didn't know. But you were going. You refused to return to Mukwonago High School that day, or ever again.

What was the point? You knew you'd never be able to speak well, you'd never be able to tell people everything you were feeling, everything you were thinking. And what you were feeling and thinking was a mess. You were taking Depakene and Peganone to prevent seizures. Your right hand didn't work properly, and sometimes, especially when you got tired, you limped and listed and there were long silences between your words. You knew you'd always put people ill at ease. What kind of life was that?

You knew what other people thought. You knew what life would be like. You knew what to do. You took a fitful shot at killing yourself. You don't like thinking about it. You don't like talking about it.

Your mother took you to the hospital, where a psychologist told her you were a "dullard." Your mother had found a one-

armed composer. She had managed to wrestle you and that goddamn air mattress into her goddamn Pinto. She had found you
the blood you needed, and taught you to speak again, and willed
you to button your own shirt. So of course she could find a doctor
who would take the time to listen to you. To see you. To know
you. And she did. He worked in Milwaukee, and he was kind and
he listened. And understood. He understood that life was hard,
and that life for someone with brain injuries was nearly intoler-
able, and that all the medications you were on took the "nearly"
out of it. He knew how you felt.

"Bret's smart," he told your mother, as if she didn't know that.
"By the time you get done talking to him, you're almost convinced suicide is a logical option."

It took time to cure those thoughts. Once, your mother found
you in your bedroom with a machete. "You want to kill yourself?" she screamed, seizing the machete. "Here, I'll help you!"
She smacked your legs with the handle.

Eventually the doctor suggested taking you off all the medications. He told your mother she might lose you, but it was a
gamble worth taking. She and you agreed.

You kept seeing the doctor. You passed your high school
equivalency exam. You prepared for the rest of your life.

You decided to take the civil-service test for a post-office job.
You asked that you be able to fill out your name and address before the test started, so you wouldn't waste so much time writing.
They refused. They thought you were trying to gain an unfair advantage. It wasn't the first time people had misjudged you, and it
wouldn't be the last.

You told your mother you were going to take a data-entry
course at Waukesha County Technical Institute, and she said
sure, if that's what you want to do. You said you'd get there yourself, and she said of course, if that's what you wanted.

You walked to West Greenfield Avenue and got on the number 9 bus, and you didn't know it, but behind the bus, slid down

in her seat to make sure she wasn't seen, was your mother. She had never felt so proud. She had never—except for days in the hospital—felt so frightened.

You, Mark, and your mom moved north to Pine Lake in 1987 when she bought a bar—The Whispering Pines—and those were good years. Your mother met a man, Oscar, fifteen years younger than her, and kind. You tended bar and got to know people, and people got to know you. Your mom and Oscar married; they lived upstairs and you and Mark lived in an apartment below. You took classes at Nicolet Area Technical College. You got A's in Computer Concepts, the Psychology of Human Relationships, Economics, and Creative Writing. Business Law and Intermediate Algebra, you got B's. Fundamentals of Speech, you got a C.

You wanted to be more than a bartender. You applied for jobs around town, but the people hiring said you should be able to type. Of course, you could type. But you couldn't do it fast enough. You filled out an application at a local gas station—it was long, and it took quite some time and you didn't like the way the person at the desk watched you labor over it—and after she thanked you, and you left, your mother saw her tear up your application and throw the pieces in the trash can.

One place that was interested in you was Drs. Foster and Smith, a pet-supply business. But the supervisor was curious. You were receiving disability insurance. Did you not know that working a steady job would jeopardize your monthly government check? Why would you want to do that? You explained to the person that you wanted to work because that's what men did. They worked. Did she have a problem with that? She did not, and she said the company would be glad to have you, and you decided that you thought you might fit in at Drs. Foster and Smith.

You started work on August 29, 1995. You were employee number 860. You worked near another young man named Marko Modic. You lifted things and you moved heavy things and it didn't take Marko long to figure out—once he got past your difficulty with language and the way, late in the day, the right side of your body stiffened, and the left side of your face froze up—that you were a smart guy. Really smart. And funny. Smarter and funnier than most everyone else in the warehouse. You and Marko would talk about politics and women and sports, and you would join the other warehouse employees one day a week to play volleyball. It didn't take you long to realize that with your balance issues and the way the right side of your body didn't work so well, you couldn't play. You stayed on the sides, making wisecracks.

Marko realized that for all your jokes, you had a chip on your shoulder. You acted like you had something to prove. When someone else would carry a five-gallon bottle of water up a flight of stairs, you would carry two jugs, one on each shoulder, right-side weakness be damned. If someone would ask about your injuries, you'd shut them down. We're all different, you would say. End of story.

Marko got to know you, but not many others did. The company hosted an annual summer picnic and an employee appreciation Christmas luncheon, but you didn't attend. Dealing with others was exhausting. And you knew that you made them uncomfortable. You knew what they were thinking when they saw you. Lunchtime, while others were knotted at tables in the cafeteria, talking about whatever people talked about, you sat in the break room, in front of the television, wolfing down your chicken and coleslaw.

People offered you rides to work, but you knew they felt beholden, and you didn't want that, so you refused. You didn't want to risk making anyone more uncomfortable. You walked to work and you walked home. You walked to the grocery store and the Laundromat and you walked to the Red Cross blood center because you wanted to be useful. You watched a few TV shows and went to bed early, and you got up and you fed Taffy and had your oatmeal and cranberries and started over again, and it was enough.

Your mother had been a hard woman, and she had done her best and she had succeeded. You were a hard man.

If only you could have explained to people all you knew—about farming and animals and your cat and the designer chickens you planned to breed, about military history, and how you knew Latin and German, how you longed for a woman's touch. . . . But you couldn't explain it to them. That was part of the problem. That was the problem. They didn't want to hear you try to explain because you made them so uncomfortable. You knew that. You knew that even if you found the cure for cancer, unless you could speak it or write it, it was useless knowledge.

You didn't want to be useless. You helped your mom and Oscar around the house. You memorized four-digit bar codes for items in the warehouse so that when someone needed something, you knew exactly where it was. You toted those gigantic jugs of water. You didn't take vacation days (partly because the paperwork required for a vacation was so daunting). When you weren't working hard, you studied. You took Introduction to Sociology and American History to 1865 and American History from 1865 and Marketing Principles and Personnel Management. You started a retirement account. The Red Cross only visited Rhinelander to collect blood four times a year, so you started visiting the Community Blood Center at Trig's Food and Drug in the RiverWalk Center, on South Courtney Street. They would take your blood every two months, unless your iron was low. If that happened, you made sure to eat more spinach and fish and Total cereal. People built their lives differently, and you had built yours. It was lonely, but you could manage. It was enough.

In 2003, when you were thirty-five, your mother and Oscar told you they had bought a farm sixty-five miles west, and they would be moving. Would you like to join them? There would be horses and chickens.

You declined. You had been working at Drs. Foster and Smith for almost eight years. Did Oscar and your mother seriously think you would consider giving up your seniority?

Your mother was so proud, yet again. And so afraid.

You stayed in Pine Lake near your brother Mark until the bar sold in 2007. Then you moved to your apartment in Rhinelander. It was the first time you would be living completely alone. You still avoided the Christmas party and the company picnic. You still turned down offers of rides to and from work. You had a job, and three Fridays a month your mother and Oscar picked you up after work and you had those weekends at the farm, and it was enough.

Then in early spring of 2010, Eric phoned from Houston, where he was teaching high school science, and he suggested you join him in a 5K run in Rhinelander. You declined. Not because you didn't think you could do it. You had been walking five miles a day, to and from work, for years, so how difficult could running be? But you knew how uncomfortable you would make the other people, the people who could speak in paragraphs, the people whose right hands didn't tire late in the day, whose smiles didn't freeze. And you worried about your balance. What if you stumbled in the middle of the race? What if you fell over? Eric persisted. "C'mon," he said, "it's a group thing, but you're alone. You're not going to bother anybody and nobody's going to bother you." Did you enter because Eric wouldn't let up, or because of something else? You're not sure.

You made it through the 5K in tennis shoes from Walmart with the soles coming loose, and that was one of the first times you realized that what you thought you knew wasn't always true. Running miles wasn't the same as walking—your legs felt like rubber bands. And no one seemed uncomfortable around you. People seemed preoccupied with how they were going to do. They said hello, and you said hello, and they smiled and you smiled. Maybe you weren't helping others, but it felt good. The race finished a couple blocks from your apartment, so you and Eric jogged over there and showered before going to the awards ceremony. People welcomed you, asked you your time (twenty-nine minutes), smiled and chatted, and it didn't really matter how slow you talked, how often you had to pause for answers. No one seemed to care. Your boss's wife was there. So were other people you knew. Five weeks later, you ran another 5K in Park Falls, Wisconsin. The night before, you woke with a cold, but you ran twenty-nine minutes again.

You bought a new pair of shoes, the kind with the big N on them. You decided you had to strengthen the right side of your body. To do that, you needed to go to the gym. You took some of the money you had been saving and you applied for a membership at a local health club, and when you pulled out your credit card and asked if the club accepted it, the guy behind the desk— a big, muscle-bound guy—looked you up and down, at your short jeans and your old jacket and at the smile frozen on your face, and he said, "Well, sure, if it's *your* card," and you turned and left. But you didn't quit. *Failure isn't getting knocked down.* You joined Anytime Fitness, in downtown Rhinelander, and your first time there—after your seven a.m. to three p.m. shift at the warehouse—the manager showed you around and explained the machines and you nodded, and you got on one of the treadmills. There was a woman on the treadmill next to you, an older woman, and she smiled and saw you were new because you were struggling to set the programs on the machine. She asked how fast you wanted to go. You knew you made people uncomfortable, but she was so nice and you didn't want to be rude, so you answered, thinking she had asked how far you intended to go. Four. You were going to go four miles. She smiled and nodded, but the truth is, she could see not just that you were new but that you were different, and she thought four miles an hour seemed a little fast. But she kept quiet when she helped you punch the buttons.

You nearly flew off the machine and the woman nearly screamed. You recovered on your own, though, and she helped you adjust the machine to a lower speed and you made it those four miles, and that woman thought about how she had never seen a stronger, more determined person in her life.

You kept at it. Your weak right side meant extra effort, extra focus, to keep from falling as you ran, but you kept at it. You had learned to button your shirt with your claw of a right hand. You had learned to play piano left-handed. Of course you were going to become a marathoner. You had heard about the Disney World Marathon and had always wanted to visit Florida, but you checked, and it was filled up. So you found one closer, the Journeys Marathon in Eagle River, and enrolled for the May 2011 event. But before it, you flew to Las Vegas and ran the Thin Mint Sprint, a 5K, at the end of January 2011. By yourself.

The day before the race, at your motel, there was a poker tournament. "Look at the dummy, look at the retard," is what you told your mother the other players were thinking. You won sixty dollars.

You ran the race, you returned to the gym, and you asked your mother if she would keep May 14 open. You wanted her to come to Eagle River to watch you run in the Journeys Marathon. You hadn't even run a 10K. You couldn't even walk from her house in Kennan to the barn without swerving. How the hell were you going to make it 26.2 miles? The hard woman told you that you were nuts and told you that you didn't want to do this, that you should run a half-marathon first.

But she and Oscar drove three hours to the race. You wore a cotton T-shirt and over that, a green cotton Whispering Pines sweatshirt that you wore when you did chores at your mother's barn. You wore nylon running pants over your shorts. You were freezing and your mother thought you might die. She knew the cutoff was six hours, and she seriously doubted you would make it and wondered how you would take this setback. After five hours, when well over half of the entrants had finished, she suggested that Oscar drive the course, to check how you were doing, and Oscar suggested that your mother needed to relax, and then she told Oscar to get in the car and go check on her boy.

Fifteen feet from the finish line you limped up to your mother and Oscar, waiting. You were exhausted, and she could see the right side of your body wasn't working too well. She could also see the joy in you. You told them about the race, how wonderful it was, how cold you were, how you were going to do more marathons, and your mother was happy and relieved, but she also couldn't help hearing people screaming all around her.

"Cross the line! Cross the finish line!"

Your time was 5:39. There were 101 finishers. You were 96th.

It's late afternoon and the last light of day is casting long shadows on the snowy streets of Rhinelander. You're getting a ride home today, so you have a little time to chat. You're sitting in Culver's, home of the ButterBurger.

It's a Wednesday, and you have just finished another day at Drs. Foster and Smith. You'll have frozen pizza for dinner and tomorrow some more canned chicken with coleslaw. You bought the can of chicken for $2.39 at Walmart and the bag of coleslaw at Trig's for 99 cents. You'll get two meals out of the chicken and at least four out of the coleslaw. You're good with money. You estimate you save $2,000 a year in cab fare alone. You have more than $50,000 in your retirement account. You had more once, from the insurance money awarded after your accident, but your retirement account means much more to you. You worked for it. Your credit rating is "excellent." You have a platinum credit card. Those are things people don't know about you.

They don't know that you traveled to Las Vegas alone years before you made the trip to run the Thin Mint Sprint. You had intended to meet a woman you'd met online there, but it hadn't worked out. And once you took a bus to Nashville for the same reason, and that hadn't worked out either. They don't know that you met someone who had also been in a psychiatric ward once—after you came home following your suicide attempt—and that you have kept in touch with her, through her problems with drugs and her troubled marriage, and that she asked you to train with her for a half-marathon (this does not make your mother happy).

You know that disappointment hurts but that nothing hurts as deeply as the injuries people inflict on themselves. You talk about terrible acts of violence in the world and you say that people who can't express themselves, who feel as if they can't tell the world who they are, those people are driven to terrible sadness and can do terrible things to themselves and others, and you sound more like a philosophy professor or a priest than a warehouse dummy.

You talk about thought and language and the Romanian woman you met online and you say "Good day" and "How are you?" in Romanian, then admit that if the conversation goes much beyond that, you're in deep trouble. Even though it's late in the day, and you're tired, your smile is bright, and infectious.

You know that taking action—whether it's reading history or reciting poetry—expands the mind, and that running conditions the body and expands a man's world, and that a man can take pride in the things he does, as long as he's doing things, and you sound like a therapist, or maybe like someone who once tried to commit suicide and then learned the folly of his thinking.

And then you say for a long time you wished you had a girl-friend but now realize that women your age usually have kids, and those women want someone with a car to help take those kids to soccer practice, and that without a car you would just be a burden, so you have accepted that you're not going to have a girlfriend. And you sound like a lot of other people who put themselves in boxes because they're afraid.

You feel bad for people who don't enter races because they think they won't do well. Does that make any sense? you ask. How are you going to do well if you don't try?

You know that speed and distance are the standard measures of a runner's success, but that like a lot of standard measures, they're wholly inadequate to measure your experience. They're wholly inadequate to measure you.

In almost eighteen years, you still haven't been to a company picnic or the employee appreciation luncheon. You don't go because you know you make people uncomfortable. Running is one thing—you're one among many, you don't have to chat, and any-one who is uncomfortable, you're not going to see again anyway.

But life is something else. What use would it be, you showing up and talking about yourself? What good could that possibly do anyone?

Bobbi Jewell almost screamed when you nearly flew off that treadmill next to her at Anytime Fitness nearly three years ago, but she helped you adjust the settings and watched you go four miles. And then she watched you go four miles the next time you were both there, and the time after that. She watched you add the elliptical trainer and the stair climber.

Bobbi is the owner of a travel agency in Rhinelander, and you stop by her business—it's your first stop once you get back in town from running trips—to show her your medals, your bling. You don't know how much you inspire her.

Marko Modic, your old pal from the warehouse, got promoted a few years after you started together. Then he got promoted again. Today he's head of human resources at Drs. Foster and Smith. He says you're smarter than 99 percent of the people at the warehouse, and he's including your supervisors and his.

He says you have changed, but in subtle ways. He says that before you started running, you would never, ever talk about the accident. Now, especially if it might help someone else, he says you'll admit that you went through a bad time in your life, that your doctors said you'd never be able to walk or talk, and that if someone else is out there and a doctor says that to him or her, then that person should find another doctor.

Marko has bad days. Who doesn't? And when those days come, he thinks about you. He thinks about what his old partner from the warehouse floor has endured, and how he's turned out, and then Marko takes a breath and he knows he'll be fine, if he just does something. He thinks about you and he takes a step forward, and you don't know that.

Five years ago, a couple down the road from your mother in Kennan had a fiftieth anniversary party, and they got a visit from their grandson, Johnny, who had been badly beaten and suffered brain injuries. They called your mother and asked if they could bring Johnny over, if he could meet you.

He was having trouble speaking. He wanted to know how you had learned to talk again. You told him that your mother loved musicals, and that vocalizing, that twisting your tongue around those unfamiliar sounds, helped you. Maybe that helped him. You don't know.

Your brother Eric started running just two years before he got you into the sport. A colleague told him he would like it. "Same old story," Eric says. "Somebody is running and she tells somebody else. Simple. And I tried it and I decided I like doing something besides nothing."

Eric runs only once or twice a week, a handful of 5K and 10K races a year. He says he was shocked when he heard you were planning to run a marathon, but he's not shocked at your success.

He says he never thought about what you could do or couldn't do, or your particular struggles or successes. You were just his little brother, and something happened, and you and the family dealt with it. It seems like everyone in your family is sort of hard. But when he does stop to think about your running, yeah, it's something. "Of course it's changed him," he says. When he begins to doubt himself—in running, or in anything—he thinks about what you have done. So yeah, of course it has changed Eric, too. Do you know that? Maybe, maybe not.

There's a lot you don't know. You don't know if you'll attend the company picnic this July, and you don't know if you'll stop in at the employee appreciation lunch at Christmastime. You don't know if you'll find love. You kind of doubt it. In the past twenty-some years, you have donated twelve gallons of blood. Nine to the Red Cross and three more to the Community Blood Center. You know it feels good, and you like the free cookies, and you like chatting with the nurses at the RiverWalk Center. Twelve gallons. You know it's doing good. But you don't know how good. There's so much you don't know.

You will deteriorate. You have scar tissue at the base of your brain, and you live with pain. When it's humid, your scar tissue swells and you get tremendous headaches. You might start losing a step tomorrow. You might start losing a lot of steps tomorrow.

Or you may not. You know that researchers have put brain-injured mice on "treadmills," and those exercising mice recover cognitively faster and more fully than nonexercising ones. You know that a doctor named Steven Flanagan, MD, chairman of the Department of Rehabilitation Medicine at NYU Langone Medical Center, figured that out. He and other scientists suspect the recovery is due to exercise-induced chemical production in the brain, chemicals that promote recovery. You know that along with this there's a growing body of evidence suggesting that people with brain injuries also may recover faster and more fully if they exercise. You know that doctors around the country recommend that patients with brain injuries, when they are able and under supervision, increase their levels of physical activity. You know that it's worked for you, that your mind and body have improved because of running.

You don't like to talk about your brain injury, or recovery, or what was, or what might have been. But you want people—especially people who are going through what you went through—to know that things can get better, that if things are getting a little better for you, they might get a little better for them.

Your mother believes you are better, and happier, since you started running. She talks about it three days before the shortest day of 2012, sitting in her kitchen, drinking coffee, four days before she and Oscar will drive to Rhinelander to pick you up, take you out for Chinese, and bring you back here to the farm.

She says you feel it's a blessing you don't remember your life before the accident, that it would only have made the past thirty-nine years more difficult. They've been difficult enough. She says you would have been anything you wanted to be—a doctor or a lawyer maybe—if that man hadn't driven his truck into you. She says you love learning and that it's got to be frustrating being a warehouse dummy. She says she wants you to return to the farm because you love the farm, not because you're frustrated in Rhinelander.

The first morning at the farm you'll wake at four-thirty a.m., as you do every morning, and you'll read in bed (lately you've been reading about the American expedition to Siberia after World War I) and then play some cribbage with your mother and Oscar, and then you'll go take care of the horses and chickens—you walk in a straight line from the house to the barn now, since you started running—and then have breakfast and then help with some bit of construction. Insulating the barn, straightening porch timbers, then pinochle, dinner, a movie on TV, and then it's bedtime. At some point in there, you'll go for a run.

Your mother drinks coffee and talks about the jalapeños she pickles and says there are great kids who don't become good boys and good boys who don't become fine men, but you have been all. She says she's not sure you would have developed into the man you are without running. In fact, she doesn't think you would have become quite as independent and confident without it. She says you might beat your time by a couple minutes or a couple seconds, but that you will beat it. She knows that improvement might not mean a lot to many people. But it means a lot to you. It means a lot to her. She was an idiot to have fought you on the running, to have doubted you. She knows that now. Your mother doesn't have difficulty seeing the idiocy in others, and she doesn't have a hard time seeing the idiocy in herself.

Your mother is a hard woman who has no time for religion, not since she learned about the priest who refused to convert her Lutheran mother, who was pregnant, to Catholicism before she married her husband in the church. The priest told your grandfather that your grandmother was a whore and that her baby would be a bastard.

Your mother is a hard woman who has no time for religion but who is sure we should all seek God, to try to understand what our gift is, to be useful. She says her gift is not panicking in difficult times, in being good at acceptance. She says your gifts are patience and perseverance. (You disagree; you say they're persistence and stubbornness.)

Your mother sits in her kitchen and speaks of death and mercy and how she was so wrong about running and about the futility of lamentation, and after three hours, she admits that she cried for you once. You were ten and she realized one afternoon that you would never whistle. It was so stupid, she says, after all you had been through. But she couldn't help it. She bawled like a baby because you would never whistle.

People who feel sorry for themselves? She understands. We all encounter injury and illness and loss and change, and we're all scared and sad and hopeless. She has certainly been all those things. And the moment she bawled like a baby might serve as an object lesson in how we all—runners and nonrunners, brain-damaged and life-battered, blessed and cursed, teenaged loan sharks and high school physics teachers alike—might handle those moments when we want to give up.

"I have sat in a bathtub full of bubbles having a glass of wine, crying and feeling sorry for myself," your mother says. "Then I got out of the goddamn bathtub and went to bed and got up the next day."

You love running for how it makes you feel. You love it for the endorphins, and how it's something that's hard, and that you can get better at. You love it because at the starting line, you can chat with anyone and so what if it's a little uncomfortable, you're not going to see them again anyway. You love it because it has changed you. You walk straighter now and you feel stronger, and you like how you can check out pretty women in shorts and no one seems to mind. You love it because running makes you realize that you were living in a box until a couple years ago—a safe box, but a box, and that since running, you see you're as good as anyone else, maybe not as fast, but trying as hard, improving as much—and having as much fun. After you finish a race you stay at the finish line, and you yell encouragement at the people still competing—the slowest, the fattest, the people with the most to gain. You know how they feel. You know they're winners, even if they don't.

For your second marathon, you ran Disney, in Orlando, in January 2012. You finished in 5:59, almost twenty minutes slower than Eagle River. But it was warm in Florida, much warmer than you expected. And you ran into a fence at mile eight—in spite of all your training, your weaker right side still throws you off as you tire—so you basically limped the last eighteen miles. You did it because you're stubborn and persistent and because you had entered the race, had grown used to the rewards of racing and you had decided damn if you were going to fly back home to Rhinelander without a medal, without bling.

You run five days a week now. When you're tired, your right foot flaps a little bit, and it lands funny, but it's not too bad. You have finished six 10Ks, a half-marathon, and three marathons. This year, you're going to run the Journeys Marathon in Eagle River for the third time, and you're shooting for a 4:22. Ten minutes a mile. You think you can do it. But you don't know.

One thing you do know, something you have learned since you ran that first 5K in those floppy tennis shoes: You're going to run more races. You're going to fly to places you never would have before. You're going to meet people you never would have met, say things you never would have said.

And you'll be fine.

Something else you know, something else you learned from running: That solitary, hard life you spent so much time and energy building? It's not enough. It never was.

You want more.

Wired

FINALIST—FEATURE
WRITING

When the software mogul John McAfee fled to a remote outpost in the jungles of Belize, it felt like something out of Apocalypse Now—and Joshua Davis was there to capture every strange, shocking, unforgettable second of it. With Davis, the reader watches as McAfee rants, raves, rules his compound, and plays Russian roulette, all the while denying drug and murder accusations. The National Magazine Award judges called this "not just a page-turner but a masterpiece." A contributing editor at Wired, Davis is the author of The Underdog, which is, as his website proclaims, "a recounting of [his] arm wrestling, bullfighting, sumo, sauna, and backward-running adventures." Wired was a finalist this year in six National Magazine Award categories, honored for everything from print design to digital storytelling.

Joshua Davis

Dangerous

On November 12, 2012, Belizean police announced that they were seeking John McAfee for questioning in connection with the murder of his neighbor. Six months earlier, I began an in-depth investigation into McAfee's life. This is the chronicle of that investigation.

Twelve weeks before the murder, John McAfee flicks open the cylinder of his Smith & Wesson revolver and empties the bullets, letting them clatter onto the table between us. A few tumble to the floor. McAfee is sixty-six, lean and fit, with veins bulging out of his forearms. His hair is bleached blond in patches, like a cheetah, and tattoos wrap around his arms and shoulders.

More than twenty-five years ago, he formed McAfee Associates, a maker of antivirus software that went on to become immensely popular and was acquired by Intel in 2010 for $7.68 billion. Now he's holed up in a bungalow on his island estate, about fifteen miles off the coast of mainland Belize. The shades are drawn so I can see only a sliver of the white sand beach and turquoise water outside. The table is piled with boxes of ammunition, fake IDs bearing his photo, Frontiersman bear deterrent, and a single blue baby pacifier.

McAfee picks a bullet off the floor and fixes me with a wide-eyed, manic intensity. "This is a bullet, right?" he says in the congenial Southern accent that has stuck with him since his boyhood in Virginia.

"Let's put the gun back," I tell him. I'd come here to try to understand why the government of Belize was accusing him of assembling a private army and entering the drug trade. It seemed implausible that a wildly successful tech entrepreneur would disappear into the Central American jungle and become a narcotrafficker. Now I'm not so sure.

But he explains that the accusations are a fabrication. "Maybe what happened didn't actually happen," he says, staring hard at me. "Can I do a demonstration?"

He loads the bullet into the gleaming silver revolver, spins the cylinder.

"This scares you, right?" he says. Then he puts the gun to his head.

My heart rate kicks up; it takes me a second to respond. "Yeah, I'm scared," I admit. "We don't have to do this."

"I know we don't," he says, the muzzle pressed against his temple. And then he pulls the trigger. Nothing happens. He pulls it three more times in rapid succession. There are only five chambers.

"Reholster the gun," I demand.

He keeps his eyes fixed on me and pulls the trigger a fifth time. Still nothing. With the gun still to his head, he starts pulling the trigger incessantly. "I can do this all day long," he says to the sound of the hammer clicking. "I can do this a thousand times. Ten thousand times. Nothing will ever happen. Why? Because you have missed something. You are operating on an assumption about reality that is wrong."

It's the same thing, he argues, with the government's accusations. They were a smoke screen—an attempt to distort reality—but there's one thing everybody agrees on: The trouble really got rolling in the humid predawn murk of April 30, 2012.

•   •   •

It was a Monday, about 4:50 a.m. A television flickered in the guard station of McAfee's newly built, 2.5-acre jungle outpost on the Belizean mainland. At the far end of the property, a muddy river flowed slowly past. Crocodiles lurked on the opposite bank, and howler monkeys screeched. In the guard station, a drunk night watchman gaped at *Blond Ambition*, a Madonna concert DVD.

The guard heard the trucks first. Then boots hitting the ground and the gate rattling as the lock was snapped with bolt cutters. He stood up and looked outside. Dozens of men in green camouflage were streaming into the compound. Many were members of Belize's Gang Suppression Unit, an elite force trained in part by the FBI and armed with Taurus MT-9 submachine guns. Formed in 2010, their mission was to dismantle criminal organizations.

The guard observed the scene silently for a moment and then sat back down. After all, the Madonna concert wasn't over yet. Outside, flashlight beams streaked across the property. "This is the police," a voice blared over a bullhorn. "Everyone out!"

Deep in the compound, McAfee burst out of a thatched-roof bungalow that stood on stilts twenty feet off the ground. He was naked and held a revolver. Things had changed since his days as a high-flying software tycoon. By 2009 he had sold almost everything he owned—estates in Hawaii, Colorado, New Mexico, and Texas as well as his ten-passenger plane—and moved into the jungle. He announced that he was searching for natural antibiotics in the rain forest and constructed a mysterious laboratory on his property. Now his jungle stronghold was under attack. The commandos were converging on him. There were thirty-one of them; he was outgunned and outmanned.

McAfee walked back inside to the seventeen-year-old in his bed. She was sitting up, naked, her long frizzy hair falling around her shoulders and framing the stars tattooed on her chest. She was terrified.

As the GSU stormed up the stairs, he put on some shorts, laid down his gun, and walked out with his hands up. The commandos collided with McAfee at the top of the stairs, slammed him against the wall, and handcuffed him.

"You're being detained on suspicion of producing methamphetamine," one of the cops said.

McAfee twisted to look at his accuser. "That's a startling hypothesis, sir," he responded. "Because I haven't sold drugs since 1983."

.   .   .

Nineteen eighty-three was a pivotal year for McAfee. He was thirty-eight and director of engineering at Omex, a company that built information storage systems in Santa Clara, California. He was also selling cocaine to his subordinates and snorting massive amounts himself. When he got too high to focus, he'd take a Quaalude. If he started to fall asleep at his desk, he'd snort some more coke to wake up. McAfee had trouble making it through the day and spent his afternoons drinking scotch to even out the tumult in his head.

He'd been a mess for a long time. He grew up in Roanoke, Virginia, where his father was a road surveyor and his mother a bank teller. His father, McAfee recalls, was a heavy drinker and "a very unhappy man" who McAfee says beat him and his mother severely. When McAfee was fifteen, his father shot himself. "Every day I wake up with him," McAfee says. "Every relationship I have, he's by my side; every mistrust, he is the negotiator of that mistrust. So my life is fucked."

McAfee started drinking heavily his first year at Roanoke College and supported himself by selling magazine subscriptions door-to-door. He would knock and announce that the lucky resident had won an absolutely free subscription; all they had to do was pay a small shipping and handling fee. "So, in fact, I am explaining to them why it's not free and why they are going to pay for it. But the ruse worked," McAfee recalls. He learned that confidence was all that mattered. He smiled, fixed them with his penetrating blue-eyed gaze, and hit them with a nonstop stream of patter. "I made a fortune," he says.

He spent his money on booze but managed to graduate and start a Ph.D. in mathematics at Northeast Louisiana State College in 1968. He got kicked out for sleeping with one of his undergraduate students (whom he later married) and ended up coding old-school punch-card programs for Univac in Bristol, Tennessee. That didn't last long, either. He was arrested for buying marijuana, and though his lawyer got him off without a conviction, he was summarily fired.

Still, he had learned enough to gin up an impressive, totally fake résumé and used it to get a job at Missouri Pacific Railroad in St. Louis. It was 1969 and the company was attempting to use an IBM computer to schedule trains. After six months, McAfee's system began to churn out optimized train-routing patterns. Unfortunately, he had also discovered LSD. He would drop acid in the morning, go to work, and route trains all day. One morning he decided to experiment with another psychedelic called DMT. He did a line, felt nothing, and decided to snort a whole bag of the orangish powder. "Within an hour my mind was shattered," McAfee says.

People asked him questions, but he didn't understand what they were saying. The computer was spitting out train schedules to the moon; he couldn't make sense of it. He ended up behind a garbage can in downtown St. Louis, hearing voices and desperately hoping that nobody would look at him. He never went back to Missouri Pacific. Part of him believes he's still on that trip, that everything since has been one giant hallucination and that one day he'll snap out of it and find himself back on his couch in St. Louis, listening to Pink Floyd's *Dark Side of the Moon*.

From then on he felt like he was always one step away from a total breakdown, which finally came at Omex in 1983. He was snorting lines of coke off his desk most mornings, polishing off a bottle of scotch every day, and living in constant fear that he would run out of drugs. His wife had left him, he'd given away his dog, and in the wake of what he calls a mutual agreement, he left Omex. He ended up shuttered in his house, with no friends, doing drugs alone for days on end and wondering whether he should kill himself just as his father had. "My life was total hell," he says.

Finally he went to a therapist, who suggested he go to Alcoholics Anonymous. He attended a meeting and started sobbing. Someone gave him a hug and told him he wasn't alone.

"That's when life really began for me," he says.

He says he's been sober ever since.

·   ·   ·

When the Madonna concert ended, McAfee's drunken guard finally emerged from his station and strolled over to find out what was going on. The police quickly surrounded him. They knew who he was: Austin "Tino" Allen had been convicted twenty-eight times for crimes ranging from robbery to assault, and he had spent most of his life in and out of prison.

The police lined everybody up against a rock wall as the sun rose. A low, heavy heat filled the jungle. Everybody began to sweat when the police fanned out to search the property. As an officer headed toward an outlying building, one of McAfee's dogs cut him off, growled, and, according to police, went in for an attack. The cop immediately shot the dog through the rib cage.

"What the fuck!" McAfee screamed. "That's my dog."

The police ignored him. They left the dead dog in the dirt while they rummaged through the compound. They found shotguns, pistols, a huge cache of ammunition, and hundreds of bottles of chemicals they couldn't identify. McAfee and the others were left in the sun for hours. (GSU commander Marco Vidal claims they were under the shade of a large tree.) By the time the police announced that they were taking several of them to jail, McAfee says his face was turning pink with sunburn. He and Allen were loaded into the back of a pickup. The truck tore off, heading southeast toward Belize City at eighty miles per hour.

McAfee tried to stay calm, but he had to admit that this was a bad situation. He had walked away from a luxurious life—mansions on multiple continents, sports cars, a private plane—only to end up in the back of a pickup cuffed to a notoriously violent man. Allen pulled McAfee close so he could be heard over the roar of the wind. McAfee tensed. "Boss, I just want to say that it's an honor to be here with you," Allen shouted. "You must be a really important person for them to send all these men to get you."

.   •   •   •

In 1986 two brothers in Pakistan coded the first known computer virus aimed at PCs. They weren't trying to destroy anything; it was simple curiosity. They wanted to see how far their creation would travel, so they included their names, addresses, and telephone numbers in the code of the virus. They named it Brain after their computer services shop in Lahore.

Within a year the phone at the shop was ringing: Brain had infected computers around the world. At the time, McAfee had been sober for four years and gotten a security clearance to work on a classified voice-recognition program at Lockheed in Sunnyvale, California. But then he came across an article in the *San Jose Mercury News* about the spread of the Pakistani Brain virus in the United States.

He found the idea terrifying. Nobody knew for sure at the time why these intrusions were occurring. It reminded him of his childhood, when his father would hit him for no reason. "I didn't know why he did it," McAfee says. "I just knew a beating could happen any time." As a boy, he wasn't able to fight back. Now, faced with a new form of attack that was hard to rationalize, he decided to do something.

He started McAfee Associates out of his 700-square-foot home in Santa Clara. His business plan: Create an antivirus program and give it away on electronic bulletin boards. McAfee didn't expect users to pay. His real aim was to get them to think the software was so necessary that they would install it on their computers at work. They did. Within five years, half of the Fortune 100 companies were running it, and they felt compelled to pay a license fee. By 1990, McAfee was making $5 million a year with very little overhead or investment.

His success was due in part to his ability to spread his own paranoia, the fear that there was always somebody about to attack. Soon after launching his company, he bought a twenty-seven-foot Winnebago, loaded it with computers, and announced that he had formed the first "antivirus paramedic unit." When he got a call from someone experiencing computer problems in the San Jose area, he drove to the site and searched for "virus residue." Like a good door-to-door salesman, there was a kernel of truth to his pitch, but he amplified and embellished the facts to sell his product. The RV therefore was not just an RV; it was "the first specially customized unit to wage effective, on-the-spot counterattacks in the virus war."

It was great publicity, executed with drama and sly wit. By the end of 1988, he was on *The MacNeil/Lehrer NewsHour* telling the country that viruses were causing so much damage, some companies were "near collapse from financial loss." He underscored the danger with his 1989 book, *Computer Viruses, Worms, Data Diddlers, Killer Programs, and Other Threats to Your System.* "The reality is so alarming that it would be very difficult to exaggerate," he wrote. "Even if no new viruses are ever created, there are already enough circulating to cause a growing problem as they reproduce. A major disaster seems inevitable."

In 1992 McAfee told almost every major news network and newspaper that the recently discovered Michelangelo virus was a huge threat; he believed it could destroy as many as 5 million computers around the world. Sales of his software spiked, but in the end only tens of thousands of infections were reported. Though McAfee was roundly criticized for his proclamation, the criticism worked in his favor, as he explained in an e-mail in 2000 to a computer-security blogger: "My business increased tenfold in the two months following the stories and six months later our revenues were 50 times greater and we had captured the lion's share of the anti-virus market."

This ability to infect others with his own paranoia made McAfee a wealthy man. In October 1992 his company debuted on Nasdaq, and his shares were suddenly worth $80 million.

· · ·

The jail cell was about ten feet by ten feet. The concrete floor was bare and cold, the smell of urine overpowering. A plastic milk container in the corner had been hacked open and was serving as a toilet. The detention center was located in the Queen Street police station, but everybody in Belize City called it the Pisshouse. In the shadows of his cell, McAfee could see the other inmates staring at him.

No charges had been filed yet, though the police had confiscated what they said were two unlicensed firearms on McAfee's property; they still couldn't identify the chemicals they had found. McAfee said he had licenses for all his firearms and explained that the chemicals were part of his antibiotic research. The police weren't buying it.

McAfee pulled twenty Belizean dollars out of his shoe and passed it through the bars to a guard. "You got a cigarette?" he asked.

McAfee hadn't smoked for ten years, but this seemed like a good time to start again. The guard handed him a book of matches and a pack of Benson & Hedges. McAfee lit one and took a deep drag. He was supposed to be living out a peaceful retirement in a tropical paradise. Now he was standing in jail, holding up his pants with one hand because the police had confiscated his belt. "Use this," Allen said, offering him a dirty plastic bag.

McAfee looked confused. "You tie your pants," Allen explained.

McAfee fed the bag through two of his belt loops, cinched it tight, and tied a knot. It worked.

"Welcome to the Pisshouse," Allen said, smiling.

•   •   •

McAfee lived in Silicon Valley for nearly twenty years. Outwardly he seemed to lead a traditional life with his second wife, Judy. He was a seasoned businessman whom startups turned to for advice. Stanford Graduate School of Business wrote two case studies highlighting his strategies. He was regularly invited to lecture at the school, and he was awarded an honorary doctorate from his alma mater, Roanoke College. In 2000 he started a yoga institute near his 10,000-square-foot mansion in the Colorado Rockies and wrote four books about spirituality. Even after his marriage fell apart in 2002, he was a respectable citizen who donated computers to schools and took out newspaper ads discouraging drug use.

But as he neared retirement age in the late 2000s, he started to feel like he was deluding himself. His properties, cars, and planes had become a burden, and he realized that he didn't want the traditional rich man's life anymore. Maintaining so many possessions was a constant distraction; it was time, he felt, to try to live more rustically. "John has always been searching for something," says Jennifer Irwin, McAfee's girlfriend at the time. She remembers him telling her once that he was trying to reach "the expansive horizon."

He was also hurting financially. The economic collapse in 2008 hit him hard, and he couldn't afford to maintain his lifestyle. By

2009 he'd auctioned off almost everything he owned, including more than 1,000 acres of land in Hawaii and the private airport he'd built in New Mexico. He was trying in part to deter people from suing him on the assumption that he had deep pockets. He was already facing a suit from a man who had tripped on his property in New Mexico. Another suit alleged that he was responsible for the death of someone who crashed during a lesson at a flight school McAfee had founded. He figured that if he were out of the country, he'd be less of a target. And he knew that, should he lose a case, it would be harder for the plaintiffs to collect money if he lived overseas.

In early 2008 McAfee started searching for property in the Caribbean. His criteria were pretty basic: He was looking for an English-speaking country near the United States with beautiful beaches. He quickly came across a villa on Ambergris Caye in Belize. In the early nineties he had visited the nation of 189,000 people and loved it. (Today the population is around 356,000.) He looked at the property on Google Earth, decided it was perfect, and bought it. The first time he saw it in person was in April 2008, when he moved in.

Soon after his arrival, McAfee began to explore the country. He was particularly fascinated by stories of a majestic Mayan city in the jungle and hired a guide to go see it. Boating up a river that snaked into the northern jungle, they stopped at a makeshift dock that jutted from the dense vegetation. McAfee jumped ashore, pushed through the vines, and caught sight of a towering, crumbling temple. Trees had grown up through the ancient buildings, encasing them in roots. Giant stone faces glared out through the foliage, mouths agape. As the men walked up the steps of the temple, the guide described how the Mayans sacrificed their prisoners, sending torrents of blood down the very stairs he and McAfee were now climbing.

McAfee was spellbound. "Belize is so raw and so clear and so in-your-face. There's an opportunity to see something about human nature that you can't really see in a politer society, because the purpose of society is to mask ourselves from each other," McAfee says. The jungle, in other words, would give him the chance to find out exactly who he was, and that opportunity was irresistible.

So in February 2010 he bought two and a half acres of swampy land along the New River, ten miles upriver from the Mayan ruins. Over the next year, he spent more than a million dollars filling in the swamp and constructing an array of thatched-roofed bungalows. While his girlfriend, Irwin, stayed on Ambergris Caye, McAfee outfitted the place like Kublai Khan's sumptuous house of pleasure. He imported ancient Tibetan art and shipped in a baby grand piano even though he had never taken lessons. There was no Internet. At night, when the construction stopped, there was just the sound of the river flowing quietly past. He sat at the piano and played exuberant odes of his own creation. "It was magical," he says.

He didn't like the idea of getting old, though, so he injected testosterone into his buttocks every other week. He felt that it gave him youthful energy and kept him lean. Plus, he wasn't looking for a quiet retirement. He started a cigar manufacturing business, a coffee distribution company, and a water taxi service that connected parts of Ambergris Caye. He continued to build more bungalows on his property even though he had no pressing need for them.

·　　·　　·

In 2010 McAfee visited a beachfront resort for lunch and met Allison Adonizio, a thirty-one-year-old microbiologist who was on vacation. In the resort's dining room, Adonizio explained that she was doing postgrad research at Harvard on how plants combat bacteria. She was particularly interested in plant compounds that appeared to prevent bacteria from causing infections by interfering with the way the microbes communicated. Eventually, Adonizio explained, the work might also lead to an entire new class of antibiotics.

McAfee was thrilled by the idea. He had fought off digital contagions, and now he could fight organic ones. It was perfect.

He immediately proposed they start a business to commercialize her research. Within minutes McAfee was talking in rapid-fire bursts about how this would transform the pharmaceutical industry and the entire world. They would save millions of lives and reinvent whole industries. Adonizio was astounded. "He offered me my dream job," she says. "My own lab, assistants. It was incredible."

Adonizio said yes on the spot, quit her research position in Boston, sold the house she had just bought, and moved to Belize. McAfee soon built a laboratory on his property and stocked it with tens of thousands of dollars' worth of equipment. Adonizio went to work trying to isolate new plant compounds that might be effective medicines, while McAfee touted the business to the international press.

But the methodical pace of Adonizio's scientific research couldn't keep up with McAfee's enthusiasm, and his attention seemed to wander. He began spending more time in Orange Walk, a town of about 13,000 people that was five miles from his compound. McAfee described it in an e-mail to friends as "the asshole of the world—dirty, hot, gray, dilapidated." He liked to walk the town's poorly paved streets and take pictures of the residents. "I gravitate to the world's outcasts," he explained in another e-mail. "Prostitutes, thieves, the handicapped. . . . For some reason I have always been fascinated by these subcultures."

Though he says he never drank alcohol, he became a regular at a saloon called Lover's Bar. The proprietor, McAfee wrote to his friends, was partial to "shatteringly bad Mexican karaoke music to which voices beyond description add a disharmony that reaches diabolic proportions." McAfee quickly noticed that the place doubled as a whorehouse, servicing, as he put it, "cane field workers, street vendors, fishermen, farmers—anyone who has managed to save up $15 for a good time."

This was the real world he was looking for, in all its horror. The bar girls were given one Belize dollar for every beer a patron bought them. To increase their earnings, some of the women would chug beers, vomit in the restroom, and return to chug more. One reported drinking fifty beers in one day. "Ninety-nine percent of people would run because they'd fear for their safety or sanity," McAfee says. "I couldn't do that. I couldn't walk away."

McAfee started spending most mornings at Lover's. After six months, he sent out another update to his friends: "My fragile connection with the world of polite society has, without a doubt, been severed," he wrote. "My attire would rank me among the worst-dressed Tijuana panhandlers. My hygiene is no better. Yesterday, for the first time, I urinated in public, in broad daylight."

McAfee knew he had entered a dangerous world. "I have no illusions," he noted in another dispatch. "We are tainted by everything we touch."

•　　　•　　　•

Evaristo "Paz" Novelo, the obese Belizean proprietor of Lover's, liked to sit at a corner table and squint at his customers through perpetually puffy eyes. He admits to a long history of operating brothels and prides himself on his ability to figure out exactly what will please his patrons. Early on, he asked whether McAfee was looking for a woman. When McAfee said no, Novelo asked whether he wanted a boy. McAfee declined again. Then Novelo showed up at McAfee's compound with a sixteen-year-old girl named Amy Emshwiller.

Emshwiller had a brassy toughness that belied her girlishness. In a matter-of-fact tone, she told McAfee that she had been abused as a child and said that her mother had forced her to sleep with dozens of men for money. "I don't fall in love," she told him. "That's not my job." She carried a gun, wore aviator sunglasses, and had on a low-cut shirt that framed her ample cleavage.

McAfee felt a swirl of emotions: lust, compassion, pity. "I am the male version of Amy," he says. "I resonated with her story because I lived it."

Emshwiller, however, felt nothing for him. "I know how to control men," she says. "I told him my story because I wanted him to feel sorry for me, and it worked." All Emshwiller saw was an easy mark. "A millionaire in freaking Belize, where people work all day just to make a dime?" she says. "Who wouldn't want to rob him?"

McAfee soon realized that Emshwiller was dangerous and unstable, but that was part of her attractiveness. "She can pretend sanity better than any woman I have ever known," he says. "And she can be alluring, she can be very beautiful, she can be butch-like. She's a chameleon." Within a month they were sleeping together, and McAfee started building a new bungalow on his property for her.

Visiting from Ambergris Caye, McAfee's girlfriend, Jennifer Irwin, was flabbergasted. She asked him to tell the girl to leave, and when McAfee refused, Irwin left the country. McAfee hardly blames her. "What I basically did was can a solid twelve-year relationship for a stark-raving madwoman," he says. "But I honestly fell in love."

One night Emshwiller decided to make her move. She slipped out of bed and pulled McAfee's Smith & Wesson out of a holster hanging from an ancient Tibetan gong in his bedroom. Her plan, if it could be called that, was to kill him and make off with as much cash as she could scrounge up. She crept to the foot of the bed, aimed, and started to pull the trigger. But at the last moment she closed her eyes, and the bullet went wide, ripping through a pillow. "I guess I didn't want to kill the bastard," she admits.

McAfee leaped out of bed and grabbed the gun before she could fire again. She ran to the bathroom, locked herself in, and asked if he was going to shoot her. He couldn't hear out of his left ear and was trying to get his bearings. Finally he told her he was going to take away her phone and TV for a month. She was furious.

"But I didn't even kill you!" she shouted.

. . .

McAfee decided it was better for Emshwiller to have her own place about a mile down the road in the village of Carmelita. So in early 2011 he built her a house in the village. Many of the homes are made of stripped tree trunks and topped with sheets of corrugated iron; 10 percent have no electricity. The village has a handful of dirt roads populated with colonies of biting ants and a grassy soccer field surrounded by palm trees and stray dogs. The town's biggest source of income: sand from a pit by the river that locals sell to construction companies.

Emshwiller, who had grown up in the area, warned McAfee that the village was not what it appeared to be. She told him that the tiny, impoverished town of 1,600 was in fact a major shipment site for drugs moving overland into Mexico, thirty-five miles to the north. As Emshwiller described it, this village in McAfee's backyard was crawling with narco-traffickers.

It was a revelation perfectly tailored to feed into McAfee's latent paranoia. "I was massively disturbed," he says. "I fell in love with the river, but then I discovered the horrors of Carmelita."

He asked Emshwiller what he should do. "She wanted me to shoot all the men in the town," McAfee says. It occurred to him that she might be using him to exact revenge on people who had wronged her, so he asked the denizens of Lover's for more information. They told him stories of killings, torture, and gang wars in the area. For McAfee, the town began to take on mythic proportions.

"Carmelita was literally the Wild West," he says. "I didn't realize that two miles away was the most corrupt village on the planet."

He decided to go on the offensive. After all, he was a smart Silicon Valley entrepreneur who had launched a multi-billion-dollar company. Even though he had lost a lot of money in the financial crisis, he was still wealthy. Maybe he couldn't maintain multiple estates around the world, but surely he could clean up one village.

He started by solving some obvious problems. Carmelita had no police station, so McAfee bought a small cement house and hired workers to install floor-to-ceiling iron bars. Then he told the national cops responsible for the area to start arresting people. The police protested that they were ill-equipped for the job, so McAfee furnished them with imported M16s, boots, pepper spray, stun guns, and batons. Eventually he started paying officers to patrol during their off-hours. The police, in essence, became McAfee's private army, and he began issuing orders. "What I'd like you to do is go into Carmelita and start getting information for me," he told the officers on his payroll. "Who's dealing drugs, and where are the drugs coming from?"

When a twenty-two-year-old villager nicknamed Burger fired a gun outside Emshwiller's house in November 2011, McAfee decided he couldn't rely on others to get the work done; he needed to take action himself. An eyewitness told him that Burger had shot at a motorcycle—it looked like a drug deal gone bad. Burger's sister said that he was firing at stray dogs that attacked him. Either way, McAfee was incensed. He drove his gray Dodge pickup to the family's wooden shack near the river and strode into the muddy yard with Emshwiller as his backup (she was carrying a matte-black air rifle with a large scope). Burger wasn't there, but his mother, sister, and brother-in-law were. "I'm giving you a last chance here," McAfee said, holding his Smith & Wesson. "Your brother will be a dead man if he doesn't turn in that gun. It doesn't matter where he goes."

"It was like he thought he was in a movie," says Amelia Allen, the shooter's sister. But she wasn't going to argue with McAfee. Her mother pulled the gun out of a bush and handed it to him.

Soon, McAfee was everywhere. He pulled over a suspicious car on the road only to discover that it was filled with elderly people and children. He offered a new flatscreen TV to a small-time marijuana peddler on the condition that the man stop dealing (the guy accepted, though the TV soon broke). "It was like John Wayne came to town," says Elvis Reynolds, former chair of the village council.

When I visited the village, Reynolds and others admitted that there were fights and petty theft but insisted that Carmelita was simply an impoverished little village, not a major transit point for international narco-traffickers, as McAfee alleges. The village leaders, for their part, were dumbfounded. Many were unfamiliar with antivirus software and had never heard of John McAfee. "I thought he would come by, introduce himself, and explain what he was doing here, but he never did," says Feliciano Salam, a soft-spoken resident who has served on the village council for two years. "He just showed up and started telling us what to do."

The fact that he was running a laboratory on his property only added to the mystery. Adonizio was continuing to research botanical compounds, but McAfee didn't want to tell the locals anything about it. In part he was worried about corporate espionage. He had seen white men in suits standing beside their cars on the heavily trafficked toll bridge near his property and was sure they were spies. "Do you realize that Glaxo, Bayer, every single drug company in the world sent people out there?" McAfee says. "I was working on a project that had some paradigm-shifting impact on the drug world. It would be insanity to talk about it."

McAfee became convinced that he was being watched at all hours. Across the river, he saw people lurking in the forest and would surveil them with binoculars. When Emshwiller visited, she never noticed anybody but repeatedly told McAfee to be careful. She heard rumors that gang members were out to "jack" him—rob and kill him. On one occasion, she recorded a village councilman discussing how to dispatch McAfee with a grenade. McAfee was wowed by her street smarts—"She is brilliant beyond description," he says—and relished the fact that she had come full circle and was now defending him. "He got himself into a very entangled, dysfunctional situation," says Katrina Ancona, the wife of McAfee's partner in the water taxi business. "We kept telling him to get out."

Adonizio was also worried about McAfee's behavior. He had initially told her that the area was perfectly safe, but now she was surrounded by armed men. When she went to talk to McAfee in his bungalow, she noticed garbage bags filled with cash and blister packs of pharmaceuticals, including Viagra. She lived just outside of Carmelita and had never had any problems. If there was any danger, she felt that it was coming from McAfee. "He turned into a very scary person," she says. She wasn't comfortable living there anymore and left the country.

George Lovell, CEO of the Ministry of National Security, was also concerned that McAfee was buying guns and hiring guards. "When I see people doing this, my question is, what are you trying to protect?" Lovell says. Marco Vidal, head of the Gang Suppression Unit, concurred. "We got information to suggest that there may have been a meth laboratory at his location," he wrote in an e-mail. "Given the intelligence on McAfee, there was no scope for making efforts to resolve the matter." He proposed a raid, and his superiors approved it.

When members of the GSU swept into McAfee's compound on April 30, 2012, they found no meth. They found no illegal drugs of any kind. They did confiscate ten weapons and 320 rounds of ammunition. Three of McAfee's security guards were operating without a security guard license, and charges were filed against them. McAfee was accused of possessing an unlicensed firearm and spent a night in the Queen Street jail, a.k.a. the Pisshouse.

But the next morning, the charges were dropped and McAfee was released. He was convinced, however, that his war on drugs had made him some powerful enemies.

He had reason to worry. According to Vidal, McAfee was still a "person of interest," primarily because the authorities still couldn't explain what he was up to. "The GSU makes no apologies for deeming a person in control of a laboratory, with no approval for manufacturing any substance, having gang connections and heavily armed security guards, as a person of interest," Vidal wrote.

Vidal's suspicions may not have been far off. Two years after moving to Belize, McAfee began posting dozens of queries on Bluelight.ru, a drug discussion forum. He explained that he had started to experiment with MDPV, a psychoactive stimulant found in bath salts, a class of designer drugs that have effects similar to amphetamines and cocaine. "When I first started doing this I accidently got a few drops on my fingers while handling a used flask and didn't sleep for four days," McAfee posted. "I had visual and auditory hallucinations and the worst paranoia of my life."

McAfee indicated, though, that the heightened sexuality justified the drug's risks and claimed to have produced fifty pounds of MDPV in 2010. "I have distributed over 3,000 doses exclusively in this country," he wrote. But neither Emshwiller, Adonizio, nor anyone else I spoke with observed him making the stuff. So how could he have produced fifty pounds without anyone noticing?

McAfee has a simple explanation: The whole thing was an elaborate prank aimed at tricking drug users into trying a notoriously noxious drug. "It was the most tongue-in-cheek thing in the fucking world," he says, and denies ever taking the substance. "If I'm gonna do drugs, I'm gonna do something that I know is good," he says. "I'm gonna grab some mushrooms, number one, and maybe get some really fine cocaine.

"But anybody who knows me knows I would never do drugs," he says.

.   .   .

In August, McAfee and I meet for a final in-person interview at his villa on Ambergris Caye. He greets me wearing a pistol strapped across his bare chest. Guards patrol the beach in front of us. He tells me that he's now living with five women who appear to be between the ages of seventeen and twenty; each has her own bungalow on the property. Emshwiller is here, though McAfee's attention is focused on the other women.

He has barely left the property since he came out of hiding in April. He says he spends his days shuttling from bungalow to bungalow, trying to mediate among the women. I ask why he doesn't leave the country, given that the Belizean government has returned his passport. "I would be perceived as running away," McAfee says. "Within three days, all of Carmelita would return to no-man's-land, and it would be the staging post for every illegal activity in northern Belize."

As McAfee tells it, he is all that stands between Carmelita and rampant criminality. The police raided him, he says, because he had run the local drug dealers out of town. These dealers had political connections and had successfully lobbied to have the police attack him. They wanted him gone. He says he also refused to make political contributions to a local politician, further antagonizing the ruling party. If he gives in, he argues, it will send a message that Belize's corrupt government can control anybody, even a rich American.

As McAfee talks, we walk across the white sand beach and into his bungalow. In many ways, his life has devolved into a complex web of contradictions. He says he's battling drugs in Carmelita, but at the same time he's trying to trick people online into taking drugs. He professes to care about laws—and castigates the police for violating his rights—but he moved to Belize in part to subvert the U.S. legal system in the event he lost a civil case. The police suggest he's a drug kingpin; I can't help but wonder if he has lost track of reality. Maybe he imagines that he can fix himself by fixing Carmelita.

His bungalow is sparsely furnished. The small open kitchen is strewn with dishes, rotting vegetables, half-drunk bottles of Coke, and boxes of Rice Krispies and Cheerios. A dog is licking a stick of butter off the counter. A bandolier of shotgun shells hangs from a chair. He pops open a plastic bottle of Lucas Pelucas, a tamarind-flavored Mexican candy, and depresses the plunger, extruding the gooey liquid through small holes in the top. "I fucking love these things," he says.

I tell him that while I was in Carmelita, the villagers described the place as quiet and slow-moving. There is crime, most admitted, but it is limited to stolen bicycles and drunken fights. It did not seem like a particularly dangerous place to me.

"Ninety-nine percent of all crimes are never, ever reported to the police," he says. "Because if the gang kills your sister and you report it, the gang will come back and kill you. Nobody says anything."

When I tell him that the locals I spoke with can remember only two murders in the past three years, he argues that I'm not asking the right questions. To illustrate his point, he takes out his pistol.

"Let's do this one more time," he says, and puts it to his head. Another round of Russian roulette. Just as before, he pulls the trigger repeatedly, the cylinder rotates, the hammer comes down, and nothing happens. "It is a real gun. It has a real bullet in one chamber," he says. And yet, he points out, my assumptions have somehow proven faulty. I'm missing something.

The same is true, he argues, with Carmelita. I'm not seeing the world as he sees it. He opens the door to the bungalow, aims the gun at the sand outside, and pulls the trigger. This time, a gunshot punctures the sound of the wind and waves. "You thought you were creating your reality," he says. "You were not. I was."

He pulls the spent cartridge out of the chamber and hands it to me. It's still warm.

• • •

Eight weeks later, my phone rings at four-thirty in the morning. I'm back in the United States and groggily pick up. "I'm sorry to wake you up at this hour, sir, but the GSU had me surrounded all night," McAfee says in a breathless rush. He explains that he's staying at Captain Morgan's Retreat, a resort on Ambergris Caye, and he decided to go for a walk at dusk. As he strolled along the beach, he heard the sound of approaching gas-powered golf carts. "You can tell the GSU vehicles because they have this low roar," he says, a hint of panic creeping into his voice. "I think they put special mufflers on them to scare people."

He dashed onto the porch of a nearby hotel room and hid behind the bushes. Then he heard someone cough on the balcony above him. "As soon as I heard that, my heart sank," he says. "They were fucking everywhere."

McAfee spends the next twenty-five minutes describing to me how the GSU silently surrounded him in the darkness. "Two of them were less than three feet away," he says "They stood unmoving. No one said a word all night long. They just surround you and stand still. Think about it. It's freaky shit, sir."

He sat there all night, he tells me, terrified that the shadowy figures he was seeing would kill him if he moved. Around four o'clock in the morning, he says, they retreated quietly and disappeared.

McAfee then walked onto the darkened beach. He thought he could see Marco Vidal, head of the GSU, motoring away in a boat. He screamed Vidal's name. (Vidal denies any GSU encounters with McAfee after the April 30 raid.)

A security guard approached and asked if he was OK. "After a while my heart was beating so fast it was like one big hum," he says. "I was bursting with perspiration."

I suggest he get some rest. He sounds frantic and scared.

"They're coming back," he says suddenly. "This is too fucking much. I'm hanging up. I'm going."

The line goes dead.

A week later, McAfee calls me from the Belizean-Mexican border. He tells me he's had enough of Belize. A day ago, he was walking down the beach on Ambergris Caye when several GSU "frogmen" walked out of the water. Later, he says, a troop of GSU officers crowded into his room but didn't say or do anything. "I have just escaped from hell," he says.

The next day he's in an $800-a-night suite at the Royal in Playa Del Carmen, Mexico. "It has a sushi restaurant," he says. "Do you realize I haven't had sushi in years?" He sounds refreshed and says he's feeling better.

Six days pass, and McAfee calls again. "Good morning, John," I say.

"Good evening, I think it is," McAfee says.

I explain that it's 9:41 a.m.

"You're kidding me," he says. "I haven't slept for a couple nights. It felt like evening to me."

"What's going on?" I ask.

"I am back from Mexico, thank God," he says, explaining that he was robbed and beaten outside of Cancun. Now he's on Ambergris Caye. "Here it's clear that they're not going to harm me, they're just trying to scare me," he says. "They have to up the ante if they're going to continue scaring me."

I talk to him repeatedly over the next week. He fires all of his bodyguards because he thinks they are informing on him. He hires William Mulligan, a British national, to take their place. McAfee figures Mulligan will have fewer connections to the authorities, despite the fact that he's married to a Belizean woman.

On Friday, November 9, 2012, I receive an e-mail from McAfee telling me that "a contingent of black-suited thugs" disembarked on the dock next to his property at ten-thirty pm. The men dispersed on the beach. "A half hour later all of my dogs had been poisoned," he writes. "Mellow, Lucky, Dipsy, and Guerrero have already died. I had to call Amy and tell her about Mellow. She is hysterical."

The next morning, November 10, 2012, McAfee calls to tell me that his dogs died horrific deaths. They were vomiting blood and convulsing on the ground. McAfee shot them to end their suffering. "It was an ugly thing," he says.

"How is Amy doing?" I ask.

"I've tried calling her twice," he says. "She's not answering. She's not doing well."

I suddenly recall a conversation I had with Emshwiller in August. She was describing someone in Carmelita who tortured dogs and, with a chill, I remember her reaction: "Mess with my dog, you're gonna get it, man," she'd said.

In another conversation, she also said she had become profoundly committed to McAfee. "If he asked me to blow someone's fucking brains out, I would," she said.

Still on the phone with me, McAfee is searching for clues to explain the dead dogs and has noticed that the fence around his property is surrounded by boot prints—"military-style boot prints," he says—and cites this as evidence that the police were involved. "I'm a paranoid person," he says. "I really am. But the whole thing is looking really weird to me."

I point out that his neighbors had been complaining about the barking. In August, Vivian Yu, operator of a bar and restaurant up the beach, asked one of McAfee's guards to do something to control the eleven dogs that roamed his property. McAfee hired a carpenter to build a fence to corral them.

Greg Faull, a neighbor two houses to the south on Ambergris Caye, was particularly incensed by the racket and aggression of McAfee's mutts. Faull was a big man—five-eleven, around 220 pounds—who owned a sports bars in Orlando, Florida, and spent part of the year in Belize. It was a tropical paradise to him, except for the nuisance McAfee's dogs created. They growled and barked incessantly at anybody who walked by on the beach.

Faull had confronted McAfee about the animals in the past. According to McAfee, Faull once threatened to shoot them, but McAfee didn't believe he'd do it. Allison Adonizio, who had stayed at Greg Faull's house when she first moved to Belize in 2010, says there was bad blood between the two men back then. "McAfee hated his guts," she wrote in an e-mail to me.

Earlier in the week, Faull had filed a formal complaint about the dogs with the mayor's office in the nearby town of San Pedro. Now, as I try to catch up on the latest details, McAfee dismisses the suggestion that any of his neighbors could have been involved in the apparent poisoning of the animals. "They're still dog lovers," he says. "And I talked to them this morning. No one here would ever poison the dogs."

He speaks specifically about Faull. "This is not something he would ever do," McAfee says. "I mean, he's an angry sort of guy, but he would never hurt a dog."

On Sunday morning, Faull is found lying face-up in a pool of blood. He's been shot once through the back of the head, execution-style. A 9-mm Luger casing lies on the ground nearby. There are no signs of forced entry. A laptop and an iPhone are missing, police say.

That afternoon, Belizean police arrive at McAfee's property to question him about Faull's death. McAfee sees them coming and is sure the authorities are intent on tormenting him again. He quickly digs a shallow trench in the sand and buries himself, pulling a cardboard box over his head. He stays there for hours.

"It was extraordinarily uncomfortable," he says.

The police confiscate all the weapons on the property and take Mulligan in for questioning. When they leave, Cassian Chavarria, McAfee's groundskeeper, tells him that Faull has been killed. According to McAfee, that was the first he heard of the murder. His initial reaction, he says, is that it was the GSU trying to kill McAfee himself. "I thought maybe they were coming for me," he says. "They mistook him for me. They got the wrong house. He's dead. They killed him. It spooked me out."

McAfee decides to go on the run and begins calling me at all hours. I ask him if he shot Faull. "No sir, no sir," he says. "That's not even funny." (Emshwiller also denies any involvement in Faull's death.)

All McAfee knew about the murder, he says, was that the police were after him, and he believed that if they caught him, he would be tortured or killed. "Once they collect me, it's the end of me," he says.

Over the next forty-eight hours, McAfee bounces from place to place around Belize, aided by a network of "people who can't be followed," he tells me. "It's complicated, and there are a lot of risks, and people could turn south at any minute." Samantha Vanegas, one of his girlfriends, is with him, and he says that they've been subsisting on Oreo Cakester cookies and cigarettes. On Tuesday morning, he says, the police raided the house next door, but they evaded capture, eventually landing in a house with no hot water and a broken toilet. There is, however, a working TV.

"We watched *Swiss Family Robinson*," he says. "It's about castaways. That's why we got into it. It was like, wow, we could do that. We could get bamboo and build something like that."

The movie had a happy ending. McAfee liked that.

The Atavist

FINALIST—REPORTING

One of the victims of Hurricane Sandy in October 2012 was the Bounty, a replica of an eighteenth-century tall ship that sank off the coast of North Carolina. Matthew Shaer's story about this disaster is, as the National Magazine Award judges said, "a tale of hubris, courage, resourcefulness, and loss that weaves together maritime history, profiles, and sturdy narrative." A staff writer at Smithsonian, Shaer also writes regularly for New York. His book, Among Righteous Men: A Tale of Vigilantes and Vindication in Hasidic Crown Heights, was published in 2011. The Atavist is a digital monthly published at atavist.com and on mobile apps. The editor is Evan Ratliff, whose story "Vanished" was nominated for a National Magazine Award and included in Best American Magazine Writing in 2010.

Matthew Shaer

The Sinking of the *Bounty*

"And tell me, wasn't that the best time, that time when we were young at sea; young and had nothing, on the sea that gives nothing, except hard knocks—and sometimes a chance to feel your strength . . ."

—Joseph Conrad, "Youth"

One. Monday, October 29, 2012, 5:30 a.m.

Five hundred feet over the Atlantic Ocean, Coast Guard Petty Officer Second Class Randy Haba jammed himself into the rear bucket seat of the Jayhawk helicopter and waited for the doomed ship to come into view. Through the window he could see the crests of the waves and a flotilla of detritus that seemed to spread out in every direction toward the horizon—wormy coils of rope, sharp splinters of yard, tatters of sailcloth. The phosphor screens of his ANVIS-9 night-vision goggles rendered the ocean neon green—a flat, unceasing green that bled into the gray-green of the clouds and the yellow-green of the sky. The kind of green that made it difficult to distinguish distance or depth of field, let alone the blink of the chest-mounted strobe that the guys up in the C-130 transport airplane had sworn was out there, somewhere in the hurricane-roiled sea.

Haba felt the helicopter lurch into a hover. The winds were blowing at close to ninety miles an hour, and in the cabin, Lieutenant Commander Steve Cerveny was fighting the sticks. "Left side," Lieutenant Jane Peña, the safety pilot, called over the radio. "Got it?"

"Roger," Haba, the crew's rescue swimmer, replied. Setting down the ANVIS-9s, he pulled on his fins, dive helmet, mask and snorkel, and thick neoprene gloves. He checked the neck seal of the flame-retardant dive suit and the pockets above the harness, which contained flares, a radio beacon, and one very sharp, spring-loaded knife.

Haba, a six-foot-three former high school football star with hard blue eyes and a weather-beaten face, had been based at the air station in Elizabeth City, North Carolina, for more than eight years, the majority of his Coast Guard career. He'd participated in plenty of rescues in the waters off Cape Hatteras, a dangerous patch of sea known by generations of mariners as the "Graveyard of the Atlantic." There, past the pastel beach houses and salt-stained crab shacks, the North Atlantic's cold Labrador current collides with the warm waters of the Gulf Stream, yielding frequent storms and high waves capable of swallowing a ship whole.

But Haba had never encountered a situation like this. An hour and a half earlier, he'd been snoozing on a lumpy leather couch at the air station when the call came in: A large wooden ship was in trouble one hundred miles east of Elizabeth City with sixteen people on board. The ship's water-removal systems were malfunctioning, and it was limping into the path of Hurricane Sandy, the vast superstorm swirling over the North Carolina coast. Haba had trotted downstairs and rendezvoused with his helicopter crew. One of the command-center staffers had printed out a picture of the ship in question from Google Images, and only when he saw it did Haba grasp how strange his morning was about to become. Because the distressed vessel wasn't a yacht. It wasn't a schooner. It looked more like a pirate ship.

Bounty, as she was known, was a working replica of the eighteenth-century tall ship of the same name, commissioned half a century earlier for a film. She measured 120 feet from stern to bow, and 128 feet from keel to masthead. Her three wooden masts held 10,000 square feet of sail. A couple of days earlier, she'd departed New London, Connecticut, under the command of Robin Walbridge, a veteran tall-ship captain. At first she'd tacked east, in an effort to avoid the worst of the storm, but at some point, Walbridge had turned the ship southwest, toward shore and Sandy's perilous center mass. Until four a.m., when the crew abandoned ship, she'd been in contact with a C-130, which was still circling overhead at 1,000 feet. After that, there was only silence on the radio.

The number of survivors was uncertain. But the C-130 crew had spotted at least one figure bobbing alone amid the debris—a small shape swaddled in an immersion suit, with a blinking strobe on his chest. The straggler, they called him. Maybe he was dead—a floater—but maybe he wasn't. Either way, Haba was about to find out. He clipped into the winch, gave a thumbs-up to the flight mechanic, and, the cable whistling behind him, dropped into the waves.

Almost immediately, he began to eat seawater. He was swimming against the current, against the wind. It didn't help that Cerveny had the Jayhawk so low. The rotor wash was spectacular, drowning out any other sound. Still, Haba paddled like hell, and a minute later, he reached the straggler. The hood of the immersion suit was pulled tight around the guy's head and all Haba could see was his face, which was covered in fresh lacerations. His skin was pale and his cheeks sunken. One arm hung limply at his side.

With some effort, Haba angled the sling under the man's other armpit, and pulled the man close to his chest. Sometimes survivors fight back, out of confusion or panic—*the surest way to drown is to fight us*, rescue swimmers like to say. But the straggler was docile, barely even able to talk, and Haba made good time back to the winch. He gave the thumbs-up to the mechanic and waited for the cable to pull them skyward. Beneath the Jayhawk, illuminated by the rising sun, the tall ship *Bounty* was slipping under the surface of the sea.

Two. Thursday, October 25, 11:00 a.m.

It amused the hands on the *Bounty*—a motley collection of retirees, bearded and tattooed twenty-somethings, and midlife re-inventionists—to watch the navy guys go all weak-kneed at the sight of the 112-foot masts. *Bounty* sailors knew every inch of that rigging, from sheets to spar. But to the local nuclear submarine crew in New London, who had come aboard that afternoon for a demonstration in square-rig sailing, it was utterly unfamiliar territory. In the end, only a few of them were brave enough to strap up and attempt a climb. The weather was calm and overcast, a pleasant fifty-eight degrees.

Later that day, after the sub crew departed, Captain Robin Walbridge convened a brief all-hands meeting. Walbridge was a naturally reserved man, but at musters he presented a calmly confident mien. Peering out over the top of his eyeglasses, a ball cap partially obscuring his brow, he outlined the course for the two weeks ahead. *Bounty* would depart New London that night—setting sail on a Friday was considered to be bad luck—and head south. If they kept up a pace of a hundred miles a day, they could easily make Florida by the second week of November.

That would allow them to meet an obligation in St. Petersburg, a tour for members of an organization that promoted awareness of Down's syndrome—and maybe even make a pit stop in Key West, where the crew could swim, hit the bars, and recharge after what was sure to be a difficult voyage south. In mid-November, the *Bounty* would sail around the tip of Florida, across the Gulf of Mexico, and into Galveston, Texas, where she'd be put up for the winter.

Walbridge was sixty-three, with unruly silver hair and meaty, callused hands. He had come relatively late to professional sea-faring after a series of stints on oil rigs and a short career as a long-haul trucker. He'd grown up in St. Johnsbury, a cloistered town in northeastern Vermont, and claimed to have first sailed at the age of eighteen, although he was tight-lipped about that part of his life; when his crew members asked his age, he would offer an array of different numbers. Perhaps something painful lurked in his past, they thought. Or perhaps Walbridge simply preferred to talk about his ships.

He'd worked on plenty over the previous two decades, all of them throwbacks in one way or another. There was the nine-teenth-century schooner *Governor Stone*; the HMS *Rose*, a tall ship built in 1970 to the specifications of eighteenth-century British Admiralty drawings; and the USS *Constitution*, the famous frigate christened by George Washington, on which Walbridge had served as a guest captain once in the 1990s. But his true love was *Bounty*, a vessel he'd captained since 1995.

Tall-ship crews are usually drawn from two cohorts of people. First there are the amateur adventurers—the retirees and arm-chair admirals, the recent college graduates putting off adult-hood. These volunteers might sail with a tall ship for a week or a few months or a year, but they are not paid; in many cases, they are actually billed for berth and board. The second cohort, the mates, tend to be experienced sailors who have decided to make a career out of tall-ship sailing. Generally speaking, they have worked their way up the totem pole, from volunteer to paid hand.

On average, the crew of *Bounty* numbered around eighteen, with a small cadre of paid officers, a paid cook, a few lower-ranking hands, and the occasional volunteer. Walbridge never discrimi-nated among the various groups. If anything, he seemed to lavish more attention on the sailors who were still learning to navigate the ship, to take in line and climb the rigging. He was intoxicated by the old-fashioned way of doing things, and he was pleased to be around those who were in the process of becoming intoxicated themselves. "He considered square-rigged sailing a truly dying art, and he was the one keeping the idea alive," one longtime *Bounty* hand has said.

And yet Walbridge was no fusty antiquarian. He had sailed the *Bounty* up and down the East Coast, through the Panama Canal and over to the West Coast, and twice across the Atlantic. Along the way, he'd seen plenty of bad weather, including a pair of hurricanes and pants-shittingly high waves that heaved across the decks, and he had acquired a certain bravado about it. Walbridge was "clearly brilliant," says a former first mate of *Bounty*, speaking on the condition of anonymity. "The kind of guy who could play three games of chess at once, who could take apart a diesel engine and put it back together with his bare hands. But the term 'prudent mariner' doesn't really enter the mix."

The former first mate recalled a series of harrowing close calls aboard the ship, including a "thirty-six-hour nightmare ordeal" off Cape Hatteras in 1998, when rough seas sent water pouring into the *Bounty*'s engine room. Both the Coast Guard and the Navy had sent vessels to the scene, and extra pumps were dropped on board to clear out the water. But in the end, Walbridge declined to be towed back to shore by the Coast Guard—fearing, the first mate believes, that it would prompt a federal investigation. Instead, *Bounty* managed to sail under her own power back to Charleston for repairs. In a few days, she was at sea again.

Around the same time that Walbridge was convening his crew on *Bounty*'s deck in New London, on October 25, a new storm, Hurricane Sandy, was arriving on the Florida coast, 1,000 miles to the south. Several crew members who were in the meeting on deck say that Walbridge believed Sandy would barrel up the coast and eventually track inland, somewhere near North Carolina. By sailing southeast before turning south, *Bounty* could stay windward of the storm. Remaining in Connecticut, Walbridge felt, wasn't an option—he subscribed to the old maxim that a ship was always safer at sea than at anchor. In a crowded port like New London, there would be practically zero "sea room," and *Bounty* would be hemmed in, dangerously close to the docks. Better to take our chances "out there," Walbridge told the crew.

It was an unusual decision—few other captains in the region, and no other tall-ship captains, were taking any such gamble. And Walbridge, likely mindful of his less experienced hands, was careful to stress that no one was obligated to stay on the *Bounty.* "I know that quite a few of you all are getting phone calls and e-mails regarding the hurricane," Chris Barksdale, the fifty-six-year-old engineer, recalls Walbridge saying. "I wouldn't blame anyone if you want to get off and I won't think any worse of you and I won't hold it against you."

Josh Scornavacchi crossed his arms and nodded. Scornavacchi, twenty-five, was short and stoutly built, with an earring in his left ear and a mop of unruly reddish hair, which he wore swept across his forehead and cowlicked up in the back. He'd grown up in land-locked Mohnton, Pennsylvania, and studied biology at Penn State before signing on as a whitewater-kayaking guide in the Lehigh Gorge. It was there that he'd caught the adventure bug and hatched a series of increasingly grandiose plans—someday he would hike Everest, float down the Amazon, travel to Congo and Papua, New Guinea. He would buy a boat and sail around the world. But in order to do that, he'd first need to learn how to sail, so in 2011 he'd signed on for a Hudson River tour aboard *Clearwater,* a sloop owned by the folk singer Pete Seeger.

After the tour, Scornavacchi returned to Mohnton, where he worked shifts at the local Red Robin and looked for another op-portunity to ship out. The world of tall ships is tight-knit, and through a friend on *Clearwater*, Scornavacchi heard of an opportunity on *Bounty*. He interviewed with John Svendsen, the ship's forty-one-year-old first mate, and in the spring of 2012, he flew to Puerto Rico to start a stint as a paid deckhand. The money wasn't much, but Scornavacchi was deeply enamored with the ship. He loved scrambling up the high-masts, loved the sight of the big canvas under sail, loved the rhythm of life on board—the nights in his gently rocking bunk and the days exploring strange new cities.

With *Bounty*, Scornavacchi had sailed from Puerto Rico to Florida, up the East Coast to Nova Scotia, and back down to Maine, stopping in dozens of ports along the way. Now he would have the chance to experience his first real hurricane. It was a prospect that had not particularly delighted his mother. Earlier that day, he had spoken to her on the phone, and listened to the way the worry made her voice heavy and syrupy. "Mom, I'm not going to die," he told her. "I promise." Walbridge was a veteran sailor, he assured her, a man who had crossed the Atlantic multiple times and maneuvered *Bounty* through some of the most dangerous passages on earth. And Walbridge was backed up by a pair of extremely able lieutenants: Svendsen, the long-haired and taciturn first mate, and second mate Matthew Sanders, an affable thirty-seven-year-old with a degree from Maine Maritime Academy. Together, Walbridge, Svendsen, and Sanders had decades of storm experience. "We trusted them," Scornavacchi recalled later. "We all did. We trusted them completely. And we trusted the boat."

In the end, none of the crew members took Walbridge up on his offer to get off in Connecticut. Around eight p.m. that evening, *Bounty* glided out of the New London harbor, past the navigational buoys and the shuddering glow of the nearby boats, her dual John Deere engines rumbling underfoot, Long Island Sound opening up before her.

Three. Friday, October 26, 8:00 a.m.

All storms start in miniature, sucking in moisture and matter as they grow, and in this respect, at least, Hurricane Sandy was no different. She had been spotted in the radar images for the first time on October 19, in the Caribbean Sea, that blue breeding ground for hurricanes, an unspectacular whorl of cloud perched southwest of Puerto Rico. Meteorologists dubbed her Tropical Depression 18. She worked her way west, along the coasts of Venezuela and Colombia, before turning north toward Jamaica. Her status was upgraded with alarming regularity, from a tropical depression to a tropical low—a cyclone with a low-pressure core—to a tropical storm. By eleven a.m. EST on October 24, she was a full-fledged hurricane.

Outside the Jamaican capital of Kingston, a city that had not seen a hurricane in twenty-four years, a man was struck and killed by falling rocks. In Haiti, floods coursed across the lowlands and swept through the post-earthquake tent cities of Port-au-Prince, claiming fifty-four lives and the homes of 20,000 people. In Cuba, eleven perished and 200,000 homes were damaged or destroyed. In the Dominican Republic, the streets of the capital city of Santo Domingo were submerged and 30,000 people evacuated.

Still accumulating size and strength, Sandy rumbled northward. By October 25, she was just southeast of Florida. News reports indicated that she could eventually reach the magnitude of Katrina and impact the entire Eastern Seaboard from the Southeast to New England. "Now is the time to update your family communication plans, check your supplies, and stay informed," a high-ranking Federal Emergency Management Agency official warned. "A hurricane isn't a point on a map—it's a big storm and its impact will be felt far from the center." The National Oceanic and Atmospheric Administration predicted gale force winds of up to seventy miles an hour in some areas and widespread storm surges—the rising of the Atlantic Ocean itself. The National Hurricane Center called for a "long-lasting event," with "two to three days of impact" after the storm had hit.

But the morning of October 26, standing on the stern deck and gazing out in the direction of the Maryland shore, Doug Faunt found it hard to believe there was a storm out there at all. The day was calm and comparatively mild, and above the *Bounty*'s towering masts, the gulls were circling. *Robin is right,* Faunt thought. *Get clear of the hurricane to the east, and then tack south. Nothing to it.* They'd be in Key West in no time, drinking Coronas on the beach. They'd be laughing.

At sixty-six, Faunt was the oldest person on *Bounty*, and the only volunteer. For most of his life, he'd been a computer engineer in Silicon Valley, a job that had made him plenty of money—not enough to be filthy rich, but enough that he was able to fully retire, without worry, shortly after his forty-eighth birthday. He'd always been an avid reader, and among his favorite books were nautical adventures, like Patrick O'Brian's *Master and Commander* novels. And so in the late 1990s, married but without kids, Faunt had set about finally fulfilling his sailing dreams. He'd taken a tour on the *Rose*, the tall ship rechristened *Surprise* for the 2003 *Master and Commander* movie starring Russell Crowe—the same vessel that Robin Walbridge had once helped helm—and sailed across the Atlantic on a century-old steel-hulled barque called the *Europa*. In his spare time, he rode motorcycles in the war-torn Balkans and backpacked through the western Sahara.

In 2008, as his marriage was disintegrating, Faunt had learned of a vacancy on *Bounty*, a ship whose history he had studied extensively. The original vessel, he knew, had been built in 1784, in the city of Hull, and christened *Bethia*, only to be purchased by the British Royal Navy and renamed HMS *Bounty* three years later. In December of 1787, *Bounty* had sailed from the port of Spithead, in Hampshire, England, under the command of William Bligh, a thirty-three-year-old lieutenant who had once served with Captain James Cook. Bligh was bound for Tahiti, where the *Bounty* would pick up a hold's worth of breadfruit trees and transport them to the West Indies. Sir Joseph Banks, a prominent naturalist with the ear of the king, hoped breadfruit, a meaty and filling food, could eventually become a staple in England; others saw it merely as a cheap source of sustenance for slaves in the colonies.

But *Bounty* was cursed almost from the outset. She ran into extremely rough weather near the southern tip of Chile, and after thirty days of unsuccessful attempts to round Cape Horn, Bligh was forced to head east, for the Cape of Good Hope and the Indian Ocean. Over the ten months it took to reach Tahiti, a deep and abiding tension developed between Bligh and his crew, especially the master's mate, Fletcher Christian.

In early April, after half a year in Tahiti, Bligh announced that the procurement of the breadfruit trees was complete—*Bounty* would set sail for Jamaica, unload her cargo, and return to England. The members of the crew boarded the ship as ordered, but unhappily; many of them had started relationships with Tahitian women, and none of them much enjoyed the prospect of a return voyage as arduous as the first. A few days later, on April 28, 1789, eighteen crewmembers under Christian's direction led Bligh out of his chamber at gunpoint and deposited him in a twenty-three-foot launch along with 22 loyal sailors.

In an exceptional display of seamanship, Bligh managed somehow to pilot the boat 3,618 nautical miles to the Dutch-held port in Timor and went on to enjoy a long if unspectacular career in the Royal Navy. The mutineers, meanwhile, sailed to Pitcairn Island via Tahiti—where they deposited a few of their number—and, after burning and sinking the *Bounty* there, established a small, self-sufficient colony. The mutineers who remained in Tahiti were eventually apprehended and sent in chains to England to stand trial. The Pitcairn crew, however, succeeded in staying out of view of the admiralty. Their outpost was only discovered in 1808, at which point almost all the mutineers were dead or gone, including Christian.

Beginning with Bligh's publication of his own account in 1790, the *Bounty* mutiny became an enduring subject of public fascination, the facts of the incident increasingly obscured beneath layers of speculation and literary invention. Charles Nordhoff and James Norman Hall's popular 1932 novel *Mutiny on the Bounty*—in which Bligh is cast as a sadistic disciplinarian and Christian a brave upstart—was adapted four times for the screen and once for the stage, with Christian portrayed by half a century's worth of leading men: Errol Flynn, Clark Gable, Marlon Brando, and Mel Gibson.

It was for Brando's outing that MGM Studios had asked the Smith & Rhuland shipyard in Lunenburg, Nova Scotia, to build a replica—the most exacting and accurate that had ever been created for a film. The shipbuilders consulted the *Bounty*'s drawings in the archives of the British Admiralty. Their only significant amendments to the original were the ship's size—the eighteenth-century ship was ninety feet from stem to stern, close quarters for a film crew—and a pair of diesel engines. Once filming concluded, Brando insisted that the ship be preserved and not burned for the final scene, as the producers had originally intended. So *Bounty* was sent to St. Petersburg, Florida, where she remained for more than twenty years.

In 1986, Ted Turner, the founder of CNN, acquired MGM's entire library of film props, including *Bounty*. In the years that followed, the ship appeared in a handful of other movies—among them a 1990 *Treasure Island* adaptation starring Charlton Heston and, later, two of the *Pirates of the Caribbean* films—but Turner had no great desire to hang on to the ship. In 1993, he donated her to the Fall River Chamber Foundation, in Massachusetts, which in turn established the Tall Ship Bounty Foundation. Robin Walbridge was brought on a year later.

Under Walbridge's direction, *Bounty* joined the community of tall ships that crisscross the globe in the summer months. It was a sort of inverse tourism circuit: The ships would lay up for a few days in one harbor, long enough for locals and visitors to admire the high masts and ballooning sails, then push off for another port of call. Maintenance, supplies, and crew salaries were financed with ticket sales, the ten bucks they charged people to climb aboard, wander belowdecks, or pose for pictures beside the replica cannons.

Before joining the replica *Bounty* as a volunteer, in 2008, Doug Faunt made it his business to read every book he could on the original ship. He kept pictures of *Bounty* around his house in Oakland and tacked additional images above his berth. The vessel bewitched him; he believed Walbridge when the captain told him that *Bounty* was "the most famous ship afloat in the entire world."

And yet Faunt was not unaware of the subpar condition in which the *Bounty* found herself at middle age. In 2001, Robert Hansen, the millionaire founder of Islandaire, an air-conditioning company, had purchased *Bounty* from the Tall Ship Bounty Foundation. He had kept Walbridge as captain and also provided a much-needed infusion of funds to help maintain the vessel and pay the sailors. But even with his respectable fortune, he seemed unable to keep up with the intensive and regular maintenance a ship of *Bounty*'s size required. There were always repairs to be done, and never enough money to do them.

Before arriving in New London, *Bounty* had spent several weeks in dry dock in Boothbay Harbor, Maine, where workers and crew members replaced some rotted planking and installed a pair of new fuel tanks. In Connecticut, two new stoves had been driven down by Tracy Simonin, an employee of the HMS Bounty Foundation, and installed by Faunt and Barksdale. *Very much a work in progress*, was how Faunt referred to the ship. Still, like practically all the hands on board, Faunt, one of *Bounty*'s volunteer engineers, believed the ship would get them to Galveston, where he had planned to undertake an array of improvements.

Now Faunt leaned against the railing on the stern deck, listening to the reassuring gurgle of the John Deeres. They were at full power, motoring fast southeast, and the entire ship shook with their effort. At the bow, his fellow sailors were double-checking the lines, shimmying up the mainmast. The wind was blowing, but not violently, and he could feel the sun on his neck.

Four. Saturday, October 27, 11:00 a.m.

The Saffir-Simpson hurricane scale separates storms into five categories. A category 1 hurricane, the weakest on the spectrum, is defined as having sustained winds of 74 miles per hour; in a category 5 storm, winds regularly reach 157 miles per hour—enough to rip the roof off a house. On Saturday, October 27, two days after *Bounty* left New London, Sandy was a mild cat. 1, flirting with tropical storm designation. And yet her low intensity belied her remarkable size. NASA satellite images taken at the time show a swirling gauze knot, with a compact core and tendrils that extended across a 1,000 mile swath of the Atlantic Ocean, from Florida to the Chesapeake Bay.

According to Laura Groves, *Bounty*'s twenty-eight-year-old boatswain—an officer in charge of equipment maintenance—beginning on Friday, the crew had printed out maps from the ship's weatherfax. They posted them in the hallway belowdecks so all hands would have a chance to track the storm's progress and the location of *Bounty* relative to it. Those maps would have shown *Bounty* approximately 200 miles from the Virginia shore, on the eastern edge of the storm. So far, so good—if the storm kept up its current pace and trajectory, the ship could still skirt the worst of the winds and bypass Sandy once she turned inland.

And yet it seemed increasingly probable that Sandy would soon clash with a fast-moving cold front, which had swept down from Canada and across the Midwest. As NOAA forecasters pointed out, the two systems, both dangerous in their own right, threatened to merge into one colossal "Frankenstorm." The prospect was terrifying. The last major hybrid storm to hit the East Coast was the Halloween Nor'easter of 1991—the "perfect storm" immortalized by Sebastian Junger—which occurred when a low-pressure system from Canada swallowed the category 2 Hurricane Grace and slammed into the coast of Massachusetts, killing thirteen people.

On the *Bounty*, sea-stowing preparations began in earnest. Anything loose, from heavy appliances to the crew's baggage, had to be lashed down. The crew furled most of the sails to reduce weight aloft, leaving only the forecourse, the lowest sail on the foremast. This was the *Bounty*'s storm sail—it would be needed to help steady the ship in a gale.

Doug Faunt spent most of the morning belowdecks. An inveterate radio geek, a couple of years earlier he'd installed a Winlink system that could be used to transmit e-mail messages via shortwave radio signals in the event of an emergency. Faunt double-checked the wires and booted up the system—all was in working order. Next he made his way aft, where the washer and dryer, previously secured, had moved six inches. They had to be tied down again, this time with extra line.

Faunt was joined for part of his shift by Claudene Christian, one of the newest members of the *Bounty* crew. Christian was forty-two, a bleach-blond former beauty queen who seemed to have lived enough lives for ten women. She had grown up in Alaska, where she'd competed in pageants from an early age. At the University of Southern California, in Los Angeles, she'd been a cheerleader—experience she parlayed into a career when she founded the company Cheerleader Doll. In 1997, the Barbie manufacturer Mattel sued Christian and her father, Rex Christian, for patent infringement, and Claudene was forced to abandon the company. According to *Los Angeles* magazine, Christian subsequently sued her own lawyer for "gross misconduct," and settled out of court for $1 million.

Suddenly flush with cash, Christian bounced around the West Coast. She sang with a band named the Mad Tea Party, did PR for a racetrack in Hermosa Beach, and became a partner in Dragons, a trackside bar. She drank heavily, dated the wrong men, and acted erratically—at one point, she reportedly purchased an expensive, life-size statue of a policeman for her front porch. In 2007, she was diagnosed with a bipolar disorder and hospitalized. Her bank account nearly depleted, she moved back home. Several years later, she discovered the sea.

She shipped out for the first time in 2011, as a cook on the *Niña*, a sixty-five-foot replica of Columbus's ship. She spent three months on board, lived for a time in rural Oklahoma—where her family had moved—and in May 2012, trucked out to Wilmington, North Carolina, to join the crew of *Bounty*. When she was growing up, Rex Christian had always told his daughter she was a descendant of Fletcher Christian, the leader of the 1789 mutiny. This may or may not have been true, but Claudene certainly believed it; it was one of the first things she told the other *Bounty* hands.

Christian was immensely popular on board *Bounty*. She was charming, warm, and unflaggingly ebullient—a "sparkplug," Faunt called her. But Faunt knew inner darkness when he saw it. His father had been an alcoholic, and his mother, who had struggled with mental illness, had committed suicide with a shotgun shortly after Faunt graduated from high school. He told Christian stories of his childhood, in South Carolina, and listened while Christian spilled the details of her own past.

For Christian, *Bounty* was a chance to start over—to make up for what she described as her "failures" in California. She threw herself into her daily duties with alacrity, taking on tasks others tried to shirk. In the evenings, sweaty and soused with salt water, she'd often join Josh Scornavacchi on deck for an impromptu jam session. Scornavacchi had brought a pair of bongos, and Christian sang along to old rock songs, her voice bright and unwavering.

Shortly before *Bounty* departed from Boothbay Harbor, Christian was promoted by Walbridge from volunteer to paid hand—a position for which she'd earn a hundred bucks a week. "Volunteer with drinking money," was how Walbridge phrased it, but Christian was immensely proud of her new position. It gave her status, but, more importantly, it validated her feeling that she belonged on the *Bounty*.

But Christian was still a green sailor, and she had never experienced bad weather at sea. The approaching storm clearly scared her in a way that it did not scare the more seasoned hands. In an e-mail conversation with her friend Rex Halbeisen after leaving Connecticut, she said she was "praying to God that going to sea was the right decision," and expressed concern with the equipment on *Bounty*. "You know me, I am not a mechanical person but the generators and engines on this ship are not the most reliable," she told Halbeisen. "They are always stewing over them. I would hate to be out to sea in a storm and the engines just quit or we have no power."

But by the time she sent a subsequent text message to her mother, probably late on Saturday night, Christian seemed to have made peace with her misgivings. "Just be sure that I am ok and HAPPY TO BE HERE on Bounty doing what I love," she wrote. "And if I do go down with the ship & the worst happens . . . Just know that I AM GENUINELY HAPPY!! And I am doing what I love! I love you."

Five. Saturday, October 27, 1:00 p.m.

By Saturday afternoon, *Bounty* was a couple of hundred miles due east of the border of North Carolina and Virginia, and Robin Walbridge made the decision to change course. He would now steer the ship southwest, toward the coast.

It was a tactic he had used before when sailing in the vicinity of large storms. "You try to get up as close to the eye as you can, and you stay down in the southeast quadrant and when it stops you stop, you don't want to get in front of it," he said in a 2012 television interview. "You'll get a good ride out of the hurricane." As third mate Dan Cleveland later recalled, Walbridge reasoned that by October 27, Bounty had made it out far enough beyond Sandy's eye that if he steered inland again, the winds whipping counterclockwise out along the margins of the storm would help propel the ship to St. Petersburg.

Walbridge reminded his senior officers that he had a good sense of how storms behaved. "He [was] never a yeller or a screamer," Cleveland later testified. "When things would go wrong, you'd never see him freak out, he'd handle situations in a calm manner. I never saw him get nervous or scared. It made you feel like you could handle things."

Cleveland, a twenty-five-year-old former landscaper who other crew members say "worshipped" Walbridge, had been through a few bad storms on Bounty, too, including one in 2008 that hit the ship as she made her way north to Louisiana from the mouth of the Panama Canal. He had heard the saying, popular among crew members, that "Bounty loves a hurricane," and although he was loath to go that far himself, he did believe that the ship handled well in strong winds. "She works hard and you work hard," was the way he put it. In the end, neither Cleveland nor the other senior officers who might have had a say in navigational matters ever objected to the new southwestern tack.

But Walbridge had made a miscalculation. His plan assumed both that the forecasts of Sandy's path would hold and that it was possible to get around Sandy at all—that she was a hurricane of normal size, a few hundred miles across. Irene, in 2011, had been 600 miles in diameter; Katrina, in 2005, measured only 415 miles from edge to edge. Skirtable distances, if your ship was well-equipped and moving fast. But Sandy was not skirtable. Meteorologists later estimated that she was the largest hurricane ever recorded in the Atlantic Basin, with a diameter of 1,000 miles, and a wind swath of 2 million square miles. If Walbridge had kept to his original southeasterly course, it was conceivable that he might have made it to Sandy's edge. Instead, now he was unwittingly sailing *Bounty* directly into her maw.

•   •   •

That afternoon, the weather worsened. Winds were now reaching over thirty miles per hour, waves were climbing to fifteen and twenty feet. A cold rain fell periodically overhead. *Bounty* rocked irregularly, making it hard to get any rest belowdecks. Even simple actions, like moving around the cabin or walking down the passageway to the head, required concentration and energy.

More distressingly, it had become clear that *Bounty* was taking on a considerable amount of water. It seeped through the ceiling and across the floorboards and through the forepeak. It spouted through the walls and squirted down from the ceiling and collected in greasy little pools in the corners of the cabins. The floors turned slippery, the stairs and ladders downright murderous. All wooden ships leak, of course, and some of the crew members comforted themselves with the fact that *Bounty* had pumped herself out of a few disasters before. There were five pumps on board—two electric, two hydraulic, and one "trash pump," a smaller unit that could be hauled around to different locations on the ship. But the hydraulic and electric pumps were working at peak capacity, and still the water was rising.

At eight a.m. on Sunday morning, after a long and mostly sleepless night, Walbridge gathered his mates in the navigation shack for a meeting. Chris Barksdale, the engineer, was also invited. Barksdale, a handyman by trade, was already seasick—later that day, when a crewmate gave him a pill for it, he vomited it back up. Walbridge pinpointed *Bounty*'s location on a map, and reviewed the plan for the day ahead: southwest and then south and straight on toward St. Petersburg.

At this point, Laura Groves later recalled, the seas were twenty-five feet and the wind was blowing at nearly sixty miles per hour. After the meeting concluded, around 8:45 a.m., she departed to help adjust the jack lines, the bow-to-stern lines that allow sailors to move safely around the deck of a storm-struck ship. Groves believed that the end was in sight, especially once they'd swung over the bottom quadrant of the hurricane and put the storm behind them. There was not yet much cause for concern, she thought.

This was not an opinion shared by Doug Faunt, who had spent Saturday night and much of Sunday morning in the engine room, monitoring the pumps. If the devices were unable to keep up with the seawater, the engine room would flood. And if the engine room flooded, *Bounty* would eventually find herself entirely at the mercy of the growing storm, batted about by the waves like a toy boat. The replica *Bounty* would be forced to rely solely on her sails, just as her namesake once had.

Faunt dashed from one engine to the next, minding the meters, tinkering with the levers, cursing under his breath. It must have been 120 degrees in that room, and humid as hell. He stripped down to his T-shirt and underwear and hiking boots, occasionally ducking through the hatch for a breath of fresh air. It was exhausting work, and at noon, he handed off the baton to another crewmember and crawled back upstairs to try to catch a few hours of sleep. When he got to his cabin, he found the room flooded and his gear soaked. He climbed naked into his sleeping bag. The bag was polyester, not cotton, and although the sensation was uncomfortable—not unlike folding your body into a used athletic sock—it did afford a bit of warmth.

Faunt had barely closed his eyes when he heard someone shout the "all hands on deck" call. You've got to be kidding me, he thought. He shouted his acknowledgment, fumbled for his sweat- and seawater-soaked clothing, and dressed in the damp darkness.

Six. Sunday, October 28, 12:30 p.m.

Josh Scornavacchi made it on deck a few minutes before Doug Faunt. Looking up at the masts, he saw the reason for the all-hands call: the forecourse was split, and the canvas was flying free. The forecourse was the *Bounty*'s storm sail; it helped steady her. It had to be furled. So Scornavacchi began to climb. He was a strong climber, comfortable with heights, but the rigging seemed to just get smaller and wetter as he shimmied upwards. The wind whipped the ropes around him into a fury, lashing him on the arms and neck hard enough to draw welts. Nevertheless, within the next hour, Scornavacchi, Laura Groves, and John Svendsen were able to secure the sail to the gaskets on the top of the yard.

While Scornavacchi was aloft, Faunt and Claudene Christian were taking up or paying out the lines as needed. The task had fallen to them partially because they were late in arriving on deck, and mostly because Faunt was fatigued and Christian couldn't be trusted aloft. Despite having been on the *Bounty* for several months, Christian was still very much a novice when it came to the workings of the ship. Faunt, who often shared shifts with her, regarded her as something of a slow learner. "It wasn't that she wasn't brave," he would later recall. "She was. She was brave and she had a lot of heart and she had passion for the *Bounty*. But you usually had to repeat things several times before she really got it."

Now she fixed Faunt with an intent stare, and complained that no one on the ship was listening to her. "What aren't they listening to?" Faunt asked. He had to holler over the roar of the storm. Behind them, thirty-foot waves were breaking over the foredeck.

"We're taking on too much water. The pumping isn't going well. We've got big problems."

"I know," he said. "We all know." There wasn't a person aboard the *Bounty* who didn't know the ship was in trouble. But it did no good to complain about it. It was better to keep your head down and do what you could to make sure everyone got out of this mess alive. Faunt tried to reassure Christian. "Listen," he said. "It's going to be fine."

.   .   .

That evening, Sandy closed in on Cape Hatteras. The storm had now merged as predicted with the easterly moving cold front. Meteorologists were reporting a noticeable drop in the atmospheric pressure off the coast of North Carolina, a sign that the storm was entering an even more dangerous phase. *Bounty*, a couple of hundred miles southeast of the cape, had found herself square in the middle of the storm system, with little hope of sailing her way back out.

As night fell over *Bounty*, visibility that had been limited enough at twilight, when a veil of rain enclosed the ship, was whittled down to practically nothing. The swells rose like battlements around her. Scornavacchi ducked through the aft hatch to check on his cabin. What he saw startled him: several boards had been ripped up from the floor and were swirling around in the wash. He understood the gravity of the situation, but he also felt strangely energized. Back home in Pennsylvania, he had longed for an adventure. Now he had found one.

Around eight p.m., the winds again tore the forecourse loose, and again Scornavacchi was sent aloft to deal with it. He scaled the foremast with extreme caution. A hard hail pelted him in the face; he could barely see, let alone hear anything. A couple of dozen feet below him, the bow of the ship shot down the trough of one wave and up the sheer face of the next. Black water coursed across the deck. Occasionally, the ship would list nearly at beam-ends, the deck at an almost perpendicular angle to the sea and the crew clinging to anything they could get their hands on.

The sail furled, Scornavacchi made his way belowdecks. There, the water had risen further still, and the crew was working microshifts to keep it at bay, a couple of minutes lying down followed by a couple of minutes working the pump. Then, suddenly, the world went sideways, then straight again. There was a scream and then a moan. Scornavacchi and his shipmates assessed the situation. Having to abandon ship was now a real possibility. But surely the *Bounty* would stay afloat, even if she were to permanently topple over on her side. Surely she wasn't about to sink just yet.

At this point, there were already two injured sailors aboard the *Bounty*. One was a twenty-seven-year-old named Adam Prokosch, who had been tossed headfirst across the mess by a particularly high wave. Christian set up a mattress in a dry part of the ship, and made Prokosch lie on his back, with his hands at his sides. It was clear that he was badly hurt; Christian worried that he might be partially paralyzed. She told him not to move.

Meanwhile, Walbridge had suffered an injury of his own, likely caused when he collided with the table in his cabin. Several sailors on board later recalled that he was moving only with extreme effort, bracing himself with both hands. Scornavacchi believes Walbridge broke his back; Faunt thinks it may have been a leg. Either would have been an ominous development. Unless you're extremely lucky, escaping a sinking ship without full ambulatory control is all but impossible.

·   ·   ·

As *Bounty*'s engineer, it was Chris Barksdale's job to maintain the generators, the pumps, and the diesel engines that powered the ship. In a subsequent interview with *Popular Mechanics*,

Barksdale recalled that the pumps became clogged early Sunday afternoon; Walbridge himself did the unclogging, but it was to little avail. The water was flooding into *Bounty* much faster than it was going out. As the ship rolled, the water in the engine room and the bilge would heave up the walls and slosh back down over the equipment. The engines sputtered, churned, and sometime after nightfall, with a dull whine, gave out completely. The *Bounty* was now adrift.

At nine p.m. Walbridge and Faunt descended to the radio room to call for help. *Bounty* was noticeably light on communications systems—most of the time, the crew members relied on their cell phones. Closer to the coast, in calm weather, this wasn't a problem. But *Bounty* was now a hundred-odd miles out to sea, and no one on board had any reception. It was too windy above-decks to conduct a conversation, which meant that the ship's satellite phone—which got no reception belowdecks—was no good either. So Walbridge and Faunt decided to issue the mayday call on the Winlink system. You almost had to laugh, Faunt thought— they were going to peck out their damn SOS via e-mail.

Still, the system worked fine, and after confirming that the message had gone through, Faunt left Walbridge and made his way forward toward the galley, bracing himself with both hands. The generators were surging badly, and the lights were flickering on and off like disco strobes. After a while, the backup generator kicked in. In the yellow glare of the emergency lights, Faunt could see the other crew members organizing emergency supplies and tending to Prokosch, who was on his back on the mattress.

The next two hours passed in a delirious blur. Salt water would get into one light fixture, and Faunt would no sooner get it clean and working again than the next one would burst. There were electrical fires to put out, pumping to do in the engine room, and loose wood to secure in the tank room, which was now fully flooded. The *Bounty* was coming apart before Faunt's eyes.

He dashed back to his cabin and took a quick inventory. He wouldn't be able to bring much with him—he was going to lose his bicycle, most of his clothing, his radio gear, his books. In the end, he settled on his rescue knife and his teddy bear, Mush, which he strapped to his chest.

Engineless, the *Bounty* spun windward up the crest of one three-story wave only to be knocked leeward by the next. At around midnight, the first Coast Guard C-130, piloted by Lieutenant Wes McIntosh, came into range, and the *Bounty* was able to establish radio contact. There was a small cheer from the navigation shack. McIntosh requested that the crew shine a light on the rigging, and Faunt activated the search beam.

For the next couple of hours, the C-130, heavy with fuel, circled overhead, sometimes at 1,000 feet and sometimes at 500. "Someone tell that guy we're 110 feet," Walbridge joked. "He's going to clip us!" There was still time for levity: according to Faunt, despite the six feet of water in the belly of the ship, Walbridge and Svendsen believed that the *Bounty* might yet be saved, if only the Coast Guard could find a way to lower some working pumps. But McIntosh could barely see half a mile in the rain, and the winds were blowing at between eighty and ninety miles an hour. A gear drop was impossible. The only thing the crew of the *Bounty* could do was hold on until morning, when a helicopter could be summoned from Elizabeth City. It seemed to Faunt an awful long time to wait.

Seven. Monday, October 29, 2:00 a.m.

Around two in the morning, the crew donned their bright-orange survival suits. Josh Scornavacchi was still not convinced that the *Bounty* would have to be abandoned, but he knew it was better to be safe than sorry. The suits—what sailors call "Gumby suits," after the bulbous, ungainly form their wearers assume—were made of heavy neoprene. They would protect against both cold water and flame, in the unlikely event that the electrical fires spread through the *Bounty*. Scornavacchi zipped the waterproof seal on the collar closed and attached a small rubberized plastic bag to his climbing harness with a carabiner. Inside the bag was his ID, a pocketknife—the essentials.

Svendsen, the first mate, was in the navigation shack, his Gumby suit only halfway zipped. He seemed to Scornavacchi to be much less concerned with his own safety than with the safety of the crew. He inspected each sailor carefully, like a commanding officer before a battle, tugging on straps, double-checking rescue lights, slapping shoulders, and patting backs.

Scornavacchi thanked Svendsen, and joined Claudene Christian near the mizzen fife rail, which surrounded the aftermost mast. The clouds he could make out overhead in the darkness were low-bellied and full, and a strong wind blew across the deck. Christian was clearly scared but putting on a brave face for her friend, and she smiled brightly at Scornavacchi.

He looked up at the ghostly lights of the C-130 circling above him in the rain. Then he felt the deck lurch violently beneath him. The *Bounty* was once again leaning perilously over on her side. Bodies slid past him in the night, some silently and acquiescently, some with horrific screams, their hands desperately clawing for a handhold, a stray piece of rigging, anything at all.

He took a deep breath and jumped.

• • •

After receiving the OK from Svendsen, Doug Faunt waddled sternward in his Gumby suit and lay down on the deck alongside Adam Prokosch, the sailor with the injured back. Prokosch was not paralyzed, as Christian had feared; he would later learn that he had separated his shoulder, broken two ribs, and severely damaged a pair of vertebrae. But it had taken time to get him up on deck, and he looked bad: his eyes were half-closed, and he had his hands crossed over his chest, kind of like a corpse.

The *Bounty* was heeling badly to starboard, forty degrees or more, Faunt guessed. He wasn't so much lying down as standing up now, with his feet on the railing, the sea frothing below him and lapping at his feet, the ship looming over him. The C-130 passed once overhead, the sound of its engines reduced by the storm to an insect-like whine. Gazing up, Faunt caught a glimpse of the big silvery wings of the plane, and the moon glowing faintly through the clouds, and then he was asleep.

That he was able to nod off on the deck of a doomed ship was a testament to the extent of his exhaustion. He had been working for forty-eight hours straight, give or take, many of them in the sweltering hell of the engine room. He was dehydrated, he was hungry, his joints ached, and his lungs burned. He was strong, but he was also sixty-six years old, and he had his limits. Faunt later figured that he might have slept for an hour, but given the speed at which the *Bounty* rolled over, it was probably half that. When he opened his eyes again, the deck was fully vertical. He bent his knees and pushed off into the sea. The storm swallowed him.

Now commenced a jarring, vicious cycle. Faunt would push his way to the surface, and a wave would drive him back under like a hammer pounding the head of a nail. The *Bounty*'s engines were submerged now, and there was plenty of diesel in the water. Faunt was an experienced diver, and he did his best not to open his mouth. But the strength of the ocean was stupendous, and he couldn't keep the salt water and diesel out of his throat. He spit out what he could and swallowed the rest.

At irregular intervals, a body in a survival suit would float past him, and Faunt would holler and wave, but it was useless. Nobody could hear him, and he couldn't distinguish one sailor from another. Zipped into the Gumby suits, they all looked the same, cartoonish orange shapes silhouetted against the dark sea. He caught hold of a life preserver, but it appeared to be tethered to something—maybe to the ship herself, he thought. He was afraid she would plunge, and that he would plunge with her. So he let go.

What surprised Faunt—what he would often think about in the days to come, first back at the Coast Guard station and then in his cluttered bedroom in Oakland—was the strange tenacity of the human brain. The brain, the mind, maybe the spirit—whatever you wanted to call it, the thing that did not allow Faunt to give up, even when he probably *should* have given up, dropping his hands and surrendering to the ocean. It simply never crossed his mind that he might be dying. The fact that it didn't, he figured, probably saved his damn life.

• • •

A sinking ship creates a funnel on the surface of the sea—planks of wood, life rafts, and human bodies can be sucked down behind her. From his training, Scornavacchi was familiar with this effect, and after jumping clear of the *Bounty*, he fought hard to get a safe distance away from her. But swimming in a Gumby suit is incredibly awkward, and his progress was maddeningly slow. The sea around him looked like a flushing toilet.

Everything he grabbed at—stray planking, strands of line— was ripped out of his hand. Gasping, his lungs filling with salt water, he fought his way back to the surface. There appeared to be no one left on board the *Bounty*, which had now fully capsized. Indeed, there appeared to be no one around at all. Before he could ponder the particulars of his plight, he was yanked underwater again by some invisible force.

In movies, sinking ships lurch through the deep like whales, their every contour visible to the camera. Scornavacchi could see nothing. It was dark enough on the surface, and an inky pitch underwater. But groping around with both hands, Scornavacchi did figure out what was pulling him down: some of the rigging had caught onto the small bag of essentials lashed to his harness. The weight of the ship pulling on him made it impossible to unhook the carabiner, and the bag was made of heavy-duty PVC plastic, which offered little hope of breaking. He was going down—five feet, then ten, fifteen. He could feel himself starting to drown, losing the ability to think or use his muscles. His lungs were filling with seawater and diesel.

Just before the *Bounty* left New London, Scornavacchi's mother had fretted about the storm. "Mom, I'm not going to die," he had told her. Now here he was, about to break his promise. He was furious with himself. He thought about his eleven-year-old brother, too, and of all the other people he would never see again. *I'm sorry,* he thought. *I'm so sorry.*

Eight. Monday, October 29, 4:15 a.m.

The two emergency life rafts on the *Bounty* were rated for twenty-five passengers each—nearly twice the number of sailors abandoning the ship. Inflated, the rafts resembled orange polyurethane igloos, with a wide base and a domed roof. Sausaged into their silvery casings, they were just a couple of feet long and pellet shaped. Now Chris Barksdale saw one of the capsules float past him. He instinctively reached out and grabbed hold of the line, he later told a reporter for *Popular Mechanics*. His other hand clutched a heavy piece of wooden grating, which the *Bounty* had shed as she sank. He was sharing the grating with a couple of other sailors, including Cleveland.

"Don't let loose!" Cleveland shouted to him.

"You don't have to worry about me letting loose of this son of a bitch," Barksdale replied. "I'm going wherever it goes."

Within an hour or so, Barksdale and Cleveland had inflated the raft and helped four other sailors inside: Drew Salapatek,

Jessica Hewitt, Laura Groves, and Adam Prokosch. They tried to be optimistic, but it wasn't easy—the storm, far from weakening, actually seemed to be blowing harder.

·   ·   ·

Several months after the sinking, Josh Scornavacchi still could not explain his salvation in practical terms. He was drowning, he was going under, he was dead—and then he was not. The bag on his harness had somehow broken free of the rigging. He climbed fast upward, pulling with his hands and kicking his feet. "I believe God did it," he says. "That he helped me in some way."

He surfaced, sputtering and coughing, alongside a makeshift raft of emergency supplies that Claudene Christian had assembled hours earlier. He clung to the side and took stock of his location. He was still dangerously close to the *Bounty*, which had rolled temporarily back to an upright position.

After a while, he saw Jessica Black, the ship's cook, drape herself over the other end of the raft. Black was clearly panicking; her face was a mask of shock. Scornavacchi was making his way toward her when he heard a sharp crack, like a rifle shot. It was a large piece of the mast, breaking loose and crashing down toward the raft. The masts on the *Bounty* weighed several tons apiece; a direct hit would have been fatal. Instead, the piece of mast fell neatly between them, and sent both sailors flying high into the air, as if they'd leapt off a trampoline.

Black vanished into the waves. Plunging back into the water, Scornavacchi cursed to himself. He'd finally found another survivor, and now she was gone. He was alone again. Worse yet, when he'd been pulled underwater, his survival suit had flooded, and his boots were loose in the legs. He was trying to tread water with the equivalent of a twenty-pound weight lashed to each ankle. And the water kept pulling him back toward the doomed *Bounty*.

The ship was equipped with hundreds of miles of rope, and now they had taken on a menacing life of their own, writhing in loops and coils in the dark water. Every time he tried to move, Scornavacchi felt one of them reaching for him. Nearby he could see the *Bounty*'s mizzenmast, the aftmost mast on the ship, lying flat across the surface of the sea. Out of other options, he hauled himself up on top of it, and held on.

Suddenly the *Bounty*, buoyed by a large swell, began to roll back upright. Scornavacchi, both hands wrapped tightly around the mizzenmast and hanging on for dear life, went with it. Soon he was more than 40 feet in the air. From somewhere out in the storm he heard a voice. "Jump," the voice said. "You've got to jump." And he did.

The next day, safe on shore, Scornavacchi would ask his shipmates who had issued the order, and receive only blank stares. No one remembered telling him to jump. No one had seen him up on the mizzenmast at all.

·　　·　　·

It was about 4:30 a.m. by the time Scornavacchi managed to reach one of the life-raft capsules. He was working to get it open when his shipmate John Jones bobbed up alongside him. Soon they were joined by two more, Mark Warner and Anna Sprague. For hours Scornavacchi had thought that everyone else was gone; now it seemed like a familiar face was popping up every few minutes. By now, Sandy's central mass was likely a little more than 400 miles southeast of Washington, D.C., according to the National Hurricane Center, and bound for New York. The worst of the storm had now passed the *Bounty*, but the strong winds and high seas had persisted.

Once the raft was inflated, the four survivors were faced with the prospect of actually boarding it. The hatch was far above the water, the rubber was slick and the whole craft was pitching wildly in the waves. They were all exhausted from battling against the ocean for hours; Scornavacchi's forearms were burning, and he found he could barely make a fist. He was helping to boost up Sprague when he heard voices nearby. On the other side of the raft were Doug Faunt, Matthew Sanders, and Jessica Black. One by one, they all piled inside and, shivering in the cold, settled down to wait. Scornavacchi, Jones, Warner, Sprague, Sanders, Black, and Faunt—seven in all. As far as they knew, they were the only surviving crew members of the tall ship *Bounty*.

· · ·

Ingested in trace amounts, salt water is not particularly harmful to the human body. But swallowed in large quantities, it wreaks havoc on metabolism, impairs the nervous system, damages the kidneys, and dangerously elevates blood pressure. By the time Faunt climbed aboard the inflatable emergency raft, he had consumed, by his estimate, a couple gallons of salt water. He could still breathe normally, and his brain was functioning, but there was an ominous ache in his stomach. He lay back on the floor of the raft and evacuated his bowels into his Gumby suit.

To either side of him, the six other survivors had assembled in a circle, leaning back against the walls in an effort to keep the raft stable. Scornavacchi and Sprague suggested a group prayer, and although the other five sailors on hand were, by Scornavacchi's reckoning, mostly atheists, everyone joined hands and asked in their own way for deliverance.

Having been involved in the communications efforts before abandoning ship, Faunt believed that help would eventually arrive. The only question was when. The *Bounty* was many miles from the shore, the weather was still squally, and there were no other ships in the area. Even the U.S. Navy had been wary enough of a run-in with Sandy that when the *Bounty* capsized, the nearest naval vessel was 260 nautical miles away. Faunt knew they could be facing a day or more in the orange raft.

Still, the crew members did their best to keep spirits high. They told stories about happier voyages aboard the *Bounty,* days when the weather was fair and the sailing smooth. They reminisced about the missing shipmates. They wondered when day would finally break. As they waited for dawn, Scornavacchi, Sprague, and Warner sang "Mingulay Boat Song," a Scottish sea chantey. Lying on his back, Faunt listened to the words:

> What care we, though, white the Minch is?
> What care we for wind or weather?
> Let her go boys; every inch is
> Sailing homeward to Mingulay.
> Wives are waiting, by the pier head,
> Or looking seaward, from the heather;
> Pull her round, boys, then you'll anchor
> 'Ere the sun sets on Mingulay.

Nine. Monday, October 29, 5:30 a.m.

By dawn, there were two Coast Guard helicopters hovering over the wreck of *Bounty.* It was Randy Haba, the rescue swimmer from the first of the two, who scooped up Doug Faunt. The first thing Faunt saw when he was hauled into the cabin of the Jayhawk was the face of John Svendsen—the straggler that Haba had spotted amid the wreckage of the *Bounty.* Svendsen had remained in the navigation shack long after the rest of the crew had jumped overboard, but eventually the *Bounty* heeled so vertiginously that he had no choice but to leap clear of the deck and into the water. Behind him, he could hear the VHF radio sputtering: *Are you still there, Bounty? Do you read me, Bounty? Come in, Bounty.*

Almost immediately, Svendsen was clocked by a falling piece of yard. He managed to shield his face, but the force of the impact shattered his hand. Maimed and badly shaken, he found himself snared by the foremast rigging, unable to wrest himself free. He felt like he was on a bad amusement park ride: Each roll of the ship lifted him dozens of feet into the air, then the next wave dropped him back into the waves, until Svendsen could barely distinguish the sky from the sea.

Working desperately with his good hand, he finally shook off the rigging and dropped into the water. Somewhere in the swirling wash, he found an orange "man overboard" buoy, the kind that inflated automatically when it hit the water, and he clung to it as hard as he could. Behind him was the ruined, heaving mass of the *Bounty*, backlit by the moon.

Faunt was ecstatic to see Svendsen—he'd worried that he had gone down with the ship. But he hardly had time to greet the first mate before the Coast Guard helicopter's mechanic, Petty Officer Third Class Mike Lufkin, was hollering in his ear. "Take off the suit," Lufkin said.

"I can't," Faunt replied. "I'll foul your bird."

"Just take it off," Lufkin said.

Faunt didn't want to expose the crew to the sight of his shit-stained Gumby, but he knew Lufkin was right. The cabin doors were open and the wind was blowing cold and Faunt was drenched. It was a recipe for hypothermia. He unzipped the suit and dropped it on the floor.

"I've really got to piss," Svendsen shouted.

"Well, it's already fouled," Faunt said, nodding toward the suit. "Might as well piss in there."

He turned away while Svendsen did his business. A few minutes later, with the Jayhawk rattling around in the rough air, an airsick Svendsen opened up the Gumby suit again and threw up inside. It was a veritable piñata of bodily fluids now, Faunt thought.

Haba was able to make three more trips to the raft to retrieve more survivors before the Jayhawk was low enough on fuel that the pilot announced he was turning back toward Elizabeth City. He had six survivors on board. It would be up to the other Jayhawk crew that had just arrived from Elizabeth City to retrieve the rest.

•   •   •

Scornavacchi, Jones, and Sanders spread out across the floor of the rubber raft in an effort to keep it steady. Without the presence of the four other bodies, the craft had turned skittish, scudding over the sea like a skipping stone. All Scornavacchi could do was hold on.

Around eight a.m., Petty Officer Third Class Dan Todd, the rescue swimmer from the second Jayhawk, poked his head into the raft's hatch. Scornavacchi allowed Todd to strap him into the basket, and leaning on his side, took in the view. He could see the flank of the *Bounty*, lying on her side, and the snarled remainders of the ten miles of line that had once kept her at sail. She was still afloat, but just barely, and she would not be for long.

The basket swung higher. There was a clank, and Scornavacchi pulled himself into the cramped cabin of the Jayhawk. Pretty soon there were eleven people crammed inside: Sanders, Jones, and Scornavacchi from the first raft; Barksdale, Cleveland, Salapatek, Hewitt, Groves, and Prokosch from the second; plus Todd and the Coast Guard flight mechanic. There wasn't enough room to move, let alone strip off the survival suits, so everyone just kind of piled on top of one another, a knot of limbs and neoprene.

Two hours later, the helicopter set down in Elizabeth City. In a single-file line, the survivors limped across the tarmac. It always felt strange to have land under your feet after a few days at sea, but this time it felt stranger than usual to Scornavacchi. He walked gingerly, letting the blood seep back into his toes. A light rain was falling. A pack of local news photographers waited nearby, jostling against hastily erected barriers. There were camera flashes, shouts, the sound of someone crying. Scornavacchi kept his head down.

Inside the Coast Guard station, Faunt went to wash the shit out of his drawers and get a change of clothes. Prokosch and Svendsen needed patching up. Scornavacchi was led to a harshly lit conference room, where his mates from the first raft were waiting. There the tallying-up began in earnest. The *Bounty* had left New London with sixteen sailors. Fourteen had been rescued. Robin Walbridge and Claudene Christian were still out there somewhere.

Among the last crew members to see them on board the ship was Laura Groves, the boatswain, who had helped conduct a headcount of the crew in the frantic last moments before abandoning ship. She would later remember that Svendsen was in the navigation shack, communicating with the C-130 pilots, and that Dan Cleveland was beside her, his Gumby suit halfway on, working on connecting a line to the capsules that held the inflatable life rafts, so they'd be easier to find if the ship capsized. Christian was on the mizzen fife rail. Walbridge was just forward of Groves, on the weather deck.

Time had gone baggy, elastic. Groves heard Svendsen shout that the foredeck was underwater, and she raced to help Cleveland get the rest of the way into his Gumby suit. Then the ship was on her side, Groves was kicking as hard as she could to keep her head above water, and Walbridge and Christian were gone.

Initially there was cause for hope. The *Bounty* had sunk only a few hours before, and the water was not particularly cold—a person in a survival suit could last for a day out there, easy. And hadn't Svendsen been plucked alone from the water? Just because Christian and Walbridge hadn't made it to a life raft, just because they weren't sitting there now in that conference room, it didn't mean they were dead. But the coastguardsmen said nothing, and as time passed, the shared optimism of the survivors dwindled.

Scornavacchi was in his room in an Elizabeth City motel when definitive word arrived. The crew from a third Coast Guard helicopter had finally found Christian in the water near the *Bounty*, but she was unresponsive, with no vital signs. Two *Bounty* crew members later said that her corpse bore the signs of severe cranial trauma: heavy bruising on one side of the face and a partially crumpled skull. That could have meant that she was killed by a blow from one of the falling masts, or it could have meant that she slipped unconscious into the water and quickly drowned. As for Walbridge, the search was ongoing. A day later, it would be called off.

Unresponsive, no vital signs. The official terminology, the way it depersonalized the dead and the lost, it unnerved Scornavacchi. He summoned an image of Christian as he had last seen her, lashing together the gear and supplies on the deck of the *Bounty*. She had looked almost peaceful there, even as the ship was going down, an easy smile on her face.

That night, Scornavacchi called his mother in Pennsylvania. She'd seen the news—she knew what had happened to the *Bounty*. "But I'm alive, Mom," he said. "I made it." He held the receiver to his ear and listened to his mother sob.

Ten. February 12, 2013, 9:00 a.m.

It was not hard to pick out Dina and Rex Christian in the crowded ballroom. They sat a couple rows back from the microphones, alongside their lawyer. To their left was a battery of television cameras, and behind them, arranged across a wide expanse of brightly patterned carpeting, were the reporters, maritime lawyers, and local sailors with a few hours to kill.

Dina Christian passed most of the hours of the Coast Guard's hearing on the *Bounty* sinking in rigid silence, sometimes dabbing her eyes with a tissue, sometimes shaking her head furiously, and sometimes leaning in to whisper to Rex, a rumpled man in his sixties. Anyone who looked closely at Dina—small, blond, with a gently upturned nose and round cheeks—would have noticed the striking resemblance she bore to her only daughter, Claudene.

The Renaissance Portsmouth Hotel and Conference Center in Portsmouth, Virginia, where the hearing was held, looms over the Elizabeth River. From the hallway outside the second floor ballroom, you could look out across the wind-chopped water to Norfolk, where a navy aircraft carrier and a handful of smaller ships, bristling with scaffolding and plastic tarp, awaited repairs. Every morning, at precisely 8:50 a.m., Coast Guard Commander Kevin Carroll, clad in his dress blues, arrived and took his place in the front of the ballroom, a few yards from where the Christians sat.

Carroll is in his forties, thickly built and tall, with a high-and-tight military style haircut and a brusque, if not entirely unfriendly, interrogative style. Three and a half months after the *Bounty*'s sinking, Carroll had been tasked with conducting the official inquiry into the incident, with sorting out the messy particulars of what exactly had gone wrong. He opened each day of testimony with a lengthy invocation of the pertinent federal regulatory code—a paragraph on marine casualties and investigations—followed by a standing moment of silence for the lost.

It had taken only a few days after the sinking for the second-guessing to begin. The questions percolated in the comments sections of articles about the incident, on the message boards and Facebook pages frequented by tall-ship buffs, in the letters pages of sailing magazines. Although they spoke fondly of him as a person, few of Robin Walbridge's fellow tall-ship captains seemed able to comprehend his decision to sail through the hurricane— or, more bafflingly, to cut across its center mass on October 28.

In an open letter to Walbridge circulated in mid-November, Jan Miles, the captain of the schooner *Pride of Baltimore II*, had compared the *Bounty*'s sinking to that of the *Fantome*, a schooner that went down off the coast of Belize in 1998, killing all thirty-one crew members aboard—the worst Atlantic sailing disaster in forty years. Like Walbridge, Miles wrote, *Fantome*'s skipper had tried to outrun a hurricane on a set of underpowered engines and placed too much faith in the accuracy of hurricane forecasts. Addressing his still-missing colleague, Miles wrote,

> You aimed all but directly at Sandy. That was reckless my friend! Was it wise or prudent to set off into the teeth of Sandy in BOUNTY[?] Did it make any sense at all? Virtually all of your professional friends and colleagues back here do not think so . . . Yeah, you were a reckless man Robin. I would not have continued to proceed as you did.

Joining Miles in his criticism were the Christians, who believed that their daughter would still be alive if Walbridge had kept *Bounty* in port. "Fact: Walbridge took [Claudene] into the worse hurricane & did not except [*sic*] help from the [Coast Guard] until it was to late for her," Dina wrote on Facebook in January. "When everyone else was in the water, she was seen holding on to the ship for dear life. Too scared to go into the water! After reading all this, how can any of you defend this Crazy Nut?"

There was one group of people who did not buy the emerging consensus that Walbridge's navigational errors and hubris were wholly responsible for the *Bounty*'s end: the ship's crew. As many of them would point out, the ship had been through bad storms before and survived them all. *Bounty* had crossed the Atlantic in foul weather, motored through gales in the Gulf, threaded some of the most treacherous passages on earth. And in each circumstance, Walbridge had acquitted himself well.

It stood to reason, then, that the sinking was not only a matter of the *Bounty*'s position relative to the hurricane on October 29—that factors beyond Walbridge's control had turned an ill-advised voyage into a doomed one. In this scenario, the blame that had fallen on Walbridge belonged more properly to Robert Hansen and the HMS Bounty Foundation.

Hansen had long struggled to adequately maintain the ship with the meager funds earned from dock tours and day sails. Patchwork measures had been undertaken to get *Bounty* from one port of call to the next. "Being a *Bounty* alumnus was kind of a point of pride," one former mate recalls. "You're part of a club. And you're part of that club because you've been sailing around the world on a boat that you've been constantly digging around in the bottom of the Lego drawer trying to put back together. Not to mix metaphors, but *Bounty* was the Bad News Bears of the tall ship world."

According to one legend circulated among new crew members, shortly before a Coast Guard inspection in the 1990s, a small fire had broken out on the *Bounty*. It allegedly smoldered for a full three days, and was smoldering still when the coastguardsmen came aboard, but the crew—in a scene that sounded like something out of a bad sitcom—was able to keep the inspectors distracted and away from the fire. "I learned a lot about how to handle boats from Robin," a former crewmember says. "And I learned far more about how to handle people."

Since 2008, Hansen had been attempting to sell the *Bounty*, and Walbridge had taken an active role in the discussions. At one point, the captain had reached out to the British billionaire playboy Richard Branson, who had sailed on the *Bounty*, asking him to buy the ship; Branson declined. Later, according to *Outside* magazine, Walbridge established contact with the Ashley DeRamus Foundation, a nonprofit organization dedicated to educating and raising awareness about people with Down's syndrome, in the hope of outfitting the *Bounty* as "a place of learning and inspiration" for special-needs visitors. In St. Petersburg, in fact, Walbridge had planned a tour for the foundation's members.

Coast Guard hearings do not have the authority to determine criminal responsibility or levy any civil penalties; Carroll was in

Portsmouth as an investigator, not a jurist. But his findings—drawn from nine full days' worth of testimony of survivors, coastguards-men, surveyors, and ship inspectors—would be admissible in civil or criminal court. And since the Christian family was widely be-lieved to be preparing a lawsuit against the HMS *Bounty* Founda-tion, the hearings had the feeling of a practice trial.

On one side were the Christians and Jacob Shisha, their lawyer, a veteran maritime litigator with a showman's demeanor and a trace of a New York accent. On the other side were Tracie Simo-nin and Robert Hansen of the Bounty Foundation, and their two attorneys, Frank Ambrosino and Leonard Langer. There was also a third, unexpected party: John Svendsen, the *Bounty*'s first mate and the first survivor who had been pulled out of the water in the gray dawn of October 29.

The Coast Guard had named Svendsen a "party in interest" in the investigation. In maritime law, this can mean one of two things. A party in interest may be a person, company, or organi-zation suspected of bearing some responsibility for the accident in question. Or it may be someone with an unusually large stake in the investigation's outcome, one way or another—someone who stands to lose or gain from the inquiry's findings, perhaps, or someone who holds the key to understanding what happened.

The Coast Guard did not specify the grounds on which Svend-sen had been summoned to Portsmouth. But whatever Carroll's reasoning, making Svendsen a principal in the investigation filled what would otherwise have been a conspicuous vacancy in the proceedings. Hansen had taken the fifth, and was not on hand for the hearing. Walbridge was lost at sea and presumed dead. So Svendsen, Walbridge's deputy, became the de facto defender of the *Bounty* and of the people who had looked after her main-tenance and charted her course that last week in October. He was the stand-in for the captain whose actions, many now be-lieved, had come at the expense of Claudene Christian's life and his own.

As a party in interest, Svendsen was given a chair near the front of the room and the opportunity to question every witness. Shisha had petitioned the Coast Guard to give the Christians the same standing, and shortly before the hearings began, Rex and Dina were granted it. The reason for Shisha's request wasn't stated. But the implications seemed obvious: By directly questioning the witnesses, he could potentially begin building a case against the HMS Bounty Foundation.

Svendsen was the first witness Carroll summoned when the hearing commenced on the morning of February 12. The first mate had sustained serious injuries to his face, hand, shoulder, and torso during the storm, and he moved slowly and deliberately to the front of the ballroom. He was dressed in a floral button-down under a black fleece, and his dirty-blond hair hung lankly to his shoulders. A conspicuous murmur arose in his wake. Seating himself in front of the microphones, Svendsen steepled his long fingers on the table and allowed Carroll to walk him through the days leading up to the sinking of *Bounty.*

Of particular concern to Carroll was Walbridge's August television interview in which he had spoken of chasing hurricanes. At the time, the comments had seemed like the boasts of a daring sailor. Now they looked a lot more like tragic foolhardiness—proof of Walbridge's poor judgment.

"Did *Bounty* chase hurricanes?" Carroll asked Svendsen bluntly.

"Not in my opinion," Svendsen replied. He maintained that Walbridge's comments had been widely misunderstood. The captain had not been advocating the "chasing of hurricanes" as a matter of pleasure or thrill, he said. He had simply been stating the truth—that hurricanes can generate a strong but manageable boost of wind power to a full-rigger like *Bounty.* "I never witnessed Robin seeking out a storm. If there was a storm, he would put the ship in the safest position in the storm," Svendsen said.

Svendsen appeared to imply that Walbridge had been correct in the abstract—"you'll get a good ride out of the hurricane"—

and wrong in the case of Sandy, which was much larger than Walbridge had assumed. As Brock Vergakis of the Associated Press later noted, Walbridge had inveighed in the same interview against ever getting "in front" of a hurricane—but by cutting southwest toward Hatteras, Walbridge had inadvertently done exactly that.

Svendsen, however, made it clear that he did not hold Walbridge entirely blameless for the sinking. He recalled that he had stressed to Walbridge the historic nature of the storm and worried aloud about the *Bounty*'s ability to withstand it. "I had mentioned other options as far as staying in and not going out to sea," Svendsen said.

These pleas were apparently offered semiprivately, in the presence of other mates, and in at least one case, privately to Walbridge. But Walbridge, Svendsen testified, had faith in the *Bounty*, and was determined to press southward. "Robin felt the ship was safer at sea," he said.

Equally striking was Svendsen's recollection that twice in the early morning hours of October 29, he had requested that Walbridge issue an abandon ship order. Twice Walbridge refused. The captain apparently believed that the *Bounty*, even without power, would remain afloat, and that the crew would be safer on board than in the life rafts. In hindsight, Walbridge had badly misjudged the condition of his ship. It was not safe at all—it was sinking fast.

Had Walbridge issued the abandon ship order earlier in the morning, when the ship was more stable, an orderly procession to the life rafts might have occurred. Instead, she began to roll over before the rafts were even fully inflated. Chaos reigned on deck, and in the end the entire crew was dumped more or less unprepared into the sea. For an inexperienced sailor like Claudene Christian, an earlier order might have meant the difference between life and death.

Eleven. Wednesday, February 13, 10:00 a.m.

Hardly anyone on board the *Bounty* during her final voyage in October had failed to note that the ship was taking on water. Even in relatively calm weather, there was always a leak—a trickle here, some seepage there. Were those leaks ordinary for a wooden ship her age? Or were they evidence that *Bounty* was dangerously dilapidated?

The task of answering those questions fell to Todd Kosakowski of the Boothbay Harbor Shipyard, who had worked on *Bounty* during the month she spent in dry dock in the fall of 2012, shortly before she sailed for St. Petersburg. The crew at Boothbay had caulked leaky seams, installed new fuel tanks, replaced rotten planks, and touched up the *Bounty*'s paint job. Kosakowski, a clean-cut man who bears a closer resemblance to an accountant than a shipyard worker, had been the manager for the project. As such, he was one of the last naval professionals to see the *Bounty* in one piece.

Kosakowski told Kevin Carroll that shortly after the *Bounty* had been brought to the shipyard, he and his workers had pulled up some planking near the mizzenmast and mainmast and found significant amounts of rot—a "dry, almost charred-looking" kind of rot, Kosakowski said.

"Did you tell Captain Walbridge?" Carroll asked.

"Yes," Kosakowski said.

"What did he say?"

"He was a little shocked when we first started looking into it," Kosakowski admitted. "His shock turned to awe when we were prodding the other framing and finding the same signs of degradation. Once we started looking at the other frames, we saw it was more widespread." Kosakowski came to believe that as much as 75 percent of the framing above the vessel's waterline was rotten.

The rotten wood needed to be removed and replaced, Kosakowski said, and he had recommended to Walbridge that he allow the shipyard crew to inspect the rest of the *Bounty,* cutting out the worst of the damage and installing fresh white oak in its place. Kosakowski testified that Walbridge agreed to a few replacements but resisted a deeper—and inevitably more costly—investigation. "[Walbridge's] response," he said, "was that they would deal with the hull at the next year's hull exam"—the annual inspection conducted by the Coast Guard. But that exam wasn't scheduled until 2014, which worried Kosakowski.

He told Carroll that he met twice more with Walbridge to talk about the rot. On that second occasion, Walbridge told Kosakowski that he wanted the issue to "stay between the two of us," Kosakowski testified, "and that he explained these problems to the owner, [and] that I didn't need to be worried."

An audible murmur passed through the crowd in the ballroom. The captain of a ship that would sail into a hurricane two months later, allegedly asking a yard worker to keep quiet the extent of the rot on his vessel—in the words of one prominent maritime safety analyst, the disclosure was nothing short of "stunning." Had Walbridge, as he promised Kosakowski, actually informed Hansen about the rot? Or had he chosen to keep Kosakowski's discovery to himself?

No one could say—one of the men was missing and the other had refused to testify or grant interviews since the wreck. But it wasn't hard to imagine the horrible bind in which this revelation would have placed the captain. For Walbridge, everything was riding on *Bounty*'s fate. His sense of identity was irrevocably linked to the ship. Had she been mothballed, it might have been devastating to him. Would he have taken that risk and told Hansen? Or would he have done whatever it took to keep *Bounty* sailing?

•   •   •

The strongest counterargument to Kosakowski's bombshell, as it happened, came from his own former colleague. Joe Jakomovicz, a veteran shipwright with a shock of white hair and a thick Maine accent, was a former yard manager of the Boothbay shipyard, where he had overseen previous repairs on the *Bounty,* including a 2006 renovation. Testifying before Carroll, Jakomovicz argued that Kosakowski was drastically overstating the extent of the rot on *Bounty.* Kosakowski, he pointed out, had "five or six years of experience," while he had forty. "I've seen worse," Jakomovicz said of the damage. "The key thing here is that it's a fifty-year-old boat," he added. "You have to realize that that's tired."

That didn't mean that the ship was seaworthy or that it wasn't—Jakomovicz was retired when the *Bounty* arrived in Boothbay in 2012—only that Jakomovicz had encountered such situations before. He remembered seeing a few photos of the *Bounty* sinking, and had marveled that, despite the rough seas, the ship had not split apart. "I said, 'My God, that boat's still floating and intact.'" Jakomovicz recalled, shaking his head. "That was surprising to me."

And yet the crew had seen it: the ocean sluicing through dozens of open seams, overwhelming the pumps. Dan Cleveland told the coastguardsmen as much in Portsmouth when it was his turn to testify later that week. Besides John Svendsen, Cleveland was the officer with perhaps the fullest understanding of *Bounty,* having spent five years on the ship, including a significant amount of time dealing with yard work and repairs. On the night the ship sank, while John Svendsen was in the navigation shack communicating with the Coast Guard, Cleveland was mostly belowdecks, trying to bail out the ailing vessel. Around midnight, Cleveland said, the ship had lost power, then flickered back to life again. But the *Bounty* was rolling hard now—hard enough that the starboard engine was temporarily underwater.

Casting about for options, Cleveland and his shipmates turned to the "trash pump," the portable gas-powered pump that could be used to supplement the overwhelmed hydraulic units. They hauled it down to the engine room, but the thing wouldn't start. "We got out the manual because we were trying to figure out if we were missing something simple," Cleveland remembered. It was funny, maybe, in the grimmest way possible—a few sailors flipping through an old instruction manual while their ship sank and the seas surged around them.

Twelve

By the end of the hearings in Portsmouth, the *Bounty*'s loss had begun to take shape, in the way that shipwrecks often do, as an unsparing aggregation of mistakes. Any one of them, had it occurred in isolation, would not likely have been fatal; it was only gathered together that they acquired such terrible weight. Had Robin Walbridge kept the ship in port, the *Bounty* might have lived to sail another day, even in her decaying state. If the *Bounty* had been in better shape, the storm might have been survivable; Sandy was extremely large, but her wind speed never rose above category 1 status, and vessels smaller than the *Bounty* have weathered much worse. If the generators had stayed online, if the pumps were able to keep up with the rising water, the *Bounty* might have limped back to shore as she did during her near-disastrous trip past Cape Hatteras in 1998. These are the hypotheticals that haunt a lost ship and her survivors.

In an interview with CNN in February, Claudia McCann, Walbridge's widow, said she believed her husband acted honorably in steering the *Bounty* south, and she has made it clear that she intends to protect his legacy. This will be no easy task—the captain's crew demonstrated loyalty in their testimony, but the story they told in spite of themselves was a damning one. In the most generous scenario, Walbridge made a single bad decision that was fatally complicated by terrible luck. But it was just as possible that he committed an act of unforgivable hubris, knowingly pushing a dilapidated ship beyond its limits and endangering the young, largely inexperienced crew he had sworn to protect.

Whether this ambiguous picture translates into legal responsibility may now be a matter for civilian courts to decide. Jacob Shisha, the Christians' attorney, says he was only attending the inquiry to "listen," but if a lawsuit is filed, the HMS Bounty Foundation will undoubtedly be the chief target. It is not inconceivable that John Svendsen, as the highest-ranking officer after Walbridge, could find himself named as a defendant as well.

In November of 2012, the surviving crew members of *Bounty* went to New York to tape a segment for ABC's *Good Morning America*. The producers shot more than an hour of tape, but used barely two minutes of it, a fact that annoyed some of the crew members. After that, they granted few interviews. Some took to switching off their phones or deleting e-mails from reporters without even reading them. Like soldiers returning from a particularly harrowing deployment, they worried that no one else would understand what they'd been through. They became even closer than they'd been on *Bounty*, sealing themselves off from the world. They started an e-mail listserv to exchange memories from their time on the ship and posted reassuring messages on each other's Facebook walls.

Thinking of you, they wrote.

It will get better, they wrote.

I'm having bad dreams, too, they wrote.

On a recent winter afternoon, Doug Faunt stood on the back porch of his house in Oakland, surveying his tangled, overgrown backyard. An aging cat wove between his legs. Even a couple of months on, his stomach still bothered him. "There's not a day that goes by that I don't think about the storm and what happened out there," he said, pushing a neon-yellow watch cap back over his brow. "I assume it will be that way for a very long time."

But the funny thing was, he also couldn't stop thinking of the things that he missed—the sound of canvas flapping overhead, the slap of saltwater on his skin. Lately he had found himself re-turning often to tall-ship forums online. Tall ships are typically taken out of commission during the winter months, laid up in October and back at sail by April or May. There was a ship sailing out of New York in the spring that he had his eye on—another full-rigger. Maybe she had room for one more sailor.

Outside

FINALIST—REPORTING

The Granite Mountain Hotshots were struggling to protect the town of Yarnell, Arizona, from an advancing wildfire when nineteen team members were killed. There was one survivor. Drawing on interviews with friends and colleagues of the dead, official reports, and the calls the men made from the scene, Kyle Dickman authoritatively reconstructs the events that led to the greatest number of firefighter deaths since 9/11. Dickman is an associate editor at Outside *and a former first responder—he began fighting wildfires when he was an eighteen-year-old college student and was later a member of the Tahoe Hotshot Crew. Founded in 1977,* Outside *has won five National Magazine Awards for General Excellence and received the award for Reporting in 1997 for Jon Krakauer's "Into Thin Air."*

Kyle Dickman

Nineteen: The Yarnell Hill Fire

arnell, Arizona, a former gold-mining town of 650 people, sits on a precipice at the western edge of the Colorado Plateau. Rising above it are the 6,000-foot peaks of the Weaver Mountains, and nearly 2,000 feet below are the flatlands and cactus of the Sonoran Desert. An hour and a half northwest of Phoenix and an hour south of Prescott, Yarnell is, according to the town's slogan, "Where the desert breeze meets the mountain air."

Weekend drivers coming into Yarnell from the south know they've hit town when they see the Ranch House Restaurant, a greasy spoon where the waitresses all look related and the clientele ride Harleys or horses. Across the street is Glen Ilah, a subdivision with a couple hundred homes owned mostly by retirees like Truman Farrell, a seventy-three-year-old air force veteran who up until two years ago was the town's volunteer fire chief.

On the night of June 28, Truman's wife, Lois, was sitting on their back patio in her usual spot by the grape trellises and the koi pond. From there the couple have a sweeping view of the Weaver range to the north, and Lois was watching a dry thunderstorm hung up on the range's crest. She saw lightning strike the ridgetop and, a short while later, wispy blue smoke drifting toward the clouds. When Lois pointed it out to Truman, he thought little of it.

•   •   •

Around seven-thirty the following night, Robert Caldwell walked through the front door of his downtown home in Prescott. "Zion!" he said as he lifted his five-year-old stepson into his arms, kissed his wife, Claire, and flopped down in a chair at the kitchen table with a can of Coors. At twenty-three, he was the youngest of three squad bosses, a senior position that put him in charge of nine men on the Granite Mountain Hotshots, a team of wildland firefighters based out of Prescott.

"Go get comfortable, would ya?" said Claire. "You smell like Robert." By this she meant go clean up because you smell like you usually do: like smoke.

Robert didn't want to get up. He'd barely been home since his last time off nearly two weeks ago, and sitting, even in his fire boots, ash-smudged work pants, and sweat-crusted Granite Mountain T-shirt, felt good. Family time was precious during the eight-month fire season, lasting from April through November. He and Claire had been married for a little less than a year, and it still felt like the honeymoon. She was the hippie chick eight years older with an easy laugh; he was the cowboy gentleman wise beyond his years. Robert had an IQ high enough for Mensa and a love of Hemingway. Hotshotting was his identity. He'd fought fire for five seasons, and after two of Granite Mountain's squad bosses left in March, he was promoted. It was one of the six full-time positions on the crew.

Since April, he and his Granite Mountain colleagues had spent twenty-six shifts on fires. The week before, they got some local press for saving a few hundred high-dollar homes from the 6,700-acre Doce Fire, a national priority that burned the crew's namesake, a 7,290-foot peak visible from nearly anywhere in Prescott. For the nation's only municipally funded hotshot crew, saving homes was a big deal, and the town was calling them heroes. The praise made the crew uncomfortable, especially Robert, who felt that getting paid to camp and work fires in the most beautiful places in the West was closer to selfish than heroic. But it was nice to be acknowledged.

That night the family ate dinner together at the kitchen table. After putting Zion to bed, Robert drank a cup of coffee while Claire did the dishes, then he pulled her into the bedroom. Before nodding off, Robert removed his wedding ring. "It's filthy," he said, showing it to Claire, who lay in the crook of his arm. Ash covered the edges, and the silver was scuffed from the handle of his Rhino, the hoe-like tool he used to dig on fires. Claire took the band and rolled it between her fingers and thought, What if someday this is all I have left?

·   ·   ·

Across town, three other Granite Mountain hotshots—Christopher MacKenzie, Garret Zuppiger, and Brendan "Donut" McDonough—arrived at the Whiskey Row Pub, a dive in Prescott's historic downtown. When the hotshots came to drink in groups, as they often did on rare days off, bartender Jeff Bunch gave them a discount. His son was a former crew member.

The trio sat by the pool tables in the back of the bar. Donut hadn't seen Garret, a red-bearded twenty-seven-year-old, or Chris, his roommate and a nine-year veteran of firefighting, in a couple of days. Strange as it was, Donut (his nickname was easier to say than his last name) had missed his hotshot brothers. He'd come down with a cold on Thursday night and taken Friday and Saturday off.

"Donut, what the fuck are you wearing?" Garret asked. He had on a pink tank top: an easy target. The hazing went around the table, moving from Donut's style to Chris's poorly trained dog, Abbey, to Garret's obsession with vinyl records, before the conversation eventually landed, as it always did, on the job.

"Any idea what the assignment is?" asked Donut. "All I heard was we got work." He was feeling better and eager to get back on the fire line. Tomorrow was Sunday, an overtime day—nearly twenty dollars an hour.

"More staging, I think," said Chris. "We've been busting little lightning fires since you left."

Seven small blazes had ignited in the mountains around Prescott during the thunderstorm the previous night. One of them, sparked by the lightning strike Lois and Truman had seen on Friday, had become a higher priority blaze after growing to one hundred acres. It had been given a name: the Yarnell Hill Fire. About the time the hotshots were finishing their beers, the incident commander, the general on the fire, had set up headquarters at the volunteer fire station in Yarnell and was ordering additional resources as fast as he could: eight engines, structure-protection specialists, air tankers, and three hotshot crews. Granite Mountain was one of them.

•   •   •

Eric Marsh woke up around 5 a.m. on Sunday at the crew's quarters, Station 7. The night before, the forty-three-year-old superintendent of Granite Mountain had eaten dinner with his wife, Amanda, at the Prescott Brewpub downtown. Afterward she drove home; he crashed at the station, a tin-sided building on a patch of blacktop six blocks from the restaurant. Sleeping there seemed easier than driving the thirty minutes to their horse ranch outside town, in nearby Chino Valley.

The crew called Eric "Papa," and at home, with Amanda, he referred to the nineteen young men as his kids. Until they got to know him, Eric intimidated most of the hotshots. He was quiet, wry, and guarded—in many ways, a typical superintendent. Amanda was his third wife, but he rarely discussed his personal life with the crew. He once drove his men sixteen hours from

Prescott to a fire in Idaho and didn't say a word until they reached the flats of the Utah desert. "I'm getting a divorce," he said, then remained silent until they reached the fire camp.

Eric grew up on a ten-acre farm in North Carolina's Blue Ridge Mountains and fell in love with hotshotting when he joined a Forest Service crew as a second-year student studying biology at Appalachian State. He graduated in 1992. Five years later, he moved to Arizona to keep fighting fires, developing a reputation as a canny and cautious firefighter. In 2003, the Prescott Fire Department hired him to help with their fuels crew.

In the years prior, the city, which is surrounded on three sides by the Prescott National Forest, was named by the Hunt Research Corporation, a California-based risk-assessment group, as one of the West's ten most likely places to be hit by a wildfire. Out of that danger grew the department's vision for a fuels crew, one that removed brush and timber growing at the edge of town to provide defensible space. Eric was good at it. He and the crew used chainsaws and chippers to clear flammable material from around hundreds of Prescott homes, setting the National Fire Protection Association's Gold Standard for defensible space in 2012. But for the longtime hotshot it wasn't enough. In the hierarchy of wildland firefighting, there are few things less glamorous than a job that demands the same backbreaking work of a fire fight but delivers none of the thrill. Turning the Granite Mountain fuels crew from a wide-eyed group of twenty men not even allowed to set foot on the fire line into certified hotshots was Eric's singular focus. He accomplished it in five years, an evolution that takes most crews twice that, some even longer.

Station 7, where the crew moved in 2011, was a point of pride for Eric. He and the wildland division of the fire department had spent the previous six years trying to convince the city council that it would be safer for Prescott to host hotshots rather than just a fuels crew. The station was proof of the department's victory.

Its new headquarters had a workshop, a gym, and a stocked gear cache with a sign on the wall that reads TOTAL COST FOR A WELL-EQUIPPED HOTSHOT: $4000. Granite Mountain's two $150,000 buggies, burly twelve-person crew hauls kitted out with cubbies for medical equipment and tools, were parked in the garage. Eric's superintendent truck, a Ford F-550 he'd customized with a welded-steel rack and brake lights in the shape of Granite Mountain's logo, was in front.

After rolling out of his sleeping bag that Sunday morning, Eric headed to the parking lot, crossing the black tiles he'd helped install in the white floor to spell out "GMIHC—Granite Mountain Interagency Hotshot Crew." When rookies stepped on the black tiles, they owed the veterans one hundred push-ups. He pulled out his JetBoil stove and a Nalgene full of Bisbee's specialty coffee grounds—both of which he always carried in his fire-line gear—and brewed up a pot of coffee. Eric had been sober for thirteen years. Coffee was his only drug, and he took it black. There was no milk or sugar on the fire line, so why get used to it any other way?

With his mug full, Eric went to the ready room, where the crew met every morning. On one wall hung a poster common in wildland fire stations. It shows pictures of wildland-fire fatalities, including the two biggest: Montana's 1949 Mann Gulch Fire (thirteen deaths) and Colorado's 1994 South Canyon Fire (fourteen deaths). In both, elite firefighters had been killed battling small blazes that grew with terrifying and unexpected speed. In both incidents, the crews burned to death after being caught off guard with no time to escape. HOW IS YOUR SITUATIONAL AWARENESS TODAY? the poster asks.

•   •   •

The Granite Mountain crew started arriving at Station 7 at five-fifteen a.m. As they awaited the briefing, they sat in the ready room and talked about family and fires. Nearly half of them had children. On the wall were two whiteboards, one covered with a handful of random facts re-upped most mornings by a third-year sawyer named Andrew Ashcraft. That morning's trivia: "A gorilla's scientific name is Gorilla, Gorilla, Gorilla" and "Milk cows that listen to music produce more milk." Robert Caldwell, who usually would have laughed while fact-checking the tidbits on his iPhone, ignored them. He'd been looking forward to days off and had a hard time leaving the house that morning.

On the other whiteboard was the Granite Mountain Hotshots Daily Physical Percentages, a half-joking, half-serious chart the crew used to take stock of each other's energy levels, a matter of safety on the line. Eric had written "68%." Donut put, "Hell ya." Robert, or Bob as he was known only on the crew, put "Moderate Duty."

By five-forty, they were all tipping back in their chairs. "We've got an assignment to Yarnell," Eric said to the men. "It's 300 acres and burning on a ridgetop in thick chaparral. It's going to be hot—real hot—and that's all I know." It was exactly the sort of short, pointed briefing the crew had come to expect from their boss. "Load up."

· · ·

The sun had risen by the time the caravan crested the Bradshaw Mountains outside Prescott and descended into Skull Valley, north of Yarnell. Eric drove up front while the buggies followed close behind, with most of the hotshots sleeping inside. Robert Caldwell rode shotgun in one, trying to ignore the music—Rammstein's "Du Hast"—blasting from the back of the truck. He texted Claire: "So much for days off. Heading to a 500-acre fire in Yarnell. Love you."

His first sighting of the Yarnell Hill Fire would have come after rounding a bend just south of Rancho El Oso Road, eight miles from the blaze and on the outskirts of the horse ranches in Peeples Valley, a dispersed community of 428 people five miles north of Yarnell. For the team's four rookies, like Robert's cousin Grant McKee, whom Robert had talked into joining the crew that winter, the fire would have seemed entirely unimpressive: a few strands of white smoke drifting near the top of the ridge. Desert fires are deceptive, though, and Robert knew it. He'd worked blazes in the redwoods of California, the spruce stands of Minnesota, and the lodgepole thickets of Montana, but chaparral, where the Yarnell Hill Fire was burning, is a mix of scrub oak and brush that grows so dense it's a struggle to walk through. When it's dry, it's a tinderbox. "It's the brush that scares me most," he used to tell his dad. "Fires just move faster in it."

Arizona, like much of the Southwest, was in a severe drought. The monsoon, a low-pressure mass of moist air that pushes up from the Gulf of California and brings afternoon rains to the region every July, was moving into Arizona, but so far the influx of moisture had done little to cool the one-hundred-plus-degree temperatures. The monsoon cycle had yet to bring any rain either, though its arrival pretty well guaranteed lightning.

The crew reached the incident commander's makeshift base at Yarnell's volunteer fire station by eight a.m. The volunteers' red trucks were in the engine bay, and a handful of 4x4 pickups from nearby state forests and local fire districts were backed into parking spaces. It was still quiet. Eric went inside for a twenty-minute briefing from the fire's operations supervisor Todd Abel, a Prescott-area firefighter with eighteen years of experience. The blaze had been divided into eastern and western divisions, and Eric was placed in charge of the west, where Granite Mountain was assigned to work. With Eric overseeing the division, which would require him to move freely around his section of the fire, command of the hotshots fell to thirty-six-year-old captain Jesse Steed.

"Men, gaggle up!" Eric called when he returned. "It's a long hike in, so bring plenty of water." Then, as he always did before leading the crew into a remote fire, he told his men to call their families.

. . .

Hotshots hike in single-file lines. Steed was up front. Behind him were the four two-man saw teams and squad boss Travis Carter, followed by Donut and the six other men carrying Pulaskis and hand tools, and finally squad bosses Robert Caldwell and Clayton Whitted, who were responsible for making sure the slowest hotshots didn't drop off the back of the line. Robert watched the boot heels of the rookie in front of him. The dust the crew kicked up stuck to the sweat on his face.

A little more than a mile in, the thin road veered left and climbed 850 feet to the crest of the Weaver Mountains, where the fire was burning. It was now nearly ten a.m. Temperatures were in the hundreds, and the last spots of shade had disappeared. Three times they stopped for water. Some hotshots, like Donut, carried thirteen quarts that day—twenty-six pounds of water that doubled the weight of their packs.

The fire, still around 300 acres, wasn't doing much when they got there. It sat atop the ridge, which ran in a crescent shape toward Peeples Valley to the north. On the west flank, to their left, the blaze was held tight against the rim rock on the range's crest. On the east flank, to their right, a few fingers of fire had burned down draws that drained toward the valley they'd hiked up.

The crew started building line, removing all the flammable fuel along the fire's eastern flank. The sawyers went first, using their chainsaws to cut brush, while the swampers, the men responsible for clearing anything that has been cut, hauled it off the line and threw it down the mountain. Donut, Robert, and the rest of the hotshots followed behind, using Pulaskis, Rhinos, and rakes to clear away leaves and needles. Steed kept one ear to the radio while helping throw brush or cut line whenever he could.

Eric, who had gone ahead to scout, stood on the peak of the ridgeline above the crew, watching the fire burn north toward Peeples Valley. It was starting to build up steam. Like all seasoned firefighters, Eric was an amateur meteorologist, and he would have noticed the few small cumulus clouds, puffy seeds of thunderstorms, building to the north of the fire. Like giant vacuums, these clouds create wind, drawing in hot air and moisture rising from the desert floor as they grow. Eric knew that the bigger those clouds got, the stronger the vacuum and the faster the flames would be pulled toward the houses in Peeples Valley. It's why the incident commander kept calling more hotshot crews, aircraft, and engines to the scene.

．　　　．　　　．

About the time Eric was scouting the fire, Marty Cole was "fiddle farting" in his garage in Chino Valley, a small ranching town just north of Prescott. He got the call to head to Yarnell to act as a safety officer, one of a few lead personnel converging on the fire.

Marty had worked for Prescott area fire departments for more than thirty years and is what's known in the business as an old salt—an arbiter of firefighting culture and tradition. He started his fire career in 1980, well before the city launched its wildland-firefighting division. Back then, firefighter culture was so tribal that city, county, and federal departments refused to leave their jurisdictions. If a fire was burning inside city limits— wildland or otherwise—it was the city's problem and nobody else's. Marty remembers one of the first burned bodies he ever saw. "A young kid burned to death in a car fire," he says. "Two blocks away, firefighters from the neighboring department sat inside their station and watched the smoke column rise."

Many of those walls have since been torn down. But the tribalism still exists, and it's strongest within the insular world of hotshots. Marty was the superintendent of Granite Mountain from 2004 to 2005, when Eric first joined and they were trying to become a hotshot crew.

It was a humbling process. At the time, every one of the roughly one hundred hotshot crews in the nation was funded by states or the feds—the Forest Service, the Bureau of Land Management, the Bureau of Indian Affairs—and many of them had decades of tradition. Granite Mountain, a startup outfit hosted by a small town in Arizona that most other hotshots had never heard of, wasn't exactly well received. The crew once showed up at a fire in Oregon in white ten-passenger vans. Real crews use buggies. When Granite Mountain went out to start work, a firefighter from another crew drew a line in the middle of the road with spray paint and wrote *Don't cross it*.

"When I left, Eric had something to prove," says Marty. "He was going to make that crew better than any other out there."

•   •   •

From his scouting position, Eric could see one of two specially outfitted DC-10s—or VLATs, very large air tankers—fly 200 feet off the ground and drop 20,000 gallons of fire retardant between the flames and Peeples Valley.

He was concerned that the blaze could pivot and start burning down the valley toward Yarnell. If that happened, the flames would be below the crew, creating the same life-threatening situation that killed thirteen men in the Mann Gulch Fire and helped spawn the ten standard firefighting orders, among them: know what your fire is doing at all times, and base all actions on current and expected fire behavior. Eric wanted to be certain that if this event unfolded, he had a dedicated lookout to warn him about it.

"Let's send Donut down to be a lookout," he told Steed. Eric picked Donut because he'd been sick—a slow day could help. "We'll send him down with Blue Ridge's supe."

The Blue Ridge Hotshots, a crew out of the Coconino National Forest, had arrived on the scene that morning, and Granite Mountain could see the crew's superintendent, Brian Frisby, on an off-road utility vehicle (UTV) motoring up the two-track in the valley to meet with Eric and coordinate their efforts.

The plan they agreed on was simple. Granite Mountain would keep building line on the fire's eastern edge while Blue Ridge used their chainsaws to widen an old road that stood between the fire and Yarnell. If the winds shifted and the blaze ran toward town, Blue Ridge could set fire to the brush between the road and the wildfire, robbing it of the fuel it needed to survive. Given the fire's steady chug to the north, it was a contingency plan.

Donut threw his gear in the back of the UTV and got a ride to a bluff in the valley that gave him a view of the fire. "Call me on tac"—a line-of-sight radio frequency—"if you need anything," the Blue Ridge supe told Donut when he dropped him off. "We've got our eyes on you."

·　　　·　　　·

Donut picked a good spot. The knoll he was perched on offered a clear view of the fire and an easy escape route. Just a few hundred yards behind him there was a safety zone, a patch of bare dirt a little larger than a tennis court that a bulldozer had cleared earlier that morning just in case things went haywire. He chose a trigger point, a small drainage a quarter of a mile away. If the fire crossed it, he'd retreat.

Not that the third-year veteran felt he was in any danger. The southern edge of the fire was nearly half a mile away, moving fifty feet an hour toward him, maybe less. He ate his MRE lunch—beef stew—and at the top of every hour "slung weather," using the red book-size kit every lookout carries to record hourly changes in conditions. He took out a thermometer on a chain, dipped the cloth-covered end into his water bottle, and swung it at arm's length for a minute to measure the humidity and temperature. At two p.m. he scratched into the kit's notebook: "104 degrees, 10 percent humidity, five to ten-mile an hour winds with gusts of 15 out of the S" and a note referencing the clouds: "Build up to the SW." Then he went back to fighting off boredom.

Donut can trace his interest in firefighting to a fire-science class he took as a fourteen-year-old kid. He came to Granite Mountain during hard times. In December 2010, he'd spent a couple of nights in jail for possession of a stolen GPS. Then, in March 2011, his girlfriend at the time gave birth to his little girl. He was working construction and taking an EMT class at the local community college at night, but on the occasions that he actually showed up for class, he mostly slept off hangovers or was still coming down from something else. "You name it, I tried it," he says.

In mid-April, he awoke from a binge feeling the full weight of fatherhood. I need to stop this now, he thought. He asked the Prescott Fire Department if they had any openings and was directed to Eric Marsh, who was looking for five replacements. Donut told Eric the whole story—the jail time, the drugs, his dream of becoming a firefighter, his new baby. He was hired on the spot. Donut thinks he got the job because Eric "saw some of himself in me."

By that time, Granite Mountain had been a full-fledged hotshot crew for three years. Eric had pulled off the feat by attracting experienced wildland firefighters, like Steed, with the one thing the Prescott Fire Department could offer that no other hotshot crew could: access to jobs on the city's red trucks. Nearly a dozen Granite Mountain alumni now worked for the department as paramedics or structural firefighters—full-time, family-friendly positions that kept them closer to home. Eric, a certified instructor in both city and wildland firefighting, facilitated that transition by offering training courses throughout the year. That was especially important this season, during something of a rebuilding year, when there were nine crew members with less than two years of experience and a pair of green squad bosses in Robert Caldwell and Travis Carter. Eric's classes got new crew members up to date on the certification Granite Mountain needed to retain its hotshot status, and the classes gave career-focused firefighters like Donut a way to become skilled hotshots and to grow out of it.

On Donut's first full fire assignment, in 2011, Granite Mountain was flown by helicopter into Arizona's Chiricahua Mountains, a range notorious among wildland firefighters for its steep and rugged terrain. He swung his Pulaski for two weeks, often working sixteen-hour days. The physical abuse nearly broke him, and most of the crew figured he'd wash.

After his first season, he'd proven himself to the rest of the men. Last year he got a tattoo on his calf of a frosted doughnut combined with Granite Mountain's logo. "Now they tell me, 'You're slower than shit and look like a Neanderthal, but we know you won't quit,'" Donut says. "They're more my brothers than my actual brother."

It's a familiar story in hotshotting: the discipline and rigor of crew life puts wayward young men on track. But Granite Mountain had a more nurturing atmosphere than most crews. Clayton Whitted, a squad boss like Robert, was a former youth pastor at the Heights Church in Prescott. During some shifts on the fire line, the crew would openly discuss Jesus or ask Clayton to tell stories from the Bible. It was through him that Donut accepted Jesus as his savior, on a fire in New Mexico two weeks before Yarnell Hill. "Clayton, Steed, Eric—those guys had it figured out. They made people better," Donut says. "I wanted a piece of that."

.　　　.　　　.

At 3:30, Claire Caldwell, Robert's wife, was at home in downtown Prescott, watering the pumpkins and sunflowers in her well-kept front yard. It was her last chore of the day, and she was rushing through it. She'd already dropped Zion off with his dad, where he'd stay the next couple of days, and planned to spend the evening relaxing on the couch with a bottle of wine and a movie.

The sky was nearly purple. Claire had just finished hosing down the garden when the wind hit. It was so strong that the sunflower blooms lay down across the raised beds. Moments later, the dry creek behind the Caldwells' house filled with water for the first time that year. She texted Robert: "Hope this rain helps you guys out! You coming home tonight? Love you."

It irritated her that he didn't respond.

.　　　.　　　.

Like many Yarnell residents, Truman Farrell was standing on the edge of Highway 89 watching the wall of fire rip north through the chaparral and junipers toward the ranches and homes in Peeples Valley.

"God, it's awful," he said to his neighbors, Dan Schroeder and Dorman Olson, who were standing beside him with their two Scottie dogs. But it was also mesmerizing, even for Truman, a veteran of both Vietnam and Desert Storm.

"Look at that!" he said, as a VLAT passed overhead and unloaded its retardant just above them. "Now that's really something to see." Little flecks of red slurry landed on his gold Honda CRV. That morning he'd made an evacuation plan with Lois. If things got bad, he'd drive the motor home, towing the CRV, and she'd drive their pickup truck. "I think we're going to watch Peeples Valley burn," he said to his neighbors.

Indeed, by midafternoon, the flames had reached the doorsteps of the outer line of houses in Peeples Valley. But none of them would burn. At approximately three-fifty p.m., the wind began to shift. The thunderstorm stopped sucking in air and started blowing it out. The vacuum was now a leaf blower. Truman compares the way the fire bellowed to a volcanic eruption—a storm within a storm that was suddenly pivoting and heading straight toward Yarnell.

"Uh-oh," he told his neighbors. "It don't look good. That's going right to Glen Ilah. We better go."

•   •   •

"Division alpha, operations. Did you copy that weather report?"

"Affirmative," replied Eric. "The winds are getting squirrelly up here. The dozer and retardant line have been compromised."

Eric, who was acting as supervisor for the heel of the fire, was scouting out front of the crew on the ridgeline above Donut when the radio traffic came through.

"Are you in a good spot?"

"Affirmative. We're in the black."

Like Eric, the rest of the crew was in the island of ash the fire had left behind the day before. The brush was incinerated, and the chance of reburn was nil. It was the safest place they could be.

The operations supervisor requested air attack fly over Granite Mountain's position. Once their location was confirmed, the focus of the fire fight shifted entirely to Yarnell. Granite Mountain was safe and sidelined.

•   •   •

Donut was less than a minute into slinging his four p.m. weather when Steed came back over the radio.

"Donut, you up?"

"Go, Steed."

"They're calling for a 180-degree wind shift and gusts of up to sixty miles per hour out of the northeast."

"Copy that."

He looked up at the approaching wall of flames and blinked. For the first time that afternoon, the wind was blowing at his face instead of his back. The flank that had been slowly backing down the valley had suddenly jumped to life. Two-foot flames had grown to twelve, and within moments the fire was running up a ridge on the east side of the valley and then south, directly at Donut.

"Steed, Donut. It hit my trigger point." The fire had crossed the drainage on the valley floor only a quarter of a mile away. "I'm bumping back to the dozer push."

"Alright, let me know when you get there. We've got eyes on you."

Donut tossed on his pack and grabbed his gear as he started wading down through the brush field and boulders toward the safety of the clearing the bulldozer had created that morning.

• • •

Eric Marsh and Granite Mountain sat in the black ash on the ridgeline above Donut and watched the fire burn for nearly an hour. They rested and ate MREs for lunch.

Chris MacKenzie, Donut's roommate, pulled out his camera and took a handful of stills. One shot was of sawyer Andrew Ashcraft taking a photo of the fire that he'd text to his wife. Another was of the column of smoke turning from bone white to black.

The hotshots who'd brought their phones texted or called their loved ones. Another sawyer, Scott Norris, who'd come to Granite Mountain this season after four years on a Forest Service hotshot crew in Payson, Arizona, texted with his girlfriend, Heather.

Heather: "I had a weird dream I proposed to Scott last night."
Then, "Oh, hi. That was meant for Sarah!"

Scott: "I'm a little old fashioned. I think I'd like to be the one to propose."

Scott: "Just watched a DC3 slurry bomber nearly collide midair with a Sikorsky helicopter."

Heather: "Holy hell! That certainly would have made the news."

Scott: "This fire is going to shit burning all over and expected 40+ mile per hour wind gust from t-storm outflow. Possibly going to burn some ranches and houses."

And finally, when the fire was racing straight at Donut, Scott texted a final photo of flames filling the valley below them: "Holy shit! This thing is running at Yarnell!"

•　　　•　　　•

Donut couldn't see the flames behind the knoll he'd just come down from, but he knew from the moment he hit the safety zone that the fire was ripping. The smoke was dark. "I see you, Donut," Steed called on the radio. It was good to hear his captain's voice. Donut was running through options in his mind. The fire was winding up and would soon cut off his escape route down the two-track the crew had hiked up from Yarnell that morning. He could hightail it back toward the rest of the crew, but one look at the 800 feet of elevation he had to climb and he thought: Fuck no, I can't outrun this.

His next option seemed worse: deploying his fire shelter, the bivy-sack-size aluminum tent that all wildland firefighters carry as a last resort. The shelters deflect heat but melt when hit directly by flames. Donut had been trained on what to do if left with no choice but to deploy. He'd throw his pack away. He'd bring a liter of water and his radio under the shelter, lie facedown and grab the fiberglass handles, and then, as he'd been instructed, he'd sing or hum or yell to anybody within earshot—just something to take his mind off the pain. He'd have to paw at the ground beneath his mouth and bury his nose in the cooler air below. Firefighters can survive interior temperatures of around 300 degrees, but not much hotter. Deployments have occurred 1,239 times since wildland firefighters started using the shelters in the 1960s, and only 22 have died.

The dozer push should have been big enough to survive a deployment, but it wasn't something Donut cared to test. In 1994, an Arizona hotshot who deployed considered beating his head against a rock to knock himself unconscious. If he lived, he figured, at least he'd avoid the pain and wake up after the storm passed.

"Steed, Donut. I'm calling Blue Ridge." He'd just keyed the mic to call when Blue Ridge's superintendent, Brian Frisby, came around the corner on his UTV. When he'd heard the weather update on the radio, he immediately left his crew to collect Donut.

Donut threw his gear in the back and handed Brian the radio: "Call Steed and Eric."

"I've got Donut. The fire's making its push. We're going to go back and bump your buggies." Brian mashed on the gas and raced toward the teams' vehicles.

.   •   •   •

The Granite Mountain crew could see Donut on the UTV racing across the flats. They could see the helicopters and air tankers pivoting from Peeples Valley to Yarnell and dozens of emergency vehicles, lights flashing, speeding down Highway 89 toward Glen Ilah, the subdivision where Truman lived. It would have been difficult for the hotshots, who had been trained to help however they can, to sit idly by and watch houses burn. They would have been thinking of their fellow firefighters placing themselves in harm's way.

With conditions changing so dramatically, Eric and the crew's leadership—Steed, Clayton, Travis, Robert—would have gathered for a moment on the ridge to discuss their options while the other hotshots sat perched on white granite boulders watching the drama unfold.

Do we hunker down in the black and do nothing but watch Yarnell burn? Or do we head down there, do some point protection, and try to save a couple of homes? Eric would have made the decision. He couldn't have imagined that, by heading for town, he was leading his crew toward a series of increasingly compromised circumstances, each more desperate than the last.

He radioed out that Granite Mountain was moving back toward Yarnell.

Donut drove Eric's supe truck to the edge of Yarnell. There, he and the Blue Ridge hotshots joined a few engine companies who were wetting and widening a contingency dozer line—a last effort to stop the fire from burning straight down Highway 89.

Donut radioed to Steed. "Buggies are parked. I'm with Blue Ridge. If you guys need anything, let me know."

"Copy. I'll see you soon." It was the last time Donut spoke to Steed.

·   ·   ·

"We've got to go *now*!" Truman yelled to Lois as he rushed toward their front door. She was coming out of the house, her arms full of things to load into their RV.

"Why?" she said. The smoke wasn't blowing over the house.

"Because if we don't, we'll die!"

Lois snapped out of it. She could now see the black smoke blowing through the oak trees outside her living room windows.

Truman grabbed a vial of holy water he'd taken from church two months before and sprinkled it on the front door, silently saying a quick prayer before he raced toward the couple's motor home.

Out front, a little white truck was circling the neighborhood. Lea Way, a local nurse practitioner, was leaning out the window warning the residents. "Everybody out! Everybody get out!"

.   .   .

Just minutes after Donut started working with the Blue Ridge crew to hastily build a new contingency line closer to town, Blue Ridge's superintendent and squad bosses told them to load back into the buggies. Fist-size embers sailed over the crew like a volley of flaming arrows. Radio transmissions were lost to the roar of the wind. Nothing more could be done. They'd lost Yarnell.

.   .   .

When the flames hit Glen Ilah, Truman and Lois had to turn on their headlights to see through the smoke as they entered the caravan of cars fleeing the subdivision. Just across the street, a tornado of fire was twirling through the neighbors' houses. Later he'd call it the day of the dragon—a ball of flame blown from the mouth of an unseen beast. He'd lived through two wars but had never felt so close to death.

Down the street, a ninety-year-old couple, the Harts, didn't know the fire was coming until they looked out the upstairs window and saw it engulf a house at the end of the street. They drove away in such a rush that they backed into a ditch and flipped the car. After they somehow crawled out, the sheriff found them walking dumbfounded toward town.

The traffic piled up at the stop sign across Highway 89 from the Ranch House Restaurant, where the Granite Mountain buggies and the Blue Ridge crew were heading. Truman came to a stop, then turned right and pointed his rig toward the safety of the desert below.

•   •   •

Since Eric's last radio transmission, Granite Mountain had covered nearly a mile on the two-track, at some point deciding to leave the safety of the black edge. The farther the crew moved down, the thicker the smoke became. When they reached a saddle above a basin below them that was 200 yards wide, Eric lost sight of the fire. A ridge to his left would have blocked his view.

The superintendent was now faced with a choice: bail off the far side of the ridge to their right, toward the questionable safety of the desert 2,000 feet below, or keep heading down to the defensible space surrounding a ranch house, the Helms place, that he could briefly see when the smoke lifted for a moment from the saddle.

He radioed to the plane circling overhead. His transmissions, normally delivered in the deadpan of a true technician, were beginning to betray his stress. Granite Mountain, he told air attack, was moving toward the ranch house they had in sight at the foot of the basin.

Get there and everything would be OK. It didn't look far. A fifteen-minute hike tops. Eric would have seen the homeowners outside, panicking as they pushed their llama and miniature donkey into the barn before they prepared to weather the inferno that was ripping toward them.

They hiked down the slope, another 500-foot descent through brush into a basin walled with giant granite boulders on three sides. Somewhere closer to the basin's floor than the saddle, the flames appeared from behind the ridge to their left.

One at a time they came face-to-face with a fire that had just burned a seemingly impossible four miles in about twenty minutes. Each of them would have known what it meant. There was no exit. Looking down through the smoke over the tops of eight-foot chaparral to a fire that was ripping uphill at them, Eric must have realized that everything he'd worked for was gone. In one decision to leave the black, he went from the superintendent of the country's only municipal hotshot crew to the only superintendent to have led nineteen elite wildland firefighters into a burnover. If he survived, he knew every hotshot crew in the nation would be up his ass. "What were you thinking, Marsh? How did you do this?" The best he could hope for was a life sentence of crippling guilt: *These kids . . . my kids . . . this situation. How did I let this happen?*

.   .   .

Still, they kept going down. He knew that trying to outrun a fire burning uphill, the decision that killed fourteen firefighters on Colorado's South Canyon Fire, wasn't an option. The fastest hotshots might make it; the slowest might not. The crew would stay together.

As fast as they could, they plowed through the chaparral, their forearms shielding their faces from the plants whipping back at them. The fire had spread across the head of the basin. Steed or one of the squad bosses radioed out, frantically calling the air-attack plane and helicopter overhead. Again and again they called. When the signal finally got through, no one could decipher the calls. Just screaming: "Granite 7!"

"Whoever is yelling over the radio needs to stop," was the response from air attack. "I can't understand you."

The crew's best chance at survival lay in a depression on the basin floor where two swales that flowed toward Yarnell met. The brush was thinnest there. Eric and Steed would have made the call. Start the chainsaws. Cut a hole in the brush big enough to deploy nineteen fire shelters. Squad bosses Robert, Clayton, and Travis would have confirmed the order with nods. This is right. This is what we have left.

A helicopter beat the air overhead, searching for the crew through the smoke. All they saw was occasional bursts of flame running and leaping up the basin.

Finally, Eric radioed air attack, his back to the superheated wind. "Our escape route has been cut off. The Granite Mountain hotshots are deploying their fire shelters." Their chainsaws were heard ripping in the background.

.   .   .

The crew would have been deliberate.

The orders provided purpose. The purpose moderated panic. They'd set down their chainsaws and gasoline outside the circle of the safety zone, so that when the fuel exploded it wouldn't damage their shelters. They'd use flares to set the brush around them on fire, a technique Wag Dodge, a Montana firefighter, famously used to save his own life on a fire that killed thirteen smoke jumpers more than sixty years earlier. It would burn the fuel out around the safety zone and keep the flames farther away from the shelters. The clearing was just sixty feet by sixty feet—a three-car garage.

They deployed their shelters in ascending order of experience. The rookies and seasonal hotshots went first; then the squad bosses, making sure their men were in. Before entering his shelter, Steed would have watched Robert, Clayton, and Travis climb into theirs. Eric went last. To protect their heads, they all pointed their feet toward the advancing flames. The grouping was so tight that the shelters touched. They followed orders. No man tried to run or buck the command. Inside the orange glow of their shelters, they would have heard each other's encouragements over the wind. They would each have had just a few moments to think. They'd wrestle their shelters as they beat the air like wind socks. They'd clench their teeth, desperately pinning the flimsy aluminum tents to the ground as the flames passed over them and the heat became unimaginable.

. . .

Donut and the Blue Ridge hotshots parked Granite Mountain's buggies at the Ranch House Restaurant and were watching the exodus of cars. The fire had overtaken the houses at the end of the street. Every few moments a propane tank exploded, throwing thirty-foot flames skyward. The helicopter beat the air above— searching for the crew through the smoke. The fire fight had ground to a halt. Donut, who had heard Eric's radio transmission moments before, was in a daze.

It took more than an hour and a half for Ranger 58, a helicopter from Arizona's Department of Public Safety, to locate the fire shelters. The first in was Eric Tarr, a paramedic. He was dropped by helicopter near the Helms place and walked 500 yards up the box canyon through the charred and barely smoking landscape. Already, more firefighters, three Forest Service men on ATVs, were converging on the basin. Minutes after arriving on the scene, Tarr checked each man's pulse and radioed out, "I have nineteen confirmed fatalities."

. . .

When the Prescott dispatch reached Wade Ward, a former Granite Mountain hotshot and the department's current public information officer, they told him he needed to get to the dispatch center as fast as possible. They didn't tell him why. As he sped to the station, all he could think of was that something had happened to his family.

When he arrived, the dispatchers were all standing at their computers, silently watching him make the long walk across the room to where a few senior-ranking Prescott fire personnel sat waiting.

"Granite Mountain deployed at the Yarnell Fire," they told him. His first thought was Eric's not going to be happy. There's going to be reams of paperwork, an investigation, and the crew's going to be put under more of a spotlight than it already was.

Then it began to sink in. These guys? Eric? Granite Mountain? No way. They're too good.

When the call came in confirming the fatalities, Wade wrote in his notebook, "No medical needed; recovery." From that point on, it was a race against Facebook and Twitter. The department called police officers, chaplains, and trauma specialists and sent them in teams of three to each of the victims' families' homes. They were dispatched in Montana, California, and a handful of cities in Arizona. Mostly, though, it was Prescott.

In its 128-year history, the city's fire department had never had a fatality. Wade had no comparable experience to fall back on. From his pocket, he grabbed the PIO's handbook for responding to tragedies and set about ticking off a checklist of tasks. Already the story was leaking.

Wade's phone began to ring, as it would for the next three months. It was a reporter in Ireland, then a reporter in New York. Both were trying to confirm what they'd already heard. Is it true? The greatest number of firefighter deaths since 9/11? The most professional wildland firefighters ever killed in a single incident?

He told them emphatically, "It is not confirmed." But when a reporter friend of his from the local newspaper called, one that he often worked with on what now seemed like such insignificant stories, he asked for his help.

"Please, let us tell the families first."

.   .   .

It was a race they couldn't win. Donut was sitting in the passenger seat of Granite Mountain's parked buggy, just staring ahead. He'd called his mother and told her that he was OK, but that's all he could say. The details escaped him.

The phones of his dead crewmates started ringing around nine p.m. One cell phone rattled in the cup holder by the front seat, where Clayton had sat. Then it was the phones of the hotshots who'd sat in the back. The calls were from girlfriends, friends, and family members. Maybe they caught wind of the tragedy on Facebook. Maybe they'd heard it second- or third-hand from somebody else. It didn't matter. The word was out. The Granite Mountain hotshots had deployed. The people were calling without any real hope that their message would ever be returned. They were calling to say goodbye.

The calls and texts kept coming, endless rings and vibrations and senseless jingles. Donut had to leave the buggy.

• • •

Marty Cole, the former superintendent of Granite Mountain and one of the two safety officers on the fire, leaned against the hood of his truck for a long time before he made up his mind that he wasn't going to the site. He'd seen enough burned bodies in his career, and could remember the faces of every one of them. "I didn't want to remember my friends like that. Not them. Not like that," he said.

Then he changed his mind. He needed to see for himself what had happened. He drove into Glen Ilah. The burn pattern seemed to have no logic. There were houses abutting the highway that were nothing but smoldering timber and houses in the middle of the neighborhood standing untouched next to thickets of unburned brush. Wilted fruit hung from the limbs of a charred apricot tree. Across from Truman and Lois's place, one of the few houses that miraculously survived, Dan and Dorman's garden was still green and producing squash. Their house was burned to the ground.

That first trip, Marty made it only to the gate of the road that led to the Helms place before he stopped, put it in reverse, and drove the six miles back to the incident command post. As he did, he replayed memories from over the years he'd worked with Eric Marsh. The hardheadedness, their arguments over trivial things like the color of crew T-shirts, his absolute faith in Eric's ability as a firefighter.

Four times he made the trip to and from the command post before arriving at the ranch house a third of a mile from the site of the tragedy. The fire had hit so hard, it broke the house's windows and oxidized the steel wagon wheels and iron bear statue on the property's perimeter. But the house was left standing. It had defensible space.

Marty walked across the blackened flats toward the basin. The bushes looked like spent matches. The soil had a texture of iced-over snow—crispy on top and powdery underneath—and there was no smoke or heat. The fire had burned so hot and fast that the mammoth granite boulders on the basin's flanks had cracked like eggshells.

What the hell were they doing here? Marty thought.

At the site, a sheriff stood guard. The hotshots' pants and packs were incinerated. Their saws, Pulaskis, and Rhinos were now deformed lumps of metal. Fourteen of their shelters had been vaporized or ripped off by the wind, and many of the men lay in the fetal position, as if they were sleeping in the blackened ash. The remaining shelters were barely recognizable. The aluminum had flaked off; the glue that held them together had melted when the temperatures hit 1,200 degrees. Five hotshots lay beneath these remnants. Robert was one of them.

Marty stood in shock and listened. Again and again he heard a hissing that ended in a crack. What is that? he thought. Then it hit him. The hotshots' radios. Somehow they were still on and functioning. He took a deep breath and went to turn them off, but the sheriff stopped him. "You can't," the officer told Marty, his hand on the old superintendent's chest. For the next three months, state and federal investigators would have to examine every detail of the crew's history up to their final moments. Something needed to be learned from this tragedy. "I've wanted to turn them off since we got here. But we have to leave it for the investigators."

·   ·   ·

Claire Caldwell was watching *Cold Mountain* in her bedroom at the back of the house. She was eating Thai lettuce wraps she'd made for dinner when a friend of hers knocked on the door. She didn't hear him. The AC was on, and the movie was turned up loud. He let himself in. When he yelled her name, she got up and went to hug him but stopped.

"It's not good," he said. "Have you seen the news?" She didn't like the look on his face.

"I don't watch fucking news."

"The boys deployed today."

"My boys? Not my boys."

"Your boys."

She fell to her knees.

No. It's not true. Deployed? She knew what that meant. But no, she thought. They're fine. They have to be. They're Granite Mountain.

Claire ran to the fridge to grab the Prescott Fire contact list. She called the most senior name she could find. Her friend drove her to Mile High middle school, where the families of the fallen had gathered in an auditorium. She learned that there was one survivor—hope. She hugged the wives of other firefighters who had already heard the news. "I'm so sorry," Claire said as she wept. "I'm so sorry."

She watched Granite Mountain alumni, strong men who had quit the crew only months before, weeping with such incapacitating grief that they could walk only with the help of friends. Still she didn't know about Robert. They were newlyweds. Most people didn't know who she was. Nobody told her.

Finally, she grabbed a uniformed officer by the shirt cuffs and asked him, "Is my husband fucking alive?"

"What's your name, Miss?"

"Claire. Claire Caldwell."

．　　　．　　　．

The hotshots were removed from the site the following morning. They were placed in body bags and covered in American flags. Eleven Prescott-area firefighters, along with the father of one of the hotshots, ceremoniously loaded the bodies into the backs of pickups and drove them to the Helms place, the safety zone they never reached. There, a pastor gave each his blessing, then the bodies were transferred to medical transport vans and driven seventy-eight miles to a hospital in Phoenix, where they were prepared for burial.

A few miles outside Yarnell, people started appearing to watch the procession. At first it was just a few standing silently by the side of the highway to offer their respects. Before long there were thousands. Police cars and fire trucks were parked at every stoplight and street corner in Phoenix. On a Monday afternoon, strangers with signs offering prayers stood shoulder to shoulder in 112-degree heat to honor the nineteen fallen hotshots.

The firefighters' loved ones grieved differently. Linda Caldwell, Robert's mother and Grant McKee's aunt, insisted she see her son's and her nephew's bodies before they were cremated. She was led into a room where they lay on gurneys with American flags draped over them. Grant was on the right, still in the fetal position. Robert lay prone and plank-like on the left. For half an hour she felt their hands and feet through the stars and stripes. She touched Robert's nose and ran her hands over his bald head. Her husband, David, couldn't bring himself to see his son's burned body. It hurt too much. Instead, he gave Robert a gift he had meant to give him the last time he saw him alive. It was a first-bound edition of Hemingway's *A Farewell to Arms*. He placed it inside Robert's coffin.

Poetry

WINNER—GENERAL
EXCELLENCE

In "Elegies," Kathleen Ossip contemplates the passing of five emblematic figures—Amy Winehouse, Steve Jobs, the painter Lucian Freud, Donna Summer, and Troy Davis (the least known of the five, Davis was executed, perhaps wrongly, for murdering a policeman). In a brief essay that appeared in Publishers Weekly in 2011, Ossip explained why she writes poetry: "When I am working on a poem . . . I'm aware of opening a space for the whole unresolved world to come in, with its contradictions and chaos." Read these poems to see what she means. Founded in 1912, Poetry won the National Magazine Award for General Excellence this year. The judges called it "a glistening jewel of a magazine, flawlessly blending the literary and visual to inform and inspire."

Kathleen Ossip

Elegies

AMY WINEHOUSE

All song is formal, and you
Maybe felt this and decided
You'd be formal too. (The eyeliner, the beehive: formal.)
When a desire to escape becomes formal,
It's dangerous. Then escape requires
Nullity, rather than a walk in the park or a movie.
Eventually, nullity gets harder and
Harder to achieve. After surgery, I had
Opiates. I pushed the button as often as I could.
Understood by music was how I felt. An escape
So complete it became a song. After that,
Elegy's the only necessary form.

STEVE JOBS

Say you lost all your money, or turned against your
	ambition.
Then you would be at peace, or
Else why does the mind punish the body?
Vengeance is mind, says the body.

Ever after, you're a mirror, "silver and exact."
Just like the bug in a string of code, the body defies the
    mind
Or looks in the mirror of the mind and shudders.
Better instruments are better because they're
Silver*ish* but intact.

TROY DAVIS

The clock is obdurate,
Random, and definite.
Obdurate the calendar.
You thump on the cot: another signature.
Did it didn't do it would do it again.
And if a *deferred* dream dies? Please sign the petition.
Very good. Let's hunt for a pen.
If you thump, there's another signature and
Signatures are given freely by the signer's hand.

LUCIAN FREUD

Lingering over
Unlovely bodies,
Couldn't help
Intuitively rendering
A whole
Nother angel.
Facts are
Relics—an
Effect worth
Undertaking: yes,
Dear daylight?

DONNA SUMMER

Discourse that night concerned the warm-blooded love
    we felt.
On the divan and in the ballroom and on the terrace,
    we felt it.
Now virtue meant liking the look of the face we lay
    next to.
Never mind the sting of the winter solstice.
All discourse that night concerned the warm-blooded love
    we felt.
Something lifted us higher. Her little finger told her so,
Untangling, with careless skill, the flora of the sexual
    grove.
Master physician with a masterly joy in wrapping up
Mud-spattered, coke-dusted wounds at midnight,
    when it's too
Early to stop dancing and go home. Our lily-minds
    soothed by her
Royalty concealed in the synthesizers in the flora of the
    sexual grove.

The New Yorker

WINNER—FICTION

In "The Embassy of Cambodia," a young woman working as a near slave for an immigrant family in suburban London struggles to comprehend the nature of cruelty. "Zadie Smith writes with incomparable passion and precise lyricism," said the National Magazine Award judges, "crafting rare meaning even from a game of badminton." Born in London in 1975, Smith has written four novels. The first, White Teeth, was included in Time's list of the hundred best English-language novels published since 1923. Her most recent novel, NW, was published in 2012. In the last forty years, The New Yorker has won the National Magazine Award for Fiction thirteen times. This year the magazine received four National Magazine Awards in addition to the Fiction prize: for Feature Writing, Essays and Criticism, and Columns and Commentary.

Zadie Smith

The Embassy
of Cambodia

0–1

Who would expect the Embassy of Cambodia? Nobody. Nobody could have expected it, or be expecting it. It's a surprise, to us all. The Embassy of Cambodia!

Next door to the embassy is a health center. On the other side, a row of private residences, most of them belonging to wealthy Arabs (or so we, the people of Willesden, contend). They have Corinthian pillars on either side of their front doors, and—it's widely believed—swimming pools out back. The embassy, by contrast, is not very grand. It is only a four- or five-bedroom North London suburban villa, built at some point in the thirties, surrounded by a red brick wall, about eight feet high. And back and forth, cresting this wall horizontally, flies a shuttlecock. They are playing badminton in the Embassy of Cambodia. Pock, smash. Pock, smash.

The only real sign that the embassy is an embassy at all is the little brass plaque on the door (which reads, "THE EMBASSY OF CAMBODIA") and the national flag of Cambodia (we assume that's what it is—what else could it be?) flying from the red tiled roof. Some say, "Oh, but it has a high wall around it, and this is what signifies that it is not a private residence, like the other houses on the street but, rather, an embassy." The people who say so are foolish. Many of the private houses have high walls, quite as high as the Embassy of Cambodia's—but they are not embassies.

0–2

On the sixth of August, Fatou walked past the embassy for the first time, on her way to a swimming pool. It is a large pool, although not quite Olympic size. To swim a mile you must complete eighty-two lengths, which, in its very tedium, often feels as much a mental exercise as a physical one. The water is kept unusually warm, to please the majority of people who patronize the health center, the kind who come not so much to swim as to lounge poolside or rest their bodies in the sauna. Fatou has swum here five or six times now, and she is often the youngest person in the pool by several decades. Generally, the clientele are white, or else South Asian or from the Middle East, but now and then Fatou finds herself in the water with fellow-Africans. When she spots these big men, paddling frantically like babies, struggling simply to stay afloat, she prides herself on her own abilities, having taught herself to swim, several years earlier, at the Carib Beach Resort, in Accra. Not in the hotel pool—no employees were allowed in the pool. No, she learned by struggling through the rough gray sea, on the other side of the resort walls. Rising and sinking, rising and sinking, on the dirty foam. No tourist ever stepped onto the beach (it was covered with trash), much less into the cold and treacherous sea. Nor did any of the other chambermaids. Only some reckless teenage boys, late at night, and Fatou, early in the morning. There is almost no way to compare swimming at Carib Beach and swimming in the health center, warm as it is, tranquil as a bath. And, as Fatou passes the Embassy of Cambodia, on her way to the pool, over the high wall she sees a shuttlecock, passed back and forth between two unseen players. The shuttlecock floats in a wide arc softly rightward, and is smashed back, and this happens again and again, the first player always somehow able to retrieve the smash and transform it, once more, into a gentle, floating arc. High above, the sun tries to force its way through a cloud ceiling, gray and filled with water. Pock, smash. Pock, smash.

0–3

When the Embassy of Cambodia first appeared in our midst, a few years ago, some of us said, "Well, if we were poets perhaps we could have written some sort of an ode about this surprising appearance of the embassy." (For embassies are usually to be found in the center of the city. This was the first one we had seen in the suburbs.) But we are not really a poetic people. We are from Willesden. Our minds tend toward the prosaic. I doubt there is a man or woman among us, for example, who—upon passing the Embassy of Cambodia for the first time—did not immediately think: "genocide."

0–4

Pock, smash. Pock, smash. This summer we watched the Olympics, becoming well attuned to grunting, and to the many other human sounds associated with effort and the triumph of the will. But the players in the garden of the Embassy of Cambodia are silent. (We can't say for sure that it is a garden—we have a limited view over the wall. It may well be a paved area, reserved for badminton.) The only sign that a game of badminton is under way at all is the motion of the shuttlecock itself, alternately being lobbed and smashed, lobbed and smashed, and always at the hour that Fatou passes on her way to the health center to swim (just after ten in the morning on Mondays). It should be explained that it is Fatou's employers—and not Fatou—who are the true members of this health club; they have no idea that she uses their guest passes in this way. (Mr. and Mrs. Derawal and their three children—aged seventeen, fifteen, and ten—live on the same street as the embassy, but the road is almost a mile long, with the embassy at one end and the Derawals at the other.) Fatou's deception is possible only because on Mondays Mr. Derawal drives to Eltham to visit his mini-market there, and Mrs. Derawal works the counter in the family's second mini-mart, in Kensal Rise. In the slim drawer of a faux–Louis XVI console, in the entrance hall of the Derawals' primary residence, one can find a stockpile of guest passes. Nobody besides Fatou seems to remember that they are there.

Since August sixth (the first occasion on which she noticed the badminton), Fatou has made a point of pausing by the bus stop opposite the embassy for five or ten minutes before she goes in to swim, idle minutes she can hardly afford (Mrs. Derawal returns to the house at lunchtime) and yet seems unable to forgo. Such is the strangely compelling aura of the embassy. Usually, Fatou gains nothing from this waiting and observing, but on a few occasions she has seen people arrive at the embassy and watched as they are buzzed through the gate. Young white people carrying rucksacks. Often they are scruffy, and wearing sandals, despite the cool weather. None of the visitors so far have been visibly Cambodian. These young people are likely looking for visas. They are buzzed in and then pass through the gate, although Fatou would really have to stand on top of the bus stop to get a view of whoever it is that lets them in. What she can say with certainty is that these occasional arrivals have absolutely no effect on the badminton, which continues in its steady pattern, first gentle, then fast, first soft and high, then hard and low.

0–5

On the twentieth of August, long after the Olympians had returned to their respective countries, Fatou noticed that a basketball hoop had appeared in the far corner of the garden, its net of synthetic white rope rising high enough to be seen over the wall.

But no basketball was ever played—at least not when Fatou was passing. The following week it had been moved closer to Fatou's side of the wall. (It must be a mobile hoop, on casters.) Fatou waited a week, two weeks, but still no basketball game replaced the badminton, which carried on as before.

0–6

When I say that we were surprised by the appearance of the Embassy of Cambodia, I don't mean to suggest that the embassy is in any way unique in its peculiarity. In fact, this long, wide street is notable for a number of curious buildings, in the context of which the Embassy of Cambodia does not seem especially strange. There is a mansion called GARYLAND, with something else in Arabic engraved below GARYLAND, and both the English and the Arabic text are inlaid in pink-and-green marble pillars that bookend a gigantic fence, far higher than the embassy's, better suited to a fortress. Dramatic golden gates open automatically to let vehicles in and out. At any one time, GARYLAND has five to seven cars parked in its driveway.

There is a house with a huge pink elephant on the doorstep, apparently made of mosaic tiles.

There is a Catholic nunnery with a single red Ford Focus parked in front. There is a Sikh institute. There is a faux-Tudor house with a pool that Mickey Rooney rented for a season, while he was performing in the West End fifteen summers ago. That house sits opposite a dingy retirement home, where one sometimes sees distressed souls, barely covered by their dressing gowns, standing on their tiny balconies, staring into the tops of the chestnut trees.

So we are hardly strangers to curious buildings, here in Willesden & Brondesbury. And yet still we find the Embassy of Cambodia a little surprising. It is not the right sort of surprise, somehow.

0–7

In a discarded *Metro* found on the floor of the Derawal kitchen, Fatou read with interest a story about a Sudanese "slave" living in a rich man's house in London. It was not the first time that Fatou had wondered if she herself was a slave, but this story, brief as it was, confirmed in her own mind that she was not. After all, it was her father, and not a kidnapper, who had taken her from Ivory Coast to Ghana, and when they reached Accra they had both found employment in the same hotel. Two years later, when she was eighteen, it was her father again who had organized her difficult passage to Libya and then on to Italy—a not insignificant financial sacrifice on his part. Also, Fatou could read English—and speak a little Italian—and this girl in the paper could not read or speak anything except the language of her tribe. And nobody beat Fatou, although Mrs. Derawal had twice slapped her in the face, and the two older children spoke to her with no respect at all and thanked her for nothing. (Sometimes she heard her name used as a term of abuse between them. "You're as black as Fatou." Or "You're as stupid as Fatou.") On the other hand, just like the girl in the newspaper, she had not seen her passport with her own eyes since she arrived at the Derawals', and she had been told from the start that her wages were to be retained by the Derawals to pay for the food and water and heat she would require during her stay, as well as to cover the rent for the room she slept in. In the final analysis, however, Fatou was not confined to the house. She had an Oyster Card, given to her by the Derawals, and was trusted to do the food shopping and other outside tasks for which she was given cash and told to return with change and receipts for everything. If she did not go out in the evenings that was only because she had no money with which to go out, and anyway knew very few people in London. Whereas the girl in the paper was not allowed to leave her employers' premises, not ever—she was a prisoner.

On Sunday mornings, for example, Fatou regularly left the house to meet her church friend Andrew Okonkwo at the 98 bus stop and go with him to worship at the Sacred Heart of Jesus, just off the Kilburn High Road. Afterward Andrew always took her to a Tunisian café, where they had coffee and cake, which Andrew, who worked as a night guard in the City, always paid for. And on Mondays Fatou swam. In very warm water, and thankful for the semi-darkness in which the health club, for some reason, kept its clientele, as if the place were a night club, or a midnight Mass. The darkness helped disguise the fact that her swimming costume was in fact a sturdy black bra and a pair of plain black cotton knickers. No, on balance she did not think she was a slave.

0–8

The woman exiting the Embassy of Cambodia did not look especially like a New Person or an Old Person—neither clearly of the city nor of the country—and of course it is a long time since this division meant anything in Cambodia. Nor did these terms mean anything to Fatou, who was curious only to catch her first sighting of a possible Cambodian anywhere near the Embassy of Cambodia. She was particularly interested in the woman's clothes, which were precise and utilitarian—a gray shirt tucked tightly into a pair of tan slacks, a blue mackintosh, a droopy rain hat—just as if she were a man, or no different from a man. Her straight black hair was cut short. She had in her hands many bags from Sainsbury's, and this Fatou found a little mysterious: where was she taking all that shopping? It also surprised her that the woman from the Embassy of Cambodia should shop in the same Willesden branch of Sainsbury's where Fatou shopped for the Derawals. She had an idea that Oriental people had their own, secret establishments. (She believed the Jews did, too.) She both admired and slightly resented this self-reliance, but had no doubt that it was the secret to holding great power, as a people. For example, when the Chinese had come to Fatou's village to take over the mine, an abiding local mystery had been: what did they eat and where did they eat it? They certainly did not buy food in the market, or from the Lebanese traders along the main road. They made their own arrangements. (Whether back home or here, the key to surviving as a people, in Fatou's opinion, was to make your own arrangements.)

But, looking again at the bags the Cambodian woman carried, Fatou wondered whether they weren't in fact very old bags— hadn't their design changed? The more she looked at them the more convinced she became that they contained not food but clothes or something else again, the outline of each bag being a little too rounded and smooth. Maybe she was simply taking out the rubbish. Fatou stood at the bus stop and watched until the Cambodian woman reached the corner, crossed, and turned left toward the high road. Meanwhile, back at the embassy the badminton continued to be played, though with a little more effort now because of a wayward wind. At one point it seemed to Fatou that the next lob would blow southward, sending the shuttlecock over the wall to land lightly in her own hands. Instead the other player, with his vicious reliability (Fatou had long ago decided that both players were men), caught the shuttlecock as it began to drift and sent it back to his opponent—another deathly, downward smash.

0–9

No doubt there are those who will be critical of the narrow, essentially local scope of Fatou's interest in the Cambodian woman from the Embassy of Cambodia, but we, the people of Willesden, have some sympathy with her attitude. The fact is if we followed the history of every little country in this world—in its dramatic as well as its quiet times—we would have no space left in which to live our own lives or to apply ourselves to our necessary tasks, never mind indulge in occasional pleasures, like swimming. Surely there is something to be said for drawing a circle around our attention and remaining within that circle. But how large should this circle be?

0–10

It was the Sunday after Fatou saw the Cambodian that she decided to put a version of this question to Andrew, as they sat in the Tunisian café eating two large fingers of dough stuffed with cream and custard and topped with a strip of chocolate icing. Specifically, she began a conversation with Andrew about the Holocaust, as Andrew was the only person she had found in London with whom she could have these deep conversations, partly because he was patient and sympathetic to her, but also because he was an educated person, currently studying for a part-time business degree at the College of North West London. With his student card he had been given free, twenty-four-hour access to the Internet.

"But more people died in Rwanda," Fatou argued. "And nobody speaks about that! Nobody!"

"Yes, I think that's true," Andrew conceded, and put the first of four sugars in his coffee. "I have to check. But, yes, millions and millions. They hide the true numbers, but you can see them online. There's always a lot of hiding; it's the same all over. It's like this bureaucratic Nigerian government—they are the greatest at numerology, hiding figures, changing them to suit their purposes. I have a name for it: I call it 'demonology.' Not 'numerology'—'demonology.'"

"Yes, but what I am saying is like this," Fatou pressed, wary of the conversation's drifting back, as it usually did, to the financial corruption of the Nigerian government. "Are we born to suffer? Sometimes I think we were born to suffer more than all the rest."

Andrew pushed his professorial glasses up his nose. "But, Fatou, you're forgetting the most important thing. Who cried most for Jesus? His mother. Who cries most for you? Your father. It's very logical, when you break it down. The Jews cry for the Jews. The Russians cry for the Russians. We cry for Africa, because we are Africans, and, even then, I'm sorry, Fatou"—Andrew's chubby face creased up in a smile—"if Nigeria plays Ivory Coast and we beat you into the ground, I'm laughing, man! I can't lie. I'm celebrating. Stomp! Stomp!" He did a little dance with his upper body, and Fatou tried, not for the first time, to imagine what he might be like as a husband, but could see only herself as the wife, and Andrew as a teenage son of hers, bright and helpful, to be sure, but a son all the same—though in reality he was three years older than she. Surely it was wrong to find his baby fat and struggling mustache so off-putting. Here was a good man! She knew that he cared for her, was clean, and had given his life to Christ. Still, some part of her rebelled against him, some unholy part.

"Hush your mouth," she said, trying to sound more playful than disgusted, and was relieved when he stopped jiggling and laid both his hands on the table, his face suddenly quite solemn.

"Believe me, that's a natural law, Fatou, pure and simple. Only God cries for us all, because we are *all* his children. It's very, very logical. You just have to think about it for a moment."

Fatou sighed, and spooned some coffee foam into her mouth. "But I still think we have more pain. I've seen it myself. Chinese people have never been slaves. They are always protected from the worst."

Andrew took off his glasses and rubbed them on the end of his shirt. Fatou could tell that he was preparing to lay knowledge upon her.

"Fatou, think about it for a moment, please: what about Hiroshima?"

It was a name Fatou had heard before, but sometimes Andrew's superior knowledge made her nervous. She would find herself struggling to remember even the things she had believed she already knew.

"The big wave . . ." she began, uncertainly—it was the wrong answer. He laughed mightily and shook his head at her.

"No, man! Big bomb. Biggest bomb in the world, made by the USA, of course. They killed five million people in *one second*. Can you imagine that? You think just because your eyes are like this"—he tugged the skin at both temples—"you're always protected? Think again. This bomb, even if it didn't blow you up, a week later it melted the skin off your bones."

Fatou realized that she had heard this story before, or some version of it. But she felt the same vague impatience with it as she did with all accounts of suffering in the distant past. For what could be done about the suffering of the past?

"OK," she said. "Maybe all people have their hard times, in the past of history, but I still say—"

"Here is a counterpoint," Andrew said, reaching out and gripping her shoulder. "Let me ask you, Fatou, seriously, think about this. I'm sorry to interrupt you, but I have thought a lot about this and I want to pass it on to you, because I know you care about things seriously, not like these people." He waved a hand at the assortment of cake eaters at other tables. "You're not like the other girls I know, just thinking about the club and their hair. You're a person who thinks. I told you before, anything you want to know about, ask me—I'll look it up, I'll do the research. I have access. Then I'll bring it to you."

"You're a very good friend to me, Andrew, I know that."

"Listen, we are friends to each other. In this world you need friends. But, Fatou, listen to my question. It's a counterpoint to what you have been saying. Tell me, why would God choose us especially for suffering when we, above all others, praise his name? Africa is the fastest-growing Christian continent! Just think about it for a minute! It doesn't even make sense!"

"But it's not him," Fatou said quietly, looking over Andrew's shoulder at the rain beating on the window. "It's the Devil."

0–11

Andrew and Fatou sat in the Tunisian coffee shop, waiting for it to stop raining, but it did not stop raining, and at 3 p.m. Fatou said she would just have to get wet. She shared Andrew's umbrella as far as the Overground, letting him pull her into his clammy, high-smelling body as they walked. At Brondesbury station Andrew had to get the train, and so they said goodbye. Several times he tried to press his umbrella on her, but Fatou knew the walk from Acton Central to Andrew's bed-sit was long and she refused to let him suffer on her account.

"Big woman. Won't let anybody protect you."

"Rain doesn't scare me."

Fatou took from her pocket a swimming cap she had found on the floor of the health-club changing room. She wound her plaits into a bun and pulled the cap over her head.

"That's a very original idea," Andrew said, laughing. "You should market that! Make your first million!"

"Peace be with you," Fatou said, and kissed him chastely on the cheek. Andrew did the same, lingering a little longer with his kiss than was necessary.

0–12

By the time Fatou reached the Derawals', only her hair was dry, but before going to get changed she rushed to the kitchen to take the lamb out of the freezer, though it was pointless—there were not enough hours before dinner—and then upstairs to collect the dirty clothes from the matching wicker baskets in four different bedrooms. There was no one in the master bedroom, or in Faizul's, or Julie's. Downstairs a television was blaring. Entering Asma's room, hearing nothing, assuming it empty, Fatou headed straight for the laundry bin in the corner. As she opened the lid she felt a hand hit her hard on the back; she turned around.

There was the youngest, Asma, in front of her, her mouth open like a trout fish. Before Fatou could understand, Asma punched the huge pile of clothes out of her hands. Fatou stooped to retrieve them. While she was kneeling on the floor, another strike came, a kick to her arm. She left the clothes where they were and got up, frightened by her own anger. But when she looked at Asma now she saw the girl gesturing frantically at her own throat, then putting her hands together in prayer, and then back to her throat once more. Her eyes were bulging. She veered suddenly to the right; she threw herself over the back of a chair. When she turned back to Fatou her face was gray and Fatou understood finally and ran to her, grabbed her round her waist, and pulled upward as she had been taught in the hotel. A marble—with an iridescent ribbon of blue at its center, like a wave—flew from the child's mouth and landed wetly in the carpet's plush.

Asma wept and drew in frantic gulps of air. Fatou gave her a hug, and worried when the clothes would get done. Together they went down to the den, where the rest of the family was watching *Britain's Got Talent* on a flat-screen TV attached to the wall. Everybody stood at the sight of Asma's wild weeping. Mr. Derawal paused the Sky box. Fatou explained about the marble.

"How many times I tell you not to put things in your mouth?" Mr. Derawal asked, and Mrs. Derawal said something in their language—Fatou heard the name of their God—and pulled Asma onto the sofa and stroked her daughter's silky black hair.

"I couldn't breathe, man! I couldn't call nobody," Asma cried. "I was gonna die!"

"What you putting marbles in your mouth for anyway, you idiot," Faizul said, and un-paused the Sky box. "What kind of chief puts a marble in her mouth? Idiot. Bet you was bricking it."

"Oi, she saved your life," said Julie, the eldest child, whom Fatou generally liked the least. "Fatou saved your life. That's deep."

"I woulda just done this," Faizul said, and performed an especially dramatic Heimlich to his own skinny body. "And if that didn't work I woulda just start pounding myself karate style, bam bam bam bam bam—"

"Faizul!" Mr. Derawal shouted, and then turned stiffly to Fatou, and spoke not to her, exactly, but to a point somewhere between her elbow and the sunburst mirror behind her head. "Thank you, Fatou. It's lucky you were there."

Fatou nodded and moved to leave, but at the doorway to the den Mrs. Derawal asked her if the lamb had defrosted and Fatou had to confess that she had only just taken it out. Mrs. Derawal said something sharply in her language. Fatou waited for something further, but Mr. Derawal only smiled awkwardly at her, and nodded as a sign that she could go now. Fatou went upstairs to collect the clothes.

0–13

"To keep you is no benefit. To destroy you is no loss" was one of the mottoes of the Khmer Rouge. It referred to the New People, those city dwellers who could not be made to give up city life and work on a farm. By returning everybody to the land, the regime hoped to create a society of Old People—that is to say, of agrarian peasants. When a New Person was relocated from the city to the country, it was vital not to show weakness in the fields. Vulnerability was punishable by death.

In Willesden, we are almost all New People, though some of us, like Fatou, were, until quite recently, Old People, working the land in our various countries of origin. Of the Old and New People of Willesden I speak; I have been chosen to speak for them, though they did not choose me and must wonder what gives me the right. I could say, "Because I was born at the crossroads of Willesden, Kilburn, and Queen's Park!" But the reply would be swift and damning: "Oh, don't be foolish, many people were born right there; it doesn't mean anything at all. We are not one people and no one can speak for us. It's all a lot of nonsense. We see you standing on the balcony, overlooking the Embassy of Cambodia, in your dressing gown, staring into the chestnut trees, looking gormless. The real reason you speak in this way is because you can't think of anything better to do."

0–14

On Monday, Fatou went swimming. She paused to watch the badminton. She thought that the arm that delivered the smashes must make a movement similar to the one she made in the pool, with her clumsy yet effective front crawl. She entered the health center and gave a guest pass to the girl behind the desk. In the dimly lit changing room, she put on her sturdy black underwear. As she swam, she thought of Carib Beach. Her father serving snapper to the guests on the deck, his bow tie always a little askew, the ugly tourists, the whole scene there. Of course, it was not surprising in the least to see old white men from Germany with beautiful local girls on their laps, but she would never forget the two old white women from England—red women, really, thanks to the sun—each of them as big as two women put together, with Kweku and Osai lying by their sides, the boys hooking their scrawny black bird-arms round the women's massive red shoulders, dancing with them in the hotel "ballroom," answering to the names Michael and David, and disappearing into the women's cabins at night. She had known the boys' real girlfriends; they were chambermaids like Fatou. Sometimes they cleaned the rooms where Kweku and Osai spent the night with the English women. And the girls themselves had "boyfriends" among the guests. It was not a holy place, that hotel. And the pool was shaped like a kidney bean: nobody could really swim in it, or showed any sign of wanting to. Mostly, they stood in it and drank cocktails. Sometimes they even had their burgers delivered to the pool. Fatou hated to watch her father crouching to hand a burger to a man waist high in water.

The only good thing that happened in Carib Beach was this: once a month, on a Sunday, the congregation of a local church poured out of a coach at the front gates, lined up fully dressed in the courtyard, and then walked into the pool for a mass baptism. The tourists were never warned, and Fatou never understood why the congregants were allowed to do it. But she loved to watch their white shirts bloat and spread across the surface of the water, and to hear the weeping and singing. At the time—though she was not then a member of that church, or of any church except the one in her heart—she had felt that this baptism was for her, too, and that it kept her safe, and that this was somehow the reason she did not become one of the "girls" at the Carib Beach Resort. For almost two years—between her father's efforts and the grace of an unseen and unacknowledged God—she did her work, and swam Sunday mornings at the crack of dawn, and got along all right. But the Devil was waiting.

She had only a month left in Accra when she entered a bedroom to clean it one morning and heard the door shut softly behind her before she could put a hand to it. He came, this time, in Russian form. Afterward, he cried and begged her not to tell anyone: his wife had gone to see the Cape Coast Castle and they were leaving the following morning. Fatou listened to his blubbering and realized that he thought the hotel would punish him for his action, or that the police would be called. That was when she knew that the Devil was stupid as well as evil. She spat in his face and left. Thinking about the Devil now made her swimming fast and angry, and for a while she easily lapped the young white man in the lane next to hers, the faster lane.

0–15

"Don't give the Devil your anger, it is his food," Andrew had said to her, when they first met, a year ago. He handed her a leaflet as she sat eating a sandwich on a bench in Kilburn Park. "Don't make it so easy for him." Without being invited, he took the seat next to hers and began going through the text of his leaflet. It was printed to look like a newspaper, and he started with the headline: "WHY IS THERE PAIN?" She liked him. They began a theological conversation. It continued in the Tunisian café, and every Sunday for several months. A lot of the things he said she had heard before from other people, and they did not succeed in changing her attitude. In the end, it was one thing that he said to her that really made the difference. It was after she'd told him this story:

"One day, at the hotel, I heard a commotion on the beach. It was early morning. I went out and I saw nine children washed up dead on the beach. Ten or eleven years old, boys and girls. They had gone into the water, but they didn't know how to swim. Some people were crying, maybe two people. Everyone else just shook their heads and carried on walking to where they were going. After a long time, the police came. The bodies were taken away. People said, 'Well, they are with God now.' Everybody carried on like before. I went back to work. The next year I arrived in Rome. I saw a boy who was about fifteen years old knocked down on his bike. He was dead. People were screaming and crying in the street. Everybody crying. They were not his family. They were only strangers. The next day, it was in the paper."

And Andrew replied, "A tap runs fast the first time you switch it on."

0–16

Twenty more laps. Fatou tried to think of the last time she had cried. It was in Rome, but it wasn't for the boy on the bike. She was cleaning toilets in a Catholic girls' school. She did not know Jesus then, so it made no difference what kind of school it was— she knew only that she was cleaning toilets. At midday, she had a fifteen-minute break. She would go to the little walled garden across the road to smoke a cigarette. One day, she was sitting on a bench near a fountain, and spotted something odd in the bushes. A tin of green paint. A gold spray can. A Statue of Liberty costume. An identity card with the name Rajib Devanga. One shoe. An empty wallet. A plastic tub with a slit cut in the top meant for coins and euro notes—empty. A little stain of what looked like blood on this tub. Until that point, she had been envious of the Bengali boys on Via Nazionale. She felt that she, too, could paint herself green and stand still for an hour. But when she tried to find out more the Bengalis would not talk to her. It was a closed shop, for brown men only. Her place was in the bathroom stalls. She thought those men had it easy. Then she saw that little sad pile of belongings in the bush and cried; for herself or for Rajib, she wasn't sure.

Now she turned onto her back in the water for the final two laps, relaxed her arms, and kicked her feet out like a frog. Water made her think of more water. "When you're baptized in our church, all sin is wiped, you start again": Andrew's promise. She had never told Andrew of the sin precisely, but she knew that he knew she was not a virgin. The day she finally became a Catholic, February 6, 2011, Andrew had taken her, hair still wet, to the Tunisian café and asked her how it felt.

She was joyful! She said, "I feel like a new person!"

But happiness like that is hard to hold on to. Back at work the next day, picking Julie's dirty underwear up off the floor inches from the wicker basket, she had to keep reminding herself of her new relationship with Jesus and how it changed everything. Didn't it change everything? The following Sunday she expressed some of her doubt, cautiously, to Andrew.

485

The Embassy of Cambodia

"But did you think you'd never feel sad again? Never angry or tired or just pissed off—sorry about my language. Come on, Fatou! Wise up, man!"

Was it wrong to hope to be happy?

0–17

Lost to these watery thoughts, Fatou got home a little later than usual and was through the door only minutes before Mrs. Derawal.

"How is Asma?" Fatou asked. She had heard the girl cry out in the night.

"My goodness, it was just a little marble," Mrs. Derawal said, and Fatou realized that it was not in her imagination: since Sunday night, neither of the adult Derawals had been able to look her in the eye. "What a fuss everybody is making. I have a list for you—it's on the table."

0–18

Fatou watched Andrew pick his way through the tables in the Tunisian café, holding a tray with a pair of mochas on it and some croissants. He hit the elbow of one man with his backside and then trailed the belt of his long, silly leather coat through the lunch of another, apologizing as he went. You could not say that he was an elegant man. But he was generous, he was thoughtful. She stood up to push a teetering croissant back onto its plate. They sat down at the same time, and smiled at each other.

"Awhile ago you asked me about Cambodia," Andrew said. "Well, it's a very interesting case." He tapped the frame of his glasses. "If you even wore a pair of these? They would kill you. Glasses meant you thought too much. They had very primitive ideas. They were enemies of logic and progress. They wanted everybody to go back to the country and live like simple people."

"But sometimes it's true that things are simpler in the country."

"In some ways. I don't really know. I've never lived in the country."

I don't really know. It was good to hear him say that! It was a good sign. She smiled cheekily at him. "People are less sinful in the country," she said, but he did not seem to see that she was flirting with him, and embarked on another lecture:

"That's true. But you can't force people to live in the country. That's what I call a Big Man Policy. I invented this phrase for my dissertation. We know all about Big Man Policies in Nigeria. They come from the top, and they crush you. There's always somebody who wants to be the Big Man, and take everything for himself, and tell everybody how to think and what to do. When, actually, it's he who is weak. But if the Big Men see that *you* see that *they* are weak they have no choice but to destroy you. That is the real tragedy."

Fatou sighed. "I never met a man who didn't want to tell everybody how to think and what to do," she said.

Andrew laughed. "Fatou, you include me? Are you a feminist now, too?"

Fatou brought her mug up to her lips and looked penetratingly at Andrew. There were good and bad kinds of weakness in men, and she had come to the conclusion that the key was to know which kind you were dealing with.

"Andrew," she said, putting her hand on his, "would you like to come swimming with me?"

0–19

Because Fatou believed that the Derawals' neighbors had been instructed to spy on her, she would not let Andrew come to the house to pick her up on Monday, instead leaving as she always did, just before ten, carrying misleading Sainsbury's bags and walking toward the health center. She spotted him from a long way off—the road was so straight and he had arrived early. He stood shivering in the drizzle. She felt sorry, but also a little prideful: it was the prospect of seeing her body that had raised this big man from his bed. Still, it was a sacrifice, she knew, for her friend to come out to meet her on a weekday morning. He worked all night long and kept the daytime for sleeping. She watched him waving at her from their agreed meeting spot, just on the corner, in front of the Embassy of Cambodia. After a while, he stopped waving—because she was still so far away—and then, a little later, he began waving again. She waved back, and when she finally reached him they surprised each other by holding hands. "I'm an excellent badminton player," Andrew said, as they passed the Embassy of Cambodia. "I would make you weep for mercy! Next time, instead of swimming we should play badminton somewhere." Next time, we should go to Paris. Next time, we should go to the moon. He was a dreamer. But there are worse things, Fatou thought, than being a dreamer.

0–20

"So you're a guest and this is your guest?" the girl behind the desk asked.

"I am a guest and this is another guest," Fatou replied.

"Yeah . . . that's not really how it works?"

"Please," Fatou said. "We've come from a long way."

"I appreciate that," the girl said. "But I really shouldn't let you in, to be honest."

"Please," Fatou said again. She could think of no other argument.

The girl took out a pen and made a mark on Fatou's guest pass.

"This one time. Don't tell no one I did this, please. One time only! I'll need to cross off two separate visits."

For one time only, then, Andrew and Fatou approached the changing rooms together and parted at the doors that led to the men's and the women's. In her changing room, Fatou got ready with lightning speed. Yet somehow he was already there on a lounger when she came out, eyes trained on the women's changing-room door, waiting for her to emerge.

"Man, this is the life!" he said, putting his arms behind his head.

"Are you getting in?" Fatou asked, and tried to place her hands, casually, in front of her groin.

"Not yet, man, I'm just taking it all in, taking it all in. You go in. I'll come in a moment."

Fatou climbed down the steps and began to swim. Not elegant, not especially fast, but consistent and determined. Every now and then she would angle her head to try to see if Andrew was still on his chair, smiling to himself. After twenty laps, she swam to where he lay and put her elbows on the tiles.

"You're not coming in? It's so warm. Like a bath."

"Sure, sure," he said. "I'll try it."

As he sat up his stomach folded in on itself, and Fatou wondered whether he had spent all that time on the lounger to avoid her seeing its precise bulk and wobble. He came toward the stairs; Fatou held out a hand to him, but he pushed it away. He made his way down and stood in the shallow end, splashing water over his shoulders like a prince fanning himself, and then crouching down into it.

"It is warm! Very nice. This is the life, man! You go, swim— I'll follow you."

Fatou kicked off, creating so much splash that she heard someone in the adjacent lane complain. At the wall, she turned and looked for Andrew. His method, such as it was, involved dipping deep under the water and hanging there like a hippo, then batting his arms till he crested for air, and then diving down again and hanging. It was a lot of energy to expend on such a short distance, and by the time he reached the wall he was panting like a maniac. His eyes—he had no goggles—were painfully red.

"It's OK," Fatou said, trying to take his hand again. "If you let me, I'll show you how." But he shrugged her off, and rubbed at his eyes.

"There's too much bloody chlorine in this pool."

"You want to leave?"

Andrew turned back to look at Fatou. His eyes were streaming. He looked, to Fatou, like a little boy trying to disguise the fact he had been crying. But then he held her hand, under the water.

"No. I'm just going to take it easy right here."

"OK," Fatou said.

"You swim. You're good. You swim."

"OK," Fatou said, and set off, and found that each lap was more distracted and rhythmless than the last. She was not used to being watched while she swam. Ten laps later, she suddenly stood up halfway down the lane and walked the rest of the distance to the wall.

"You want to go in the Jacuzzi?" she asked him, pointing to it. In the hot tub sat a woman dressed in a soaking tracksuit, her head covered with a head scarf. A man next to the woman, perhaps her husband, stared at Fatou and said something to her. He was so hairy he was almost as covered as she was. Together they rose up out of the water and left. He was wearing the tiniest of Speedos, the kind Fatou had feared Andrew might wear, and was grateful he had not. Andrew's shorts were perfectly nice, knee length, red and solid, and looked good against his skin.

"No," Andrew said. "It's great just to be here with you, watching the world go by."

0–21

That same evening, Fatou was fired. Not for the guest passes—the Derawals never found out how many miles Fatu had traveled on their membership. In fact, it was hard for Fatou to understand exactly why she was being fired, as Mrs. Derawal herself did not seem able to explain it very precisely.

"What you don't understand is that we have no need for a nanny," she said, standing in the doorway of Fatou's room—there was not really enough space in there for two people to stand without one of them being practically on the bed. "The children are grown. We need a housekeeper, one who cleans properly. These days, you care more about the children than the cleaning," Mrs. Derawal added, though Fatou had never cared for the children, not even slightly. "And that is of no use to us."

Fatou said nothing. She was thinking that she did not have a proper suitcase and would have to take her things from Mrs. Derawal's house in plastic bags.

"And so you will want to find somewhere else to live as soon as possible," Mrs. Derawal said. "My husband's cousin is coming to stay in this room on Friday—this Friday."

Fatou thought about that for a moment. Then she said, "Can I please use the phone for one call?"

Mrs. Derawal inspected a piece of wood that had flaked from the doorframe. But she nodded.

"And I would like to have my passport, please."

"Excuse me?"

"My passport, please."

At last Mrs. Derawal looked at Fatou, right into her eyes, but her face was twisted, as if Fatou had just reached over and slapped her. Anyone could see the Devil had climbed inside poor Mrs. Derawal. He was lighting her up with a pure fury.

"For goodness' sake, girl, I don't have your passport! What would I want with your passport? It's probably in a drawer in the kitchen somewhere. Is that my job now, too, to look for your things?"

Fatou was left alone. She packed her things into the decoy shopping bags she usually took to the swimming pool. While she was doing this, someone pushed her passport under the door. An hour later, she carried her bags downstairs and went directly to the phone in the hall. Faizul walked by and lifted his hand for a high-five. Fatou ignored him and dialed Andrew's number. From her friend's voice she knew that she had woken him, but he was not even the slightest bit angry. He listened to all she had to say and seemed to understand, too, without her having to say so, that at this moment she could not speak freely. After she had said her part, he asked a few quick technical questions and then explained clearly and carefully what was to happen.

"It will all be OK. They need cleaners in my offices—I will ask for you. In the meantime, you come here. We'll sleep in shifts. You can trust me. I respect you, Fatou."

But she did not have her Oyster Card; it was in the kitchen, on the fridge under a magnet of Florida, and she would rather die than go in there. Fine: he could meet her at six p.m., at the Brondesbury Overground station. Fatou looked at the grandfather clock in front of her: she had four hours to kill.

"Six o' clock," she repeated. She put the phone down, took the rest of the guest passes from the drawer of the Louis XVI console, and left the house.

"Weighed down a bit today," the girl at the desk of the health club said, nodding at Fatou's collection of plastic bags. Fatou held out a guest pass for a stamp and did not smile. "See you next time," this same girl said, an hour and a half later, as Fatou strode past, still weighed down and still unwilling to be grateful for past favors. Gratitude was just another kind of servitude. Better to make your own arrangements.

Walking out into the cold gray, Fatou felt a sense of brightness, of being washed clean, that neither the weather nor her new circumstance could dim. Still, her limbs were weary and her hair was wet; she would probably catch a cold, waiting out here. It was only four-thirty. She put her bags on the pavement and sat down next to them, just by the bus stop opposite the Embassy of

Cambodia. Buses came and went, slowing down for her and then jerking forward when they realized that she had no interest in getting up and on. Many of us walked past her that afternoon, or spotted her as we rode the bus, or through the windscreens of our cars, or from our balconies. Naturally, we wondered what this girl was doing, sitting on damp pavement in the middle of the day. We worried for her. We tend to assume the worst, here in Willesden. We watched her watching the shuttlecock. Pock, smash. Pock, smash. As if one player could imagine only a violent conclusion and the other only a hopeful return.

Permissions

Contributors

STEVEN BRILL is cofounder and CEO of Journalism Online, developer of Press+, an e-commerce platform that offers digital publishers flexible subscription models to collect revenue from their online readers. During thirty years as a media entrepreneur, Brill founded and ran Court TV, *The American Lawyer* magazine and ten regional legal newspapers, and *Brill's Content* magazine. A graduate of Yale College and Yale Law School, he has written for *The New Yorker, Time, Harpers,* and the *New York Times Magazine,* among other magazines and news sites. Brill is currently expanding his work on "Bitter Pill" with regular columns focusing on the rollout and implementation of the Affordable Care Act. The culmination of his reporting will be published later this year in a book by Random House. The author of three books, Brill also teaches journalism at Yale, where he founded the Yale Journalism Initiative to help encourage talented young people to consider the journalism profession. The initiative has trained and motivated more than one hundred Yale Journalism Scholars who are employed at some of the world's most prestigious news organizations.

MAX CHAFKIN is a contributing writer with *Fast Company.* His work has also appeared in *Vanity Fair,* the *New York Times Magazine, Men's Journal,* and *Inc.* He also coproduces *The Rewrite,* a podcast about writing and journalism. He is a graduate of Yale University and lives with his wife in Jackson Heights, New York.

In 2001, **JOSHUA DAVIS** became part of the U.S. Arm-Wrestling Team after placing fourth out of four in the lightweight division at the National Arm-Wrestling Finals. As a result, he traveled with the U.S. team to Poland to compete in the World Arm-Wrestling Championship, where he placed 9/2/2014th out of eighteen (the eighteenth guy didn't show up). Josh has never won a competitive arm-wrestling match. Josh's memoir, *The Underdog*, details his journey through a series of increasingly unusual competitions. For a decade he has been a contributing editor at *Wired*, where he has tracked rumors of genetically modified cocaine behind rebel lines in Colombia, investigated the world's largest diamond heist in Antwerp, and documented the rise of networked warfare in Iraq in 2003. He is also the cofounder of *Epic Magazine* (epicmagazine.com).

Kyle Dickman is a contributing editor at *Outside* magazine. He spent five seasons fighting wildland fires, including one with California's Tahoe Hotshots. He lives in Santa Fe with his wife, Turin.

Steve Friedman (stevefriedman.net) is the author of four books and the coauthor of two. A writer at large for *Runner's World* and *Bicycling* magazines, he has also written for *Esquire*, *GQ*, *Outside*, the *New York Times*, the *Washington Post*, *New York*, and many other publications. His stories have been published in *The Best American Sports Writing* multiple times and *The Best American Travel Writing* and cited as "notable" in *The Best American Essays*. He grew up in St. Louis, graduated from Stanford University, and lives in New York City.

Tom Junod has been a writer at large for *Esquire* since 1997. He has been a finalist for the National Magazine Award eleven times and has won twice. He has also won a James Beard Award for essay writing. On the occasion of *Esquire*'s seventy-fifth anniversary, his 2003 story, "The Falling Man," was selected as one of the seven best articles in the history of the magazine. A graduate of the State University of New York at Albany, he lives in Marietta, Georgia, with his wife and daughter and sings in a band called Cousin Billy.

ARIEL LEVY joined *The New Yorker* as a staff writer in 2008. Her profile subjects have included Cindy McCain, the Olympic boxer Claressa Shields, the longtime Italian prime minister Silvio Berlusconi, and Nora Ephron. Her work has been anthologized in *The Best American Essays 2008* and *The Best American Travel Writing 2011*. In 2012, she was a visiting critic at the American Academy in Rome. Levy teaches at the Fine Arts Work Center in Provincetown, Massachusetts. Before joining the magazine, she was a contributing editor at *New York* magazine for twelve years.

BARRY LOPEZ, an essayist and short story writer, is the author of fourteen books of fiction and nonfiction. He is the recipient of numerous literary and cultural awards and honors, including the National Book Award for *Arctic Dreams*.

LISA MILLER is a staff writer at *New York* magazine, covering social trends, parenting, and religion, among other topics. She is the former religion columnist for the *Washington Post*, former senior editor of *Newsweek* magazine, and author of *Heaven: Our Enduring Fascination with the Afterlife*. She graduated from Oberlin College and lives in Brooklyn.

LUKE MOGELSON lived in Afghanistan between June 2011 and December 2013, writing for the *New York Times Magazine*. He has also reported from the war in Syria. He currently lives in Mexico, where he is working on a collection of short stories.

EMILY NUSSBAUM is the television critic for *The New Yorker*. She lives in Brooklyn.

KATHLEEN OSSIP is the author of *The Do-Over*, which will be published in 2015; *The Cold War*, which was one of *Publishers Weekly's* best books of 2011; *The Search Engine*, which was selected by Derek Walcott for the American Poetry Review / Honickman First Book Prize; and *Cinephrastics*, a chapbook of movie poems. Her poems have appeared in *The Best American Poetry, Poetry, Paris Review, American Poetry Review, Boston Review*, the *Washington Post, The Believer, A Public Space*, and *Poetry Review* (London). She teaches at the New School in New York and online for the Poetry School of London. She has received a fellowship from the New York Foundation for the Arts.

JANET REITMAN is a contributing editor at *Rolling Stone* and has been writing for the magazine since 2002. Her work has also appeared in *GQ, Men's Journal, ESPN the Magazine, Marie Claire*, and the *Los Angeles Times*, among other national publications, and has been nominated for numerous awards, including two National Magazine Awards. In 2007, Reitman was a finalist for her investigative feature "Inside Scientology," an extensive inside look at one of America's most secretive religions. Her 2011 book, *Inside Scientology*, based on the original *Rolling Stone* article, was a *New York Times* Notable Book and a nationwide best-seller. Reitman specializes in investigative and narrative nonfiction, focusing on national security, terrorism, foreign policy, and youth culture and activism. Based in New York, she is a graduate of the University of California, Santa Cruz, and the Columbia University Graduate School of Journalism.

WITOLD RYBCZYNSKI is a writer and emeritus professor of architecture at the University of Pennsylvania. He has contributed to *The Atlantic, The New Yorker, The New York Review of Books*, and the *New York Time* and has been an architecture critic for *Saturday Night, Wigwag*, and *Slate*. The recipient of the 2007 Vincent Scully Prize, Rybczynski has written eighteen books, including the J. Anthony Lukas Prize–winning *A Clearing in the Distance; Home: A Short History of an Idea; Last Harvest; Makeshift Me-*

tropolis; and *How Architecture Works: A Humanist's Toolkit*, which was a finalist for the Marfield Prize for writing on the arts. From 2004 to 2012, Rybczynski served on the U.S. Commission of Fine Arts. In 2014 he received the National Design Award for Design Mind from the Cooper-Hewitt National Design Museum.

MATTHEW SHAER is a staff writer at *Smithsonian* magazine and a regular contributor to *New York*. His reporting has appeared in *Harper's*, *The New Republic*, *Popular Science*, and *Men's Journal*, among other publications.

ZADIE SMITH was born in northwest London in 1975 and divides her time between London and New York. Her first novel, *White Teeth*, was the winner of the Whitbread First Novel Award, the Guardian First Book Award, the James Tait Black Memorial Prize for Fiction, and the Commonwealth Writers' First Book Award. Her second novel, *The Autograph Man*, won the Jewish Quarterly Wingate Literary Prize. Zadie Smith's third novel, *On Beauty*, was short-listed for the Man Booker Prize and won the Commonwealth Writers' Best Book Award (Eurasia Section) and the Orange Prize for Fiction. Her most recent novel, *NW*, was published in 2012 and has been short-listed for the Royal Society of Literature Ondaatje Prize and the Women's Prize for Fiction.

WRIGHT THOMPSON is an Emmy-winning senior writer for ESPN. He has been featured in eight editions of *The Best American Sports Writing* and lives in Oxford, Mississippi.

JEAN M. TWENGE is a professor of psychology at San Diego State University and the author of *The Impatient Woman's Guide to Getting Pregnant*.